Neuroscience in Criminal Justice Systems

This edited collection shows the tangible and positive impacts neuroscience is having in specific jurisdictions for individuals involved in the criminal justice system as witnesses, victims, defendants, and legal practitioners. Over the last 30 years, neuroscience has significantly informed legal, philosophical, and doctrinal discussions by deepening our understanding of the relationships between the brain, mind, and criminality. By embracing a practical and realist approach, this book explores the fundamental question of what and how neuroscience has been concretely contributing to criminal justice, with a specific focus on international systems. Notably, the volume brings together perspectives to discuss neuroscience's positive impact on the global criminal justice process. It provides an overview of different legal dimensions that have been thus far positively impacted by neuroscience, as well as some discussion on its future applications to improve the treatment of system-impacted people. To this aim, the book covers two key areas: (1) criminal trials; and (2) punishment, treatment, and reform. This work will appeal to academics, criminal lawyers, judges, policymakers, and reformers interested in how neuroscience contributes to meaningful changes in the criminal justice system. The reader will gain significant insights into neuroscience's present and immediate future contributions to different dimensions of the criminal justice process through original exploration by legal academics and practitioners.

Hannah Wishart is Senior Lecturer in Law at the University of Sunderland, U.K.

Colleen M. Berryessa is Associate Professor at the School of Criminal Justice at Rutgers University, U.S.

Routledge Contemporary Issues in Criminal Justice and Procedure

Series Editor Ed Johnston is an Associate Professor of Criminal Justice and Procedure at the *University of Northampton, U.K.*

Justifying Punishment
Perspectives from Post-Communist Europe
Edited by Jakub Drápal

International Perspectives of Neuroscience in the Youth Justice Courtroom
Edited by Hannah Wishart and Ray Arthur

Poor Defence Lawyering in Criminal Proceedings
A Comparative View
Edited by Ashlee Beazley, Michele Panzavolta and Andrew Sanders

The Digital Courtroom
Participation, Attendance, Engagement and Consumption
Lisa Flower

Justice Denied: Exploring Inequities in the Legal System
Edited by Ed Johnston and Claire-Michelle Smyth

Access to Justice for Persons with Psychosocial Disabilities
A Comparative Analysis of Participation in the Kenyan Criminal Justice System
Paul Ochieng Juma

Neuroscience in Criminal Justice Systems
The Positive Impact of Neurojustice
Edited by Hannah Wishart and Colleen M. Berryessa

See more at https://www.routledge.com/Routledge-Contemporary-Issues-in-Criminal-Justice-and-Procedure/book-series/CONTEMPCJP

Neuroscience in Criminal Justice Systems

The Positive Impact of Neurojustice

Edited by Hannah Wishart and Colleen M. Berryessa

Routledge
Taylor & Francis Group
LONDON AND NEW YORK

First published 2026

by Routledge
4 Park Square, Milton Park, Abingdon, Oxon OX14 4RN

and by Routledge
605 Third Avenue, New York, NY 10158

Routledge is an imprint of the Taylor & Francis Group, an informa business

British Library Cataloguing-in-Publication Data
A catalogue record for this book is available from the British Library

Library of Congress Cataloging-in-Publication Data
Names: Wishart, Hannah editor | Berryessa, Colleen M. editor
Title: Neuroscience in criminal justice systems : the positive impact of neurojustice / edited by Hannah Wishart and Colleen M. Berryessa.
Description: Abingdon, Oxon [UK] ; New York, NY : Routledge, 2026. | Series: Routledge contemporary issues in criminal justice and procedure | Includes bibliographical references and index.
Identifiers: LCCN 2025044469 (print) | LCCN 2025044470 (ebook) | ISBN 9781032827599 hardback | ISBN 9781032836164 paperback | ISBN 9781003510246 ebook
Subjects: LCSH: Neurosciences—Law and legislation | Neurosciences—Law and legislation—Criminal provisions | Neurosciences—Law and legislation—European Union countries | Criminal justice, Administration of—Psychological aspects | Criminals—Rehabilitation | Criminal psychology | Cognitive science
Classification: LCC K487.S3 N49 2026 (print) | LCC K487.S3 (ebook)
LC record available at https://lccn.loc.gov/2025044469
LC ebook record available at https://lccn.loc.gov/2025044470

ISBN: 978-1-032-82759-9 (hbk)
ISBN: 978-1-032-83616-4 (pbk)
ISBN: 978-1-003-51024-6 (ebk)

DOI: 10.4324/9781003510246

Typeset in Galliard
by Apex CoVantage, LLC

Contents

About the Editors

Hannah Wishart is Senior Lecturer in Law at the University of Sunderland. She is co-author of the following books: *Neurolaw in the Courtroom: Comparative Perspectives on Vulnerable Defendants* (Routledge) and *International Perspectives of Neuroscience in the Youth Justice Courtroom* (Routledge). Hannah has published peer-reviewed journal articles on the relevance of neuroscience in youth justice, the abolition of the doctrine of *doli incapax*, and the unfair treatment of developmentally immature children in the English criminal justice system. Hannah's research interests include youth justice, neurolaw, legal defences, and adolescent brain development.

Colleen M. Berryessa is Associate Professor at the Rutgers University School of Criminal Justice. She utilises both qualitative and quantitative methods to consider how psychological processes, perceptions, attitudes, and social contexts affect the criminal justice system, particularly related to courts, sentencing, and forms of punishment broadly defined. She received a Ph.D. in criminology from the University of Pennsylvania, a B.A. in government and mind, brain, and behavior from Harvard University, and served as a CIRGE research fellow at Stanford University.

Contributors

Ray Arthur is a professor of law at Northumbria University who specialises in researching children's right to self-determination in justice settings and developing a broader understanding of the experiences of troubled and vulnerable young people. This interdisciplinary research embraces innovative methodologies to shape and advance the research of children's rights and family justice in novel child-centric ways, empowering young people by giving them a voice to their experiences. He has previously worked at Teesside University, the Open University, the University of Birmingham, and the University of Limerick.

Joshua Budhu is a neuro-oncologist and the Nicholls-Biondi Diversity Clinical Scientist Faculty Scholar at Memorial Sloan Kettering Cancer Center, and an assistant professor of neurology at Weill Cornell Medical College in New York City.

Carolina R. Caliman is a Ph.D. candidate at the Rutgers University School of Criminal Justice. Her research focuses on courts and sentencing, examining the perceptions and decision-making processes of courtroom actors. She is particularly interested in the intersection of law and psychology, including mental health and substance addiction, as well as the impacts of expungement policies and clean slate legislation on legal outcomes and public opinion. She received a M.A. in criminal justice from Rutgers University and a Bachelor of Laws (LL.B.) from the Federal University of Espírito Santo in Brazil.

Gregg D. Caruso is Professor of Ethics and Director of the Patrick J. Waide Center for Applied Ethics at Fairfield University. He is also Honorary Professor of Philosophy at Macquarie University and Co-Director of the Justice Without Retribution Network at the University of Aberdeen. His research focuses on free will, moral responsibility, punishment, business ethics, philosophy of law, moral psychology, philosophy of mind, neuroethics, and applied issues in moral, legal, and political philosophy. His books include *How to Live Well Without Free Will* (forthcoming), *Neurolaw* (2024), *Moral Responsibility Reconsidered* (with Derk Pereboom, 2022), *Rejecting*

Retributivism: Free Will, Punishment, and Criminal Justice (2021), *Just Deserts: Debating Free Will* (with Denial Dennett, 2021), *Public Health and Safety: The Social Determinant of Health and Criminal Behavior* (2017), and *Free Will and Consciousness: A Determinist Account of the Illusion of Free Will* (2012).

Amanda V. Chen is currently a student at Harvard Medical School and will attend Harvard Law School in the fall of 2026. She graduated from Dartmouth College in 2021 with a degree in psychology and founded Dartmouth's first mental health peer support program. Amanda is currently a research assistant for Dr. Stephanie Tabashneck. After graduating from law school, Amanda plans to bring her psychology and medicine background to her legal work.

Jean Grace Choi is a registered optometrist with TPA endorsement (allowing her to prescribe medication for ocular conditions) and enrolled Barrister and Solicitor of the High Court of New Zealand. She graduated from optometry in 2014, law with honours in 2024, taught clinical optometry at the Faculty of Health and Medical Sciences, and currently works as a research fellow assisting Professor Mark Henaghan at the University of Auckland Law School. Jean has a particular research interest in the intersection of medicine and the law, including neuroscience.

Olivia Choy is an assistant professor of psychology at Nanyang Technological University, Singapore. She received her Ph.D. in criminology from the University of Pennsylvania. Her research focuses on examining biological factors together with psychological and social-environmental variables to gain a more complete understanding of the development and treatment of antisocial behavior in children and adults. Specifically, she studies psychophysiological factors, brain mechanisms using non-invasive brain stimulation and neuroimaging methods, and nutrition in relation to crime and antisocial behavior.

Federica Coppola is an assistant professor of law at IE Law School (Madrid, Spain) and a research affiliate at the Department of Criminal Law at the Max Planck Institute for the Study of Crime, Security, and Law (Freiburg, Germany), which she originally joined as a senior researcher in 2021. She holds a JD summa cum laude from the University of Bologna, an LL.M. in international, comparative, and European laws, and a Ph.D. in law from the European University Institute. Following her Ph.D., she was Robert A. Burt Presidential Scholar in Society and Neuroscience at Columbia University in New York and a lecturer in criminal law and neuroscience at Columbia Law School. Federica's areas of expertise include criminal law theory, sentencing and punishment, criminal constitutional law, criminal and social justice, and neurolaw. She is the author of *The Emotional Brain and the Guilty Mind* (Hart Publishing, 2021) and the co-editor of *Social Rehabilitation and Criminal Justice* (Routledge, 2024).

Brianna da Silva Bhatia is an internal medicine physician in Portland, Oregon. She served as the SARS-CoV-2 (COVID-19) health strategist at Physicians for Human Rights (PHR).

Deborah W. Denno is the Arthur A. McGivney Professor of Law and Founding Director of the Neuroscience and Law Center at Fordham Law School. She received her B.A. from the University of Virginia, her M.A. from the University of Toronto, her Ph.D. in sociology with a specialty in criminology from the University of Pennsylvania, and her J.D. from the University of Pennsylvania Law School. Her forthcoming book, *Changing Law's Mind: How Neuroscience Can Help Us Punish Criminals More Fairly and Effectively* (Oxford University Press), focuses on her empirical study of all criminal cases (totaling nearly 9,000 cases) that addressed social neuroscientific evidence over 12 decades (1900–2020). In 2024, Professor Denno received the ABA Criminal Justice Section's Raeder-Taslitz Award.

Mark Henaghan is a professor of law at the University of Auckland in Aotearoa, New Zealand, Fellow of the Royal Society of New Zealand, and Co-Director of the Academic Liaison Team of the International Academy of Family Lawyers. Mark specialises in all aspects of family law, including neuroscience in the criminal justice system.

Sjors Ligthart is an associate professor of criminal law at Tilburg University, the Netherlands, and a principal investigator of the project "Mental Liberty in the Age of Modern Technology: Towards Absolute Protection of the Mind?" (VI.Veni.231 R.022). He is a postdoctoral researcher at the Willem Pompe Institute for Criminal Law and Criminology, Utrecht University, the Netherlands, on the research project "Law and Ethics of Neurotechnology in Criminal Justice" (VI.C.201.067). He is the author of *Coercive Brain-Reading in Criminal Justice: An Analysis of European Human Rights Law* (Cambridge University Press, 2022) and co-author of *Minds, Freedoms and Rights: On Neurorehabilitation in Criminal Justice* (Cambridge University Press, 2025).

Katherine J. McLachlan is a senior lecturer and Teaching Program Director of Criminology at Flinders University. She has extensive experience working across criminal justice and social welfare agencies focused on child protection and child exploitation, youth justice, police intelligence, crime policy and research, victim support, and corrections. She is currently a member of the Parole Board of South Australia and has interviewed hundreds of people who have offended. She is an award-winning teacher and senior fellow, Advance HE with a professional interest in victimology, trauma-informed practice, sentencing, and violence against women and children.

Gerben Meynen is Professor of Ethics, in particular bioethics, Department of Philosophy, VU University Amsterdam, and Professor of Forensic Psychiatry, Willem Pompe Institute for Criminal Law and Criminology and Utrecht

Centre for Accountability and Liability Law (UCALL), Utrecht University. He co-edited *Neurolaw: Advances in Neuroscience, Justice and Security* (Palgrave MacMillan, 2021) and *Brain and Crime*, Volume 197 in the Elsevier series *Handbook of Clinical Neurology* (2023). In 2021, he received a Vici grant from the Dutch Research Council (NWO) for the project "Law and Ethics of Neurotechnology in Criminal Justice" (VI.C.201.067). He also works as a psychiatrist.

Joanna Naples-Mitchell is an international human rights lawyer. She currently serves as U.S. Research Advisor at Physicians for Human Rights (PHR) and Director of the Redress Program at the Zomia Center. She has previously worked for Human Rights Watch and the Human Rights and Special Prosecutions Section of the Criminal Division of the U.S. Department of Justice. She holds a law degree from New York University School of Law and a bachelor's degree from Harvard University. She is admitted to practice law in the state of New York.

Altaf Saadi is a neurologist at Massachusetts General Hospital and associate professor of neurology at Harvard Medical School. She is a medical expert for Physicians for Human Rights (PHR) and co-authored a PHR report on "Excited delirium" alongside Ms. Naples-Mitchell and Dr. da Silva Bhatia. She has also leveraged her neurological expertise to speak against the use of carotid neck restraints by law enforcement, the medical harms of police attack dog bites, and the harms of hospital police. In addition to her work with PHR, she has provided medical expertise to other leading human rights and civil rights organisations, including the American Civil Liberties Union (ACLU), National Immigrant Justice Center, Human Rights First, and Disability Rights California, among others. Her national recognition includes the 2023 Bernard Lown Award for Social Responsibility, a national award for health justice leadership. She received her M.D. from Harvard Medical School, a Master's in health policy and management from the UCLA Fielding School of Public Health, and a B.A. in psychology and international studies from Yale University.

Elizabeth Shaw is a senior lecturer in the School of Law at the University of Aberdeen. She is a co-director of the Justice Without Retribution Network. Her research interests are interdisciplinary, involving criminal law, philosophy, and neuroscience. She is a co-editor of *Free Will Skepticism in Law and Society* (Cambridge University Press, 2019) and *The Routledge Handbook of the Philosophy and Science of Punishment* (Routledge, 2021) and author of *Punishment and Moral Uncertainty: Seeking Convergence on Criminal Justice* (Cambridge University Press, forthcoming).

Stephanie Tabashneck is a forensic psychologist and attorney in Cambridge, Massachusetts. She is a senior fellow in law and applied neuroscience at the Center for Law, Brain and Behavior at Massachusetts General Hospital at Harvard Medical School and the Petrie-Flom Center for Health Law Policy at Harvard Law School. She is president of the Massachusetts Association of Family and Conciliation Courts and a past member of the Ethics Committee for the American Psychological Association. She presents regionally and nationally on psychology and law topics. Recent publications include the book *Substance Use and Parenting: Best Practices for Family Court Practitioners*, a white paper on the *Science of Late Adolescence: A Guide for Judges, Attorneys, and Policy Makers*, and an article on the opioid crisis and family drug courts.

Mia A. Thomaidou is a Neuroscience and Society Fellow at the Dana Foundation. She completed a post-doctoral fellowship at Rutgers University, School of Criminal Justice between 2022–2024. Mia completed her Ph.D. in the field of behavioral neuroscience in the Netherlands and holds a BSc in cognitive neuroscience from the University of Westminster in London and two MSc degrees, in neuropsychology and criminal justice. Her current work focuses on applications of science in the context of criminal justice, policy, and society more generally. She also has a particular interest in data science and the potentials of artificial intelligence and algorithmic decision-making to transform the landscape of criminal justice by facilitating impartiality, fairness, and efficiency.

Naomi van de Pol is a Ph.D. researcher at the Willem Pompe Institute for Criminal Law and Criminology (WPI) and the Utrecht Centre for Accountability and Liability Law (UCALL), Utrecht University. Her research is part of the project "Law and Ethics of Neurotechnology in Criminal Justice" (VI.C.201.067), exploring the human rights protection for the mind and the fundamental rights involved in using neurotechnology to predict and prevent recidivism in criminal justice. She also serves as the managing editor of the *Netherlands Quarterly of Human Rights*.

Sandy S. Xie is a Ph.D. candidate in the School of Criminal Justice at Rutgers University—Newark. She received her M.S. in criminology from the University of Pennsylvania and her B.A. in criminology with minors in sociology and neuroscience from the Pennsylvania State University. Her research focuses on neuroscience and neuroethics, biopsychosocial criminology, responsibility and morality, mental health, bias and stigma, and public perceptions.

Abbreviations

ABD	Acute Behavioural Disturbance
ACC	Anterior Cingulate Cortex
ACE	Adverse Childhood Experiences
ACEP	American College of Emergency Physicians
ASD	Autism Spectrum Disorder
ASERT	Autism Services, Education, Resources, and Training Collaborative
ADHD	Attention Deficit Hyperactivity Disorder
AMA	American Medical Association
APA	American Psychiatric Association
ATI	Alternatives to Incarceration
BART	Bay Area Rapid Transit
CBT	Cognitive Behavioural Therapy
CEPOL	European Police College
CF	Correctional Facility
CIT	Crisis Intervention Training
CITs	Crisis Intervention Teams
CLE	Continuing Legal Education
CPTSD	Complex Post-Traumatic Stress Disorder
CRAFT	Community Reinforcement Approach and Family Training
CT	Computed Tomography
DAT	Dopamine Transporter Expression
DDA	Doctrine of Doing and Allowing
DOC	Department of Corrections
DSM	*Diagnostic and Statistical Manual of Mental Disorders*
DSM-5	*Diagnostic and Statistical Manual of Mental Disorders*, 5th Ed.
DSM-5-TR	*Diagnostic and Statistical Manual of Mental Disorders*, 5th Ed. Text Revision
ECHR	European Convention on Human Rights
ECtHR	European Court of Human Rights
EEG	Electroencephalography
EMCDDA	European Monitoring Centre for Drugs and Drug Addiction
EUDA	European Union Drugs Agency
FASD	Foetal Alcohol Syndrome Disorder

fMRI	functional Magnetic Resonance Imaging
G2i	Group-to-Individual Issue
HPA	Hypothalamic-Pituitary Adrenal
HSP70	Heat Shock Protein-70
ICC	International Criminal Court
ICD	*International Classification of Diseases*
ICD-9	*International Classification of Diseases*, 9th Revision
ID	Intellectually Disabled
IDEAL	Infant Development and Lifestyle
IPICD	Institute for the Prevention of In-Custody Deaths
LENC	Law and Ethics of Neurotechnology in Criminal Justice
LRO	Limited Rehabilitation Opportunity
M110	Measure 110
MACR	Minimum Age of Criminal Responsibility
MHTR	Mental Health Treatment Requirements
MRI	Magnetic Resonance Imaging
NOX2	NADPH oxidase
NPS	National Probation Service
NWO	Dutch Research Council
PCSC	Police, Crime, Sentencing and Courts Act
PET	Positron Emission Tomography
PDPM	Portuguese Drug Policy Model
PFC	Prefrontal Cortex
PHR	Physicians for Human Rights
PLRA	Prison Litigation Reform Act
PTSD	Post-Traumatic Stress Disorder
RCT	Randomised Controlled Trial
SIM	Sequential Intercept Model
SJC	Supreme Judicial Court
SUD	Substance Use Disorder
TBI	Traumatic Brain Injury
tDCS	transcranial Direct Current Stimulation
U.K.	United Kingdom
UN	United Nations
U.S.	United States of America
YAL	Young Adult List
YOT	Youth Offending Team

Table of Statutes

C.A. Assembly Bill No. 360 (an act to add Section 1156.5 to the Evidence Code, and to add Chapter 3.5, commencing with Section 24400, to Division 20 of the Health and Safety Code) (2023).

'Engrossed Senate Bill 5476' (*State of Washington*) Criminal Procedure (Mentally Impaired Persons) Act (2003).

Evidence Act (2006).

Intellectual Disability (Compulsory Care and Rehabilitation) Act (2003).

Pennsylvania Judicial Code, Title 42 (2017).

The Age of Criminal Responsibility (Scotland) Act (2019).

The Age of Criminal Responsibility Bill (2019–2021).

The Children Act (1989).

The Children and Young Persons Act (1969).

The Crime and Disorder Act (1998).

The Police, Crime, Sentencing and Courts Act (2022).

The Prison Litigation Reform Act Pub. L. No. 104–134, tit. VIII, 110 Stat. 1321–66 (1996) (codified as amended in scattered sections of the U.S. Code)

The Sentencing Act (2002).

U.S. Constitution, Eighth Amendment (1791).

U.S. Model Penal Code (1960).

Table of Cases

Apodaka et al. v. Raemish et al. / Lowe et al. v. Raemish et al. 586 U. S. ___ (2018).
Ashker v. Governor of California [2014] No. C 09-5796 CW (N.D. Cal. Jun. 2, 2014).
Beers-Capitol v. Whetzel [2001] 3d Cir 256 F.3d 120.
BW v. Commonwealth of Australia [2023] NZHC 1587.
C v. Director of Public Prosecutions [1994] 3 All ER 190.
Callwood v. Jones [2018] U.S. Supreme Court 39 S. Ct. 100.
Churchward v. R [2011] NZCA 531.
Clark v. Coupe [2022] 3d Cir No. 21-2310.
Coleman v. Brown [2014] E.D. Cal 28 F. Supp. 3d 1068, 1109.
Commonwealth v. Eldred [2018] Mass SJC No SJC-12279.
Cox v. Glanz [2015] 800 F.3d 1231 (2015).
Crane v. Utah DOC [2022] 15 F.4th 1296.
Daubert v. Merrell Dow Pharmaceuticals, Inc., 509 [1993] U.S. Supreme Court U.S. 579.
Davis v. Ayala [2015] 567 U.S. 257.
Declaration of Steven B Karch, MO, FFELM, Rosa v. TASER International, Inc. [2009] N.D. Cal No. C-05-03577 JF/HRL.
Deposition of Vincent J.M. Di Maio, M.D. at 159:19–21.
Dickey v. R [2023] NZCA 2.
Farmer v. Brennan [1994] 511 U.S. 825, 834.
Finley v. Huss et al. [2024] 6th Cir No. 23-1083.
Frye v. United States [1923] DC Cir *293 F 1013.*
G. H. et al. v. Florida Dept. of Juvenile Justice (ongoing), Class Action Complaint (filed on May 9, 2019) <https://www.splcenter.org/sites/default/files/doc._2_-_complaint.pdf>
Gallacher v. R [2024] NZCA 335.
Goode v. Baggett [2020] 5th Cir 811 F. App'x 227.
Graham v. Florida [2010] 560 U.S. 48.
Gregory v. County of Maui [2006] 9th Cir 414 F. Supp. 2d 965.

Hammond v. Pennsylvania DOC (ongoing), Class Action Complaint (filed on March 3 2024) <https://abolitionistlawcenter.org/wp-content/uploads/2024/03/Hammond-v.-DOC-030424-Complaint.pdf>.
Harrison v. County of Alameda [2014] N.D. Cal No. C11-2868 JST.
Harvard et al. v. Florida DOC (ongoing), Class Action Complaint (filed on August 5, 2019) <https://fji.law/wp-content/uploads/2019/05/Class-Action-Complaint-for-Declaratory-and-Injunctive-Relief-07205539xB3B17.pdf>.
Hope v. Harris [2022] U.S. 21.
Hoyt v. Cooks et al. [2012] 11th Cir 672 F.3d 972, 976.
Jones' El v. Berge [2001] W.D. Wis. 164 F. Supp. 2d 1096.
Jordan v. Gardner [1993] 9th Cir 986 F.2d 1521, 1529 (en banc).
M v. R [2024] NZCA 451.
Maaka-Wanahi v. Police [2023] NZHC 3291.
Madrid v. Gomez [1995] N.D. Cal. 889 F. Supp. 1146.
Mann v. Taser International [2009] 11th Cir 588 F.3d 1291.
Marquez v. City of Phoenix [2012] 9th Cir 693 F.3d 1167; [2006] 9th Cir 414 F. Supp. 2d 965.
Miller v. Alabama [2012] USSC 10-9646
New Zealand Police v. Morrison [2019] NZDC 13977.
Ngamoki v. R [2022] NZCA 171.
Odle v. Calderon [1996] N.D. Cal. 919 F Supp 1367.
Odle v. Woodford [2001] 9th Cir 238 F3d 1084.
Palakovic v. Wetzel [2017] 3d Cir 854 F. 3d 209.
People v. Buss [1999] Ill 718 NE2d 1.
People v. Odle [1988] Cal 754 P2d 184.
Peoples v. Annucci [2016] SDNY 180 F. Supp. 3d 294.
Peppers v. Washington County, Tenn. [2017] 6th Cir 686 Fed. App'x. 328.
Peroza-Benitez v. Smith [2021] 3d Cir 994 F.3d 157, 165.
Pirolozzi v. Stanbro, F Supp 2d [2009] U.S. Dist LEXIS 42575, 2009 WL 1441070 (N.D).
Platt v. R [2010] NZCA 43.
Pora v. R [2015] UKPC 9, [2016] 1 NZLR 277.
Porter v. McCollum, 558 US 30 [2009] United States Supreme Court 08-10537.
R v. Abbott [1964] 1 Q.B 489.
R v. Bonython 38 SASR [1984] Supreme Court of South Australia.
R v. Clarke and Ors [2018] EWCA Crim 185, [2018] 1 Cr App R (S) 52.
R v. Fawcett [2021] NZHC 2406.
R v. Geoghegan (Kieran) [2019] EWCA Crim 787.
R v. L [2019] *EWCA Crim 1326.*
R v. Markham and Edwards [2017] EWCA Crim 739.
R v. Pritchard [1836] 7 C & P 303.
R v. Tupoumalohi [2024] NZHC 3278.
R v. ZA [2023] EWCA Crim 596.

Roper v. Simmons [2005] 543 U.S. 551.
Sanders v. Melvin [2017] 7th Cir 873 F.3d 957; [2022] 7th Cir No. 20-3276.
Scarver v. Litscher [2005] *W.D. Wis.* 371 F. Supp. 2d 986, 1003 (W.D. Wis. 2005); aff'd, [2006] 7th Cir. 434 F.3d 972.
Scher v. Engelke [1991] 8th Cir. 943 F.2d 921, 924.
Schmidt and Šmigol v. Estonia [2023] App. no 3501/20 and two others (ECtHR, 28 November 2023).
Shakka v. Smith [1995] 4th Cir 71 F.3d 162, 166.
State v. Blake [2021] Wash Sup Ct, No 96873-0.
State v. Burr [2008] N.J. 948 A.2d 627, 634.
Taylor v. Riojas [2020] 592 U.S. 7.
Thomas v. Farley [1994] 7th Cir. 31 F.3d 557, 559.
Thomas v. Tice, 948 F.3d 133 (3d Cir. 2020).
Thorpe et al. v. Virginia DOC (ongoing), Class Action Complaint (filed on June 5, 2019) <https://www.acluva.org/sites/default/files/field_documents/2019_05_06_001_complaint.pdf>
Thorpe v. Clarke [2022] et al. 37 F.4th 926 (2022).
Toevs v. Reid [2012] 685 F.3d 903, 916.
United States v. Runyon [2021] 4th Cir 994 F3d 192, 204.
United States v. D.W. [2016] EDNY 198 F. Supp. 3d 18.
United States v. Bannister [2011] EDNY 786 F. Supp. 2d 617.
V W v. Nichelini [2017] ED CA WL 34246.
W. Austl. v. Mack [2012] WASC 127, 41.
Wallace v. Baldwin [2018] 7th Cir 895 F.3d 481.
Wilkinson v. Austin [2005] 545 U.S. 209, 222.
Williams v. Sec'y Pa. Dept. Corr [2017] 3d Cir 848 F.3d 549.
Wilson v. Seiter [1991] 501 U.S. 294, 301–02.
Zhang v. R [2019] NZCA 507, [2019] 3 NZLR 648

Introduction

Hannah Wishart and Colleen M. Berryessa

The chapters in this edited volume demonstrate the tangible and positive impact that neuroscience has had and continues to have on individuals involved in the criminal justice system—witnesses, victims, defendants, and legal practitioners—in specific jurisdictions worldwide. Over the last 30 years, analyses of neuroscience—'a branch of the life sciences that studies the brain and nervous system'[1]—and its potential impacts on international criminal justice have figured prominently in interdisciplinary academic debates and law school curricula.[2] Neuroscience has significantly informed legal, philosophical, and doctrinal discussions by deepening our understanding of the relationships between the brain, mind, and criminality. Most leading international legal scholars have examined the relevance of neuroscience within the criminal justice system in their specific jurisdictions and particular subgroups of individuals, such as children and young people. These original arguments have spurred proposed reforms in legal frameworks and processes regarding unfitness to plead, culpability, sentencing, and risk assessment in countries such as Australia,[3] the Netherlands,[4] New Zealand,[5] the United Kingdom,[6] and the United States of America.[7]

1 B. Garland, *Neuroscience and the Law: Brain, Mind, and the Scales of Justice* (Chicago University Press, Chicargo, 2004) 206.

2 Notable universities that embed neuroscience and law modules include Harvard Law School (U.S.), The Open University (U.K.), and Maastricht University (Netherlands).

3 A. Alimardani, J. Chin, 'Neurolaw in Australia: The Use of Neuroscience in Australian Criminal Proceedings' (2019) 12 *Neuroethics* 255–270.

4 See, for example, S. Ligthart, 'Coercive Neuroimaging, Criminal Law, and Privacy: A European Perspective' (2019) 6(1) *Journal of Law and the Biosciences* 289–309.

5 See, for example, M. Henaghan, J. Choi, 'Promising Steps in Aotearoa New Zealand Criminal Law to Recognise Neurodiversity' in H. Wishart, C. Berryessa (eds), *International Perspectives of Neuroscience in the Youth Justice Courtroom* (Routledge, London, 2025) 55–71.

6 P. Catley, L. Claydon, 'The Use of Neuroscientific Evidence in the Courtroom by Those Accused of Criminal Offenses in England and Wales' (2015) 2(3) *Journal of Law and the Biosciences* 510–549.

7 See, for example, D. Denno, 'The Place for Neuroscience in Criminal Law' in D. Patterson, M. S. Pardo (eds), *Philosophical Foundations of Law and Neuroscience* (Oxford University

DOI: 10.4324/9781003510246-1

However, examinations of how neuroscience has positively transformed the landscape of the criminal justice system through such reforms have scarcely addressed the experiences of system-impacted individuals, including youths, trauma-affected persons, and autistic defendants. To date, no book has offered an in-depth exploration of the positive socio-legal impacts and future applications of neuroscience in global criminal justice, aimed at improving the treatment of individuals impacted by the system. International legal scholars have extensively examined the practical relevance and application of neuroscience in criminal justice systems worldwide. Increasingly, novel arguments about mental (in)competency, guilt, legal insanity, and neuroscience-informed expert medical evidence have arisen.

Although valuable in a theoretical context, many discussions have remained practically inconclusive, and applications of neuroscience as legal evidence in courts have been limited. This book is needed because no other literature has surveyed what neuroscience has positively contributed to current and pragmatic applications across jurisdictions involving a wide range of people in criminal justice to date; it has focused on how neuroscience can impact the law (theoretically and practically) in the future and why a neuroscientific-centred approach to policy reform is required. The idea for the collection arose when the editors examined the literature and identified a gap, as no single piece of research surveys the positive and realistic applications of neuroscience for specific populations in contemporary international criminal justice.[8]

By embracing a practical and realist perspective, this edited collection is the first to answer the fundamental (yet underexplored) question of what and how neuroscience has positively and concretely contributed to criminal justice. Notably, the volume brings together worldwide perspectives to discuss the positive impact of neuroscience on the global criminal justice system for witnesses, victims, defendants, and legal practitioners across different stages of the criminal justice system. These chapters are organised under two subheadings: the criminal trial (Chapters 1 to 4) and punishment, treatment, and reform (Chapters 5 to 12).

In Chapter 1, Hannah Wishart and Ray Arthur examine the contributions of neuroscientific evidence of adolescent brain development to youth justice law and policy in England and Wales. They will show that the youth justice system in England and Wales continues not to support children and young people's developmental immaturity and lack of capacity. In English law, children are held criminally responsible and punished for their actions from 10 years of age because it is assumed that they possess the legally relevant capacities

Press, New York, 2016) 69–83; O. D. Jones, F. X. Shen, 'Law and Neuroscience in the United States' in T. M. Spranger (ed), *International Neurolaw a Comparative Analysis* (Spranger, Heidelberg, 2012) 349–380.

8 We would like to acknowledge Federica Coppola for her invaluable insights and early contribution to this project. Without her guidance and insights, this project would not have been possible.

necessary for blame. However, the latest neuroscientific evidence suggests that maturation is a long and complex process that stretches into adulthood. The developmental differences in the brain's biochemistry and anatomy limit children's ability to perceive risks, control impulses, understand consequences, and control emotions. The prefrontal lobe is involved in controlling aggression and other behavioural impulses related to criminal responsibility. Yet, this lobe is the last area to mature, developing in the twenties rather than the teen years. They argue that this evidence highlights that the children's inexperience and under-developed powers of self-control and reasoning make them prone to acting in ways they cannot help, understand, or intend. These insights suggest that some children may be exempt from criminal responsibility, and abolishing the defence of *doli incapax* was a short-sighted move. They claim that the English youth justice system should support the child's development by more explicitly considering the Child First imperative of promoting their status as capacity-evolving persons. Thus, it is concluded that English law should introduce a developmental immaturity defence.

In Chapter 2, Deborah W. Denno explains that at its broadest, neuroscience encompasses all information pertaining to the brain and its functions, a definition that also includes different types of brain injury. Folded into this definition is what constitutes 'brain injury.' In the United States and internationally, there has been an increase in the use of neuroscientific evidence to assess defendants' brain injuries in court, often as a means to determine punishment. With a substantial portion of the criminal population suffering from some form of brain injury, examining such evidence can reveal its impact on assessing defendants' mental states and innovative sentencing. This chapter focuses on the results of Denno's 12-decade Neuroscience Study and other empirical research analysing criminal cases in the United States and other countries, including Canada, England and Wales, the Netherlands, and Slovenia. Through comparative study, she argues that we can turn a critical eye toward how the criminal justice system treats brain-injured defendants and what the future holds for such ever-evolving evidence.

In Chapter 3, Joanna Naples-Mitchell, Brianna da Silva Bhatia, Joshua Budhu, and Altaf Saadi describe the 'excited delirium' defence, which has been widely used as justification for aggressive law enforcement tactics and as an explanation for deaths in law enforcement custody, and how its lack of scientific basis leads to misapplications of neuroscience. Particularly, the use of 'excited delirium' has reached a critical turning point in recent years, catalysed by the Black Lives Matter protests of summer 2020 and, in response, physician advocacy efforts. They review the history of 'excited delirium,' how it has been propagated in the United States and globally as pseudoscience, and how advocates, researchers, and healthcare professionals have worked in concert to drive significant policy and cultural changes. Overall, neuroscientists, physicians, and other healthcare professionals must acknowledge how science can be misused to perpetuate harm and racism. Dispelling the term and concept both within law enforcement communities and the criminal justice system at large is essential to ensuring accurate forensic investigations, preventing future harm, and upholding principles of evidence-based justice.

In Chapter 4, Naomi van de Pol, Gerben Meynen, and Sjors Ligthart argue that neuroscientific information retrieved by neuroimaging technologies has made positive contributions to the assessment of legal responsibility, risk, and treatment in Dutch criminal trials, particularly by drawing from examples from Dutch case law. In the Netherlands, neuroimaging has been increasingly used to help determine a defendant's criminal responsibility and legal insanity, with the Institute for Forensic Psychiatry and Psychology of the Dutch Ministry of Justice and Security recently pleading for expanding the use of neuroimaging in forensic examinations of criminal suspects. The authors also look to the future in which neurotechnology in criminal justice can present risks and opportunities for convicted persons' human rights, particularly to ensure that rights protect people *against* potential risks and *support* opportunities presented by emerging neurotechnologies. Overall, this chapter suggests that neurotechnologies can help improve legal judgements during criminal trials and be applied to individual cases to optimise and personalise treatment and care after conviction.

In Chapter 5, Elizabeth Shaw and Gregg D. Caruso articulate the concept of 'neuroprediction' in criminal justice, examining the possibilities for and concerns surrounding using neuroprediction in actuarial risk assessments in criminal trials. Drawing from theories of retributivism, consequentialism, and non-consequentialist social protection, they describe why the use of neuroprediction may be opposed by retributivists, but that consequentialists may be more willing to embrace this technology. The chapter offers insights from the philosophy of punishment and debates surrounding free will, demonstrating how neuroscience can enhance criminal justice policy related to risk assessment and also has the potential to inform penal theory and reform moving forward.

In Chapter 6, Katherine J. McLachlan examines the relevance of psychological and neurophysiological trauma in sentencing, specifically in reducing moral culpability and the impact on deterrence, as well as informing effective sanctions in Australia. She wrestles with how and why defendants with backgrounds of trauma might have their trauma-related 'mental disorders or abnormalities' influence their sentencing outcomes, particularly focusing on the application of principles from a Victorian Court of Appeal case that has been the leading Australian authority on the relevance of mental impairments in sentencing. By applying this framework to cases moving forward, evidence-informed sentencing that focuses on trauma as an individualised 'mental impairment' can lead to better sentencing outcomes for defendants across jurisdictions. The issues raised in this chapter are of interest to jurisdictions such as Canada, the United States (U.S.), the United Kingdom (U.K.), and Aotearoa, New Zealand, given the parallels in the sentencing calculus across countries with a Westminster system of law.

In Chapter 7, Mark Henaghan and Jean Grace Choi illustrate how specific lower courts in Aotearoa, New Zealand, have adopted principles from neurodisability jurisprudence to protect vulnerable defendants throughout Aotearoa, New Zealand, with a particular focus on Foetal Alcohol Syndrome Disorder (FASD) and the emerging issue of methamphetamine exposure in utero. In Aotearoa, New Zealand, the impact of neuroscience has been limited in the higher courts due to the lack of neuroscience experts available on FASD and the limited community support upon release. However, the Young Adult List, a specialist lower court, has begun to adopt a range of neuroscience understandings to improve procedural fairness for neurodivergent defendants. This not only enables procedural fairness and a therapeutic approach but also helps to increase knowledge of neuroscience and neurodiversity within court processes.

In Chapter 8, Sandy S. Xie and Olivia Choy examine the ethical dilemmas associated with treating mental health in prison. As individuals with mental health issues continue to proliferate within incarcerated populations, alternatives to imprisonment or as part of a reduced prison sentence, such as diversion to a mental health court, prescription drugs or other medical remedies to manage symptoms, or non-invasive brain-based interventions, have become more common. Although these alternatives may seem promising, they come with the potential ethical and philosophical risks of turning treatment into punishment. After reviewing these risks and possible concerns, the authors conclude that neuroscience and other scientific research can still be utilised to establish outcomes that are more conducive to mental health stability, personal growth, and crime reduction if we also acknowledge the challenges and concerns that arise from the overlap of mental health and the criminal justice system.

In Chapter 9, Federica Coppola discusses how social neuroscience can be used to challenge prolonged solitary confinement in prison litigation in the United States. Solitary confinement is still widely applied and considered constitutionally legitimate. Coppola illustrates how emerging research on the neurobiological damages of extreme isolation provides new and unique legal challenges to solitary confinement, as well as informs key normative arguments that support the recognition of prolonged solitary confinement as a cruel and unusual punishment. The chapter concludes with a call for utilising neuroscientific evidence to challenge solitary confinement as a whole and to support its total abolition. Indeed, neuroscientific research should continue to support the adoption of alternative measures to solitary confinement, emphasising the positive effects of healthy social environments and connections on mental health and behavioural well-being.

In Chapter 10, Carolina R. Caliman and Colleen M. Berryessa describe how neuroscience can aid legal decision-makers to better understand the moral responsibility of defendants with Autism Spectrum Disorder (ASD) and how it can shape more equitable and just legal decision-making during the sentencing proceedings of diagnosed defendants in the U.S. As defendants with ASD face a myriad of difficulties at every stage of the legal process, neuroscience has begun to cultivate better models of care and service innovations for sentencing modifications for defendants with ASD. Specifically, programs in the U.S. states of Pennsylvania and Alabama are paving the way for applying neuroscience to cases involving defendants with ASD, as well as integrating neuroscience into the Sequential Intercept Model (SIM) in sentencing decisions for defendants with ASD. Although the applications and the use of neuroscience within these avenues and in specific jurisdictions have been limited, it represents a valuable tool to inform members of the court on the more appropriate and considerate treatment of defendants with ASD, and international jurisdictions should be able to readily adopt such principles in their jurisdictions as well.

In Chapter 11, Amanda V. Chen and Stephanie Tabashneck discuss how evidence-based criminal justice policies informed by neuroscience can contribute to better outcomes for individuals with substance use disorders (SUD) and the community at large moving forward. Although some countries have taken steps towards some form of decriminalisation after decades of punitive treatment of drug-related offences, some countries, such as Portugal, the Netherlands, and certain U.S. states, have begun to take more medically informed harm reduction approaches to addressing substance abuse. The use of such approaches has led to both increases in treatment and reduced rates of drug use, suggesting the potential success of evidence-based criminal justice policies informed by neuroscience. Even so, policymakers must integrate evidence-based treatments comprehensively with justice systems moving forward.

In Chapter 12, Mia A. Thomaidou draws from other chapters and international examples to discuss the positive impacts of neuroscience education for criminal justice decision-makers to better inform punishment decisions, remedy the treatment of people with mental health problems in prisons, and potentially lead to more effective responses to crime. Given the growing integration of neuroscience into criminal justice settings, scientific comprehension by legal professionals has become imperative. Hence, adequate scientific training can meaningfully impact the comprehension of neuroscience at the criminal trial and aftercare stages. The chapter concludes by presenting a vision for a scientifically informed criminal justice system and offers policy recommendations for the sustainable integration of neuroscience and law.

In conclusion, this edited volume thoughtfully explores the past, present, and future of how neuroscience can inform the criminal justice system to improve the treatment of specific groups of people in discernible and progressive ways, particularly in criminal trials and aftercare. Indeed, globally, neuroscience is being applied in criminal justice systems to allow defendants to be more equitably understood and justly treated. We hope this book and its contributions can speak to an international audience of academics, criminal lawyers, judges, policymakers, advocates, and reformers, equipping them with knowledge about present and immediate future contributions of neuroscience to various dimensions of the criminal justice process. Although we acknowledge that neuroscience is not a magic bullet and should not be viewed as the one-stop solution to all legal issues within the criminal justice system, it, along with the chapters in this book, can help policymakers improve how individuals are treated within it.

1 How Has Neuroscience Positively Contributed to English Youth Justice?

Hannah Wishart and Ray Arthur

Introduction

The rapid expansion of neuroscientific insights into adolescent brain development, revealing that the brain does not reach complete maturity until early adulthood, has garnered significant interest from policymakers and the youth justice system. Over the past 20 years, as noted by Mia A. Thomaidou,[1] the impact of neuroscience on policy has become firmly established in criminal justice systems worldwide, especially in the United States (U.S.). This trend, particularly in youth justice, was notably reinforced by the Supreme Court's landmark ruling in *Roper v. Simmons* (2005), which abolished the death penalty for those under 18 convicted of murder.[2] The United Nations Committee on the Rights of the Child (UN Committee), in *General Comment No. 24* (2019), affirmed that state parties should elevate their MACRs and must 'take note of recent scientific findings.'[3] Given the successful use of neuroscience as a tool for policy reform in the U.S., it was anticipated that neuroscience would also make a similar affirmative contribution to the youth justice system in England and Wales.[4] Charlotte Walsh, in 2011, claimed that there would be a

> lure of a parallel reliance . . . given how neatly these discoveries can be made to mesh with arguments in support of raising the age of criminal responsibility, reinstating the principle of *doli incapax* (or something akin to it) and the advocation of de-carceration.[5]

1 M. Thomaidou, 'Neuroscience Education in the Criminal Justice System' in H. Wishart, C. Berryessa (eds), *Neuroscience in Criminal Justice Systems: The Positive Impact of Neurojustice* (Routledge, Oxon, 2025) chapter 12, p. 209.

2 *Roper v. Simmons*, 543 U.S. 551 (2005) (No. 03-633).

3 United Nations Committee on the Rights of the Child, 'General Comment No. 24' (2019) CRC/C/GC/24 (UN Committee, 2019) 27.

4 C. Walsh, 'Youth Justice and Neuroscience a Dual-Use Dilemma' (2011) 51 *British Journal of Criminology* 21.

5 Ibid. 22.

DOI: 10.4324/9781003510246-2

Since Walsh's statement, a significant body of literature has emerged discussing how neuroscience can aid reform arguments in the English youth justice system. The literature specifically addresses arguments for raising the minimum age of criminal responsibility (MACR) and introducing a developmental immaturity defence with the support of neuroscience research on adolescent brain development.[6] For instance, Claire McDiarmid contended that a defence mechanism is necessary to safeguard young individuals who commit offences within the criminal process, proposing a bespoke defence for those under 18, grounded in the latest neuroscientific evidence.[7] In Parliament, Lord Dholakia similarly referenced neuroscientific evidence on adolescent brain development in the House of Lords to advocate for the passage of the Age of Criminal Responsibility Bill (2019–2021), raising the MACR from 10 to 12 years.[8] Nevertheless, neuroscience has not had the same beneficial impact on the English youth justice system as it has in the U.S.

Child appellants in England and Wales have used neuroscientific research as fresh evidence on appeal as part of a child appellant's defence to reduce their responsibility from murder to manslaughter in English courts.[9] However, neuroscience has not been widely recognised or accepted as admissible in all cases by the judiciary. Neuroscience has also not been used to support positive reforms of the common law for children and young people, as was demonstrated in the U.S. case of *Roper*.[10] The MACR has not increased despite Lord Dholakia's efforts with the Age of Criminal Responsibility Bills and support from the academic community and the UN Committee.[11] The defence of *doli incapax* was abolished in 1998,[12] and no alternative age-inspired defence has replaced it, despite recommendations by the Law Commission and academics in agreement with the neuroscientific literature and the Youth Justice Board's adoption of 'Child First' as a guiding principle of the English and Welsh youth justice system.[13]

6 Law Commission, *Criminal Liability: Insanity and Automatism* (Discussion Paper, July 2013); C. McDiarmid. 'An Age of Complexity: Children and Criminal Responsibility in Law' (2013) 13(2) *Youth Justice* 145–160; C. McDiarmid, 'After the Age of Criminal Responsibility: A Defence for Children Who Offend' (2016) 67(3) *Northern Ireland Legal Quarterly* 327–341.

7 See, generally, McDiarmid (2016).

8 Lord Dholakia, Age of Criminal Responsibility Bill [HL] (Hansard, Volume 783, 8 September 2017) col. 2188 <https://hansard.parliament.uk/Lords/2017-09-08/debates/D3E4D198-43BB-4B60-9FF0-CFF5B0EA1CB6/AgeOfCriminalResponsibilityBill>

9 Note that neuroscience has been used more widely by children and adults as evidence in criminal trials. See further, P. Catley, L. Claydon, 'The Use of Neuroscientific Evidence in the Courtroom by Those Accused of Criminal Offences in England and Wales' (2015) 2(3) *Journal of Law and Biosciences* 510–549.

10 For example, *R v. L* (2019) EWCA Crim 1326.

11 A. Brown, A. Charles, 'The Minimum Age of Criminal Responsibility: The Need for a Holistic Approach' (2019) 21 *Youth Justice* 3; UN Committee on the Rights of the Child (2019) at 27.

12 Section 34 of the Crime and Disorder Act (1998).

13 See, generally, Law Com (2013); McDiarmid (2016); Youth Justice Board, *A Guide to Child First* (Youth Justice Board, 2022) <https://yjresourcehub.uk/wp-content/uploads/media/Child_First_Overview_and_Guide_April_2022_YJB.pdf> accessed February 2025.

This chapter examines how neuroscience has been used effectively and ineffectively applied to reform youth justice in England and Wales by considering key examples of its application in the courts and Parliament. It will recognise how important neuroscientific findings on adolescent brain development are to understandings of children's capacity and behaviour within the English youth justice system. It will also explore meaningful ways in which neuroscience can positively contribute to the future development of the English youth justice system for children and young people.

Neuroscientific Understandings of the Adolescent Brain

Cognitive neuroscience investigates the functional and structural changes during adolescence as the brain develops and matures. The advent of neuroimaging tools, such as Magnetic Resonance Imaging (MRI) and Functional Magnetic Resonance Imaging (fMRI), has significantly transformed our understanding of brain maturation over the past two decades. It was previously thought that the most significant phase of brain maturation was during the first five to eight years of childhood, concluding by early adolescence. However, brain imaging reveals that adolescence is a crucial period characterised by significant and complex brain development, commencing with the onset of puberty and continuing into early adulthood, with the complete maturation of the prefrontal cortex occurring around the mid-twenties.[14]

It has long been established that the brain's overall volume and development remain relatively constant from early childhood; however, significant changes and improvements occur in its structure, connectivity, and function during adolescence. The brain undertakes two neurodevelopmental processes simultaneously, and the key to making these changes is essential for overall brain maturity and improved cognitive function by increasing the brain's white matter, which consists of neural fibres called axons bundled in a white myelin substance. These fibres transmit electrical impulses and signals cell by cell across brain regions, enabling the brain to become more efficient when performing tasks (e.g., making decisions) as it matures incrementally.[15]

These processes are particularly vital in the prefrontal cortex, which is best recognised as the brain's centre for executive function and is the last to attain full maturity due to its intricate structure. The brain follows a progressive hierarchical development model, meaning that the primary sensorimotor areas of the cortex are prioritised in early life and are the first to achieve complete

14 Walsh (2011) 22; Royal College of Psychiatrists, *Additional Submission to Justice Select Committee Inquiry into Children and Young People in Custody* (June 2020) 1 <https://committees.parliament.uk/publications/2010/documents/19436/default/> accessed December 2024.

15 H. Wishart, R. Arthur, T. Butts, 'Outlining the Relationship Between the English Youth Justice System and the Developmental Neurobiology of the Human Brain' in H. Wishart, R. Arthur (eds), *International Perspectives of Neuroscience in the Youth Justice Courtroom* (Routledge, Oxon, 2025) 29–32.

maturity. Meanwhile, unimodal associative regions (e.g., the prefrontal and temporal cortices)[16] take longer to develop and are, therefore, the last to reach maturity, as the brain employs a 'top-down' informational approach to develop executive function and enhance decision-making capabilities.[17]

The long-drawn-out maturation of the prefrontal cortex and related areas of the adolescent brain results in immaturity, diminished cognitive capacity, and deficits in children's decision-making. The prefrontal cortex is critical for processing past experiences, emotions, and information, and contextualising environments from other areas of the cortex, enabling a person to make rational and controlled decisions.[18] Due to its underdevelopment, adolescents are more likely to process information using the amygdala because

> the prefrontal lobe operates like the brakes on a car, most adolescents would be driving cars with very thin brake shoes. It is not that the entire mechanism is missing, but that it is not operating at full strength.[19]

Subsequently, adolescents are not risk-averse, impulsive, and emotional, and seek out risk-taking activities such as criminal behaviour and actions that produce instant rewards.[20]

The (Non-)Application of Neuroscience in the English Youth Justice System

As noted previously, the impact of neuroscience on the development of youth justice laws and policies has been particularly noteworthy in the jurisprudence of the United States Supreme Court in cases such as *Roper v. Simmons* (2005), which declared the juvenile death penalty was unconstitutional, and *Graham v. Florida* (2010),[21] in which the U.S. Supreme Court ruled that it was unconstitutional to sentence a juvenile to life without the opportunity for parole for a crime that did not involve homicide. This section will examine the extent to

16 For a detailed understanding of adolescent brain development, see A. Galvan, *The Neuroscience of Adolescence* (Cambridge University Press, Online, 2017).

17 B. Larsen, B. Luna, 'Adolescence as a Neurobiological Critical Period for the Development of High-Order Cognition' (2018) 94 *Neuroscience & Biobehavioral Reviews* 179–195; A. Keller et al., 'Hierarchical Functional Systems Development Supports Executive Function' (2023) 27(2) *Trends in Cognitive Sciences* 160–174.

18 N. Fogelson, M. Shah et al., 'Prefrontal Cortex Is Critical for Contextual Processing: Evidence from Brain Lessons' (2009) 132(11) *Brain* 3002.

19 J. Rutherford, 'Juvenile Justice Caught between *The Exorcist* and *A Clockwork Orange*' (2002) 51 *Depaul Law Review* 727.

20 H. Howard, H. Wishart, '"Seen and Not Heard": In Defence of Children, Neuroscience, and Effective Participation at Trial' in H. Wishart, R. Arthur (eds), *International Perspectives of Neuroscience in the Youth Justice Courtroom* (Routledge, Oxon, 2025) 50.

21 *Graham v. Florida* 560 U.S. 48 (2010).

which developments in neuroscientific research have impacted law and policy in England and Wales.

Neuroscience, Parliament, and Policy Reform

Neuroscience has been used to support policy reform in Parliament; however, not all of these efforts have resulted in positive outcomes for children and young people, as evidenced by the enactment of legislation that enshrines their best interests and places their welfare at the heart of the English youth justice system. One such example is the Police, Crime, Sentencing and Courts Act (2022) (PCSC),[22] which lowered the minimum starting point for children and increased the minimum term starting point that young people must serve in detention for being convicted of murder.

This Act replaced the 12-year minimum term starting point that applied to children and young people convicted of murder aged 10 to 17 with a set of age-bracketed starting points that reflect adult starting points with an 8-year starting point for those aged 14 and below, a 10-year starting point for 15- and 16-year-olds, and a 14-year starting point for 17-year-olds.[23] The Government reasoned that 'the fixed 12-year starting point for children . . . [did] not account for the seriousness of the crime, nor [did] it reflect the different stages of development children go through between the ages of 10 and 17.'[24] Thus, the Government argued that removing the 12-year minimum term would be fairer to those 'closer to the age of 18, who will have higher starting points, while younger children will have lower starting points to reflect their reduced maturity and development,'[25] leading to 'a more gradual shift to adult sentences, reducing the gap that currently exists.' The Government explained that 'a 17-year-old, a week before they turn 18, is likely to have more concept of responsibility than an 11-year-old'; thus, this was a reasonable justification.[26]

However, the Act has faced significant criticism for not considering the developmental immaturity of young people. Claudia Sturt, Chief Executive of the Youth Justice Board, provided oral evidence to the Joint Committee on Human Rights regarding the PCSC Bill in the Houses of Parliament. She argued that aligning the starting points with those allocated for individuals aged 18 and over who are convicted of murder means that someone under 18 can receive a whole life order for a murder conviction, which is similar in length to that of an adult's sentence. In her view, this poses a problem as the Act does not address the fact

22 Section 127 of the Police, Crime, Sentencing and Courts Act (2022).

23 Section 127 5A(2).

24 Ministry of Justice, *A Smarter Approach to Sentencing* Consultation Paper 292 (HMSO, London, September 2020) 91.

25 Ibid. 92.

26 Joint Committee on Human Rights, *Legislative Scrutiny: Police, Crime, Sentencing and Courts Bill (Parts 7 and 8): Sentencing and Remand of Children and Young People* (Parliament Publications, 23 September 2021) para. 35.

that 16- and 17-year-olds are young people '. . . and [it][27] does not consider their childhood or developmental stage; it treats them as if they are adults.'[28]

Similarly, Lord Dholakia provided the same rationale, considering the latest neuroscientific research to support the introduction of the Age of Criminal Responsibility Bill (2019–2021), which was designed to increase the MACR from 10 to 12 years of age. The MACR in England and Wales was established at 10 years by the Children and Young Persons Act (1963). As a result, children under this age are exempt from criminal liability, as they are deemed morally incapable of responsibility and, therefore, lack the blameworthiness required for criminal liability. This, unfortunately, means that children aged 10 years and older can be held criminally liable for their actions, which Lord Dholakia has explained is a problem because 'there is no other area of law—whether it is the age for where we regard children as fully competent to take informed decisions until later in adolescence. The age of criminal responsibility is an anomalous exception' in England and Wales.[29]

Traditionally, the English youth justice system did not prosecute young people once they had achieved the MACR. Instead, the rebuttable presumption of *doli incapax* was invoked. According to the rebuttable presumption of *doli incapax*, children were only to be held criminally responsible if, in addition to committing the *actus reus* and *mens rea* of a criminal offence, the prosecution also proved, beyond a reasonable doubt, that when doing the act, the child knew that what they were doing was seriously wrong. During the 1990s, the presumption of *doli incapax* was considered 'not in the interests of justice, or victims or of the young people themselves.'[30] The presumption was said to be 'wholly out of date'[31] and 'out of touch with today's society and contrary to common sense'[32] as it allowed young offenders 'to run rings around the court system, and to avoid proper sanctions.'[33] Instead, 'the child is, and must be, capable of being held to account'[34] because Section 34 of the Crime and Disorder Act 1998 abolished the presumption of *doli incapax*.[35]

27 Added for emphasis.

28 'Joint Committee on Human Rights Oral Evidence: Legislative Scrutiny of the Police, Crime, Sentencing and Courts Bill, and Youth Justice' (HC 451, 30 June 2021, published 6 June 2021) per Claudia Sturt, p.4. <https://committees.parliament.uk/oralevidence/2491/html/>

29 House of Lords Debate, *Age of Criminal Responsibility Bill*, vol. 749, col 477 (Lord Dholakia, 8 November 2013) <https://hansard.parliament.uk/lords/2013-11-08/debates/13110858000393/AgeOfCriminalResponsibilityBill(HL)>.

30 Home Office, *No More Excuses: A New Approach to Tackling Youth Crime* (TSO, 1997), [4.4].

31 House of Lords Debate, vol. 585, col 1323 (12 February 1998), per Lord Williams of Mostyn <https://hansard.parliament.uk/Lords/1998-02-12/debates/7ab3c6d3-228b-47a9-a098-c66fa85a6e52/LordsChamber>.

32 *C v. Director of Public Prosecutions* [1994] 3 All ER 190, 196.

33 House of Commons Debate, vol. 294 col 390 (19 May 1997), per Jack Straw <https://hansard.parliament.uk/Commons/1997-05-14>.

34 Ibid.

35 Section 34 of the Crime and Disorder Act 1998 states that: 'The rebuttable presumption of criminal law that a child aged ten or over is incapable of committing an offence is hereby abolished.'

This is further compounded by the fact that the MACR in England and Wales is one of the world's lowest thresholds of criminal responsibility. Conversely, in Scotland, the MACR is 12 years of age; by contrast, in Europe, the MACR, on average, ranges from 14 to 16 years of age.[36] In fact, the UN Committee on the Rights of the Child (UN Committee) has proposed on numerous occasions that state parties ought to increase their MACRs to a minimum of 14 years of age because 'developmental and neuroscience evidence indicates that adolescent brains continue to mature even beyond the teenage years, affecting certain kinds of decision-making.'[37] Yet, the Government believes that 'setting the age of criminal responsibility at 10 for England and Wales provides appropriate flexibility in dealing with children who offend, allowing for early intervention in a child's life, to prevent subsequent offending,'[38] and there is no desire to introduce an age-related defence like *doli incapax*.

In Mitigation at Sentencing

To some extent, neuroscience has positively contributed to sentencing procedures used by the judiciary to determine the sentences of children and young people convicted of criminal offences. In 2017, the Sentencing Council issued specific guidance for the courts to consider in recognition of the young offender's age and degree of (im)maturity at the sentencing stage, because their young brains are still maturing until around 25 years of age.[39] The Sentencing Council stated that courts should acknowledge that 'the emotional and developmental age of an offender is of at least importance to their chronological age (if not greater)'[40] because adolescence is a vital period marked by significant and intricate brain development.[41] The Sentencing Council has therefore advised that the courts consider age and immaturity, for 'it is

36 Section 1 of the Age of Criminal Responsibility (Scotland) Act (2019); House of Lords Debate, *Age of Criminal Responsibility Bill [HL]*, Second Reading, col 1553-54 (Lord Dholakia, 29 January 2016) <https://hansard.parliament.uk/Lords/2016-01-29/debates/16012936000411/AgeOfCriminalResponsibilityBill>.

37 UN Committee (2019) 22.

38 Baroness Bennett of Manor Castle, After Clause 138, Police, Crime, Sentencing and Courts Act 2022 (Report stage, Amendment) at 90 <https://bills.parliament.uk/bills/2839/stages/15878/amendments/89993> accessed February 2025.

39 Sentencing Council, Sentencing Children and Young People (Sentencing Council, 1 June 2017) para. 1.4–1.5 <https://www.sentencingcouncil.org.uk/overarching-guides/magistrates-court/item/sentencing-children-and-young-people/> For young adult guidance, see Sentencing Council Guidance, M13 Age (Sentencing Council, 1 October 2019) <https://www.sentencingcouncil.org.uk/droppable/item/m13-age/> accessed January 2025.

40 Sentencing Council, *Sentencing Children and Young People Definitive Guideline* (Sentencing Council, 2017) 4.

41 See, also, Royal College of Psychiatrists, *Additional Submission to Justice Select Committee Inquiry into Children and Young People in Custody* (June 2020) 1 <https://committees.parliament.uk/publications/2010/documents/19436/default/> accessed December 2024.

important to bear in mind any factors that may diminish the culpability of a child or young person.'[42]

This was recently confirmed by Mrs. Justice May in *R v. ZA* (2023),[43] in which the court considered an appeal against the sentences of several children and argued that the sentences were inappropriate because the lower courts failed to apply the most appropriate sentencing guidance for children/young people. In acknowledging the neuroscience, she stated that

> the brains of young people are still developing up to the age of 25, particularly in the areas of the frontal cortex and hippocampus. These areas are the seat of emotional control, restraint, awareness of risk and the ability to appreciate the consequences of one's own and others' actions; in short, the processes of thought engaged in by, and the hallmark of, mature and responsible adults.[44]

This case reiterated that a distinct approach must be adopted when determining children's sentences by highlighting the latest neuroscientific research.

Positive considerations of neuroscience can also be found in case law before *ZA*,[45] for example, in *R v. Clarke Ors* (2018), where the court examined a scientific article published in the *Lancet Journal* confirming that children mature at different rates and beyond 18 years of age.[46] However, there have also been instances where the courts have examined and excluded published neuroscientific journal articles due to the research's insufficient probative value on appeal. For example, in *R v. L* (2019),[47] where the Court of Appeal considered and rejected the appeal of fresh evidence comprising neuroscientific research involving a 15-year-old appellant convicted of murder and sentenced to 14 years in detention for stabbing and killing another 15-year-old.[48] Lord Justice Davis observed that

> the courts (as, indeed, are most parents) are well aware that the brain develops and responsibility grows as children grow into adulthood. It is known that teenagers are much more likely to make reckless, antisocial and irresponsible decisions without thought of the consequences.

As a result, he claimed that

> these sentiments . . . reflected in the various papers . . . produced to us . . . lend no real support to some general proposition that, assuming no

42 Sentencing Council (2017) para. 1.5.
43 *R v. ZA* [2023] EWCA Crim 596.
44 Ibid. 52.
45 *R v. Geoghegan (Kieran)* [2019] EWCA Crim 787.
46 *R v. Clarke and Ors* [2018] EWCA Crim 185, [2018] 1 Cr App R (S) 52 at [5].
47 *R v. L* [2019] EWCA Crim 1326.
48 [2019] EWCA Crim 1326.

> cognitive deficit, teenagers are in all cases not to be considered responsible for their actions.[49]

Although general judicial guidance indicates that young age and cognitive immaturity should be considered as mitigating factors when determining sentences for children, there have been several cases where the courts have referenced neuroscience in appeal decisions, leading to favourable outcomes for child appellants. However, as evidenced in *L*, the courts may be reluctant to treat neuroscientific studies as fresh evidence in all cases to support a child's appeal for reduced culpability, as these studies typically provide broad insights into adolescent behaviour rather than specific evidence regarding an individual's cognitive deficits or degree of immaturity.

The Future Application of Neuroscience in English Youth Justice

Neuroscience may no longer be 'sitting at the courtroom door'[50] as the courts and policymakers have examined its scientific findings. To date, there has been a clear lack of progress in integrating neuroscience to create positive policy reform for children. The PCSC Act has resulted in 17-year-olds convicted of murder being sentenced to a longer minimum term starting point of 14 years. Lord Dholakia's latest reiteration of the Age of Criminal Responsibility Bill (2019–2021) has been tabled. There is little prospect of any reform of the age of criminal responsibility in England and Wales. However, there remains hope that Parliament and the courts will continue to implement neuroscience, leading to tangible and positive changes in the lives of children under English law. This section examines significant ways neuroscience can support arguments for policy reform, from raising the MACR to ending with proposals for implementing a developmental immaturity defence for children.

Increasing the Minimum Age of Criminal Responsibility

Children of 10 years are not adults, and the more a young person is involved with crime, the more significant the gap with adults tends to be. The low age of criminal responsibility fails in both its protective function towards young people and its crucial communicative function regarding how we treat the youngest and some of the most vulnerable within our society. It ignores the evidence that the child's inexperience and under-developed powers of self-control and reasoning make them prone to acting in ways they cannot help,

49 Ibid. 41.

50 B. Garland, M. S. Frankel, 'Considering Convergence: A Policy Dialogue about Behavioral Genetics, Neuroscience, and Law' in N. A. Farahany (ed), *The Impact of Behavioral Sciences on Criminal Law* (Oxford University Press, 2009) (Accessed via Oxford Scholarship Online) 158.

understand, or intend. Because the prefrontal lobe is not fully mature and is still developing during adolescence, teens are almost inevitably overly emotional, more prone to risk-taking, and subject to wide mood swings, immature judgement, decreased risk perception, and impaired future-time perspective.[51]

Furthermore, their functioning with respect to considering issues empathically from the perspective of others, capacity for autonomy and resisting pressure from others, and their ability to experience guilt and shame are under-developed.[52] This contributes to the tendency to make harmful choices to themselves and others. Thus, there is a scientific basis for increasing the MACR in England and Wales.

Yet successive governments continue to assert that 10 is the appropriate MACR in England and Wales: '[v]ictims of serious crimes committed by 10 and 11 year-olds must feel assured that those responsible can be proceeded against by the courts'[53] and that 'setting the age of criminal responsibility at 10 provides flexibility in dealing with children and allows for early intervention in a child's life.'[54] The low age of criminal responsibility is presented as a courtesy to children and a gateway to early intervention. The low MACR assumes that criminal-justice-involved children are as rational and fully responsible as adults and marginalises the critical developmental differences between children and adults.

Reforming Fitness to Plead Procedure

The current fitness to plead procedures do not offer much support to young people, as these procedures apply to trial on indictment only, that is, Crown Court cases only. Only a relatively small number of children are sentenced in this type of court compared with magistrates' courts. Approximately 5% of all sentencing occasions of children are at the Crown Court. This equates to 1,800 sentencing occasions involving around 460 children. This proportion has remained stable over the last ten years, varying between 4% and 5%.[55]

51 K. L. Modecki, 'Addressing Gaps in the Maturity and Judgment Literature: Age Differences and Delinquency' (2008) 32 *Law and Human Behaviour* 78; Rutherford, (2002) 727.

52 N. Stone 'Old Heads Upon Young Shoulders: "Compassion to Human Infirmity" following R v. JTB' (2010) 32(3) *Journal of Social Welfare & Family Law* 287, 292.

53 House of Lords Debate, *Age of Criminal Responsibility Bill* (vol. 783, Col 2211, Baroness Vere of Norbiton (Con), 8 September 2017) <https://hansard.parliament.uk/Lords/2017-09-08/debates/D3E4D198-43BB-4B60-9FF0-CFF5B0EA1CB6/AgeOfCriminalResponsibilityBill#:~:text=Volume%20783%3A%20debated%20on%20Friday%208%20September%202017&text=That%20the%20Bill%20be%20now%20read%20a%20second%20time.&text=school%20can%20be%20prosecuted%20and,in%20the%20adult%20Crown%20Court>.

54 Ministry of Justice submission to House of Commons Justice Committee, *Children and Young People in Custody (Part 1): Entry into the Youth Justice System*, Twelfth Report of Session 2019–21, (HC 306, 2020) para 62.

55 Youth Justice Statistics 2022–2023 (25 January 2024) <https://www.gov.uk/government/statistics/youth-justice-statistics-2022-to-2023/youth-justice-statistics-2022-to-2023-accessible-version#sentencing-of-children>.

The test for fitness to plead sets quite a high threshold for finding an accused who is unfit to plead.[56] The question of fitness will depend on the defendant's ability to understand the difference between guilty and not guilty pleas, follow the evidence in the proceedings, instruct counsel, and challenge jurors. However, he need not necessarily be able to act in his own best interests. An understanding on the defendant's part that what he or she had done was wrong is not part of the legal test for unfitness to plead; it merely requires that the defendant has a rudimentary understanding of the trial process.

Studies indicate that there is a threefold increase in the likelihood that children who are involved in the criminal justice system experience mental health issues more than their peers in the general population.[57] Among those who enter the system, 30% exhibit borderline learning difficulties, while 60% struggle with significant literacy issues, communication disorders, language deficits, and comprehension problems.[58] Additionally, a quarter of these children have an average IQ below 70. According to Howard and Wishart,

> This is particularly problematic for those who appear in court, as it places them at a disadvantage in giving evidence in the witness box, as "the jury is often swayed by the defendant in the witness box, with likeability and eloquent presentation thought to the influence the jury's perception."[59]

Children are also susceptible to making false confessions and pleading guilty to crimes, even if they were not involved, because they are incentivised by short-term benefits (e.g., receiving a lesser sentence).[60] The unfitness test offers no consideration of the degree of maturity of cognitive abilities or the development of social-emotional capacities, factors that directly impact a young person's ability to use information to make sound judgments and decisions.

In October 2023, the Government responded to the Law Commission's report on 'Unfitness to Plead.' The government accepted the recommendation

56 *R v. Pritchard* (1836) 7 C & P 303.

57 Justice Committee, *Sentencing Guideline: Overarching Principles-Sentencing Youths, Memorandum Submitted by Sainsbury Centre for Mental Health* (April 2009) para 2.1 <https://publications.parliament.uk/pa/cm200809/cmselect/cmjust/497/497we09.htm#note125> accessed February 2024.

58 R. Harrington, S. Bailey, *Mental Health Needs and Effectiveness of Provision for Young Offenders in Custody and in the Community* (Youth Justice Board, London, 2005); K. Bryan, G. Garvani, J. Gregory, K. Kilner, 'Language Difficulties and Criminal Justice: The Need for Earlier Identification' (2015) 50(6) *International Journal of Language and Communication Disorders*, 763.

59 Howard and Wishart (2025) 51.

60 L. C. Mallory, E. P. Shulman, E. Cauffman, 'Interrogations, Confessions, and Guilty Pleas Among Serious Adolescent Offenders' (2014) 38(3) *Law and Human Behavior* 181–193; L. J. Grove, J. Kukucka, 'Do Laypeople Recognize Youth as a Risk Factor for False Confession? A Test of the "Common Sense Hypothesis"' (2021) 28(2) *Psychiatry, Psychology and Law*, 185–205; Howard and Wishart (2025) 50–51.

that there be a reformulation of the legal test as an assessment of the defendant's capacity to participate effectively in a trial, rather than focusing on the defendant's intellectual abilities, acknowledging that such reform would accommodate advances in psychiatric and psychological thinking. The government also accepted the recommendation that the legal framework for addressing unfitness to plead be expanded into the magistrates' and youth courts, and it is committed to bringing forward legislation 'when parliamentary time allows.'[61] However, it is not yet known when (if at all) the Government will develop legislation to reform the unfitness to plead procedure and the Crown Court test.[62]

Introducing a 'Developmental Immaturity' Defence

The UN Committee in General Comment No. 24 (2019) has discouraged member states from using a rebuttable presumption within a *doli incapax*–styled defence because these kinds of devices leave 'much to the discretion of the court, . . . [resulting][63] in discriminatory practice.'[64] However, the UN Committee has acknowledged, alongside an increase in the MACR, that children with developmental delays, disabilities, and neurodevelopmental disorders should be given special consideration and assessed on a case-by-case basis to determine whether they should be exposed to the criminal justice system.[65] As the Royal Society observes, 'there is huge individual variability in the timing and patterning of brain development,'[66] to such an extent that a child can 'demonstrate vastly different cognitive capacities for understanding'[67] from other children in the same age group. A child's capacity for understanding and self-control is intertwined with their age, sex, and brain development, and influenced by factors such as genetics and the environment.[68] The Law Commission noted, in particular, that some children 'will have a level of developmental maturity that is much lower than the norm for a person of their age, albeit that their level of immaturity is not so extreme as to constitute a recognised medical condition.'[69] It, therefore, makes sense that developmentally immature children who lack the capacity for criminal responsibility are offered a defence. More specifically, a defence that excuses those without capacity

61 Policy Paper, *Government Response to the Law Commission Report on 'Unfitness to Plead'* (25 October 2023) <https://www.gov.uk/government/publications/government-response-to-the-law-commission-report-unfitness-to-plead>.

62 Dated February 2025.

63 Added for emphasis.

64 UN Committee (2019) para. 26.

65 Ibid. at para. 28.

66 The Royal Society, *Brain Waves Module 4: Neuroscience & the Law* (Royal Society, 2011) 13.

67 N. J. Lennings, C. J. Lennings, 'Assessing Serious Harm under the Doctrine of Doli Incapax: A Case Study' (2014) 21 *Psychiatry, Psychology and Law* 793.

68 S. J. Blakemore, T. Robbins, 'Decision-Making in the Adolescent Brain' (2012) 15(9) *Nature Neuroscience* 1185.

69 Law Com (2013) para. 9.10.

or reduced capacity with genuine issues of developmental immaturity rather than reintroduce a *doli incapax* presumption into English law, which is unsupported by the UN Committee and previously abolished for reasons outlined in this chapter. In 2013, the Law Commission proposed introducing the following 'developmental immaturity' defence in law:

> In light of this, it is arguable that a person should not bear criminal responsibility for what would otherwise be an offence when he or she *wholly* lacked the relevant capacities by virtue of developmental immaturity. The relevant capacities could be those which apply in our proposed defence of "not criminally responsible by reason of recognised medical condition," namely,
>
> (1) rationally to form a judgment in relation to what he or she is charged with having done;
> (2) to appreciate the wrongfulness of what he or she is charged with having done; or
> (3) to control his or her physical acts in relation to what he or she is charged with having done.[70]

The idea that developmental immaturity should form an exculpatory defence and provide persons who suffer from it with a complete general defence has received some support from legal academics. Yet, it has been subjected to significant criticism due to its narrow scope.[71] For example, De Than and Elvin argued that

> this was a revision and rebranding of their earlier and unenacted recommendation of the addition of a 'developmental immaturity' limb to the diminished responsibility defence (under Section 52 of the Coroners and Justice Act (2009),[72] but with a stricter approach since the lack of capability must be total.[73]

The Law Commission justified the requirement of a complete lack of capacity for those who suffer developmental immaturity because 'a person may lack capacity in this sense is that he or she has not developed the

70 Ibid. at 9.4.

71 McDiarmid (2016) 329; H. Keating, 'How Should the Criminal Law Respond to the "Special Status" of Children?' in J. J Child, R. A. Duff (eds), *Criminal Law Reform Now* (Hart Publishing, Oxford, 2021) 171.

72 Added for emphasis.

73 C. De Than, J. Elvin, 'How Should the Criminal Law Deal with People Who Have "Partial Capacity?"' in B. Livings, A. Reed, N. Wake (eds), *Mental Condition Defences and the Criminal Justice System: Perspectives from Law and Medicine* (Cambridge Scholars Press, Cambridge, UK, 2015) 311.

relevant capacities of understanding and self-control' due to developmental immaturity.[74]

Developmental delays are best viewed as brain and cognitive underdevelopment affecting a child's maturity level. In some cases, an individual's developmental maturity can exceed the norm for their age, and their immaturity may lead to a complete lack of capacity.[75] This defence could be an essential tool for those who suffer from developmental immaturity and a total lack of capacity to either form a rational judgment, understand the wrongfulness or exercise self-control over their actions. As McDiarmid stresses, 'a defence would make it easier to ensure that, where it is relevant, evidence supporting a claim of lack of capacity, arising as a result of developmental immaturity, is available to the court'[76] because, 'unlike a MACR, a defence is not a blanket exemption from criminal liability. No child defendant would have to plead it and, indeed, making the plea is no guarantee of success, which depends on the evidence.'[77]

However, the Law Commission framed the defence in such a way that it would require a person to suffer a total lack of legally relevant capacities due to developmental immaturity; the very nature of their degree of capacity will determine whether such a person would be afforded a successful plea, which is problematic. As De Than and Elvin argued, 'a requirement of total lack of capability in relation to cognition or control has a serious risk of rendering a defence largely meaningless and of mimicking the current law's lack of regard for medical reality.'[78] This is problematic because if English law enacts this proposed defence, it will prevent individuals who possess a degree of immaturity higher than the norm for a person of the same age and who do not have a level of immaturity that results in a complete lack of legal capacities from successfully pleading the defence. In this case, developmentally immature individuals who committed homicides, such as *R v. Abbott* (1964)[79] and *R v. Markham* (2017),[80] and suffered substantial impairments rather than a complete loss of legally relevant capacities due to developmental delays would be excluded from successfully pleading the defence simply because their degree of immaturity did not cause them to suffer a total lack of mental capacity, despite being recognised as developmentally immature. Thus, there is space for developmental immaturity defences that recognise those who suffer from a total loss of capacity and children who lack some capacity.

74 Law Com (2013) paras. 9.1 and 9.3.
75 Law Com (2013) para 9.10.
76 McDiarmid (2016) at 329.
77 Ibid. at 338.
78 De Than and Elvin (2015) 311.
79 *R v. Abbott* [1964] 1 Q.B 489.
80 *R v. Markham and Edwards* [2017] EWCA Crim 739.

Final Remarks

Developmental immaturity is relevant to responsibility assessments and can be normal or abnormal. As observed, a child/young person's brain development is intertwined with their competency, developmental delays, life experiences and behaviour. As Coppola argued, because 'the ability to act for normative reasons, or to be normatively rational, does not simply require knowledge or understanding of the moral appropriateness of one's behaviour against the normative standards of right and wrong.'[81]

Neuroscience has been used to support arguments for increasing the MACR. Neuroscience confirms that brain immaturity impacts practical rationality in everyday contexts (not just for the *mens rea* of murder) because it can create a degree of incapacity in the child's ability to understand the nature of their conduct, exercise self-control, and form a rational judgment. Brain immaturity and rational capacities are therefore relevant to a person's ability to engage in criminal conduct and answer 'the normative demands of the criminal law.'[82] Considering neuroscience evidence, it is increasingly questionable why Parliamentarians still believe that 'children of ten and above are, for the most part, able to differentiate between bad behaviour and serious wrongdoing' and that the current MACR 'allows flexibility to deal with young offenders.'[83] However, on numerous occasions, Parliament has considered several iterations of Lord Dholakia's Age of Criminal Responsibility Bill, yet none have been enacted into law.

Thomas Crofts is optimistic that legal practitioners and academics will continue to make future calls to increase the MACR in England and Wales, supported by robust neuroscientific evidence on adolescent development. Croft believes that there is 'an emotional response and a scientific, research-based call for change' that might act as a catalyst to increase the MACR.[84] Even if the Government were willing to increase the MACR, it would raise the question of which new age would be appropriate to treat children/young people as criminally responsible for committing offences. Numerous proposed threshold ages for the MACR exist in the legal literature, from Lord Dholakia's increase to 12 years of age[85] to Keating's suggestion of an incremental change to the MACR, first to 13 years, then 14 years.[86] The latest neuroscientific evidence

81 F. Coppola, *The Emotional Brain and the Guilty Mind: Novel Paradigms of Culpability and Punishment* (Hart Publishing, Oxford, 2020) 136.

82 N. Lacey, 'Space, Time and Function: Intersecting Principles of Responsibility Across the Terrain of Criminal Justice' (2007) 1 *Criminal Law and Philosophy* 236.

83 Per Lord Faulks, *Hansard House of Lords Debate* (vol. 768, cols 1573, 1577, 1575, 29 January 2016) <https://hansard.parliament.uk/Lords/2016-01-29/debates/16012936000411/AgeOfCriminalResponsibilityBill>.

84 T. Crofts, 'Will Australia Raise the Minimum Age of Criminal Responsibility' (2019) 43 *Criminal Law Journal* 39.

85 Age of Criminal Responsibility Bill (2019–2021).

86 Keating in Child and Duff (2021) 178.

on adolescent brain development reveals that children/young people develop at their own speed and different rates. Most individuals lack varying capabilities based on factors such as sex, age, epigenetics, and individual development. Thus, finding a suitable age would be difficult because there is no magic age at which most children/young people reach a reasonable degree of maturity and competence. Alongside any increase in the MACR, there would also need to be a commitment to diverting children away from the youth criminal justice system and into the childcare system.

The Children Act 1989 removed from the youth court the power to order a young person into the care of a local authority.[87] Nevertheless, Schedule 2 of the Children Act 1989 requires local authorities to take reasonable steps to encourage children in their area not to commit criminal offences.[88] *Guidance* suggests that in addition to intermediate treatment for those at risk of offending, this might involve offering advice and support services for parents, providing family support services, family centres, daycare, and accommodation, and ensuring that children in need gain maximum life benefits from educational opportunities, healthcare, and social care, leading to reduced rates of offending by such children.[89] The Children Act 1989 provides local authorities with a statutory mandate to call upon other departments within local government, such as any other local authority, any local education authority, any local housing authority, and any health authority, special health authority, primary care trust, or National Health Service (NHS) trust to assist them in their duties to provide services for children and to prevent youth crime (under section 27 Children Act 1989). This important provision of the Children Act 1989 seeks to ensure that the various arms of the public service should cooperate. Any authority whose help is requested must comply with the request, provided it is compatible with their own statutory or other duties and does not unduly prejudice the discharge of any of their functions (contrary to section 27(2) of the Children Act 1989).

The principle of inter-agency cooperation to prevent youth crime is also reaffirmed in section 37 of the Crime and Disorder Act 1998, which places all those carrying out functions in relation to the youth justice system under a statutory duty to have regard to the new principal aim of preventing offending by children and young people.[90] Paragraph 4 of the 'framework document'

87 Children Act (1989): sections 90(1) and (2) respectively repealed Children and Young Persons Act (1969): section 1(2)(f) and section 7(7).

88 Schedule 2, paragraph 7(a)(ii) provides that every local authority shall take reasonable steps designed to reduce the need to bring criminal proceeding against such children and paragraph 7(b) requires local authorities to encourage children within their area not to commit criminal offences.

89 Department of Health 1991 The Children Act 1989 Guidance and Regulations Volume 2 Family Support, Day Care and Educational Provision for Young Children, (HMSO, London).

90 Crime and Disorder Act (1998), Section 37(1): 'It shall be the principal aim of the youth justice system to prevent offending by children and young people.' Section 37(2): 'In addition to

for the Crime and Disorder Act 1998 explains the incorporation of this aim into the statute; it argues that the youth justice system has for 'too long been seen to be separate from wider youth crime prevention work' and that the new statutory aim makes clear the 'important link that there should be between the work of the youth justice system and wider work to help prevent children and young people offending.'[91] The White Paper *No More Excuses*, which preceded the 1998 Act, stressed that 'preventing offending promotes the welfare of the individual young offender and protects the public.'[92] In 2020, the *Prevention and Diversion Project* was jointly commissioned by the National Probation Service (NPS), Youth Justice Board (YJB), and the Association of Youth Offending Team (YOT) Managers. *The Prevention and Diversion Project* developed a new definition of prevention that involves providing support and interventions to children (and their parents/carers) who may be displaying behaviours that point to their underlying needs or vulnerability. The aim is to address unmet needs, promote positive outcomes, and stop children from entering the formal youth justice system.[93]

All of these laws, provisions, and standards strengthen the obligations upon state actors to embed safeguarding and the best interests of the child in their practices with children, to promote children's development of a pro-social identity, to engage with a diversionary ethos, and to ensure all work with children is constructive and future-focused. This view of young people recognises that the child offender lacks capacity, and, consequently, there is a need for both the family and the state to take responsibility for children's needs and to respond to youth offending by providing young people with the necessary tools to grow into competent adults.

---

any other duty to which they are subject, it shall be the duty of all persons and bodies carrying out functions in relation to the youth justice system to have regard to that aim.'

91 See, generally, Home Office, *Youth Justice: Preventing Offending* (HMSO, London, 1998).

92 Home Office (1997) 2.2.

93 Youth Justice Board, *Prevention and Diversion Scoping Survey* (Youth Justice Board, London, 2021) para 2.

2 The Neuroscience of Brain Injury in Criminal Cases

An International Scope

Deborah W. Denno

Introduction

At its broadest, neuroscientific evidence encompasses all information pertaining to the brain and its functions.[1] Folded into this definition are brain injuries, typically 'caused by a bump, blow, or jolt to the head' or by a 'penetrating' source, such as a gunshot wound.[2] Survivors of brain injuries can experience health problems as severe and lifelong as a chronic disease.[3] With brain injuries impacting a large portion of the criminal population worldwide,[4] this chapter

1 D. Aono, G. Yaffe, H. Kober, 'Neuroscientific Evidence in the Courtroom: A Review' (2019) 4(40) *Cognitive Res.: Principles and Implications* 3. Other references have more specific definitions of 'neuroscience.' According to one source, for example, 'neuroscience' is '[t]he scientific study of the structure and function of the nervous system; includes experimental and clinical studies of animals and humans.' O. D. Jones, J. D. Schall, F. X. Shen, *Law and Neuroscience* (2nd ed., Aspen Publishing, 2020) 931.

2 U.S. Centers for Disease Control and Prevention, 'About Moderate and Severe TBI' *Traumatic Brain Injury & Concussion* <https://www.cdc.gov/traumatic-brain-injury/about/moderate-severe-tbi.html> accessed 22 November 2024.

3 Ibid.

4 E. Durand, M. Chevignard, A. Ruet, A. Dereix, C. Jourdan, P. Pradat-Diehl, 'History of Traumatic Brain Injury in Prison Populations: A Systematic Review' (2017) 60(2) *Annals of Physical and Rehabilitation Medicine*, 95–101; S. Hunter, L. E. Kois, A. T. Peck, E. B. Elbogen, C. LaDuke, 'The Prevalence of Traumatic Brain Injury (TBI) Among People Impacted by the Criminal Legal System: An Updated Meta-Analysis and Subgroup Analyses' (2023) 47(5) *Law and Human Behavior* 539–565 <https://doi.org/10.1037/lhb0000543>; D. O. Lewis, J. H. Pincus, M. Feldman, L. Jackson, B. Bard, 'Psychiatric, Neurological, and Psychoeducational Characteristics of 15 Death Row Inmates in the United States' (1986) 143(7) *The American Journal of Psychiatry* 838–845; B. S. Schneider, D. B. Arciniegas, C. Harenski, G. Janez, B. Clarke, K. A. Kiehl, M. Koenigs, 'The Prevalence, Characteristics, and Psychiatric Correlates of Traumatic Brain Injury in Incarcerated Individuals: An Examination in Two Independent Samples' (2021) 35(14) *Brain Injury*, 1690–1701; E. J. Shiroma, P. L. Ferguson, E. E. Pickelsimer, 'Prevalence of Traumatic Brain Injury in an Offender Population: A Meta-Analysis' (2010) 16(2) *Journal of Correctional Health Care* 147–159; U.S. Centers for Disease Control and Prevention, 'TBI and Correctional Facilities' *Traumatic Brain Injury & Concussion* <https://www.cdc.gov/traumatic-brain-injury/health-equity/correctional-facilities.html> accessed 21 November 2024.

DOI: 10.4324/9781003510246-3

takes a critical look at the brain injury cases within my United States (U.S.) Neuroscience Study[5] and compares the results with empirical research conducted in six different countries: Australia,[6] Canada,[7] England and Wales,[8] the Netherlands,[9] and Slovenia.[10] Altogether, the studies show a double-edged-sword continuum of how various criminal justice systems treat brain-injured defendants, why countries differ in their approaches, and what the future holds for such influential and ever-evolving information.

For purposes of consistency, the discussion that follows treats 'brain injury' as synonymous with 'head injury' and 'brain damage' and focuses on external causes, such as blunt force injuries (like a car accident) or penetrations (such as a gunshot wound). The term also includes more internal-type sources of brain injury, such as dementia or alcohol-induced brain damage. Likewise, there are differing definitions and consequences of 'brain injury' depending on the injury's type and seriousness and whether it can be classified as 'traumatic brain injury' (TBI).[11] Unlike some mental illnesses, a defendant's brain injury can often be detected and confirmed with the use of various neuroscience tools, such as neuroimaging and psychological or neurological testing. These relatively more objective types of tests can bolster accurate diagnoses, offering courts more concrete evidence for appropriate sentencing, treatment, and rehabilitation strategies.[12]

5 D. W. Denno, 'The Myth of the Double-Edged Sword: An Empirical Study of Neuroscience Evidence in Criminal Cases' (2015) 56(2) *Boston College Law Review* 493; D. W. Denno, 'How Experts Have Dominated the Neuroscience Narrative in Criminal Cases for Twelve Decades: A Warning for the Future' (2022) 63 *William & Mary Law Review* 1215.

6 A. Alimardani, J. Chin, 'Neurolaw in Australia: The Use of Neuroscience in Australian Criminal Proceedings' (2019) 12(3) *Neuroethics* 255; A. Alimardani, 'An Empirical Study of the Use of Neuroscience in Sentencing in New South Wales, Australia' (2023) 14 *Frontiers in Psychology* 1.

7 J. A. Chandler, 'The Use of Neuroscientific Evidence in Canadian Criminal Proceedings' (2015) 2(3) *Journal of Law and Biosciences* 550.

8 P. Catley, L. Claydon, 'The Use of Neuroscientific Evidence in the Courtroom by Those Accused of Criminal Offenses in England and Wales' (2015) 2(3) *Journal of Law and Biosciences* 510.

9 C. H. de Kogel, E. J. M. C. Westgeest, 'Neuroscientific and Behavioral Genetic Information in Criminal Cases in the Netherlands' (2015) 2(3) *Journal of Law and Biosciences* 580.

10 M. Hafner, 'Judging Homicide Defendants by Their Brains: An Empirical Study on the Use of Neuroscience in Homicide Trials in Slovenia' (2019) 6(1) *Journal of Law and Biosciences* 226.

11 See, for example, '§73.06 Management of head injury: Overview' in 4 Medical Malpractice: Guide to Medical Issues §73.06, Matthew Bender & Company, Inc. (2024); National Institute of Neurological Disorders and Stroke, '*Traumatic Brain Injury: Hope Through Research*' (2020) <https://catalog.ninds.nih.gov/sites/default/files/publications/traumatic-brain-injury-hope-through-research_1.pdf> accessed 22 November 2024; '§39.18 Traumatic brain injury, listing 11.18' in 5 Social Security Practice Guide §39.18, Matthew Bender & Company, Inc. (2024); and Erin B. Wasserman, Kevin M. Guskiewicz, '§24C.02 TBI Defined' in 1 Forensic Sciences §24C.02, Matthew Bender & Company, Inc. (2024).

12 Denno (n 5) 1260, 1279.

The first section of this chapter describes and compares the international studies. Despite some of their methodological differences, all studies included a defendant's brain injuries as a component of their definition of neuroscience. The second section analyses how these studies assess brain-injured defendants, pinpointing the reigning perspective of the double-edged sword. The double-edged sword concept suggests that when neuroscientific evidence is presented in a case, it may produce 'a more lenient sentence in some instances but a harsher punishment in others.'[13] In considering brain injury specifically, there appear to be especially revealing insights into the double-edged sword effect. Likewise, different countries' criminal justice systems react more leniently or harshly to brain injury evidence in their sentencing of criminal defendants, which this chapter illustrates by way of a theoretical continuum. For example, Slovenia represents one end of the continuum with a mitigating outlook on brain injury and an optimistic view that brain-injured defendants can be rehabilitated. In contrast, England and Wales constitute the other end of the continuum with a more aggravating and punitive perspective toward defendants with brain injuries. This continuum also highlights courts' potential biases and misjudgments concerning whether they believe defendants' brain injuries can be improved with rehabilitation—a perspective backed by science—or whether they view such injuries as permanent, making rehabilitation unlikely and defendants a 'future danger' at risk of recidivism.[14]

My U.S. Neuroscientific Study and international research show that the neuroscientific underpinnings of brain injury evidence are an invaluable guide to countering judges' and juries' potentially false and biased assumptions about brain-injured defendants. These revelations pertain particularly to wrong-headed suggestions that brain injuries are permanent and unchangeable and, therefore, defendants are more dangerous and less treatable. This chapter calls for greater awareness generally of neuroscience in legal systems and the critical need for attorneys to introduce sound and reliable brain injury science in their cases to enhance more just and accurate sentencing practices.

Neuroscientific Evidence in Criminal Cases Worldwide

This chapter's selected studies empirically investigated how the criminal justice systems in their respective countries used neuroscientific evidence, including indicators of brain injuries. Although the studies differed in a variety of ways

13 Alimardani (n 6) 10; see also Denno (n 5) and O. D. Jones, F. X. Shen, 'Law and Neuroscience in the United States' in T. Spranger (ed), *International Neurolaw: A Comparative Analysis* (Springer-Verlag Berlin Heidelberg, 2012) 349, 362 (both discussing the double-edged sword).

14 A. Liontas, 'Reckoning with the Connection between Brain Injuries and Criminal Behavior' (*New York Times*, 30 November 2024) <https://www.nytimes.com/2024/11/30/opinion/brain-injury-incarcerations-crime.html?unlocked_article_code=1.eE4._cGN.2HRAjdpXmHgf&smid=url-share> accessed 30 November 2024.

methodologically, their substantially shared approaches enable a type of comparison that pieces together the purpose and impact of brain injury information in the courtroom and how it may be employed in the future.[15]

As Table 2.1 shows, all studies examined their country's application of neuroscientific evidence during a particular time frame.[16] All relied on data from

Table 2.1 Study Methodologies

Study	*Timespan and Cases*	*Database Used*	*Definition of 'Neuroscience'*
Australia Alimardani & Chin (2019) Alimardani (2023)	All available criminal cases up to 2019 779 cases initially considered All available criminal sentencing cases up to 2016 331 cases	CaseLaw, Australasian Legal Information Institute ("AustLII"), and the Australian Neurolaw Database	Adopted a broad definition that included neuroimaging evidence and non-neuroimaging evidence
England and Wales Catley & Claydon (2015)	2005–2012 (8 years) 204 cases	Lexis Library	Cited the Royal Society's definition, which is described in part as 'the study of the brain and nervous system,' and pinpointed cases with a basis in cognitive neuroscience
Canada Chandler (2015)	2008–2012 (5 years) 133 cases	LexisNexis Quicklaw	Excluded a definition but focused on cases involving evidence of brain injury or cognitive impairment linked to a neurological cause
United States Denno (2015)—(2022)	1992–2012 (20 years) 800 cases 1900–2020 (120 years) 8,358 cases	Westlaw & Lexis	Used a broad definition that included neuroimaging tests, non-neuroimaging tests, and expert testimony

(Continued)

15 More detailed methodological comparisons of these studies (apart from the research in Australia) can be found in D. W. Denno, 'Empirical Use of Neuroscientific Evidence in Criminal Justice' *The Encyclopedia of Behavioral Neuroscience* (2nd ed., Amsterdam, Netherlands: Elsevier, Sergio Della Salla, ed., 2022) 719; D. W. Denno, 'Vulnerable Defendants and Neuroscience in Courtrooms Throughout the World' in H. Wishart, C. M. Berryessa (eds), *Neurolaw in the Courtroom: Comparative Perspectives on Vulnerable Defendants (Series in Contemporary Issues in Criminal Justice and Procedure)* (1st ed., Routledge, New York, 2023) 3–20.

16 The research in Australia did not specify a start date for the study's time frame, instead indicating that the study examined all available cases in the Australian databases up to 2016. Alimardani (n 6) and Alimardani (n 6). Alimardani's 2023 article only looked at the New South Wales jurisdiction.

Table 2.1 (Continued)

Study	*Timespan and Cases*	*Database Used*	*Definition of 'Neuroscience'*
Slovenia Hafner (2019)	1991–2015 (24 years) 89 cases	Slovenian case law database 'sodnapraksa. si' used initially, then requested cases directly from courts	Examined cases discussing brain damage, neurological diseases and dysfunctions, or organic mental, personality, and behavioral disorders
The Netherlands de Kogel & Westgeest (2015)	2000–2012 (12 years) 231 cases	Dutch case law database 'Rechtspraak.nl'	Defined as involving assessments of the brain, neuropsychological assessments, or neurobiological predisposition or brain damage; also included a separate definition for behavioral genetic information

widely used legal databases, such as Westlaw or Lexis, or their country's specialised legal database. As expected, studies incorporated varying definitions of 'neuroscience' that corresponded with their goals and the type of information available in their respective databases. Yet, as Table 2.2 notes, on a more operational level, most studies investigated two types of neuroscientific evidence that attorneys introduced into the courtroom: (1) neuroimaging tests, such as MRI, CT, and PET scans, which image the brain's structure and function; and (2) non-neuroimaging tests, including psychometric tests, which measure the brain's structure and function without imagining.[17] In addition, most criminal cases in all studies depended on expert witnesses who discussed a defendant's cognitive abilities and medical history, with or without depending on neuroscientific testing.[18] It is often through the use of testifying experts that researchers can assess the impact of a defendant's brain injuries or other disorders on a defendant's behaviour. That behaviour predominantly involved a crime of violence, as Table 2.2 indicates.

The type of crime, such as one involving violence, could also influence the phase at which attorneys would present neuroscientific evidence (pretrial, trial, or sentencing). Phases are a critical component of how this information could impact defendants, as Table 2.3 delineates. For example, if evidence is presented at the pretrial phase by either the defence or the prosecution, it may be an effort to garner a plea bargain or dismiss a case. At the trial phase, which determines guilt or innocence or anything in-between, such as the acceptance

17 For more detail (apart from the research in Australia), see Denno (n 15) and Denno (n 15).
18 Denno (n 15) 721.

Table 2.2 Types of Neuroscientific Evidence Introduced Into Court

Study	*Type of Crime*	*Types of Evidence Introduced*
Australia Alimardani & Chin (2019) Alimardani (2023)	Not specified	Neuropsychological testing; neuropsychiatric test, psychometric testing; frontal lobe abnormality; hemorrhage; **brain injury**; **head injury**; cerebral insult
England and Wales Catley & Claydon (2015)	Homicide; crimes of violence; crimes of dishonesty; sexual offenses; drug offenses; driving offenses; Other	Neuroimaging; **head injury and brain damage**; family history; cognitive impairment; developmental immaturity; alcohol dependency syndrome
Canada Chandler (2015)	Homicide; crimes of violence; sexual offenses; drug offenses; driving offenses; property offenses; other	Prenatal alcohol exposure; neuropsychological testing; **traumatic brain injuries**; neuroimaging; dementia; epilepsy; birth trauma; parasomnia; tumor
United States Denno (2015)—(2020)	Death penalty; homicide; crimes of violence; sexual offenses; drug offenses; driving offenses; property offenses; crimes involving children; other	**Brain damage**; **head injury**; low IQ/mental retardation; toxic exposure; neuroimaging; adult personality/behavioral disorders; mental/behavioral disorders due to psychoactive substance abuse; organic mental disorders; schizophrenia, schizotypal, and delusional disorders
Slovenia Hafner (2019)	Homicide only	**Brain damage**; age-related impairments; neurological diseases and dysfunctions; organic mental disorders; organic personality disorders; behavioral disorders; neuroimaging
The Netherlands de Kogel & Westgeest (2015)	Crimes of violence; sexual offenses; drug offenses; property offenses; other	Neuroimaging; neuro-endocrinological assessment; neurobiological predisposition; **damage to the brain**; heritability factors; genetic predisposition; family history indicating biological origin; addiction

Table 2.3 Purpose and Use of Neuroscientific Evidence in Criminal Proceedings

Study	*Phase of Criminal Proceedings Where Neuroscience Was Used * Phase Most Used*	*Most Common Purpose for Neuroscientific Evidence*	*Most Common Purpose for Mitigating Neuroscientific Evidence*	*Prosecutor's Use of Neuroscientific Evidence*
Australia Alimardani & Chin (2019) Alimardani (2023)	Pretrial; trial/guilt; sentencing *(did not specify where most used)	Mitigation	Used for leniency in sentencing (relating to moral culpability and general deterrence)	Stated that regardless of the impact (mitigation or aggravation), prosecutors have a duty to provide all relevant materials to the court that would assist in the determination of a sentence with any evidence, including neuroscience evidence
England and Wales Catley & Claydon (2015)	Pretrial; guilt; *sentencing	Aggravation by way of victim evidence	Drawn upon to quash convictions, to lead to convictions for lesser offenses, and to lead to reduced sentences with the most successful application during appeals of sentence	Employed by the prosecution to provide evidence of a victim's injuries or cause of death or injury; however, the study's focus concerned the defense's use of mitigating evidence
Canada Chandler (2015)	Pretrial; guilt; *sentencing	Mitigation	Employed for assessing moral blameworthiness during the sentencing phase, particularly for violent crimes	Excluded any discussion of the prosecution's use of neuroscientific evidence
United States Denno (2015)–(2020)	Pretrial; guilt; *sentencing (mostly for death penalty cases)	Mitigation	Implemented to mitigate punishments, especially during the penalty phase for death penalty cases	Prosecutors rarely use neuroscientific evidence but if used it is in these two ways: to suggest a defendant's propensity to commit crimes and as evidence of a victim's injuries or cause of death
Slovenia Hafner (2019)	Pretrial; guilt; *sentencing	Mitigation	Applied to mitigate or reduce sentencing	Excluded any discussion of the prosecution's use of neuroscientific evidence, but did report that neuroscientific evidence was never used as an aggravating factor
The Netherlands de Kogel & Westgeest (2015)	Pretrial; guilt; *sentencing	Mitigation	Incorporated to show diminished accountability for the offense	Excluded any discussion of the prosecution's use of neuroscientific evidence

of the insanity or diminished capacity defences, the evidence could be used to suggest why a defendant may not have the requisite mental state for committing the crime charged or why they may have acted in self-defence. Lastly, neuroscientific evidence could be employed at the sentencing phase to inform the determination of the defendant's penalty, assuming the defendant is convicted at trial.

Table 2.3 shows that, for all countries, neuroscientific evidence was incorporated at all three phases of a criminal proceeding. Yet, it was consistently most widely applied during the sentencing phase.[19] Notably, at all phases, the most common purpose for neuroscientific evidence was to mitigate the level of the crime for which a defendant was charged (for example, to lessen a murder down to manslaughter) or to reduce a defendant's sentence. The exception was Catley and Claydon's study of England and Wales. Their research revealed that, while neuroscientific evidence could mitigate, the evidence was most commonly employed by prosecutors to aggravate a defendant's sentence by specifying the extent of a victim's injuries or cause of death. My U.S. Neuroscience Study reported that prosecutors applied neuroscientific evidence for a similar purpose (to clarify the extent of the victim's injuries) but with less frequency than was found in Catley and Claydon's research.[20]

The Australian study also noted the use of neuroscientific evidence by prosecutors, explaining that because 'prosecutors have a duty to provide all relevant evidence to the court that would assist in a determination of a sentence,' they then 'have a duty to present neuroscientific evidence at criminal hearings regardless of the influence that it may have on the punishment and whether it may reduce or aggravate the sentence.'[21] According to the authors, defence attorneys may fail to introduce neuroscientific evidence out of a concern that prosecutors may use it to aggravate the punishment[22]—a practice also documented in my U.S. Neuroscience Study. However, other studies may have excluded examining the prosecutor's role in this respect, considering it outside their scope and leaving unanswered how much this issue differed across countries.

Other country-specific factors impacted the use of neuroscientific evidence in court cases. For example, in my U.S. Neuroscience Study, nearly one-half of the defendants faced the death penalty, and the other half were mostly incarcerated for life or long sentences.[23] Thus, in the U.S., neuroscientific evidence is more widely introduced at the sentencing phase as mitigation evidence, even though U.S. attorneys also incorporate such evidence at the pretrial and guilt phases. Regardless, the non-death penalty countries also used neuroscientific evidence most commonly at the sentencing phase.

19 The study in Australia looked only at the sentencing phase of its selected cases. Alimardani (n 6).

20 D. W. Denno, 'Concocting Criminal Intent' (2017) 105(2) *Georgetown Law Review* 323.

21 Alimardani (n 6) 14.

22 Ibid.

23 Denno (n 5) and Denno (n 5).

Lastly, every country addressed some form of brain injury evidence and its impact, as indicated in Tables 2.2 and 2.4. Each country appears to treat such evidence differently depending on the goals and perspectives of its respective criminal justice system. The second section of this chapter discusses these variations in more depth, emphasising how each country falls within the framework of a double-edged-sword continuum that reflects a calculation between mitigation, aggravation, and defendant rehabilitation.

Table 2.4 Brain Injury, Rehabilitation, and the Double-Edged Sword Effect

Study	*Brain Injury as a Mitigating Factor*	*Brain Injury as an Aggravating Factor*	*Existence of a Double-Edged Sword Effect for Brain Injury*
Australia Alimardani & Chin (2019) Alimardani (2023)	Mitigating for culpability	Aggravating for risk of recidivism and danger to society	A Double-Edged Sword Plus Effect: Mitigation with Rehabilitation
England and Wales Catley & Claydon (2015)	Mitigating for culpability	Aggravating for dangerousness posed to the public	A Double-Edged Sword Effect
Canada Chandler (2015)	Mitigating for culpability	Aggravating for risk of recidivism	A Double-Edged Sword Plus Effect: Aggravation with Risk of Dangerousness
United States Denno (2015)–(2020)	Mitigating for culpability	Rarely used as an aggravating factor, but if it was raised, it was in the context of future dangerous	No Substantial Evidence of a Double-Edged Sword Effect
Slovenia Hafner (2019)	Mitigating for culpability	No formal finding for aggravation but could be considered aggravating with regard to requiring compulsory treatment due to potential dangerousness	No Double-Edged Sword Effect: Mitigation and Rehabilitation
The Netherlands de Kogel & Westgeest (2015)	Mitigating for culpability	Aggravating for risk of recidivism	A Double-Edged Sword Plus Effect: Aggravation Unless with Rehabilitation

The Special Case of Brain Injury

An overview of how different countries utilise neuroscientific evidence provides context for the special case of a defendant's brain injury. First, such a focus shows that neuroscientific evidence is not a one-size-fits-all concept, as indicated in Table 2.1. Criminal justice actors, including judges and juries, may interpret some kinds of neuroscientific factors as more fixed and unchangeable and, therefore, less amenable to rehabilitation. Because a serious brain injury can be a chronic condition that can manifest in different ways across a lifetime, it may seem (wrongly so) more permanent and predictive of a defendant's future dangerous behaviour. Second, this proclivity suggests that defence attorneys must learn the intricacies of introducing various types of neuroscientific evidence in court. Lastly, brain injury is a particularly effective vehicle for illustrating the importance of neuroscience and the complexities of the double-edged sword effect. For all of these reasons, I conducted a specific study of U.S. brain injury cases, which the following sections describe.

The Double-Edged Sword Concept: A Closer Look

The double-edged sword concept refers to the influence of neuroscientific evidence on judicial outcomes that can induce either mitigation or aggravation of a sentence, depending on how courts interpret the circumstances. All of the studies this chapter analyses address this concept in some capacity. A closer look at *Odle v. Calderon*,[24] a particularly serious U.S. brain injury case, helps explain how neuroscientific evidence can clarify the impact of a defendant's brain injury on criminal justice actors and whether that injury may be interpreted as a double-edged sword.

In *Odle*, the defendant, James Odle, was convicted of the first-degree murder of two different people, including a police officer, after Odle had been drinking and taking drugs.[25] He was then sentenced to death.[26] Odle brought forth an ineffective assistance of counsel claim, which he won on appeal, arguing that his counsel failed to present expert testimony at trial related to Odle's mental condition and statutory mitigating factors.[27]

That evidence included the results from an EEG test conducted on Odle that suggested Odle suffered from brain damage.[28] As the court noted, Odle was 'missing a piece of his brain the size of a grapefruit,' and his brain deficits

24 919 F Supp 1367, 1376 (ND Cal 1996).

25 *People v. Odle*, 754 P2d 184, 187 (Cal 1988).

26 B. Egelko, 'Double Murderer on Death Row Dies,' B3, at Death Row prisoner James Odle, who killed Amber Swartz-Garcia's father, dead at 71' *San Francisco Chronicle* (22 December 2020) <https://www.sfchronicle.com/crime/article/Death-row-prisoner-James-Odle-who-killed-Amber-15820763.php> accessed 30 November 2024.

27 *Odle v. Woodford*, 238 F3d 1084, 1089 (9th Cir 2001).

28 Ibid. 1088.

were obvious.[29] EEG results also corroborated expert and lay witness testimony describing Odle's erratic behaviour and brain disorders.[30]

Odle's background revealed that his mental deficiencies commenced in 1973 when he was in a car accident and experienced 'severe trauma to his brain.'[31] As a result, a surgeon 'performed a temporal lobe lobectomy, removing a 3 x 3 x 4 inch piece of his brain.'[32] According to the defence expert, 'Odle's brain injury would probably cause behavioral disturbances beyond his control,' a 'diagnosis consistent with Odle's complaints, documented during his hospitalizations, that he often felt unable to control his impulses.'[33] Indeed, after the surgery, Odle was committed to a mental hospital three times over seven years and twice attempted suicide while in jail or prison before he engaged in the murders in 1980.[34]

Odle was initially determined to be competent to stand trial because he remained calm during the trial. Remarkably, neither his attorney nor the trial judge questioned his capacity.[35] Yet, after a federal appellate court reversed that finding of competency, Odle and his lawyers continued to litigate his case to substantiate his ongoing mental disability and prevent his execution. In 2020, with litigation ongoing, Odle died of natural causes on death row.[36]

The varied interpretations of Odle's competency to stand trial illustrate the significance of the neuroscience of brain injury in criminal cases. First, Odle's trial lawyer never questioned his competency and therefore withheld from consideration compelling evidence of Odle's substantial impairment. Second, the federal court's overturning of Odle's competency decision suggested such information was powerfully mitigating because of the alternative explanations and hypotheses it could have provided for Odle's crimes. Presumably, without such evidence of brain damage, a jury could have viewed Odle's violent conduct as far more threatening and dangerous.[37]

Odle lies at the core of the 'double-edged sword' conflict concerning how the criminal justice system views the intersection of neuroscience and criminal law. In some countries, this tension may be all the more pronounced in cases involving a defendant's brain injuries. Although introducing neuroscientific evidence can diminish a defendant's level of blameworthiness because it humanises or explains a defendant's behaviour, its double-edged

29 Ibid. 1089.
30 Ibid. 1087–1088.
31 Ibid. 1087.
32 Ibid.
33 Ibid. 1088.
34 Egelko (n 26).
35 Egelko (n 26).
36 Egelko (n 26).
37 *Odle v. Woodford* (n 27) 1088.

sword potential can also bolster 'judgments about [the defendant's] risk and dangerousness.'[38]

Notably, most studies did not find that court systems fully embraced the concept of a double-edged sword or that prosecutors routinely applied neuroscience as an aggravating factor.[39] My U.S. Neuroscience Study in particular showed that prosecutors seldom incorporate neuroscientific evidence to support a claim relating to a defendant's future dangerousness.[40] Nonetheless, evidence of a defendant's brain injury could trigger an exception in some countries, depending on that country's overall philosophy.

Country Differences in the Use of the Double-Edged Sword

A comparison of international studies shows that countries generally appear to operate along an approximate continuum of mitigation and aggravation in terms of their embrace (or not) of the double-edged sword concept with respect to brain injuries. With the help of Table 2.4, this section examines all countries, starting with those that favour mitigation most and concluding with those that veer closer to aggravation. Within the scope of this continuum, I found that some countries were more apt to treat a brain injury as mitigating if the defense could show 'something more' on the defendant's behalf, such as the defendant's likely success at rehabilitation, in which case I would label the country as 'rehabilitation plus.' Of course, my overview depends heavily on how other authors characterised their findings and the extent to which they pinpointed brain injury cases.

Slovenia: No Double-Edged Sword Effect: Mitigation and Rehabilitation

Among all countries, the Slovenian study stood out because its results revealed no double-edged sword effect, and the Slovenian system focused on mitigation and rehabilitation. In the 89 Slovenian homicide cases involving neuroscientific evidence, there was 'no evidence of the double-edged sword of neuroscience effect,' and neuroscience was never introduced into a case as an aggravating factor.[41] Instead, about one-fifth of the studied defendants were sentenced to compulsory psychiatric treatment, a disposition purportedly not intended to punish but to protect society (and the defendant) and provide rehabilitative treatment.[42] Similarly, while neuroscientific evidence was used to establish a defendant's future dangerousness in about one-quarter of the cases, this tactic was not designed to promote more severe sentences in Slovenia 'in

38 Chandler (n 7) 574.

39 Denno 'Vulnerable Defendants and Neuroscience in Courtrooms throughout the World' (n 15).

40 Denno (n 5) 544.

41 Hafner (n 10) 239–240.

42 Ibid. 241.

the same way as observers of the double-edged sword effect report for other countries.'[43]

The Slovenian study mentioned a limited number of cases concerning a defendant's brain injury or brain damage. Of those cases, most injuries were attributable to a self-induced or 'internal' condition, such as the defendant's extensive drug or alcohol abuse[44] or stroke or cerebral atrophy,[45] rather than an external injury, such as a blow to the head. Regardless, the study's account of the Slovenian system suggests that even if these injuries were considered chronic or unchangeable, they would not be viewed differently from other neuroscientific disorders. As the study explained, 'courts never presumed in advance that the defendant's dangerous behavior rooting in his neurological condition could not be changed.'[46] Likewise, 'the criminal justice system never gave up—at least expressly—on the idea of rehabilitation even for the perpetrators of [the] most severe crimes.'[47]

The United States: No Substantial Evidence of a Double-Edged Sword Effect

In most cases of extreme violence in the United States, the potential of a defendant's rehabilitation is far less, if ever, a factor with respect to neuroscientific evidence because the death penalty or the prospect of a harsh sentence looms. Generally, individuals are either going to be executed, remain on death row for years, or be incarcerated for a lifetime or close to it.[48] Therefore, rehabilitation is not considered relevant in the way it could be in non-death penalty countries where sentences are far less severe.

Regardless of this punitive bent, my U.S. Neuroscience Study did not show substantial evidence of a double-edged sword framework. In cases in which neuroscientific evidence was an issue, defence attorneys mostly wanted to introduce such evidence on behalf of their clients to mitigate their clients' punishment or criminal charges. In contrast, prosecutors wanted to exclude neuroscientific evidence, except in cases in which the evidence pertained to victims' injuries, especially Shaken Baby Syndrome.[49] In the few cases in which prosecutors used neuroscientific evidence to suggest aggravation, defence attorneys predominantly introduced evidence in ineffective or damaging ways, only to be employed against their clients by prosecutors.[50]

43 Ibid. 241–242.
44 Ibid. 236.
45 Ibid. 244.
46 Ibid. 242.
47 Ibid. 242.
48 Denno (n 5).
49 D. W. Denno, 'How Prosecutors and Defense Attorneys Differ in Their Use of Neuroscience Evidence' (2016) 84 *Fordham Law Review* 453–479; Denno (n 20).
50 Denno (n 5).

In reviewing the various empirical studies discussed in this chapter, brain injuries provided insights into the double-edged sword effect that were not as apparent when considering the impact of neuroscientific evidence generally. For this chapter, I wanted to know if the concept of a double-edged sword would be more pronounced in cases involving a brain injury in my U.S. Neuroscience Study, given that brain injuries could be viewed as less mitigating. Therefore, I examined all listed brain injury scenarios in my U.S. Neuroscience Study's universe of 7,776 defendant cases during the 12 decades from 1900 to 2020.[51] There were four key findings:

- While a substantial percentage of incarcerated individuals have brain injuries,[52] a defendant's brain injury will not always be one of the items mentioned in a criminal case involving neuroscientific evidence from Westlaw or Lexis because so many other factors may be more relevant. Of the 7,776 defendant cases in my U.S. Neuroscience Study, 601 cases (7.73%) were found to raise information about a defendant's brain injury.[53]
- Not surprisingly, cases mentioning a brain injury increased over time (from 1990 to 2020). There are three potential reasons for this finding: (1) brain injuries among defendants have actually increased; (2) such injuries have become medically more detectable; or (3) criminal cases are more apt to include the term "brain injury" in their list of neuroscientific evidence. Regardless of the reason, from 1900 to 1980, cases mentioned a defendant having a brain injury only 4–5% percent of the time, whereas that number grew incrementally over the decades to 14% by 2020, accounting for the increase in neuroscience cases generally.[54]
- A comparison of brain injury cases to cases in which no brain injury was mentioned revealed no difference in prosecutors' willingness to argue that a defendant was a future danger. In both categories of cases (brain-injured and non-brain-injured), a future dangerousness issue related to neuroscience was rare, occurring only 4% of the time. For example, only 26 cases (4%) of the 601 brain injury defendant cases concerned future dangerousness.[55]
- Of these 26 future dangerousness brain injury cases, 17 (65%) cases had a future dangerousness issue that was explicitly related to the defendant's brain injury, and 9 (35%) cases had a future dangerousness issue that was

51 See Denno (n 5) for a fuller description of the twelve-decade neuroscience study.

52 See the articles listed in (n 4).

53 Information on file with the author.

54 Information on file with the author.

55 A future dangerousness issue related to neuroscience was presented in 343 (4%) of the 7,776 defendant neuroscience cases. The 343 number comes from adding the 26 brain injury–related future dangerousness cases and the 317 non-brain injury–related future dangerousness cases. The 4% figure remained stable even when I subtracted out the 26 cases from the 343 cases.

not associated with the defendant's brain injury and instead pertained to another neuroscientific condition that the defendant possessed.

Although there was no substantial evidence of a double-edged sword effect in the U.S. Neuroscience Study, including in brain injury cases, that does not mean it did not exist. When relevant, such an approach would highlight the intractability of a defendant's brain injury, such as the prosecution's position in *People v. Buss*.[56] Yet, this intractability argument was unsuccessful in *United States v. Runyon*.[57] There, the court dismissed a claim of ineffective assistance of counsel when defence counsel omitted key neuroscientific information on the defendant's behalf. On appeal, defence expert testimony suggested that Runyon's history of head injuries, including car accidents and a blast injury, may have caused mild, diffuse brain damage, particularly in the brainstem and frontal lobe.[58] Defence counsel also tried to dampen any suggestion of Runyon's future dangerousness with mitigating expert testimony stating that Runyon posed little risk of violence when incarcerated.[59] Although the prosecution countered that strategy, stating that Runyon's evidence of brain injury was 'weak' and 'double-edged,'[60] and the court found that the defence counsel's actions were reasonable,[61] the Circuit Court concluded differently. It remanded the case on the basis that defence counsel failed to investigate Runyon's mental health evidence and should have done so.[62]

Overall, *Buss* and *Runyon* demonstrate how a double-edged sword interplay works because both cases consider mitigation and future dangerousness arguments, albeit with differing outcomes. Although the cases are outliers—future dangerousness is infrequent when neuroscience is involved—it bears emphasising how much the U.S. differs from a country like Slovenia, which prioritises both mitigation and rehabilitation. That said, U.S. Courts have consistently held that investigating a defendant's cognitive and intellectual deficiencies is a key part of the mitigation inquiry, especially in death penalty cases.[63] Although ineffective assistance of counsel claims are challenging to prove, they are more successful when a defence attorney either fails to introduce neuroscientific evidence or handles it incompetently, given the U.S. Supreme Court's recognition of the mitigating value of neuroscientific evidence in criminal cases.[64]

56 718 NE2d 1 (Ill 1999).
57 994 F3d 192, 204 (4th Cir. 2021).
58 Ibid.
59 Ibid. 214, 220.
60 Ibid. 204.
61 Ibid.
62 Ibid. 207–210.
63 Denno (n 5) 506.
64 Ibid.

Australia: A Double-Edged Sword Plus Effect: Mitigation With Rehabilitation

Both Australian studies (2019, 2023) specifically addressed the double-edged sword concept in the criminal cases they examined. According to the 2019 study, Australia has acknowledged the concept of a double-edged sword involving neuroscientific evidence 'since at least 1979.'[65] Likewise, the 2019 study noted two 'highly cited judgments,' where evidence of the defendant's brain damage was both a mitigating factor that reduced the defendant's culpability and an aggravating factor that bolstered arguments that the defendant was a future danger to society.[66] In balancing both factors, the courts seemingly reached a compromise verdict, finding the defendant guilty of manslaughter while 'acting under a substantial abnormality of the mind arising from his brain damage.'[67]

In the 2023 study focusing solely on sentencing cases in South Wales, results showed that neuroscientific evidence was 'substantially' more mitigating than aggravating.[68] In those cases where neuroscientific evidence impacted the sentence, the sentence was far more apt to support leniency (85%). In turn, there was only one case in which neuroscientific evidence was associated with a harsher sentence and did not also support a more lenient sentence. Likewise, only a small percentage of cases (5%) concluded that 'neuroscience tended towards both mitigating and aggravating the sentence.'[69]

The Australian criminal justice system takes seriously a defendant's potential for rehabilitation. A brain injury closely associated with the defendant's criminality may suggest that the defendant is a future danger; however, if the court considers the injury treatable and the defendant amenable to rehabilitation, the court may view the defendant as someone unlikely to offend again.[70] Although the Australian studies appear less optimistic generally than the Slovenian study regarding rehabilitation, the Australian findings do seem to suggest an overall positive attitude toward a defendant's rehabilitation for brain injury, thereby fitting into the 'mitigation plus' category.

Perspectives toward the double-edged sword concept may also be inconsistent depending on the institution evaluating it. According to one Australian report, for example, courts hold a 'concerning attitude . . . towards rehabilitation of offenders with an acquired brain injury, that nothing works for them (i.e., therapeutic nihilism), while there are many studies that suggest otherwise.'[71] Regardless, it is clear that courts consider the rehabilitative potential of neuroscientific evidence in brain injury cases. In *R v. Peterson*, for

65 Alimardani (n 6) 263.
66 Ibid (citing *Veen v. R* and *Veen v. R* (No 2).
67 Ibid.
68 Alimardani (n 6) 5.
69 Ibid. 10.
70 Ibid.
71 Ibid. 5.

example, the defence successfully argued for a partial defence of self-defence based on the defendant's brain damage in a case in which the defendant was accused of murdering his friend.[72] Described as 'a man of limited intellectual ability,' two psychiatrists explained that the defendant also suffered from 'executive dysfunction caused by frontal lobe damage,' which impaired his capacity to control his behaviour and foresee the consequences of his actions.[73] To reach a partial defence, the Supreme Court of Western Australia considered the medical evidence explaining the defendant's frontal lobe injury, especially in their evaluation of the reliability, voluntariness, and fairness of the admissions he made to the police.[74]

Ultimately, the 2023 Australian study found that neuroscientific evidence primarily led to mitigation in most cases and was 'rarely used as evidence for the offender's risk of recidivism.'[75] Indeed, even when courts viewed the defendant as a potential danger, they considered the defendant's prospects for rehabilitation.

The Netherlands: A Double-Edged Sword Plus Effect: Aggravation Unless With Rehabilitation

The Netherlands study by de Kogel and Westgeest noted the presence of a double-edged sword effect in some cases, yet stressed that the impact would likely be most substantial in those 'with a high risk of severe violence.'[76] Likewise, the Dutch courts were amenable to evidence showing that defendants could potentially reduce their risk of recidivism. According to assessments in one case, for example, experts found a defendant's organic brain defects to be generally untreatable but could see the defendant's chances for improvement with rehabilitation efforts that may reduce the defendant's risk of recidivism.[77] Indeed, in some circumstances, courts viewed cases involving brain damage differently, suggesting that such defendants could be 'extra vulnerable' to an extreme emotional state and that attorneys could tailor their defences accordingly.[78]

De Kogel and Westgeest reviewed a number of brain injury cases involving prefrontal brain damage in which courts considered that the consequences of such damage could affect a defendant's behavioural choices and therefore be mitigating. In one of the cases,[79] the court determined that the defendant's prefrontal brain damage negated his level of premeditation for stabbing and

72 Alimardani (n 6).
73 Ibid. 529.
74 Ibid. 260.
75 Ibid. 263.
76 de Kogel (n 9) 601.
77 Ibid. 594.
78 Ibid. 596–597.
79 Ibid. 593 (discussing Court's Hertogenbosch Sept. 5, 2007, ECL:RBSHE:2007:BB2861).

killing his wife, thus reducing his sentence from murder to manslaughter. The court relied heavily on the neurologist's expert testimony, concluding that the defendant could not control his impulses and stop his behaviour after it began.[80] Although the court explained that a defendant would typically have sufficient time to ponder his actions in such a situation, the court credited the neuroscientific testimony for concluding otherwise, noting that 'premeditation was not proven.'[81]

Overall, the Netherlands study suggests that the concept of the double-edged sword is particularly noticeable in brain injury cases. Because brain damage can mitigate the defendant's blameworthiness but aggravate the defendant's sentencing due to a purportedly untreatable condition, the circumstance suggests a recidivism risk. That said, there is also a doubled-edged sword 'plus' effect, indicating that sentencing mitigation is still possible, especially because Dutch courts are open to evidence that the defendant has 'opportunities' to improve and therefore counter any proclivity to recidivate.

Canada: A Double-Edged Sword Plus Effect: 'Aggravation and Risk of Dangerousness'

For a range of reasons, neuroscientific evidence was most commonly introduced in Canada to diagnose conditions related to a defendant's fetal alcohol spectrum disorders (FASDs) and their resultant brain-damaging effects.[82] Although the Canadian study acknowledges that evidence of other types of brain injury was not frequently introduced into court,[83] that statistic did not mean that such injuries did not exist in the criminal population, only that prenatal alcohol exposure was 'more commonly raised and better documented.'[84]

Likewise, in Canada, neuroscientific evidence could have created risks for the defendant if introduced, as the likelihood of mitigation was nearly equivalent to the likelihood of aggravation.[85] For example, focusing on cases involving prenatal alcohol syndrome, evidence of resulting brain damage could be mitigating, but judges also perceived it as 'a source of increased risk of

80 Ibid. 593.

81 Ibid. 593. In addition, de Kogel and Westgeest surveyed a range of other brain injury cases in which courts recognized either that a defendant could potentially recidivate because of their condition and resultant lack of impulse control, or be amendable to rehabilitation therefore a reduced sentence, all highly dependent on the conclusions and recommendations of expert witnesses.

82 Chandler (n 7) 557. For a thorough discussion of this association, see Denno (n 14).

83 Chandler (n 7) 558.

84 Ibid. 557.

85 Ibid. 569 (noting that neuroscientific evidence either hindered (34%) or mitigated (38%) sentencing decisions in criminal cases similarly).

recidivism or pessimism about treatment.'[86] This view was especially pronounced for more serious crimes with potential public safety concerns.[87]

In the Canadian study, because FASD is a factor in many cases, it is a challenge to pinpoint its specific influence on the country's overall criminal justice system. Likewise, it is difficult to assess whether judges are responding pessimistically to the FASD matter itself or to the condition of a defendant's brain injury because the influences are so tightly intertwined. One particular case provides a clue. In *R v. Steppan*, the defendant presented a lack of a specific FASD diagnosis and seemingly received a more lenient sentence as a result. As the study explains, for Steppan, 'the hope for success in treatment may have been tied to the evidence that his cognitive limitations were not too severe, but it may also have been positively affected by the lack of an FASD diagnosis.'[88] In essence, additional research is needed to clarify 'whether an explicit diagnosis of brain damage as an explanation for cognitive limitations and behavioral problems produces greater pessimism about rehabilitation than the observation of those symptoms alone.'[89]

Regardless of this association, the double-edged sword analysis is alive and well in Canada. Although neuroscientific evidence 'tends to reduce moral blameworthiness . . . it also tends to increase judgements about risk and dangerousness, given the view (expressed often in the cases reviewed here) that brain injuries can sometimes be managed but not cured.'[90] The dearth of existing alternatives to incarceration in Canada aggravates this dilemma. Even when Canadian judges view a defendant's brain damage as mitigating, appropriate services for treatment and containment simply do not exist.[91] Thus, opportunities to rehabilitate brain-injured defendants remain stymied far more by the pragmatism of institutional impediments than by the signs of judicial resistance.

England and Wales: A Double-Edged Sword Effect

Catley and Claydon's study of England and Wales did not explicitly address the concept of a 'double-edged sword,' hence this chapter provides a briefer analysis of their work. Yet, their findings thoroughly explained how the prosecution and defence both used neuroscientific evidence. Like other studies, the defence incorporated neuroscientific evidence to mitigate a defendant's culpability and punishment. In contrast, the prosecution (not the defence) was more likely to introduce neuroscientific evidence generally—not about the defendant per se, but instead to examine the extent of a *victim's* brain injury to

86 Ibid. 564.
87 Ibid.
88 Ibid. 572.
89 Ibid.
90 Ibid. 574.
91 Ibid.

better bolster a case against the defendant.[92] By detailing the victim's injuries or cause of death, the prosecutor would have more information to support their recommended sentence.[93]

Defendant brain injury cases involving neuroscientific evidence illustrate the complexity of information concerning various factors and influences. For example, in *R v. Hendy*, a diminished responsibility case in which a jury convicted the 16-year-old defendant of murder,[94] testifying experts explained that Hendy's earlier brain injury from a road accident may have led to temporal lobe damage and affected his ability to control his behaviour.[95] The circumstances were exacerbated all the more by Hendy's heavy drinking.[96] Further testing of Hendy, by way of an EEG test indicating left temporal lobe damage, and later neuropsychometric testing, convinced the Court of Appeal to overturn Hendy's murder conviction and substitute a manslaughter conviction due to diminished responsibility.[97] However, rather than incarceration, Hendy was provided with a hospital order during sentencing under the Mental Health Act of 1983,[98] an outcome that the study found troubling and that suggests a double-edged sword perspective. As the Catley and Claydon study explained, the neuroscientific evidence introduced on Hendy's behalf allowed him to avoid a criminal conviction. Yet, it also enhanced the impression of his risk of harm, leading to the court's 'imposition of a restriction order without limit of time.'[99]

It is unclear whether a hospital order was less punitive for Hendy. The order could be viewed as mitigating, especially compared to the solutions other countries provide through rehabilitation. That said, in England and Wales, the prosecution is still more likely than the defence to introduce neuroscientific evidence, and both countries have a limited capacity for rehabilitation. Thus, England and Wales fall on the furthest extreme on the double-edged sword continuum regarding using neuroscientific evidence.

Conclusion

Neuroscience is an excellent entry into the significant discussions of our time, especially how the law will evolve to move society forward and incorporate insights about brain injuries. This chapter's analysis of how the criminal justice systems of six countries use neuroscientific evidence shows a resonating theme across countries that is pronounced but not always accurate. Neuroscientific research can correct this misalignment and, in many ways, it already has.

92 Catley (n 8).
93 Ibid.
94 Ibid. 525–526 (discussing *R v. Hendy* [2006] EWCA 819).
95 Ibid. 526.
96 Ibid.
97 Ibid 527.
98 Ibid; see Mental Health Act of 1983, ss 37 and 41.
99 Catley (n 8) 527.

In essence, key criminal justice actors commonly embrace the concept of a double-edged sword, the belief that neuroscience can offer either a mitigating or an aggravating interpretation of a defendant's cognitive challenges and adjust a potential punishment accordingly. This belief appears to be particularly striking in defendant brain injury cases, based on the unsupported assumption that brain injuries are fixed and permanent, and injured defendants are dangerous and untreatable. Yet, the results of my 12-decade U.S. Neuroscience Study and the empirical research conducted in six countries show that the double-edged sword concept does not fully reflect reality; instead, it is an outdated framework fueled by potentially deleterious misunderstandings. The criminal justice system's use of neuroscience deserves credit for enlightening case decision-making and correcting what could otherwise be distorted views.

Throughout this chapter, the positives of neuroscience have prevailed, especially when they are associated with the brain injury sciences. Not only is there growing evidence that even severe brain injuries can be successfully treated,[100] but most courts in most countries are also more apt to view a defendant's brain injury evidence as mitigating rather than aggravating or as a future danger. Likewise, the majority of the studies this chapter analyses did not report that court systems fully share the premise of a double-edged sword or that prosecutors routinely used neuroscience as an aggravator. Although prosecutors may employ various purported strategies to make such arguments, many courts do not accept them, or there are institutional impediments that can explain why they do (for example, a lack of alternatives to incarceration). Assuming neuroscientific evidence becomes more sophisticated, this double-edged sword focus may increasingly subside, as Slovenia's criminal justice system has demonstrated.

This chapter's studies show that the risk of the double-edged sword effect is too low for defence attorneys to justify withholding neuroscientific evidence concerning a defendant's brain injury, even when the injury appears to be permanent or untreatable. At a minimum, neuroscientific information can give courts a better understanding of a defendant's behaviour, enhancing appropriate decision-making and sentencing. Increasingly, criminal justice actors have opportunities to become aware of the latest discoveries and recognise the impact of neuroscience in all phases of the criminal justice systems worldwide.[101]

100 See Hunter (n 4) 539–565; Colorado Division of Criminal Justice, '*OVP: Victims of a Violent Crime Brain Injury Task Force*' (2024) <https://dcj.colorado.gov/dcj-offices/ovp/vic-vilnt-crime-brain-injury-tf> accessed 7 December 2024; Liontas (n 14).

101 I am most grateful to Megan Martucci and Erica Valencia-Graham for their immensely helpful comments and contributions, and to reference librarian Kathleen Thompson for her excellent research. I also thank Colleen M. Berryessa, Hannah Wishart, and Karen Steele for their insightful input. I am indebted to five sources for research funding: Fordham University School of Law, Fordham's Neuroscience and Law Center, Mr. and Mrs. John R. Costantino, the Gerald M. Edelman Post-Graduate Fellowship in Neuroscience, and the Roger Sachs Family Foundation. No individual or organization acknowledged in this chapter necessarily supports the chapter's interpretations or conclusions. I take responsibility for any mistakes or misjudgments.

3 'Excited Delirium' in Law Enforcement Contexts

Scientific, Legal, and Ethical Concerns

Joanna Naples-Mitchell, Brianna da Silva Bhatia, Joshua Budhu, and Altaf Saadi

Introduction

The in-custody killing of George Floyd during the summer of 2020 ignited an unprecedented wave of national and global demonstrations in support of the Black Lives Matter movement, and against police violence and systemic racism. In recent years, the deaths of George Floyd, Angelo Quinto, Manuel Ellis, Zachary Bear Heels, Elijah McClain, Natasha McKenna, and Daniel Prude have been attributed to 'excited delirium' rather than to the conduct of law enforcement officers.[1] Although concerns about the questionable basis of 'excited delirium' existed before these high-profile deaths, the resulting social movement prompted physicians, legal scholars, and advocacy groups like Physicians for Human Rights (PHR) to delve deeper into the origins and use of

1 S. Glenn, '"Can't Breathe": Tacoma Police Restraint of Manuel Ellis Caused His Death, Medical Examiner Reports' (*The Seattle Times*, 3 June 2020) <https://www.seattletimes.com/seattle-news/cant-breathe-tacoma-police-restraint-of-manuel-ellis-caused-his-death-medical-examiner-reports/> accessed 29 November 2024; Associated Press News, 'Family Rallies for Man Killed in 2017 Omaha Police Struggle' (*Associated Press News*, 6 June 2021) <https://apnews.com/article/ne-state-wire-omaha-28d4820fecb111234d641f609db031f3> accessed 29 November 2024; CBS News Colorado, '"Excited Delirium": Elijah McClain's Mother Talks To "60 Minutes" about Use Of Ketamine To Sedate Suspects—CBS Colorado' (14 December 2020) <https://www.cbsnews.com/colorado/news/excited-delirium-elijah-mcclain-60-minutes-ketamine-sedate-suspects/> accessed 29 November 2024; J. Jouvenal, '"Excited Delirium" Cited in Dozens of Deaths in Police Custody: Is It Real or a Cover for Brutality?' (*Washington Post*, 7 May 2015) <https://www.washingtonpost.com/local/crime/existence-of-excited-delirium-ruling-in-va-womans-death-has-experts-split/2015/05/06/b1cc9499-ddaa-474c-9e8a-9ae89a9ae679_story.html> accessed 29 November 2024; see, generally, K. W. Crenshaw, A. J. Ritchie, R. Anspach and others, 'Say Her Name: Resisting Police Brutality against Black Women' (2015) *Columbia Law School Faculty Scholarship;* L. Voytko-Best, 'Daniel Prude's Autopsy Report Says "Excited Delirium," a Controversial Diagnosis, Contributed To His Death' (*Forbes*, 3 September 2020) <https://www.forbes.com/sites/lisettevoytko/2020/09/03/daniel-prudes-autopsy-report-says-excited-delirium-a-controversial-diagnosis-contributed-to-his-death/> accessed 29 November 2024.

DOI: 10.4324/9781003510246-4

'excited delirium' in the United States and use the momentum to push for change around use of the diagnosis.[2]

When did the term 'excited delirium' evolve to describe a distinct type of delirium or become a cause of death? How did the corresponding term 'excited delirium syndrome' proliferate amongst medical examiners and coroners, and in explaining deaths in police custody? PHR examined these questions in a March 2022 report, from which parts of this chapter are adapted,[3] concluding that 'excited delirium' is not a valid diagnosis and should not be used as a cause of death. Following the report's publication, PHR and partners undertook a groundbreaking advocacy campaign, leveraging research and medical expertise to persuade medical and law enforcement associations to disavow the use of 'excited delirium.' Over the next several years, a number of medical and law enforcement groups have renounced 'excited delirium,' underscoring the power of health professional mobilisation. 'Excited delirium' is no longer recognised by any major U.S. medical association.

Origins and History

Wetli and Fishbain

The introduction of the term 'excited delirium' in the 1980s has been attributed to Drs. David Fishbain and Charles Wetli. Fishbain was the director of psychiatric emergency services at the University of Miami, and Wetli was a forensic pathologist. In 1981, Wetli and Fishbain co-authored a case report detailing cocaine intoxication in a person who had swallowed packets of cocaine.[4] The authors described the resulting delirium—an acute change in attention and cognition (see section on Delirium)—as a medical emergency. Wetli and Fishbain characterised this 'acute excited delirium' as reversible, transient, and with an array of possible causes. They elaborated that there are 'two types of delirium: stuporous . . . and excited.'[5] We conclude that Wetli

2 See, generally, B. da Silva Bhatia et Al., *Excited Delirium and Deaths in Police Custody March 2022 the Deadly Impact of a Baseless Diagnosis* (*Physicians for Human Rights*, March 2022); M. O'Hare, J. Budhu, A. Saadi, 'Perspective | Police Keep Using "Excited Delirium" to Justify Brutality: It's Junk Science' (*The Washington Post*, 17 July 2020) <https://www.washingtonpost.com/outlook/chokehold-police-excited-delirium/2020/07/17/fe907ec8-c6bc-11ea-b037-f9711f89ee46_story.html> accessed 4 December 2024.

3 B. da Silva Bhatia et al. (n 2). We acknowledge our Physicians for Human Rights (PHR) report coauthors Michele Heisler, MD, MPA, PHR medical director and professor of internal medicine and of public health at the University of Michigan, and Julia Sherwin, JD, civil rights lawyer, for their important work on the original report from which this is adapted. We also thank additional PHR colleagues for their contributions to the research, writing, and editing of the original report.

4 D. A. Fishbain, C. V. Wetli, 'Cocaine Intoxication, Delirium, and Death in a Body Packer' (1981) 10 *Annals of Emergency Medicine* 531.

5 Ibid. 532.

and Fishbain initially used 'excited' as an adjective to portray the hyperactive form of delirium. Notably, they stated that the treatment of delirium is of the underlying illness and concluded that the delirium presentation hides the 'medical nature.'

Later, in 1985, Wetli and Fishbain published a case series on cocaine-induced psychosis.[6] This series described seven people who used cocaine (six men and one woman) who exhibited fear, panic, violent behaviour, hyperactivity, hyperthermia, and/or unexpected strength. All of them had been restrained (six by police, in some cases with the assistance of bystanders, and one by emergency room staff), and all died suddenly with respiratory arrest, with five of them reportedly dying in police custody. Autopsies did not reveal any 'anatomic cause of death.' In this publication, Wetli and Fishbain again described 'excited delirium' as a 'medical emergency but with a psychiatric presentation' and noted that the 'prognosis depends on the underlying cause of the delirium.'[7]

A short time later, Wetli began using 'excited delirium' as a distinct cause of death and diagnosis—treating it as a unique condition, separate from the established, medically recognised delirium, which is defined by the presence of an underlying medical cause that must be identified and treated (see Section 3.1). There is, however, no indication in his writings that he had access to new scientific evidence underpinning this change.

Serial Murders of Black Women in Miami

In the years that followed his publications on cocaine-induced 'excited delirium,' Wetli began to seek new applications of his theories in his work as deputy chief medical examiner in Miami.

Between September 1986 and November 1988, 12 Black women were found dead in the same geographic area of Miami.[8] Wetli and several of his colleagues found that almost all had low levels of cocaine upon toxicology testing, and they classified the majority of the deaths as accidents from cocaine intoxication.[9] Shortly thereafter, Wetli began to publicise his theory that the women had died due to the combination of sex with cocaine.[10] Wetli speculated that the women consumed small amounts of cocaine and then died

6 C. V. Wetli, D. A. Fishbain, 'Cocaine-Induced Psychosis and Sudden Death in Recreational Cocaine Users' (1985) 30 *Journal of Forensic Sciences* 873; R. W. Byard, 'Ongoing Issues with the Diagnosis of Excited Delirium' (2018) 14 *Forensic Science, Medicine, and Pathology* 149; A. Truscott, 'A Knee in the Neck of Excited Delirium' (2008) 178(6) *Canadian Medical Association Journal* 669.

7 Wetli et al. (1985) 878.

8 A. Walker, H. Dewar, 'Cocaine-Sex Deaths in Dade Probed' (*Miami News*, 24 November 1988).

9 Ibid.

10 Ibid.

from sexual excitement, which he described as the female manifestation of the 'cocaine psychosis' he had previously identified in men.[11] He said that 'for some reason, the male of the species becomes psychotic and the female of the species dies in relation to sex.'[12] As to why all the women dying were Black, he further speculated, without any scientific basis, 'we might find out that cocaine in combination with a certain (blood) type (more common in blacks) is lethal.'[13]

On December 12, 1988—less than a month after Wetli began to publicise this theory—14-year-old Antoinette Burns was found dead.[14] Wetli, who performed the initial autopsy, believed that she, too, had died from a combination of sex and cocaine use, despite a negative toxicology report.[15,16] In March of 1989, police investigators confronted Wetli's supervisor, chief medical examiner Dr. Joseph Davis, with evidence they believed pointed to homicide.[17] Consequently, Davis began to reexamine case files.[18] Later that month, Davis announced his conclusion that the deaths of all of the women—19 by that point and including Ms. Burns—were homicides.[19]

Unfortunately, this new evidence and reclassification did not stop the use of 'excited delirium.' One year after Davis's reclassification of the deaths as homicides, Wetli continued to assert that at least some of the women had died from a combination of sex and cocaine.[20] Wetli also continued to promote a corresponding theory of Black male death from cocaine-related delirium.[21]

Wetli's mischaracterisation of the murders of Black women in Miami—and the racism and misogyny that seemed to inform it—failed to discredit his other equally racialised and gendered theory of sudden Black male death from cocaine.[22] Instead, the use of the term 'excited delirium' grew.

11 Ibid.

12 Ibid.

13 Ibid.

14 P. Collins, B. McPhail, 'Seventeen Dead So Far' (*New Times*, 3 May 1989).

15 D. Gehrke, 'Missed Calls, Close Calls Mar Serial Killings Case' (*Miami Herald*, 26 April 1990); 'Investigation Report (Antoinette Burns. M.E. Case No. 7703575)' (Metropolitan Dade County Medical Examiner Department, 1988) Medical Examiner Department Report 7703575. (Accessed provided courtesy of Julia Sherwin).

16 B. Bearak, 'Eerie Deaths of 17 Women Baffle Miami' (*Los Angeles Times*, 14 May 1989) <https://www.latimes.com/archives/la-xpm-1989-05-14-mn-413-story.html> accessed 2 December 2024; D. Gehrke, '18 Killings Leave Families Struggling with Uncertainty' (*Miami Herald*, 18 June 1989).

17 See, generally, R. Rymer, 'Murder Without a Trace' (1990) *Health* 55–56.

18 Ibid.

19 R. Goudreau, 'Somebody Killed 19 Women' (*Miami Herald*, 31 May 1989).

20 See, generally, Rymer (1990); G. Garcia-Roberts, 'Is Excited Delirium Killing Coked-up, Stun-Gunned Miamians?' (*Miami New Times*, 15 July 2010) <https://www.miaminewtimes.com/news/is-excited-delirium-killing-coked-up-stun-gunned-miamians-6367399> accessed 2 December 2024.

21 Rymer (n 20).

22 Osagie K. Obasogie, *Excited Delirium and Police Use of Force—Virginia Law Review* (28 December 2021) <https://virginialawreview.org/articles/excited-delirium-and-police-use-of-force/> accessed 29 November 2024.

Publication of Excited Delirium Syndrome

In 2005, Theresa Di Maio, a psychiatric nurse, and her husband, Dr. Vincent Di Maio, a forensic pathologist serving as the chief medical examiner of Bexar County, Texas, and editor of the *American Journal of Medicine and Pathology*, published a book on 'excited delirium syndrome.'[23] They defined the term as 'the sudden death of an individual during or following an episode of excited delirium, in which an autopsy fails to . . . explain the death.'[24] They defined 'excited delirium' as 'delirium involving combative or violent behavior' caused by 'normal physiologic reactions of the body to stress gone awry.'[25] The Di Maios discussed the history and origins of 'excited delirium' via summarised case reports from primarily the 1930s and 1940s, in most cases describing women in psychiatric institutions.

Role of TASER

TASER/Axon is a U.S. company that develops technology products and weapons for the military, law enforcement, and civilians, including 'Taser,' a line of so-called 'less-lethal' electroshock 'stun' weapons. In 2007, TASER purchased 1,000 to 1,500 copies of Di Maio's book on 'excited delirium syndrome' and distributed them for free, along with other materials on 'excited delirium,' for free, to medical examiners and police chiefs.[26] Given that there were only around 500 full-time forensic pathologists in the United States at the time,[27] TASER's large purchase in 2007 alone likely saturated the forensic pathology community with the 'excited delirium syndrome' theory.[28] Di Maio had also testified as a paid expert for TASER/Axon multiple times.[29]

American College of Emergency Physicians (ACEP) White Paper

In 2005, TASER's national litigation counsel,[30] Michael Brave, co-founded a corporation entitled the Institute for the Prevention of In-Custody Deaths

23 See, generally, T. G. DiMaio, V. J. M. DiMaio, *Excited Delirium Syndrome: Cause of Death and Prevention* (CRC Press, Taylor & Franics Group, Boca Raton, 2005).

24 Ibid.

25 Ibid.

26 Deposition of Vincent J.M. Di Maio, M.D. at 159:19–21, *Harrison v. County of Alameda*, No. C11-2868 JST (N.D. Cal. Jan. 24, 2014); B. Yeung, 'Taser's Delirium Defense' (*Mother Jones*, March/April 2009) <https://www.motherjones.com/politics/2009/02/tasers-delirium-defense/> accessed 3 December 2024; Garcia-Roberts (n.20).

27 Scientific Working Group on Medicolegal Death Investigation, *Increasing the Supply of Forensic Pathologists in the United States* (Scientific Working Group on Medicolegal Death Investigation, 2012).

28 L. Wamsley, 'Taser Changes Its Name to Axon and Offers Free Body Cameras for Police' (*NPR*, 7 April 2017) <https://www.npr.org/sections/thetwo-way/2017/04/07/522878573/were-more-than-stun-guns-says-taser-as-it-changes-company-name> accessed 2 December 2024.

29 Deposition of Vincent J.M. Di Maio, M.D. at 159:19–21, *Harrison v. County of Alameda*, no. C11-2868 JST (N.D. Cal. Jan. 24, 2014).

30 O. El. Akkad, J. Leeder, 'How Taser International Wins in the Courtroom' (*The Globe and Mail*, 28 November 2007) <https://www.theglobeandmail.com/news/national/

(IPICD) with another individual, John Peters, paid by TASER to be an expert and consultant on cases they were involved with due to Taser-related deaths.[31] In October 2008, IPICD held its '3rd Annual Sudden Death, Excited Delirium & In-Custody Death Conference.' IPICD advertised the conference as 'the first consensus conference that focuses upon excited delirium.'

The conference speakers included TASER and/or restraint death defence experts and consultants, such as Drs. Di Maio, Wetli, Theodore Chan, Gary Vilke, Steven Karch,[32] and Deborah Mash.[33] These physicians are part of what the *New York Times*, in a December 26, 2021 investigative report, described as a 'small but influential cadre of scientists, lawyers, physicians and other police experts whose research and testimony are frequently used to absolve officers of blame for deaths.'[34] Forming a 'cottage industry of exoneration,' many of the dozen or so individuals in this group have ties with TASER/Axon and/or work as defence experts in death-in-custody litigation.[35]

The results of the 2008 IPICD conference were published as the 'White Paper Report on Excited Delirium Syndrome' by the American College of Emergency Physicians on September 10, 2009.[36] The co-authors of the white paper included Chan, Mash, and Vilke, as well as TASER's medical director, Dr. Jeffrey Ho.[37] Despite the close links between the paper's co-authors and TASER, these were not disclosed in the white paper report, and PHR was

---

how-taser-international-wins-in-the-courtroom/article20406364/> accessed 2 December 2024; S. Nasiripour, 'Zapping Taser' (*Reveal*, 1 December 2008) <http://revealnews.org/article/zapping-taser/> accessed 2 December 2024; T. Reid and others, 'Shock Tactics: As Taser Warns of Risks, Cities Bear a Burden in Court' (*Reuters*, 23 August 2017) <https://www.reuters.com/investigates/special-report/usa-taser-legal/> accessed 2 December 2024; J. Valentino-DeVries and others, 'How Paid Experts Help Exonerate Police after Deaths in Custody—The New York Times' (*The New York Times*, 2021) <https://www.nytimes.com/2021/12/26/us/police-deaths-in-custody-blame.html> accessed 2 December 2024.

31 See, generally, J. Sherwin, *Initial List of Officers, Directors and Resident Agent* (Institute for the Prevention of In-Custody Death, Inc, 2005).

32 *Declaration of Steven B Karch, MO, FFELM, Rosa v. TASER International, Inc*, No. C-05-03577 JF/HRL (N.D. Cal. Jun. 1, 2009).

33 T. Reid and others (n 30); P. Eisler, T. Reid, J. Szep, 'Shock Tactics: Taser Inserts Itself in Probes Involving Its Stun Guns' (*Reuters*, 24 August 2017) <https://www.reuters.com/investigates/special-report/usa-taser-experts/> accessed 3 December 2024.

34 Valentino-DeVries and others (n 30).

35 Ibid.

36 The Excited Delirium (ExDS) Task Force, *White Paper Report on Excited Delirium Syndrome Office of Justice Programs* (American College of Emergency Physicians, 238235, 2009) <https://www.ojp.gov/ncjrs/virtual-library/abstracts/white-paper-report-excited-delirium-syndrome> accessed 2 December 2024.

37 A. Mannix, 'After Conflict-of-Interest Concerns, HCMC Ends Deal with Taser Manufacturer' (*The Minnesota Star Tribune*, 19 June 2019) <https://www.startribune.com/after-conflict-of-interest-concerns-hcmc-ends-deal-with-taser-manufacturer/511528142> accessed 2 December 2024; C. Gilbert, A. Caputo, G. Hing, 'Tasers Are Less Reliable than Their Maker Has Claimed: The Results Can Be Deadly' (*APM Reports*, 9 May 2019) <https://www.apmreports.org/episode/2019/05/09/when-tasers-fail> accessed 2 December 2024.

unable to find conflict-of-interest statements or disclosures in any related documentation.

The white paper report acknowledged that the pathophysiology of 'excited delirium syndrome' is not understood, that there are no tests or standard diagnostic criteria, and that the medical treatment for the 'syndrome' is unknown. The authors provided *International Classification of Diseases, Ninth Revision* (*ICD-9*) codes such as manic excitement, delirium of mixed origin, agitation, delirium, and abnormal excitement, which 'describe the same entity as excited delirium syndrome.' They failed to consider that if manic excitement, delirium of mixed origin, agitation, and abnormal excitement are the same entity as 'excited delirium,' then 'excited delirium' cannot be a unique entity. Their report also does not consider that the forms of delirium or manic excitement in the *ICD-9* are not regarded as lethal if treated. The *Diagnostic and Statistical Manual of Mental Disorders* (*DSM-5*), the primary diagnostic tool used by clinicians for psychiatric diagnosis, recognises 'delirium' as a clinical entity, with 'hyperactive,' 'hypoactive,' and 'mixed' delirium subtypes, but these do not align with 'excited delirium.'[38]

The white paper report offered 10 specific features suggesting the presence of 'excited delirium' (pain tolerance, agitation, not responding to police presence, superhuman strength, rapid breathing, not tiring despite heavy physical exertion, naked/inappropriately clothed, sweating profusely, hot to the touch, and attraction to/destruction of glass/reflective surfaces). However, it provided no direct citations to the medical literature as to the origins or accuracy of these 10 features in predicting or diagnosing 'excited delirium,' nor did it comment on the validity of these features as a screening tool. The descriptions of certain symptoms and signs also played into racist tropes that people of colour possess 'superhuman strength' and are 'impervious to pain.'[39] This was especially concerning given that Wetli had asserted without evidence, 18 years prior, that 70% of people who died of cocaine-induced delirium were Black men and that 'it may be genetic.'[40]

In 2011, the same group of authors published a reiteration of the white paper report in the academic, peer-reviewed literature, titled 'Excited delirium syndrome: defining based on a review of the literature.'[41] Based on a review of 18 articles, 10 written by the paper's authors, the authors again identified 10 features of 'excited delirium.'[42] At no point did the authors discuss the lack of and consequent need to develop and test screening tools

38 Mannix (n 37); Gilbert, Caputo and Hing (n 37).

39 A. S. Byju, 'Excited Delirium: How Cops Invented a Disease' (2021) *Current Affairs* <https://www.currentaffairs.org/news/2021/04/excited-delirium-how-cops-invented-a-disease> accessed 2 December 2024.

40 Rymer (n 20).

41 G. M. Vilke, M. L. DeBard et al., 'Excited Delirium Syndrome (ExDS): Defining Based on a Review of the Literature' (2012) 43(5) *Journal of Emergency Medicine* 897–905.

42 Ibid.

for 'excited delirium' that are valid (able to identify diseased and non-diseased individuals accurately) or reliable (repeat measurements yield the same result). Once again, they also provided no statements of conflicts of interest or disclosures.

In 2021, Walsh et al. (an independent group of authors) analysed the language of the 2009 ACEP report and found that it relied on racial stereotypes.[43] They discussed the role of language, encouraging biased diagnosis and treatment, and called upon ACEP to formally retire the 2009 report, which it ultimately did (see section on Mobilisation for Change).

Medicine

Delirium

Delirium is a well-established clinical syndrome in medicine, with defined diagnostic criteria, known risk factors, and a growing body of research into its pathophysiology. The *DSM-5* outlines delirium as an acute disturbance in attention and cognition, typically with a fluctuating course and underlying medical cause.[44] Unlike 'excited delirium,' medical delirium is recognised across specialities, including geriatrics, neurology, and psychiatry, and is subject to continual empirical refinement.

Medical Literature

PHR's examination of the peer-reviewed medical literature on 'excited delirium,' published in their 2022 report, found that a small group of people authored articles supporting this diagnosis, many of them with ties to TASER/Axon and/or other conflicts of interest. Most of the studies cross-reference each other and highlight non-peer-reviewed sources, such as the Di Maio and Di Maio book *Excited Delirium Syndrome*, which is not a scientific or medical textbook, is not peer-reviewed, and draws unsubstantiated conclusions.[45]

Most of the reviewed literature suggests a relationship between 'excited delirium,' death, and restraint. However, these studies have small sample sizes alongside other limitations. The extensive review conducted by Strommer et al. included studies up to April 2020 and summarised 'excited delirium' characteristics. They found that restraint was described in 90% of all deaths in the 'excited'

43 B. Myrick Walsh, I. K. Agboola and others et al, 'Revisiting "Excited Delirium": Does the Diagnosis Reflect and Promote Racial Bias?' (2023) 24 *Western Journal of Emergency Medicine* 152.

44 D. A. Regier, E. A. Kuhl, D. J. Kupfer, 'The DSM-5: Classification and Criteria Changes' (2013) 12 *World Psychiatry* 92.

45 See, generally, T. G. DiaMaio, V. J. M. DiMaio, *Excited Delirium Syndrome Causes of Death and Prevention* (CRC Press, Boca Raton, 2005).

or agitated delirium medical literature and that cases involving restraint were 7.4 times more likely to result in death than were those without restraint.[46]

We are unable to make conclusive determinations about whether restraint or positional asphyxia is the most likely true cause of death for people said to have died from 'excited delirium' while agitated and forcibly restrained. We are not aware of any rigorous scientific research that examines the prevalence of death for people with 'excited delirium' who are not physically restrained.

Notably, in a December 26, 2021, investigation in *The New York Times*, the authors analysed more than 230 scientific papers on restraints, body position, and 'excited delirium' in the National Library of Medicine database, published since the 1980s. They found that nearly three-quarters of the studies that included at least one author who was in the network of TASER/defence experts 'regularly supported the idea that restraint techniques were safe or that the deaths of people who had been restrained were caused by health problems.' Meanwhile, 'only about a quarter of the studies that did not involve anyone from the network backed that conclusion. More commonly, the other studies said some restraint techniques increased the risk of death.'[47]

Attempts to Explore Neuroscience

Some researchers have attempted to give 'excited delirium' scientific legitimacy by grounding it in neuroscience, but their efforts have failed to produce credible or consistent evidence. A 2009 study from Mash and Wetli argued that 'excited delirium' results from dopaminergic hyperactivity and extreme neurochemical stress. Their post-mortem analysis, conducted primarily on individuals with positive toxicology for cocaine, reported elevated levels of heat shock protein-70 (HSP70).[48] However, subsequent work has found that HSP70 is elevated in the brains of individuals who die from drug intoxication or hyperthermia,[49] suggesting that its presence reflects a nonspecific stress response rather than a distinct pathophysiological process.[50]

In that paper and previous work, Mash also expounds on a dopamine hypothesis. She proposes multiple mechanisms, including decreased dopamine transporter expression (DAT), overexpression of α-synuclein, and alterations

46 E. M. F. Strömmer et al., 'The Role of Restraint in Fatal Excited Delirium: A Research Synthesis and Pooled Analysis' (2020) 16 *Forensic Science, Medicine, and Pathology* 680.

47 Valentino-DeVries and others (n 30).

48 See, generally, D. C. Mash and others, 'Brain Biomarkers for Identifying Excited Delirium as a Cause of Sudden Death' (2009) 190 *Forensic Science International* e13–19.

49 M. M. Johnson and others, 'Increased Heat Shock Protein 70 Gene Expression in the Brains of Cocaine-Related Fatalities May Be Reflective of Postdrug Survival and Intervention Rather than Excited Delirium' (2012) 57 *Journal of Forensic Sciences* 1519.

50 B. Ondruschka and others, 'Drug- and/or Trauma-Induced Hyperthermia? Characterization of HSP70 and Myoglobin Expression' (2018) 13 *PLoS One* e0194442.

in opioid receptors.[51] These studies have focused almost exclusively on decedents with cocaine exposure, potentially conflating the acute and chronic effects of cocaine with 'excited delirium.'[52] Although small in scale and limited in scope, they have nonetheless been used to legitimise 'excited delirium' as a discrete diagnosis—even in cases where no toxicological evidence of cocaine or other stimulants is present.

Other studies, including those invoking NADPH oxidase (NOX2)–mediated oxidative stress, follow a similar pattern: small sample sizes, mostly drawn from cocaine-related deaths, and a failure to distinguish between causation and correlation.[53] These papers often propose mechanistic explanations for excited delirium without controlling for key confounders like drug toxicity, and without applying basic standards of causal inference. Given the lack of replication and the serious implications of invoking 'excited delirium' in forensic and legal contexts, it is striking that these proposed biological mechanisms were accepted at face value by some, without the rigorous validation and independent confirmation that would ordinarily be required in other areas of science. Therefore, there is currently insufficient evidence to support the existence of a distinct neuroscientific pathway for 'excited delirium' as a separate clinical condition. In this context, neuroscience does not debunk the diagnosis of 'excited delirium'; rather, it shows how neuroscience and neuroscientists can be used to legitimise diagnoses promoted by questionable interests, such as law enforcement agencies seeking to justify deaths and violence in police custody.

Racism in Neuroscience

The push to frame 'excited delirium' as a biological syndrome has not occurred in isolation. Its use in cases involving the deaths of Black men and other people from minoritised groups in police custody reflects how neuroscience and medicine have reinforced racial hierarchies, often under the guise of scientific objectivity. This pattern has deep historical roots.

In the 19th century, physicians coined pseudoscientific diagnoses like drapetomania, described as a mental illness causing enslaved people to flee captivity, and used phrenology to claim biological inferiority based on skull shape.[54] In the 20th century, the diagnosis of schizophrenia underwent a dramatic racial and gender shift, becoming disproportionately applied to

51 D. C. Mash J. K. Staley, 'D3 Dopamine and Kappa Opioid Receptor Alterations in Human Brain of Cocaine-Overdose Victims' (1999) 877 *Annals of the New York Academy of Sciences* 507.

52 D. C. Mash and others, 'Cocaine Abusers Have an Overexpression of α-Synuclein in Dopamine Neurons' (2003) 23 *The Journal of Neuroscience* 2564.

53 S. Schiavone and others, 'Involvement of the NADPH Oxidase NOX2-Derived Brain Oxidative Stress in an Unusual Fatal Case of Cocaine-Related Neurotoxicity Associated With Excited Delirium Syndrome' (2016) 36 *Journal of Clinical Psychopharmacology* 513.

54 È. Edwards-Grossi, C. D. E. Willoughby, 'Slavery and Its Afterlives in US Psychiatry' (2024) 114 *American Journal of Public Health* S250.

African American men, particularly those involved in or associated with the civil rights movement. This trend is explored in the book *Protest Psychosis*, which highlights how the diagnosis was used to pathologise Black political resistance.[55] Racism persists in modern neuroscience, although exclusion has evolved from overt pseudoscience to structural neglect embedded in research methods and technologies. For example, standard EEG caps often fail to accommodate coarse or tightly coiled hair textures, leading to poor signal quality or participant exclusion, disproportionately affecting Black individuals.[56] Neuroimaging databases, biometric algorithms, and brain–computer interface models continue to draw from homogenous, predominantly white populations.[57] As a result, researchers not only underrepresent systematically marginalised groups in brain science but also produce findings and tools that risk reinforcing bias when deployed in clinical, educational, or carceral settings.

Improving outcomes for all individuals, within clinical settings and beyond, requires recognising how neuroscience and neuroscientists can contribute to perpetuating racism and harmful stereotypes—and that they are not immune to the influence of broader social forces.

Legal Cases

'Excited delirium' is frequently asserted as a defence by police officers who kill people during restraint.[58] With notable exceptions, such as the murder prosecutions of the Minneapolis police officers who killed George Floyd, law enforcement officers are usually not criminally prosecuted for restraint-related deaths.[59]

A review of legal cases discussing 'excited delirium' suggests that the term appears to be primarily associated with cases involving interactions between individuals and law enforcement. Despite significant challenges to 'excited delirium's' validity within the medical community—and the limited context in which it arises—the term has been admitted in U.S. courts as a legitimate

55 See, generally, J. M. Metzl, *The Protest Psychosis: How Schizophrenia Became a Black Disease* (Beacon Press, Boston, 2009).

56 L. Sanders, 'New Electrodes Better Capture Brain Waves of People with Natural Hair | Science News' (*Science News*, 11 March 2020) <https://www.sciencenews.org/article/electrodes-brain-waves-eeg-black-african-american-natural-hair> accessed 6 August 2025.

57 J. A. Ricard and others, 'Confronting Racially Exclusionary Practices in the Acquisition and Analyses of Neuroimaging Data' (2023) 26 *Nature Neuroscience* 4.

58 A. Chang, 'Police Repeatedly Cite "Excited Delirium" In Killings, But It Has No Real Definition' (*NPR*, 7 April 2021) <https://www.npr.org/2021/04/07/985128452/police-repeatedly-cite-excited-delirium-in-kilings-but-it-has-no-real-definitio> accessed 2 December 2024.

59 K. Wedell, C. Kelly, C. McManus, C. Fernando, 'George Floyd Is Not Alone. "I Can't Breathe" Uttered by Dozens in Fatal Police Holds across U.S.' (*USA TODAY*, 25 June 2020) <https://www.usatoday.com/in-depth/news/investigations/2020/06/13/george-floyd-not-alone-dozens-said-cant-breathe-police-holds/3137373001/> accessed 2 December 2024.

diagnosis, including as a direct cause of death.[60] 'Excited delirium' in a police setting has been considered a reasonable medical diagnosis for an extremely broad array of signs and symptoms. It might be described as a state of agitation, excitability, or paranoia.[61] It might include bizarre behaviour, confusion, delusions, hyperactivity, incoherence, or yelling.[62] It is often, although not necessarily, associated with drug use.[63]

Courts have admitted 'excited delirium' theory as evidence, allowing law enforcement to use it as a defence in civil rights cases involving police brutality or wrongful death. Some courts have used qualified immunity to shield officers from accountability, as deaths attributed to 'excited delirium' justify force that might otherwise be deemed excessive, given the associations with 'superhuman strength' and being 'impervious to pain.'[64] Similarly, deaths that might otherwise be attributed to asphyxiation because of excessive force may instead be explained away as natural or accidental due to the victim's 'excited delirium.'[65]

The pervasiveness of 'excited delirium' within law enforcement policies and training manuals has resulted in several lawsuits against police officers for violating their training and mishandling a person claimed to be in 'excited delirium.' By introducing evidence that officers failed to follow training in this manner, plaintiff's attorneys validate law enforcement protocols on 'excited delirium,' perpetuating the term's acceptance in courts at the expense of future victims of police violence.

Several underlying risks are presented by the pervasiveness of 'excited delirium' within law enforcement policies and training manuals. Myocardial infarctions (heart attacks), drug or substance overdose and withdrawal, oxygen deprivation, and acute psychosis have all been bundled by some law enforcement agencies or trainers under the diagnosis of 'excited delirium.' Yet, these require quite different medical interventions in an emergency, in contrast to the trained responses to 'excited delirium.' In this way, 'excited delirium' has not only impeded possible treatment for individuals but also obscured the true cause of death and provided cover to those responsible.

60 Obasogie (n 22).

61 *Mann v. Taser International* [2009] 11th Cir 588 F.3d 1291.

62 *Hoyt v. Cooks et al.* [2012] 11th Cir 672 F.3d 972, 976.

63 *Goode v. Baggett* [2020] 5th Cir 811 F. App'x 227.

64 *Callwood v. Jones* [2018] U.S. Supreme Court 39 S. Ct. 100.

65 *Gregory v. County of Maui* [2006] 9th Cir 414 F. Supp. 2d 965 (D. Haw. 2006); *Pirolozzi v. Stanbro, F Supp 2d* [2009] US Dist LEXIS 42575, 2009 WL 1441070 (N.D); *Marquez v. City of Phoenix* [2012] 9th Cir 693 F.3d 1167; [2006] 9th Cir 414 F. Supp. 2d 965 (D. Haw. 2006); *Peppers v. Washington County, Tenn* [2017] 6th Cir 686 Fed. App'x. 328; *V W v. Nichelini* [2017] United States District Court Eastern District of California WL 34246 (E.D. CA Feb. 2, 2017).

Publication of PHR Report

In March 2022, PHR published its findings in a report titled, *'Excited Delirium' and Deaths in Policy Custody: The Deadly Impact of a Baseless Diagnosis.* PHR concluded that 'excited delirium' is not a valid, independent medical diagnosis and should not be a cause of death. The term lacks a clear or consistent definition, established aetiology, or agreed-upon pathophysiology. Consequently, there are no diagnostic standards for 'excited delirium.' The scant body of literature mentioning the term was deemed riddled with conflicts of interest, often undisclosed, involving law enforcement or organisations like TASER International (Axon Enterprise).

Moreover, the diagnosis of 'excited delirium' was shown to be primarily applied to deaths occurring during encounters with law enforcement. The report highlights how if any other medical condition were to occur only or even mostly in a particular environment or context, a scientific approach would require an interrogation of that environment as a contributing or causative factor—in this case, law enforcement actions and police custody.

Lacking the reliable definitions and criteria required for scientific validity, the report also discussed how a diagnosis of 'excited delirium' yields no actionable steps or guidance for treatment. Instead of addressing underlying medical or psychiatric conditions using a medical approach, this label justifies actions such as choking and restraints, contrary to medical standards. People presenting with agitation, confusion, rapid breathing, elevated heart rate, or sweats have an underlying diagnosis, and their condition should be found and treated medically.

Mobilisation for Change

In December 2020, following the Black Lives Matter protests that summer, the American Psychiatric Association (APA) advocated for the U.S. Department of Health and Human Services to conduct a nationwide investigation of all cases labelled 'excited delirium.' In June 2021, the American Medical Association (AMA) elaborated that the term 'excited delirium' has been used to justify inappropriate and discriminatory actions. Both associations advocated for the cessation of using the term 'excited delirium' unless a clear set of diagnostic criteria could be established, rigorous studies were undertaken, and the data were made available. In 2020 and 2021, respectively, the APA and AMA released statements denouncing 'excited delirium' and its use as justification for excessive police use of force.[66]

66 Council on Psychiatry and Law, *Position Statement on Concerns about Use of the Term "Excited Delirium" and Appropriate Medical Management in Out-of-Hospital Contexts* (American Psychiatric Association, APA Official Actions, 2020); American Medical Association, 'New AMA Policy Opposes "Excited Delirium" Diagnosis' (*American Medical Association*, 14 June 2021) <https://www.ama-assn.org/press-center/press-releases/new-ama-policy-opposes-excited-delirium-diagnosis> accessed 2 December 2024.

PHR used this momentum to launch an advocacy campaign asking ACEP and the National Association of Medical Examiners (NAME) to rescind their previous endorsements of 'excited delirium.' In the context of a nationwide reckoning over racial justice, this new physician advocacy push—closely coordinated with impacted families and other scholars—gained traction previous efforts had not.

In the spring of 2022, the American Academy of Emergency Medicine published a statement opposing the use of 'excited delirium.' Around the same time, Patrick Caceres, an investigator with the Bay Area Rapid Transit (BART) Office of the Independent Police Auditor, began to research the topic, encountering the recent medical association statements and PHR's report.[67] He shared his research with his colleagues, which resulted in the BART police department removing 'excited delirium' from the policy manual and barring its use in written reports.[68]

In February 2023, PHR presented its report at the American Academy of Forensic Sciences annual conference. In March 2023, NAME released a statement withdrawing its support for 'excited delirium.'[69] In April 2023, ACEP followed suit but stopped short of rescinding its 2009 white paper.[70] Over the summer, ACEP's members mobilised, introducing a resolution for a vote at the organisation's annual meeting in October 2023 that would formally retire the white paper.[71] On October 12, ACEP approved the resolution and released an updated statement clarifying that the white paper should no longer be cited.[72]

67 M. Friedrich, 'Medical Groups Disavow Discredited Excuse for Deaths in the Criminal Justice System' (*Arnold Venutres*, 26 January 2024) <https://www.arnoldventures.org/stories/medical-groups-disavow-discredited-excuse-for-deaths-in-the-criminal-justice-system>.

68 Bay Area Rapid Transit, '"Excited Delirium" Removed from BART Police Department Police Manual and Will No Longer be Used in Written Reports' (*Bay Areas Rapid Transit*, 18 August 2022) <https://www.bart.gov/news/articles/2022/news20220818>.

69 Physicians for Human Rights, 'PHR Welcomes National Association of Medical Examiners (NAME) Policy Reversal on "Excited Delirium" as a Cause of Death' (*Press Release*, 31 March 2023) <https://phr.org/news/phr-welcomes-national-association-of-medical-examiners-name-policy-reversal-on-excited-delirium-as-a-cause-of-death>.

70 Physicians for Human Rights, 'PHR Welcomes American College of Emergency Physicians (ACEP) Policy Reversal on "Excited Delirium," Calls for Further Actions' (*Press Release*, 9 May 2023) <https://phr.org/news/physicians-of-human-rights-welcomes-american-college-of-emergency-physicians-acep-policy-reversal-on-excited-delirium-calls-for-further-action/>.

71 M. Hawryluk, R. Rayasam, 'Police Blame Some Deaths on "Excited Delirium." ER Docs Consider Pulling the Plug on the Term' (*KFF Health News*, 2 October 2023) <https://kffhealthnews.org/news/article/police-blame-some-deaths-on-excited-delirium-er-docs-consider-pulling-the-plug-on-the-term>.

72 M. Hawryluk, R. Rayasam, 'Doctors Abandon a Diagnosis Used to Justify Police Custody Deaths. It Might Live On, Anyway' (*KFF Health News*, 16 October 2023) <https://kffhealthnews.org/news/article/excited-delirium-diagnosis-police-custody-deaths-emergency-doctors-renounce>; Physicians for Human Rights, 'Emergency Medicine Association Finally Withdraws Its Approval of Policy Paper Endorsing "Excited Delirium" as Cause of Death' (*Physicians for Human Rights*, Press Release, 13 October 2023) <https://phr.org/news/emergency-medicine-association-finally-withdraws-its-approval-of-policy-paper-endorsing-excited-delirium-as-cause-of-death/>.

From 2023–2024, this advocacy push also prompted new statements disavowing the use of 'excited delirium' from other national medical associations, including the American College of Medical Toxicology, the College of American Pathologists, and the American Academy of Neurology,[73] as well as law enforcement stakeholders such as the Colorado Peace Officers Standards and Training Board and the private training company Lexipol.[74]

As medical and law enforcement opposition grew, multiple state legislatures began to consider laws banning the use of 'excited delirium' in the context of death investigations, policing, and litigation. The family of Angelo Quinto, working with the office of California State Assembly member Mike Gipson, led the way with landmark legislation in California. In October 2023, California became the first state in the United States to ban the use of 'excited delirium.' The states of Colorado and Minnesota later followed, with bills also introduced in New York and Hawaii.[75]

International Reach

'Excited delirium' and a closely associated term, 'acute behavioural disturbance' (ABD), have also received attention in the wake of in-custody deaths

73 The College of American Pathologists, 'CAP Supports Discontinuing Term "Excited Delirium" as Cause of Death' (*The NewsMarket*, 13 October 2023) <https://newsroom.cap.org/latest-news/cap-supports-discontinuing-term-excited-delirium-as-cause-of-death/s/c29dd694-6877-428a-95b4-d5fc5c0d82cc> accessed 2 December 2024; E. K. Ritzl, A. Saadi and others et al., 'AAN Position Statement on Excited Delirium' (*American Academy of Neuroscience*, 2024) <https://www.aan.com/advocacy/excited-delirium-position-statement> accessed 2 December 2024; American Academy of Emergency Medicine, *AAEM Excited Delirium Statement* <https://apps.aaem.org/UserFiles/RevisedAAEMExcitedDelirium9.21.22.pdf> accessed July 2025.

74 Bay Area Rapid Transit, '"Excited Delirium" Removed from BART Police Department Policy Manual and Will No Longer Be Used in Written Reports' (*Bay Area Rapid Transit*, 18 August 2022) <https://www.bart.gov/news/articles/2022/news20220818> accessed 2 December 2024; A. Sherry, 'Colorado Strikes "Excited Delirium" from All Law Enforcement Diagnosis, Training Documents' (*Colorado Public Radio*, 1 December 2023) <https://www.cpr.org/2023/12/01/colorado-strikes-excited-delirium-as-law-enforcement-diagnosis/> accessed 2 December 2024; Lexipol Team, 'Understanding Excited Delirium: 4 Takeaways for Law Enforcement' (*Lexipol*, 3 November 2023) <https://www.lexipol.com/resources/blog/understanding-excited-delirium-4-takeaways-for-law-enforcement-officers-2/> accessed 2 December 2024.

75 Gipson and others, Assembly Bill No. 360, An act to add Section 1156.5 to the Evidence Code, and to add Chapter 3.5 (commencing with Section 24400) to Division 20 of the Health and Safety Code, relating to excited delirium 2023 [360]; A. Mannix, 'Minnesota Gov. Walz Signs Law Banning "Excited Delirium" for Police' (*Star Tribune*, 5 June 2024) <https://www.startribune.com/minnesota-gov-walz-signs-law-banning-excited-delirium-for-police/600371297> accessed 2 December 2024; R. Rayasam, 'As More States Target Disavowed "Excited Delirium" Diagnosis, Police Groups Push Back' (*KFF Health News*, 18 March 2024) <https://kffhealthnews.org/news/article/excited-delirium-police-deaths-state-legislation-bans/> accessed 2 December 2024.

in Australia,[76] Canada,[77] the United Kingdom,[78] and elsewhere. In 2020, the Royal College of Pathologists in the United Kingdom issued guidance on 'excited delirium,' stating, " 'Excited Delirium' should never be used as a term that, by itself, can be identified as the cause of death. The use of Excited Delirium as a term in guidance to police officers should also be avoided.'[79] In 2022, the Royal College of Psychiatrists released a position statement on ABD and 'excited delirium,' holding that ABD should never be used as a diagnosis or cause of death and that 'excited delirium' should not be used at all.[80] Canadian coroners' groups have also begun to move away from reliance on the concept.[81]

Conclusion

The term 'excited delirium' lacks a consistent clinical definition, a clear pathophysiological basis, and formal recognition by the medical community. Introduced in the 1980s to explain sudden deaths during encounters with law enforcement, its origins are mired in racism, and the initial cases have since been discredited. Yet the term has persisted, seemingly because of the convenience it offers in attributing in-custody deaths to a supposed medical syndrome rather than to the circumstances of restraint or use of force.

Its continued use has led to the misattribution of hundreds of deaths and has been incorporated into some law enforcement training programs, despite having no basis in established medical science. 'Excited delirium' is not a recognized diagnosis in the *ICD* or *DSM*, nor is it supported by any leading medical organization. Its persistence obscures true causes of death, shields institutions from accountability, and undermines the integrity of both medical

76 R. Kurmelovs, '"Excited Delirium": How a Disputed US Term Found Its Way to Australian Deaths-in-Custody Inquests' (*The Guardian*, 3 July 2021) <https://www.theguardian.com/australia-news/2021/jul/04/excited-delirium-how-a-disputed-us-term-found-its-way-to-australian-deaths-in-custody-inquests> accessed 2 December 2024.

77 J. Kiedrowski, R.-F. Melchers, 'An Independent Review of the Adoption and Use of Conducted Energy Weapons by the Royal Canadian Mounted Police' (*Royal Canadian Mounted Police*, 5 June 2008) <https://web.archive.org/web/20091231091631/http:/www.rcmp-grc.gc.ca/ccaps-spcca/cew-ai/kiedrowski-report-rapport-eng.htm> accessed 2 December 2024; Garcia-Roberts (n 20); Panel of Mental Health and Medical Experts Review of Excited Delirium, *Report of the Panel of Mental Health and Medical Experts Review of Excited Delirium* (*Government of Nova Scotia*, 30 June 2009).

78 The Royal College of Pathologists, 'Forensic Science Regulator Guidance The Use of "Excited Delirium" as a Cause of Death' (*The Royal College of Pathologists*, Birmingham, 31 October 2020).

79 Ibid.

80 Royal College of Psychiatrists, 'Acute Behavioural Disturbance' and 'Excited Delirium' PS02/22 (Royal College of Psychiatrists, Position Statement, September 2022).

81 B. Lindsay, 'Canadian Coroners Starting to Reject Excited Delirium as Cause of Police-Related Deaths' (*CBC News*, 17 April 2023) <https://www.cbc.ca/news/health/coroners-excited-delirium-1.6811083> accessed 3 December 2024.

and legal investigations. Recognizing these harms, several states, including California, Minnesota, and Colorado, have banned 'excited delirium' as an official cause of death in forensic investigations, reflecting a broader movement toward scientific and ethical reform.

The recent paradigm shift around 'excited delirium' in the United States underscores the power of collective action, when independent physicians, researchers, and affected community members can come together to push for change. Among the major U.S. medical associations, there is now a consensus that 'excited delirium' is not a valid, independent medical diagnosis, and should not be used as a cause of death. These organisations, along with other health experts, have denounced the term as lacking scientific validity and ethical standing.

Ultimately, it is time for the criminal justice system to move beyond the flawed and scientifically unsupported concept of 'excited delirium.' At the same time, neuroscientists, physicians, and other healthcare professionals must acknowledge how science can be misused to perpetuate harm and racism—'excited delirium' being a troubling yet telling example. Retiring it as a diagnosis and legal defence is essential to ensuring accurate forensic investigations, preventing future harm, and upholding principles of evidence-based justice.

4 From Neurolaw to Neurorights

The Impact of Neuroscience on Dutch Criminal Justice and Considerations About the Future

Naomi van de Pol, Gerben Meynen, and Sjors Ligthart

Introduction

Neuroscience is a rapidly expanding field that has started to permeate different societal domains. Primarily, neurotechnologies such as neuroimaging and brain stimulation are employed in the medical sector, for instance, for the diagnosis and treatment of neurological conditions such as brain tumours, epilepsy, and Parkinson's disease.[1] Meanwhile, such technologies are also increasingly considered and used in the criminal justice sector. For instance, neuroimaging in criminal justice is used to address questions of criminal responsibility and *mens rea*.[2] This development has given rise to the field of neurolaw, which investigates the (potential) impact of neuroscientific developments on the law and legal practices. Understanding how neuroscience may enhance—or has enhanced—criminal law leads us to examine its impact through three distinct lenses: revision, assessment, and intervention.[3] In the second section, we will discuss these three areas in detail, with a particular focus on their actual contribution to criminal law in the Netherlands.

Apart from criminal law, neurotechnological developments have also influenced our understanding of human rights law. For over a decade, academics have explored not only the potential risks—such as how emerging neurotechnology could enable others to interfere with our private mental states, including thoughts, emotions, and desires—but also the opportunities they present.

1 J. Yuan and others, 'Machine Learning Applications on Neuroimaging for Diagnosis and Prognosis of Epilepsy: A Review' (2022) 368 *Journal of Neuroscience Methods* 109441; N. Bidesi and others, 'The Role of Neuroimaging in Parkinson's Disease' (2021) 159 *Journal of Neurochemistry* 660.

2 N. A. Farahany, 'Neuroscience and Behavioral Genetics in US Criminal Law' (2015) 2 *Journal of Law and the Biosciences* 485; K. De Kogel, L. Westgeest, 'Neuroscientific and Behavioral Genetic Information in Criminal Cases in the Netherlands' (2015) 2(3) *Journal of Law and the Biosciences* 580.

3 G. Meynen, 'Forensic Psychiatry and Neurolaw' (2019) 65 *International Journal of Law and Psychiatry* 101345; Gregg D. Caruso, *Neurolaw* (Cambridge University Press, Cambridge, 2024) 3.

DOI: 10.4324/9781003510246-5

Although human rights law should protect against unsolicited interference with our minds,[4] particularly in the context of criminal justice,[5] scholars are also considering how neurotechnology could reinforce certain rights and serve as a lens for rethinking legal frameworks more broadly.[6] This dual perspective highlights the need for human rights to serve both as a safeguard *against* the risks of neurotechnologies and as a framework *for* recognising the positive implications these technologies offer.

To achieve this, different scholars have argued for "updating" the established framework of human rights, for example, by recognising specific human rights to protect the mind, such as a right to mental self-determination.[7] As we will consider in the third section, such a right not only protects against unwanted interferences, but it also includes a positive dimension, in the way that it grants rightsholders the freedom to self-determine their inner realms, *inter alia*, by using neurotechnology. We will consider potential legal foundations of such a right, focusing on the European Convention on Human Rights, and explore how the right could possibly facilitate the positive impact of neuroscience and technology on the criminal justice sector. But first, let us turn to the impact neuroscience has had so far on criminal justice in the Netherlands.

Neurolaw: Research and Practice in the Netherlands

The field of neurolaw investigates how developments in neuroscience could shape and improve legal standards and procedures, addressing three areas of impact: revision, assessment, and intervention. We address these areas in what follows, focusing on developments in the Netherlands.

Revision

Within the revision domain, the central question is whether neuroscience gives reason to reform the law or legal practices. An important topic in this domain has been that—allegedly—neuroscience shows that all of our mental content

4 See, for example, J. C. Bublitz, R. Merkel, 'Crimes against Minds' (2014) 8 *Criminal Law and Philosophy* 51.

5 S. Ligthart, *Coercive Brain-Reading in Criminal Justice* (Cambridge University Press, Cambridge, 2022) 3.

6 R. G. Boire, 'On Cognitive Liberty' (2001) 2 *Journal of Cognitive Liberties* 7; W. Sententia, 'Neuroethical Considerations: Cognitive Liberty and Converging Technologies for Improving Human Cognition' (2004) 1013 *Annals of the New York Academy of Sciences* 221.

7 M. Ienca, R. Andorno, 'Towards New Human Rights in the Age of Neuroscience and Neurotechnology' (2017) 13 *Life Sciences, Society and Policy* 1, 8; N. A. Farahany, *The Battle for Your Brain: Defending the Right to Think Freely in the Age of Neurotechnology* (St. Martin's Press, New York, 2023) 211–214; J. C. Bublitz, 'The Nascent Right to Psychological Integrity and Mental Self-Determination' in A. von Arnauld, K. von der Decken, M. Susi (eds), *Cambridge Handbook of New Human Rights* (Cambridge University Press, Cambridge, 2020) 387.

and behaviour are determined by brain processes and that—again, allegedly—therefore there is no room for free will.[8] Because free will is often regarded as essential for moral and legal responsibility (and, therefore, punishment), the absence of free will would imply that no one could be held criminally responsible and no one could justifiably be punished.[9] Even though this topic has sparked lively debate, to our knowledge, no legal revisions have been (directly) motivated by this line of reasoning.[10]

However, this differs from another topic: the maturing adolescent brain. Neuroscientists have observed that the human brain continues to develop until a person's mid-twenties.[11] The fact that in many teenagers and other adolescents the brain is not yet "matured", it has been argued, should be reflected in sentencing in criminal law. This line of reasoning seems to have influenced U.S. Supreme Court rulings on adolescents, although there is a debate about the extent of its actual impact on the Court's decisions.[12] Meanwhile, in the Netherlands, neuroscientific findings clearly contributed to a change in the law, by the establishment of so-called *adolescentenstrafrecht* (adolescent criminal law).[13] Adolescent criminal law entails that:

> As of 1 April 2014, young offenders aged 16 to 22 can be tried either as a juvenile or as an adult, under adolescent criminal law. This allows the court to take the offender's development into account. Some juveniles need a tough approach, while others benefit more from guidance, even though they may be older.[14]

Thus, it could be argued, neurotechnology has contributed to the criminal law framework by enabling more tailored sentences, taking into account that adolescents are still developing. In fact, in his paper on neurolaw and adolescent criminal law, Schleim concludes that 'To my knowledge, neuroscience has

8 G. Meynen, 'Neurolaw' (2014) 17 *Ethical Theory and Moral Practice* 819; J. Green, J. Cohen, 'For the Law, Neuroscience Changes Nothing and Everything' (2004) 359 *Philosophical Transactions of the Royal Society of London B: Biological Sciences* 1775.

9 A. Bigenwald, V. Chambon, 'Criminal Responsibility and Neuroscience' (2019) 10 *Frontiers in Psychology* 1406.

10 Ibid.

11 L. Steinberg, 'The Influence of Neuroscience on US Supreme Court Decisions about Adolescents' Criminal Culpability' (2013) 14(7) *Nature Reviews Neuroscience* 513.

12 Ibid; S. J. Morse, 'Neuroscience, Free Will, and Criminal Responsibility' in W. Glannon (ed), *Free Will and the Brain: Neuroscientific, Philosophical, and Legal Perspectives* (Cambridge University Press, Cambridge, 2015) 251.

13 S. Schleim, 'Real Neurolaw in the Netherlands' (2020) 11 *Frontiers in Psychology* 1762. Of note, Schleim is critical of the way in which neuroscientific data have been used to justify this revision of criminal law.

14 'Penalties for Juvenile Offenders' (*Government of the Netherlands*) <https://www.government.nl/topics/sentences-and-non-punitive-orders/penalties-juvenile-offenders> accessed 16 August 2024. Our translation.

never before influenced lawmaking in such a direct and explicit way as in the new Dutch adolescent criminal law.'[15] The introduction of adolescent criminal law in the Netherlands not only has practical implications for prosecutors, defence lawyers and judges (and of course defendants and victims), but also for behavioural experts (often psychiatrists and psychologists). If a defendant is between the ages of 16 and 22, experts are consulted to determine whether there is reason to take the defendant's development into account in light of the adolescent criminal law provisions, and if so, in what way.

Assessment

When we move to the assessment domain, it is of particular interest that neuroimaging has been used in actual court cases. In 2015, a special issue of the *Journal of Law and the Biosciences* was devoted to actual applications of neuroscience and neurotechnology in court cases in the United States, the Netherlands, Canada, and England and Wales. In the contribution concerning the Netherlands, De Kogel and Westgeest reported that neuroscientific or genetic information had been used in more than 200 cases between 2000 and 2012.[16] The authors also examined the legal questions for which the information was utilised. They reported that the information was used to answer questions about, among others: evidence for committing the offence (7 cases), competency to stand trial (4 cases), accountability (72 cases) and criminal recidivism risk (15 cases).[17] Regarding the accountability cases, they wrote that the defendant's responsibility was often considered 'diminished' based on neuroscientific or genetic information.[18]

The publication by De Kogel and Westgeest, ten years ago, made clear that neuroscience was at that time (highly) relevant in at least some cases in Dutch criminal law. Meanwhile, if one looks at the number of cases they found, approximately 200 in 12 years, that would mean less than 20 annually—a small number compared to the approximately 90,000 criminal cases handled in the Netherlands yearly.[19] This low percentage is also reflected in a study by Kempes and others, who examined pretrial forensic reports of adolescent and young adult offenders (aged 12 to 25) between 2005 and 2015.[20] Their unique study used a large database containing thousands of forensic reports. Out of 34,304 reports in that period, only 232 contained

15 Schleim (n 13).
16 De Kogel and Westgeest (n 2) 584.
17 Ibid. 587.
18 Ibid. 594.
19 As the authors make clear, in view of their methodology, there may be some underestimation of the actual number. Still, it is likely that it is not very far from the truth.
20 M. Kempes and others, 'Neurobiological Information and Consideration in Dutch Pre-Trial Forensic Reports of Juvenile Criminal Offenders' (2019) 18(3) *International Journal of Forensic Mental Health* 212.

a diagnosis of acquired brain injury, neurological disorder or genetic abnormality in the paragraph "diagnostic and forensic considerations". They wrote that: 'Each year, less than 1% of all forensic reports contained a diagnosis of acquired brain injury, neurological disorder or genetic abnormality in the paragraph on diagnostic and forensic considerations with no increase over time.'[21] They also made an interesting observation:

> Surprisingly, in almost half of the forensics reports in which neurobiological information was present this was not mentioned in the considerations of the forensic expert on criminal responsibility. Moreover, even if the forensic expert mentioned a relation between a neurobiological factor and the index offense, this information was often not considered further in the question regarding the risk of recidivism (35%) and in the question regarding both risk and risk management (56%).[22]

So, at least until 2015, neurobiological factors were rarely considered in forensic psychiatric evaluations. If they were considered, they were often not addressed regarding the questions that ultimately matter to the judges in court. Kempes and others state that: 'When neurobiological factors are considered with regard to criminal responsibility, forensic experts ***should pay more attention*** to also consider them in the questions regarding recidivism risk and risk management.'[23]

To our knowledge, no more recent studies have been performed in the Netherlands that provide information about the use—in particular in terms of frequency—of neurodata in forensic psychiatric reports or court cases.

Still, it is noteworthy that today, the Pieter Baan Centre, the Dutch forensic observation clinic under the Ministry of Justice and Security, where 220 defendants (often in more serious cases) are being evaluated each year, uses neuro-evaluation in about one in every five or six cases on average.[24] Interestingly, the Netherlands Institute for Forensic Psychiatry and Psychology, which is also part of the Dutch Ministry of Justice and Security, has recently started both a neuro helpdesk (*neuroloket*) and neuro outpatient clinic (*neuropoli*). The neuro helpdesk can be contacted by behavioural experts who have practical, rather than theoretical, questions about the need or helpfulness of (additional) neuro-evaluation while performing assessments of defendants. The neuro outpatient clinic, meanwhile, entails that defendants who are evaluated anywhere in the country can be evaluated at the Pieter Baan Centre during one day, offering the possibility to combine neurological examination,

21 Ibid. 215.

22 Ibid. 217.

23 Ibid. 218. Emphasis added.

24 C. van de Grift, 'Experts willen meer aandacht voor mogelijke hersenschade van verdachten' (*NOS*, 17 October 2022) <https://nos.nl/nieuwsuur/artikel/2448737-experts-willen-meer-aandacht-voor-mogelijke-hersenschade-van-verdachten> accessed 16 August 2024.

neuropsychological testing, as well as neuroimaging.[25] In our view, it is important that neurological evaluation, neuropsychology, and brain imaging are integrated—and that, more specifically, neuroimages are not considered in isolation.[26] The fact that the Dutch Ministry of Justice and Security now provides these options shows the concrete impact of neuroscience on forensic and criminal justice practice. Given these developments, it is not unlikely that the use and actual impact of neuroscience and neurotechnology in Dutch criminal cases will improve soon. It would be interesting to see if the study performed by De Kogel and Westgeest some 12 years ago could be repeated in the coming years.

Intervention

Neurotechnology cannot only *obtain information* from the brain (e.g., by visualising), but it can also be used to *change* the brain. To our knowledge, neurotechnological interventions, such as neurostimulation, have not (yet) been used in forensic psychiatric practice or elsewhere in criminal justice. However, it may be of interest that, in the Netherlands, some pioneering research has been done regarding the possibility of neuromodulation in a forensic population.[27] More specifically, Sergiou and others used transcranial Direct Current Stimulation (tDCS) in an offender population and observed that self-reported aggression decreased after tDCS.[28] This finding clearly does not warrant any definitive conclusions; it is "proof of principle" at best, and further research would certainly be required to determine the value of neuromodulation for forensic purposes.[29] However, it is pertinent that neurotechnology to influence behavioural traits (that are relevant from a criminal justice perspective) is now actually studied in forensic psychiatric patients. In other words, neuroscience has actual impact on research that is being performed in the forensic population.

25 K. Bouma, 'Het criminele brein: Pieter Baan centrum duikt in neuropoli in de hersenen van verdachten' (*De Volkskrant*, 23 June 2023) <https://www.volkskrant.nl/wetenschap/het-criminele-brein-pieter-baan-centrum-duikt-in-neuropoli-in-de-hersenen-van-verdachten~bda3c47b/> accessed 26 August 2024.

26 G. Meynen, *Legal insanity* (Springer International Publishing, Cham, 2016) 125 and 143.

27 C. S. Sergiou and others, 'Transcranial Direct Current Stimulation Targeting the Ventromedial Prefrontal Cortex Reduces Reactive Aggression and Modulates Electrophysiological Responses in a Forensic Population' (2022) 7 *Biological Psychiatry: Cognitive Neuroscience and Neuroimaging* 95.

28 See also: R. Knehans and others, 'Modulating Behavioural and Self-Reported Aggression with Non-Invasive Brain Stimulation: A Literature Review' (2022) 12(2) *Brain Sciences* 200.

29 Some interventions that alter the brain, such as psychopharmaceuticals, are already in use. However, neurotechnological interventions offer the potential advantage of more precisely targeting specific brain areas and having fewer and less intense side effects compared to medication.

Normative Concerns

As this brief overview makes clear, neuroscience has made an actual impact on criminal justice in the Netherlands. Criminal law has been reformed, such as through the introduction of adolescent criminal law, and neuro-evaluation has a place not only in actual criminal cases but also at an organisational level, where the Ministry of Justice and Security has established a neuro helpdesk and a neuro outpatient clinic. In addition, neuromodulation has been used in research to diminish aggression in a forensic population. This impact is suggestive of even greater influence in the future.

Obviously, these developments concerning neurotechnology in criminal justice have not occurred in isolation. Neurotechnology has started to permeate various sectors of society. This has led to enthusiasm, challenges, and concerns.[30] For a long time, the discussion around neurotechnology focused primarily on *protection against* techniques that may infringe upon personal interests, such as privacy, identity, and mental self-determination. However, there is now growing consideration of the *opportunities* and positive implications of neurotechnologies, and, accordingly, a right *to have access to* neurotechnologies. Initially, this conversation was mainly driven by ethicists, but increasingly, it has attracted legal attention and policy development.[31] For example, a report by the Advisory Committee of the UN Human Rights Council emphasised the importance of balancing the potential harm and the 'spectrum of opportunities offered by neurotechnologies in terms of improving people's life and well-being.'[32]

The potential opportunities and risks posed by the use of neurotechnology in our society (among which in criminal justice) have sparked a debate about the sustainability of existing human rights. The debate regards whether humans (including defendants and offenders) are sufficiently protected against the risks of emerging neurotechnologies and entitled to the benefits they may offer.[33] In general, two positions can be distinguished. First, there are scholars who believe that the current human rights framework provides adequate protection vis-à-vis emerging technologies, because existing provisions can be interpreted to include protection for the mind.[34] Others, however, argue that

30 See on neurotechnology vis-à-vis criminal justice and in particular its challenges, for example, S. H. Geukes and others, 'Neurotechnology in Criminal Justice: Key Points for Neuroscientists and Engineers' (2024) 21(1) *Journal of Neural Engineering* 013001.

31 Bublitz (n 7); see S. Ligthart, E. Dore-Horgan, G. Meynen, *Minds, Freedoms and Rights: On Neurorehabilitation in Criminal Justice* (Cambridge University Press, Cambridge, 2025), in press.

32 United Nations General Assembly, 'Report of the Human Rights Advisory Committee on the Impact, Opportunities and Challenges of Neurotechnology with Regard to the Promotion and Protection of All Human Rights' (8 August 2024) UN Doc A/HRC/57/61, para 54.

33 S. Ligthart and others, 'Minding Rights: Mapping Ethical and Legal Foundations of "Neurorights"' (2023) 32(4) *Cambridge Quarterly of Healthcare Ethics* 461.

34 S. Michałowski, 'Critical Reflections on the Need for a Right to Mental Self-Determination' in A. von Arnauld, K. von der Decken, M. Susi (eds), *Cambridge Handbook of New Human*

the current framework does not suffice. Some have advocated for the creation of new human rights—so-called neurorights.[35] Adapting (the interpretation of) human rights in view of emerging neurotechnology would fall within the revision domain of neurolaw. Interestingly, while debates on legal revisions are so far mainly motivated by *knowledge* from neuroscience—such as the understanding that the brain matures in our mid-twenties—the neurorights revision debate is motivated by the *practical possibilities* of emerging neurotechnologies.

In the neurorights debate, specific attention is given to a right to mental self-determination (sometimes also referred to as a right to cognitive liberty),[36] which could protect individuals against the risks of neurointerventions, while allowing them to *benefit* from the opportunities presented by neurotechnologies. We will consider this right in more detail in the following section, with a focus on the European Convention on Human Rights (ECHR), the human rights framework relevant for more than 700 million Europeans, including people in the Netherlands. The interpretation—and possible revision—of human rights may well impact on what is and is not possible regarding neurotechnological applications in criminal justice. More precisely, they may not only determine whether it would be legally permitted to use neurostimulation—i f proven technologically safe and effective—in an offender population, but also whether offenders may have a *right to be offered* such an intervention.[37]

Neurorights: Towards a Right to Mental Self-Determination

Mental Self-Determination in the Literature

To the best of our knowledge, the first to mention a right to mental self-determination in the context of emerging neurotechnologies was Bublitz in 2011.[38] He argued that:

> When the natural boundaries of the mind, the skull, can be surmounted by neurotechnologies, normative boundaries have to be established. Thus, the law should recognise a mind-protecting right. . . . I think the

Rights (Cambridge University Press, Cambridge, 2020) 404; J. C. Bublitz, 'Neurotechnologies and Human Rights' (2024) 28 *The International Journal of Human Rights* 782.

35 Ienca and Andorno (n 7); R. Yuste, J. Genser, S. Herrmann, 'It's Time for Neuro-Rights; New Human Rights for the Age of Neurotechnology' (2021) 18 *Horizons* 154.

36 Bublitz (n 7); N. A. Farahany, 'The Costs of Changing Our Minds' (2019) 69 *Emory Law Journal* 75, 103.

37 E. Dore-Horgan, 'Do Criminal Offenders Have a Right to Neurorehabilitation?' (2023) 17(2) *Criminal Law Philosophy* 429.

38 J. C. Bublitz, 'If Man's True Palace Is His Mind, What Is Its Adequate Protection? On a Right to Mental Self-Determination and Limits of Interventions Into Other Minds' in B. van den Berg, L. Klaming (eds), *Technologies on the Stand* (Wolf Legal Publishers, Nijmegen, 2011) 89.

best abstract formulation of the protected interest is mental sovereignty or mental self-determination, to be understood in opposition to heteronomous influences on mental functions.[39]

In later publications, Bublitz describes mental self-determination as a broad right to 'self-determine what is in and on one's mind,'[40] which, in the context of neurotechnologies, entails a right to 'alter one's mental states with the help of neurotools, as well as to refuse to do so.'[41] Thus, the right to mental self-determination encompasses protection for all mental states in two related dimensions. The first dimension grants *positive* entitlements, including the right of individuals to self-determine their inner realm, such as the content of their thoughts, consciousness, or other mental phenomena, including the right to freely change their mental states using neurotechnologies. The second dimension gives people the right to freely exercise their mental capacities, placing *negative* obligations on others not to interfere therewith and protecting against the coercive or unconsented use of neurotechnologies.[42] A similar view of mental self-determination is offered by Farahany and other scholars who, while not explicitly using the term 'mental self-determination', have examined the dual right to make choices about one's own mind and to be free from mental interference.[43]

The literature about a right to mental self-determination prompts research into the legal foundations of such a right, which has so far been limited. Bublitz and Merkel have argued that, although the law mainly protects 'bodies and brains' rather than 'minds and mental states,' a right to mental self-determination is already implicitly woven into the law's structure.[44] Furthermore, Bublitz has identified some anchor points of the right in current law, such as the freedom of thought and the right to mental integrity.[45] Michalowski, in response to Bublitz, has posited that the protection afforded to autonomy and mental integrity by the right to respect for private life (Article 8 ECHR) mirrors a right to mental self-determination.[46] Additionally, other scholars have noted that the right to mental self-determination, as a specification of Article 8 ECHR, receives increasing support.[47] For example, the

39 Ibid. 106; see also: Boire (n 6); Sententia (n 6).

40 Bublitz (n 7) 389.

41 J. C. Bublitz, 'My Mind Is Mine!? Cognitive Liberty as a Legal Concept' in E. Hildt, A. G. Franke (eds), *Cognitive Enhancement* (vol. 1, Springer, Dordrecht, 2013) 233.

42 See, for example, Bublitz and Merkel (n 4); Ligthart and others (n 33) 468.

43 Farahany (n 7); Farahany (n 36) 75, 98 and 103; Ienca and Andorno (n 7); Sententia (n 6); P. Sommaggio and others, 'Cognitive Liberty: A First Step towards a Human Neuro-Rights Declaration' (2017) 3 *BioLaw Journal* 27.

44 Bublitz and Merkel (n 4).

45 Bublitz (n 7) 389.

46 Ibid 405; Michalowski (n 34).

47 Ligthart and others (n 33) 473; S. Ligthart and others, 'Closed-Loop Brain Devices in Offender Rehabilitation' (2021) 30 *Cambridge Quarterly of Healthcare Ethics* 669; P. Kellmeyer and others, 'The Effects of Closed-Loop Medical Devices on the Autonomy and Accountability of Persons and Systems' (2016) 25 *Cambridge Quarterly of Healthcare Ethics* 623.

Committee on Bioethics of the Council of Europe defined mental integrity under Article 8 ECHR as 'the ability of individuals to exercise control over what happens to them with regard to, *inter alia*, their body, their mental state, and the related personal data.'[48]

Thus, from the legal literature, it seems possible that a right to mental self-determination could, in principle, be accommodated by the ECHR. However, the literature so far is not based on a thorough analysis of the case law of the European Court of Human Rights (ECtHR) and focuses almost exclusively on the negative dimension of the right, warranting further research. The following section will explore whether mental self-determination—particularly its positive dimension—has a foundation in the law, deriving from the protection of mental integrity and personal autonomy by Article 8 ECHR and the right to freedom of thought, protected by Article 9 ECHR.

Mental Self-Determination in the ECHR

The Right to Personal Autonomy

In the search for legal foundations of a right to mental self-determination, personal autonomy emerges as a fundamental interest protected by Article 8 ECHR.[49] The first basis for a specific legal right to autonomy can be found in the case *Pretty v. the United Kingdom*.[50] The applicant, a terminally ill woman, complained to the ECtHR that her right to self-determination was infringed because she was refused the ability to control the timing and circumstances of her death together with her husband.[51] The ECtHR connected self-determination to personal autonomy, defined as 'the ability to conduct one's life in a manner of one's own choosing.'[52] Therefore, various authors consider the two rights synonymous.[53]

The Court has clarified that personal autonomy includes not only choices entailing positive effects for the individual's body and mind, but also 'the

48 Committee on Bioethics of the Council of Europe, *Strategic Action Plan on Human Rights and Technologies in Biomedicine* (2020–2025), Adopted by the Committee on Bioethics (DH-BIO) at its 16th meeting (19–21 November 2019), para 22.

49 K. Lõhmus, *Caring Autonomy: European Human Rights Law and the Challenges of Individualism* (Cambridge University Press, Cambridge, 2015) 15; J. Marshall, *Personal Freedom Through Human Rights Law* (Brill Nijhoff, Leiden, 2008) 49.

50 *Pretty v. the United Kingdom* App No 2346/02 (ECHR, 29 April 2002).

51 Ibid, para 58.

52 Ibid, paras 61–62; I. Roagna, *Protecting the Right to Respect for Private and Family Life under the European Convention on Human Rights* (Council of Europe, Strasbourg, 2012) 15.

53 Likewise, *mental* autonomy and mental self-determination may be closely linked. Although there is no explicit reference in the ECtHR's case law to mental autonomy, it is reasonable to assume that it exists as a specification of personal autonomy, given the living instrument doctrine and the fact that the ECtHR almost always refers to autonomy in broad terms. See, for example, J. Marshall (n 49); L. Vardanyan, O. Hamuľák, H. Kocharyan, 'Personal Autonomy and Human Corporeality' (2024) 27 *Internet of Things* 101279.

opportunity to pursue activities perceived to be of a physically or morally harmful or dangerous nature for the individual concerned.'[54] As a result, patients have the right to refuse treatment, even if such treatment would be beneficial to their health or even life-saving.[55] This shows that the right to personal autonomy primarily imposes a negative obligation on States to refrain from forcibly subjecting individuals to medical treatment without valid consent, reflecting the negative dimension of mental self-determination: protection against involuntary interferences.[56]

Although the positive dimension of mental self-determination—a right to freely change one's mind—is less prominently featured in the ECtHR's case law on autonomy, some notable anchor points can still be identified. For instance, the Court has clarified that personal autonomy refers to the ability to live one's life in a manner of one's own choosing. Article 8 ECHR protects personal development, including the ability to develop and fulfil one's personality according to one's own choices.[57] Therefore, Article 8 ECHR encompasses a right to self-determine various aspects of life, including mental and emotional aspects such as personality, reflecting the positive dimension of a right to mental self-determination.

This positive dimension of mental self-determination is also apparent in the case law concerning positive obligations based on the right to autonomy.[58] For example, to ensure that individuals with a disability or disease can live their lives autonomously, the ECtHR decided that States have an obligation to provide a certain level of care.[59] Moreover, to protect individuals' sexual autonomy and gender identity, States must provide transgender people with legal recognition of their gender.[60] These examples show that under various circumstances, States hold positive obligations to provide, to a certain extent,

54 *Pretty* (n 50), para 62.

55 See, for example, *Arskaya v. Ukraine* App no 45076/05 (ECHR, 5 December 2013), para 69; *Y.P. v. Russia* App no 43399/13 (ECHR, 20 September 2022).

56 Or without proper justification under Article 8(2) ECHR; see E. Wicks, 'The Right to Refuse Medical Treatment under the European Convention on Human Rights' (2001) 9 *Medical Law Review* 17; W. Buelens, C. Herijgers, S. Illegems, 'The View of the European Court of Human Rights on Competent Patients' Right of Informed Consent' (2016) 23 *European Journal of Health Law* 481, 483.

57 *Bruggeman and Scheuten v. Germany* App no 6959/75 (ECmHR, 12 July 1997), para 55; *Kyriakides v. Cyprus* App no 39058/05 (ECHR 16 October 2008), para 48.

58 Marshall (n 49) 54.

59 *McDonald v. the United Kingdom* App no 4241/12 (ECHR, 20 May 2014); *Di Trizio v. Switzerland* App no 7186/09 (ECHR, 2 February 2016).

60 P. Johnson, 'LGBT Rights at the Council of Europe and the European Court of Human Rights' in J. Marshall (ed), *Personal Identity and the European Court of Human Rights* (Routledge, London, 2022) 99, 114; D. Valentiner, 'The Human Right to Sexual Autonomy' (2021) 22 *German Law Journal* 703, 708–710; *Christine Goodwin v. the United Kingdom* App no 28957/95 (ECHR [GC] 11 July 2002).

the necessary conditions for a person to exercise their autonomy and develop their personality in various situations.[61]

If States indeed must guarantee individuals' mental self-determination, they bear a responsibility to provide a legal and administrative framework that allows individuals to control their mental states. On the one hand, this could include a negative duty to refrain from employing neurotechnology without obtaining the subject's valid consent. On the other hand, neurotechnology could also play a part in helping offenders regain greater agency over their mental states, potentially facilitating their rehabilitation.[62] For instance, neurointerventions may in the future help offenders address psychological barriers to mental control, such as (substance) addiction, irresistible sexual urges, or a lack of impulse control.[63] In such instances, offenders may, perhaps, have a right to be offered neurointerventions that support their mental self-determination.

The Right to Mental Integrity

In addition to personal autonomy, the right to mental integrity under Article 8 ECHR could also safeguard mental self-determination.[64] Mental integrity is featured in cases involving medical treatment, especially non-consensual psychological and psychiatric interventions.[65] Mental integrity grants patients the right to control one's mental states by being able to consent to or refuse psychological and psychiatric treatment.[66] Such treatment can profoundly impact a person's capacity to control their mind, owing to both its intended therapeutic effects and potential mental side effects. For example, antipsychotic medication can have side effects impairing mental control by causing drowsiness, fatigue, memory deficits, and reduced emotional responsiveness. The fact that medical procedures that potentially reduce a patient's mental control can

61 M. Donnelly, *Healthcare Decision-Making and the Law* (Cambridge University Press, Cambridge, 2011) 41 and 78.

62 Ligthart, Dore-Horgan and Meynen (n 31).

63 T. Douglas and others, 'Coercion, Incarceration and Chemical Castration: An Argument From Autonomy' (2013) 10 *Bioethical Inquiry* 393, 399; Jesper Ryberg. *Neurointerventions, Crime and Punishment* (Oxford University Press, New York, 2020) 36–37.

64 The Court also uses 'psychological integrity' and 'moral integrity' to refer to the same concept; *X and Y v. the Netherlands* App no 8978/80 (ECHR, 26 March 1985), para 22; D. Harris and others, *Harris, O'Boyle and Warbrick: Law of the European Convention on Human Rights* (5th ed., Oxford University Press, Oxford, 2023) 525; M. E. Villiger, *Handbook on the European Convention on Human Rights* (Brill Nijhoff, Leiden, 2022) 442.

65 See, for example, *Matter v. Slovakia* App no 31534/96 (ECHR, 5 July 1999); *Shopov v. Bulgaria* App no 11373/04 (ECHR, 2 September 2010), para 41; *Fyodorov and Fyodorova v. Ukraine* App no 39229/03 (ECHR, 7 July 2011); *Pranjić-M-Lukić v. Bosnia and Herzegovina* App no 4938/16 (ECHR, 2 June 2020), para 63.

66 Ibid, see also: *Storck v. Germany* App no 61603/00 (ECHR, 16 June 2005), para 144 and 178; *G.B. and R.B. v. the Republic of Moldova* App no 16761/09 (ECHR, 8 December 2012), para 29.

infringe on mental integrity under Article 8 ECHR underscores that mental integrity encompasses the negative aspect of mental self-determination.

It can be argued that on the basis of the ECtHR's case law on mental integrity under Article 8 ECHR, also a more positive dimension of the right to mental self-determination can be found.[67] Relevant cases are not about the administration of forced medical treatment but rather about a lack of (access to) adequate treatment for mental health conditions. The Grand Chamber has established a 'positive obligation . . . to take appropriate measures to protect the life and health of those within their jurisdiction,'[68] which was found to be especially relevant in the case of prisoners who required medical assistance.[69] This obligation can be reasonably interpreted to extend to safeguarding both the physical and mental health of individuals. For example, in *Bensaid v. the United Kingdom*, the applicant faced deportation to Algeria and complained that he would be unable to receive adequate treatment for his schizophrenia there.[70] The ECtHR found that 'mental health must also be regarded as a crucial part of private life associated with the aspect of moral integrity,' and therefore the State should not obstruct access to treatment for those who want to manage their health condition.[71]

Treatment for mental health conditions could be considered a form of regaining control over one's mind, as it often involves modifying cognitive processes, emotional responses, and mental states. For example, it would be in line with the ECtHR's interpretation of Article 8 ECHR to argue that some neurointerventions can be conducive to mental integrity (and autonomy), that is, when they are employed to treat certain mental disorders—which may, sometimes, also contribute to reducing a convicted person's risk of reoffending. As such, in a (forensic) medical context, mental integrity seems to entail a limited version of the positive dimension of the right to mental self-determination: a right to freely alter one's mind to recover from mental disorders, including those that contribute to one's risk of reoffending.[72]

67 See *Bensaid v. the United Kingdom* App no 44599/98 (ECHR, 6 February 2001); *Dolenec v. Croatia* App no 25282/06 (ECHR, 26 November 2009).

68 *Vavřička and Others v. Czech Republic* App nos 47621/13 and 5 others (ECHR, 8 April 2021), para 282.

69 See, for example, *Sławomir Musiał v. Poland* App no 28300/06 (ECHR, 20 January 2009), para 87; *Guide on the Case-Law of the European Convention on Human Rights: Prisoners' Rights* (Council of Europe/European Court of Human Rights, Strasbourg, 2024), paras 144–157.

70 *Bensaid* (n 67).

71 Ibid, para 47; see also: *Dolenec* (n 67); *Guide on Article 8 of the European Convention on Human Rights: Right to Respect for Private and Family Life, Home and Correspondence* (Council of Europe/European Court of Human Rights, Strasbourg, 2024) 44.

72 See also: Marshall (n 49) 184.

The Right to Freedom of Thought

In the literature, the protection of mental self-determination (or, cognitive liberty) is often associated with the right to freedom of thought.[73] For example, as Bublitz writes, 'the scope of freedom of thought defines the realm and limits of mental self-determination.'[74]

In the European context, Article 9 ECHR guarantees the right to freedom of thought, conscience and religion. This article provides absolute protection to the so-called *forum internum*, the internal realm of the individual's mind that is considered off-limits for State interventions.[75] According to the Council of Europe, this right aims to 'prevent State indoctrination of individuals and to permit the development, refinement and substitution of personal thought, conscience and religion.'[76] Thus, the freedom of thought, conscience and religion reflects both the negative dimension (protection against State control over thoughts)[77] and the positive dimension (the freedom to develop the *forum internum*) of mental self-determination. Although scholars have observed a limited number of cases concerning the *forum internum* and criticised the ECtHR's minimal engagement with this aspect,[78] it is generally accepted that Article 9 ECHR includes a right to develop one's thoughts, conscience and beliefs. For example, Grabenwarter writes that freedom of thought aims to protect the 'inner core of self-determination.'[79] Moreover, regarding the right to freedom of thought in the meaning of Article 18 of the International Covenant on Civil Political Rights, Nowak has clarified that it includes a right 'to develop autonomously thoughts and a conscience free from impermissible external influence.'[80]

Note that the scope of the legal protection of mental self-determination through the right to freedom of thought would partly depend on how one defines the notion of "thought"—an issue currently under debate.[81] Whether

73 See, for example, Bublitz (n 7); Farahany (n 7).

74 J. C. Bublitz, 'Cognitive Liberty or the International Human Right to Freedom of Thought' in J. Clausen, N. Levy (eds), *Handbook of Neuroethics* (Springer Science, Dordrecht, 2015) 1330.

75 Harris and others (n 64) 573.

76 J. Murdoch, *Freedom of thought, Conscience and Religion* (Human rights handbooks No. 9, Council of Europe, Strasbourg, 2007) 13.

77 See also: N. Hertz, 'Neurorights—Do We Need New Human Rights? A Reconsideration of the Right to Freedom of Thought' (2023) 16(1) *Neuroethics* 5.

78 Ibid, J. C. Bublitz, 'Freedom of Thought as an International Human Right: Elements of a Theory of a Living Right' in M. J. Blitz, J. C. Bublitz (eds), *The Law and Ethics of Freedom of Thought* (vol. 1, Palgrave Studies in Law, Neuroscience, and Human Behavior, Cham, 2021) 57; P. O'Callaghan, B. Shiner, 'The Right to Freedom of Thought in the European Convention on Human Rights' (2021) 8 *European Journal of Comparative Law and Governance* 112.

79 C. Grabenwarter, *The European Convention on Human Rights* (Hart Publishing, Oxford, 2014) 237.

80 M. Nowak, *U.N. Covenant on Civil and Political Rights* (2nd rev. ed., Engel, Kehl, 2005) 412.

81 See, for example, the positions defended by both Bublitz and Ligthart in M. J. Blitz, J. C. Bublitz (eds), *The Law and Ethics of Freedom of Thought Vol. 2* (Palgrave McMillan, Cham, 2025), in press.

freedom of thought protects mental phenomena that are usually not considered a thought is unclear. One could think of *feelings, tendencies, behavioural control, risk-taking, empathic abilities,* and *emotional responses*—potential targets for reducing risks of recidivism in convicted persons, e.g., with neurotechnology.[82] The general rule of interpretation of Article 31(1) of the Vienna Convention seems to oppose such a broad interpretation of thought, prescribing that 'ordinary meaning' should be given to the terms of a treaty in light of its object and purpose.[83] Because mental phenomena such as feelings, behavioural inclinations, and empathic abilities are not normally captured by the common understanding of thought, enhancing these mental entities through neurotechnology will plausibly fall *outside* the scope of the absolute right to freedom of thought.

Conclusion

In the Netherlands, neuroscience has already had a tangible impact on the legal system and forensic practices. Neuroscientific findings have contributed to the establishment of adolescent criminal law, and neuroimaging has been used in criminal court cases to address questions concerning criminal accountability and recidivism risk. Furthermore, the Netherlands Institute for Forensic Psychiatry and Psychology—part of the Dutch Ministry of Justice and Security—has recently started both a neuro helpdesk for forensic experts and a neuro outpatient clinic. In addition, neuromodulation has been studied in a Dutch forensic population to reduce aggression.

Given that neurotechnologies in criminal justice can have a profound influence on personal interests such as privacy, identity, and personal integrity, it is essential to explore these developments from a human rights perspective. This need for scrutiny is broadly recognised in the literature and underpins the 'neurorights debate,' which centres on whether existing legal frameworks sufficiently protect individuals against the profound implications of emerging neurotechnologies while also granting them sufficient rights to benefit from the positive potential of such technologies. A key consideration in this debate is the right to mental self-determination—allowing individuals to control what happens in and to their minds. The outcome of this debate, which could lead to new interpretations of or even revisions of existing rights, may have a direct impact on the legal boundaries of employing emerging neurotechnologies in criminal justice, also in the Netherlands.

As explored in this chapter, the right to mental self-determination appears to have some foundations within the ECHR framework, particularly in the right to respect for private life (Article 8 ECHR) and the freedom of thought

82 Ligthart, Dore-Horgan and Meynen (n 31).

83 J. C. Bublitz, 'What is Thought? Interpreting and Constructing Article 18 ICCPR in Light of the Vienna Convention' in Blitz and Bublitz (n 81).

(Article 9 ECHR). This case law reflects the negative dimension of the right: States are obliged to refrain from interfering with individuals' minds through coercive medical treatments, which could include neurotechnology. However, the ECtHR case law also provides evidence of the *positive* dimension of the right, which is crucial to appreciate the opportunities that neurotechnologies bring to criminal justice. This means that, depending on how the neurorights debate evolves, people in the criminal justice system may not only receive (more) protection, but they may also be entitled to offers of neurotechnologies, for instance, to diminish the impact of mental illness on their mental health and risk of reoffending.

Acknowledgements

This publication is part of the project Law and Ethics of Neurotechnology in Criminal Justice (LENC) (with project number VI.C.201.067) of the research program Vici, which is financed by the Dutch Research Council (NWO).

5 Neuroprediction

The Future of Crime Prevention or Fostering Injustice?

Elizabeth Shaw and Gregg D. Caruso

Introduction

Neuroprediction in the context of criminal justice refers to the use of neuroscience and neuroimaging techniques to predict an individual's likelihood of engaging in criminal behaviour in the future. It involves analysing brain activity, structure, or function to assess an individual's propensity for violence, recidivism, or other antisocial behaviours.[1] In this chapter, we examine future possibilities for the use of neuroprediction, address concerns about the use of neuroprediction, and analyse how different penal theories can go about addressing these concerns. We focus mainly on retributive and social protection theories, but also briefly discuss consequentialist theories. We argue that social protection theories can offer adequate constraints on the use of neuroprediction, and that such theories have distinct advantages over retributive and consequentialist approaches to neuroprediction.

In the first section, we begin by introducing the concept of neuroprediction and briefly discuss the accuracy and potential of neuropredictive technologies—with a particular focus on how they could enhance current structured actuarial risk assessments in the future. In the second section, we explore the ethical implications of neuroprediction through the lens of different penal theories, examining under what conditions, if any, its use might be considered morally acceptable. We compare retributive and social protection theories, highlighting reasons why retributivists might oppose the use of neuroprediction. In the third section, we argue that social protection theories can, contrary to some criticisms, effectively safeguard individual rights while providing necessary limits on using neuropredictive tools. Finally, in the fourth section, we test the robustness of our approach by applying it to two specific neuropredictive scenarios and comparing the outcomes with the recommendations of retributivism.

1 T. Nadelhoffer et al., 'Neuroprediction, Violence, and the Law: Setting the Stage' (2012) 5(1) *Neuroethics* 67.

DOI: 10.4324/9781003510246-6

Neuroprediction: Current Practice and Future Possibilities

Decisions about public safety and the prevention of violence are more likely to succeed when they are based on accurate predictions of who will engage in violence and under what circumstances. Traditionally, offender risk estimates were determined using unstructured clinical judgments by trained forensic psychologists—a subjective technique that has since been shown to perform a little better than chance.[2] Recently, structured actuarial risk assessment techniques have improved the accuracy of offender placement decisions by quantifying the offender's degree of fit with a known validation sample. Structured actuarial risk assessment is any evidence-based technique that generates probabilistic predictions about the ostensible offender's engaging in certain behaviour—e.g., violence, reoffending, relapsing, or responding to treatment.[3] Today, more than 20 U.S. states require their courts to use these statistical tools in offender sentencing and placement decisions.[4]

Despite the potential advantages of structured actuarial risk assessments, critics fear these tools may lead to negative consequences if they do not exhibit sufficiently accurate predictions or do not treat individuals fairly and with respect. One key concern is that current risk assessment tools tend to be algorithmic. They use big data and statistical analyses to derive correlates of criminal offending and package them into computational algorithms. If the data being used, however, is already biased because of, say, the over-policing of black and brown communities or historical biases elsewhere in the legal system, then the predictions produced by these tools will reflect and reinforce existing cultural biases. For this reason, the potential for race-based discrimination is an emerging concern regarding the use of algorithmic risk assessment methods.[5]

Soon, however, neuropredictive technologies may allow us to improve existing methods by including unique neurobiological markers in our risk assessments. Scientists, for instance, are beginning to examine 'whether the inclusion of neurobiological and/or genetic markers can improve predictive models based solely on non-biological evidence.'[6]

A growing number of theorists have suggested that, in the near future, neuropredictive technologies may be able to further improve our risk assessment

2 See E. Aharoni et al., 'Ethical Implications of Neurobiological Informed Risk Assessment for Criminal Justice Decisions: A Case for Pragmatism' in F. De Brigard, W. Sinnott-Armstrong (eds), *Neuroscience and Philosophy* (MIT Press, 2022), chapter 6.

3 F. Taxman, 'The Partially Clothed Emperor: Evidence-Based Practices' (2018) 34(97) *Journal of Contemporary Criminal Justice* 97: Aharoni et al. (n 2).

4 Aharoni et al. (n 2), 161–162.

5 M. Hamilton, 'Investigating Algorithmic Risk and Race' (2021a) 5(1) *UCLA Criminal Justice Law Review* 53; M. Hamilton, 'Evaluating Algorithmic Risk Assessment' (2021b) 24(2) *New Criminal Law Review* 156.

6 Aharoni et al. (n 2), 168.

methods, both in terms of accuracy and counterbalancing human bias.[7] Neuroscientists have made tremendous progress in identifying and exploring some of the neural correlates of violence and aggression in the past two decades.[8] Certain patterns in brain function and structure, for instance, have been linked to traits such as impulsivity, aggression, and lack of empathy, which could be associated with criminal behaviour. Using techniques such as functional magnetic resonance imaging MRI (fMRI) or electroencephalography (EEG), we may one day be able to predict violent behaviour and recidivism based on abnormalities in brain regions involved in decision-making, impulse control, and emotional regulation associated with a heightened risk of (re)offending. Neuroprediction holds promise in the study of psychopathy, a personality disorder linked to higher rates of criminal behaviour. Research has shown that individuals with psychopathic traits often have differences in brain areas related to empathy, morality, and emotional processing.[9] This has led to efforts to identify neurobiological markers that might predict violent or criminal tendencies in such individuals.[10]

Preliminary studies on neuroprediction have already shown some promise. A series of studies conducted by Aharoni and colleagues found that in a sample of 96 adult offenders who engaged in an impulse control task while undergoing fMRI, brain activity within the anterior cingulate cortex (ACC) prospectively predicted being rearrested later. Offenders with relatively low ACC activity had roughly double the odds of getting rearrested for a violent or nonviolent crime as those with high activity, controlling for other known risk factors. Using advanced statistical techniques, these neuropredictive models demonstrated relatively high accuracy—that is, the probability that a true positive was correctly classified exceeded 75%.[11] Other studies have reported similar predictive effects using different models of brain function.[12] Together,

7 Nadelhoffer et al. (n 1); Aharoni et al. (n 2).

8 See A. Raine, *The Anatomy of Violence: The Biological Roots of Crime* (Vintage, New York, 2014).

9 J. Anderson, K. Kiehl, 'Psychopathy: Developmental Perspectives and Their Implications for Treatment' (2014) 32(1) *Restorative Neurology Neuroscience* 103.

10 R. De Oliveira-Souza et al., 'Psychopathy as a Disorder of the Moral Brain: Fronto Temporo-Limbic Grey Matter Reductions Demonstrated by Vox-Based Morphometry' (2008) 40(3) *NeuroImage* 1202; A. Glen et al., 'Increased Volume of the Striatum in Psychopathic Individuals' (2010) 67 *Biological Psychiatry* 52; See A. Raine, A. Glenn, *Psychopathy: An Introduction to Biological Findings and their Implications* (NYU Press, New York, 2014); See, generally, A. Raine, A. Glenn, *Psychopathy: An Introduction to Biological Findings and their Implications* (NYU Press, New York, 2014); V. Leutgeb et al, 'Brain Abnormalities in High-Risk Violent Offenders and their Association with Psychopathic Traits and Criminal Recidivism' (2015) 12(308) *Neuroscience* 194.

11 E. Aharoni et al., 'Predictive Accuracy in the Neuroprediction of Rearrest' (2014) 9(4) *Social Neuroscience* 332.

12 K. Kiehl et al., 'Age of Gray Matters: Neuroprediction of Recidivism' (2018) 19 *NeuroImage: Clinical* 813; C. Delfin et al., 'Prediction of Recidivism in a Long-Term Follow-Up of Forensic Psychiatric Patients: Incremental Effects of Neuroimaging Data' (2019) 14(5) *PLoS One* e0217127.

'these studies provide preliminary evidence that brain factors such as ACC function may serve as candidate biomarkers for antisocial behaviour.'[13]

It is quite possible, then, that in the future we will be able to improve existing actuarial risk assessment tools by incorporating neuropredictive technologies, which could help in making decisions related to sentencing, parole, or rehabilitation programs. Because neuropredictive technologies are based on the individual's unique neurobiological markers rather than on current structured actuarial risk assessments, they hold the potential for reducing human and algorithmic bias.

Neuroprediction: Retributivism Versus Societal Protection

Although neuroprediction in criminal justice offers potential advantages, such as more accurate risk assessment and better-targeted interventions, many fear that it could lead to human rights violations, disregard for human dignity, and the preemptive detention of individuals judged at high risk of violence.[14]

Different penal theories have different implications about whether neuroprediction would ever be ethically acceptable and, if so, under what conditions. For some theorists, the main problem with this practice lies in the 'prediction' part rather than the 'neuro' part. For example, 'pure' retributivist Michael Moore argues that rather than aim to prevent future crimes, an offender's punishment should be based purely on how much he deserves to suffer for the crime he has already committed.[15] Although most retributivists, unlike Moore, accept that crime prevention should play some role in sentencing, they often worry that basing the sentence on predicted recidivism risk could lead to disproportionate sentencing. 'Negative' retributivists insist that innocent people should not be punished and that people should be punished no more severely than they deserve.[16] Negative retributivists might therefore welcome predictive technologies if they were only used to justify releasing someone somewhat earlier than the maximum deserved detention period. They would oppose preventive detention that lasted longer than would be proportionate to their past crime. (Those who endorse negative retributivism usually also believe that desert plays some positive role in justifying punishment, albeit the state might be permitted to inflict less than the offender deserves.)[17]

13 Aharoni (n 2), 170.

14 D. Soto et al., 'Neurorights vs Neuroprediction and Lie Detection: The Imperative Limits to Criminal Law' (2022) 13 *Frontiers in Psychology* 1030439.

15 See M. Moore, *Placing Blame* (Oxford University Press, New York, 1997).

16 See Z. Hoskins, A. Duff, Legal Punishment' in E. Zalta (ed), *The Stanford Encyclopedia of Philosophy* (Spring Edition, 2024) <https://plato.stanford.edu/archives/spr2024/entries/legal-punishment/>.

17 See, e.g., J. Lemos, *Free Will's Value: Criminal Justice, Pride, and Love* (Routledge, New York, 2023).

In contrast, a growing number of theorists have rejected retributivism on the basis that it depends on a conception of basic desert moral responsibility that is deeply flawed.[18] Basic desert moral responsibility is the kind of responsibility needed to make the harm of blame and punishment deserved and fundamentally so.[19] It is the kind of moral responsibility required to justify retributive punishment. To be morally responsible in the retributive sense for a criminal act is to deserve to suffer some hardship simply because of the nature of the act, regardless of whether this promotes beneficial consequences. Sceptics of basic desert moral responsibility sometimes invoke neuroscience to support their critique of retributivism.[20] Neuroscientists currently adopt the philosophical assumption that 'all behaviour is caused by our brains.'[21] Suppose everyone's motivations, personality, and deliberations are entirely determined by their brains' development (and the way the brain responds to their situation), which in turn was caused to develop in that exact way by genetic and environmental factors beyond their control. In that case, the question arises whether retributive punishment is truly 'deserved.' As the third section of this chapter will explain, responsibility sceptics typically endorse a theory of criminal sanctions based on societal protection, within which neuroprediction might seem to fit more comfortably than within a retributive framework.[22]

Consequentialist theories may also be more receptive to the use of neuroprediction. These theories argue that punishment is justified if it produces beneficial social outcomes, such as reducing crime, protecting society, or deterring would-be offenders. Because neuroprediction can be seen as a tool that helps

18 See, generally, D. Pereboom, *Living Without Free Will* (Cambridge University Press, New York, 2001); D. Pereboom, *Free Will, Agency, and Meaning in Life* (Oxford University Press, New York, 2014); D. Pereboom, G. D. Caruso, 'Hard-Incompatibilism Existentialism: Neuroscience, Punishment, and Meaning in Life' in G. D. Caruso, O. Flanagan (eds), *Neuroexistentialism: Meaning, Morals, and Purpose in the Age of Neuroscience* (Oxford University Press, New York, 2018); G. D. Caruso, 'Justice Without Retribution: An Epistemic Argument against Retributive Criminal Punishment' (2020) 13(1) *Neuroethics* 13; G. D. Caruso, *Rejecting Retributivism: Free Will, Punishment, and Criminal Justice* (Cambridge University Press, New York, 2021a).

19 Pereboom (n 18).

20 See R. Sapolsky, *Determined: A Science of Life without Free Will* (Penguin Press, New York, 2023).

21 See A. Raine, A. Glenn, *Psychopathy: An Introduction to Biological Findings and Their Implications* (NYU Press, New York, 2014).

22 G. D. Caruso, 'Retributivism, Free Will Skepticism, and the Public Health-Quarantine Model: Replies to Kennedy, Walen, Corrado, Sifferd, Pereboom, and Shaw' (2021b) 46(2) *Journal of Legal Philosophy* 161; G. D. Caruso, 'Free Will Skepticism and Criminal Behavior: A Public Health-Quarantine Model' (2016) 32(1) *Philosophical Review* 25; G. D. Caruso, 'Preemptive Incapacitation, Victim's Rights, Desert, and Respect for Persons: Replies to McCormick and Donelson' (2023) 10(3) *Journal of Practical Ethics* 29; Caruso (n 18); Pereboom (n 18); Pereboom and Caruso (n 18); see, also, G. D. Caruso, D. Pereboom, 'A Non-Punitive Alternative to Punishment' in Focquaert et al. (eds), *Routledge Handbook of the Philosophy of Science of Punishment* (Routledge, New York, 2020).

achieve beneficial social outcomes, consequentialist theories are more likely to support its use. Consequentialists might argue that if neuroprediction can help identify individuals at higher risk of reoffending, it can assist in targeting interventions or preemptively detaining high-risk offenders, thereby reducing the overall crime rate and ensuring greater public safety. Furthermore, knowing that one's behaviour could be assessed using neuroscientific technologies might act as a general deterrent to others in society. If offenders know that their risk of reoffending can be predicted, they might be less likely to engage in criminal behaviour.

In response, retributivists may allege that both social protection theorists and consequentialists lack the conceptual resources to oppose or place adequate constraints on the objectionable use of preemptive detention (detaining an individual before they have committed a crime) and indefinite preventive detention (if an individual is deemed to be at high risk of violent recidivism). Furthermore, the neuroscientific argument for scepticism about basic desert moral responsibility suggests another way penal theorists may resist neuroprediction—i.e., by questioning the acceptability of the 'neuro' part of neuroprediction. The version of retributivism based on a libertarian conception of free will is at odds with the idea of neuroprediction of behaviour (and the deterministic or quasi-deterministic assumptions about human action that arguably underlie this technique). According to libertarianism, human actions are not predetermined by brain processes or anything else, and the ability of agents to rise above biological and environmental pressures and make indeterministic free choices is an important source of human dignity. According to libertarianism, a person's free choice is like the traditional view of what 'Eve was when she bit the apple. Perfectly free to do otherwise. So perfectly free, in fact, that even God couldn't tell which way she'd jump.'[23] For this kind of libertarian, to try to read a person's brain and preempt morally important choices, disrespects agency; and viewing a person as a 'biological machine' undermines human dignity.

Appealing to libertarian free will is therefore one way to oppose neuroprediction and defend retributivism against sceptical challenges to free will and basic desert moral responsibility. We contend, however, that this path is ill-advised for three reasons. First, strong philosophical and scientific reasons exist for believing agents lack libertarian free will. This is because the leading accounts of libertarian free will-event-causal libertarianism and agent-causal-libertarianism face significant philosophical and scientific challenges.[24] Second, most libertarians acknowledge that we lack sufficient evidentiary grounds to believe human beings have the kind of free will and moral responsibility needed

23 J. Fodor, 'Review of *Freedom Evolves*' (2003) 5 *London Review of Books* <https://www.lrb.co.uk/the-paper/v25/n05/jerry-fodor/why-would-mother-nature-bother>.

24 Pereboom (n 18); Caruso (n 18); See G. D. Caruso, *Free Will and Consciousness: A Determinist Account of the Illusion of Free Will* (Lexington Books, Lanham, Maryland, 2012).

to justify retributive punishment. Libertarian John Lemos, for instance, candidly admits: 'It is my view that at this point in time we simply don't have sufficient experimental/empirical evidence nor sufficient metaphysical nor logical nor intuitive evidence to establish that libertarian free will exists' (2018: 6).[25] Similarly, Al Mele, who offers a competing libertarian account, refuses to endorse his own view since he too admits: 'I do not know of strong evidence that human brains work as they would need to work if a theoretically attractive event-causal libertarian view is true.'[26] These acknowledgements are essential because they reveal that belief in libertarian free will does not meet the high epistemic standard needed to justify retributive punishment.

Because legal punishment inflicts significant harm on individuals, the justification for such harm must meet a high epistemic standard. If it is significantly probable that one's justification for harming another is unsound, then, prima facie, that behaviour is seriously wrong. The burden of proof, therefore, lies on those who want to inflict harm on others to provide reasonable justification for such harm. This means that retributivists who want to justify legal punishment on the assumption that agents are free and morally responsible (and hence justly deserve to suffer for the wrongs they have done) must justify that assumption. They must justify that assumption in a way that meets a high epistemic standard of proof, since the harms caused by legal punishment are often quite severe. It is not enough to point to the mere possibility that agents possess libertarian free will or to assume that compatibilists' accounts of free will successfully preserve basic desert moral responsibility. Nor is it enough to say that the sceptical arguments against free will and basic desert moral responsibility fail to be conclusive. Instead, a positive and convincing case must be made that agents are morally responsible in the basic desert sense, since it is the backward-looking desert of agents that retributivists take to justify the harm caused by punishment. Given that both libertarian and compatibilist accounts of free will face significant and unresolved difficulties, we maintain that in the face of uncertainty about the existence of free will, it is, *prima facie*, seriously morally wrong to retributively punish wrongdoers on the philosophically questionable assumption that they deserve it.[27]

25 J. Lemos, *A Pragmatic Approach to Libertarian Free Will* (Routledge, 2018) 6. For discussion of similar statements see, e.g. Pereboom (n 18); Caruso (n 18); Caruso (n 24).

26 A. Mele, *Aspects of Agency: Decisions, Abilities, Explanations, and Free Will* (Oxford University Press, New York, 2017), 205.

27 We should note that this epistemic argument applies only to *positive* retributivists who hold that individuals who commit crimes deserve punishment in proportion to the wrongdoing they've committed. It does not apply to *negative* retributivists who appeal to the notion of desert *only* as a constraint on punishment. This latter view, however, is considered by many retributivists to be 'too weak to guide criminal law' and as amounting to nothing more than 'desert-free consequentialism side constrained by negative desert'—L. Alexander et al., *Crime and Culpability: A Theory of Criminal Law* (Cambridge University Press, New York, 2009), 7. See B. Vilhauer, 'Free Will and Reasonable Doubt' (2009) 46(2) *American Philosophical Quarterly* 131; B. Vilhauer, 'Taking Free Will Skepticism Seriously' (2012) 62(249) *The*

Third, and perhaps most important for our present purposes, we contend that social protection theories can preserve human dignity and provide adequate constraints on neuroprediction without appeal to libertarian (or compatibilist) free will. In the following section, we briefly sketch the public health-quarantine model, as developed by Derk Pereboom and Gregg D. Caruso,[28] and use it to represent the kind of social protection theories we have in mind. We then respond to retributive concerns about the supposed threat that neuroprediction poses to individual rights and dignity. We argue that, contra critics, social protection theories can effectively safeguard individual rights while providing necessary limits on the use of neuropredictive tools.

Can Social Protection Theories Place Adequate Constraints on Neuroprediction?

The public health-quarantine model is one kind of social protection theory. It offers a non-retributive approach to addressing criminal behaviour, based on public health ethics and focused on prevention and social justice. The theory is based on an analogy with quarantine and draws a comparison between the treatment of dangerous criminals and the treatment of carriers of dangerous diseases. In its simplest form, it can be stated as follows: (1) Moral responsibility sceptics maintain that criminals are not morally responsible for their actions in the basic desert sense; (2) plainly, many carriers of dangerous diseases are not responsible in this or in any other sense for having contracted these diseases; (3) yet, we generally agree that it is sometimes permissible to quarantine them, and the justification for doing so is the right of self-protection and prevention of harm to others; (4) for similar reasons, even if a dangerous criminal is not morally responsible for their crimes in the basic desert sense (perhaps because no one is ever in this way morally responsible), it could be as legitimate to incapacitate them as to quarantine the non-responsible carrier of a dangerous disease.[29]

The model's core maintains that the incapacitation of the seriously dangerous is justified on the grounds of the right of self-defence and defence of others. Just as the state is justified in quarantining individuals carrying contagious diseases to protect society, it is likewise justified in incapacitating the criminally dangerous with the minimum harm required for adequate protection. The resulting account would not justify the sort of criminal punishment whose legitimacy is most dubious, such as death or confinement in the most common kinds of prisons in our society. The model also specifies attention to

Philosophical Quarterly 833; E. Shaw, *Free Will, Punishment, and Criminal Responsibility*, PhD thesis (Edinburgh University, 2014); Caruso (2020, 2021a) (n.18); E. Shaw, 'Neuroscience, Criminal Sentencing, and Human Rights' (2021) 63 *William and Mary Law Review* 1409.

28 See Pereboom (n 18); Caruso (n 18); Pereboom and Caruso (n 18); Caruso and Pereboom (n 24).

29 Pereboom (n 18).

the well-being of criminals, which would change much of current policy. Furthermore, the public health component of the theory prioritizes prevention and social justice and aims at identifying and acting on the social determinants of health and criminal behaviour.[30] This combined approach to dealing with criminal behaviour is arguably sufficient for dealing with dangerous criminals and avoids the harms to communities, imprisoned people, and the families of detaining non-dangerous people simply to inflict retributive suffering.

However, one objection that has been raised against social protection views is that they cannot preserve the rights and dignity of persons. John Lemos, for instance, has argued that 'the human capacity for moral responsibility gives human beings a special dignity and worth that is fundamental to a proper system of morality grounded on the concept of respect for persons.'[31] He further maintains that theories of criminal justice that reject basic desert moral responsibility cannot protect this special dignity and worth.[32] According to Lemos, possession of libertarian free will is necessary for basic desert moral responsibility and to make sense of holding persons responsible in the just desert sense.'[33] Alternatives to criminal justice that reject libertarian free will, he contends, cannot adequately protect the rights and dignity of persons in the context of criminal justice. In particular, he argues that views like the public health-quarantine model lack 'the theoretical means to build an argument against lowering evidentiary standards for criminal conviction so as to provide better protections against crime.'[34] Yet, lowering the evidentiary bar would fail to respect the dignity and worth of persons, since it would be a 'great injustice to rob innocent people of their freedom when they are innocent and have committed no crimes.'[35] According to Lemos, the only way to protect the rights and dignity of persons is to appeal to the notion of just deserts and the principle that 'people who've committed no crimes don't deserve this kind of treatment.'[36]

A similar objection can be raised against using neuroprediction by social protection theories. Critics could argue that even if a few false positives occur, it would still be safer for society to preemptively incapacitate individuals assessed at high risk of committing violent offences. The concern here is similar to the movie *Minority Report*, which is set in a dystopian future where a specialised police force called PreCrime prevents crimes before they happen. What if neuroprediction became so reliable that we could one day

30 See G. D Caruso, *Public Health and Safety: The Social Determinants of Health and Criminal Behavior* (ResearchLinks Books, London, 2017); Caruso (n 18).

31 J. Lemos, *Freedom, Responsibility, and Determinism: A Philosophical Dialogue* (Hackett, Indianapolis, Indiana, 2013), 78.

32 Ibid; J. Lemos, 'Moral Concerns about Responsibility Denial and the Quarantine of Violent Criminals' (2016) 35 *Law and Philosophy* 461.

33 Lemos (n 32), 147.

34 Ibid. 150–151.

35 Ibid. 151

36 Ibid.

preemptively incapacitate individuals who are going to commit violent crimes? Critics argue that social protection theories are unable to give a principled reason for opposing preemptive incapacitation, yet preemptive incapacitation intuitively violates the rights of individuals, the presumption of innocence, and the retributivist conviction that individuals who have not committed any crimes do not deserve to have their liberty restricted or removed.

Although we take this concern seriously, we maintain that social protection theories can adequately preserve the rights and dignity of persons. First, it is crucial to recognise that the public health-quarantine model is not a strict consequentialist theory. Rather, it justifies incapacitation on the grounds of the right of self-defence and defence of others. That we have this right has broad appeal, much broader than utilitarianism or consequentialism more generally has. In addition, this makes the view more resilient to several objections. One advantage it has over consequentialist deterrence theories is that it has more restrictions placed on using people merely as a means. For instance, as it is illegitimate to treat carriers of a disease more harmfully than is necessary to neutralise the danger they pose, treating those with violent criminal tendencies more harshly than is required to protect society will be illegitimate as well. The model requires that we adopt the principle of least infringement, which holds that the least restrictive measures should be taken to protect public health and safety. This ensures that criminal sanctions will be proportionate to the danger posed by an individual, and sanctions that exceed this upper bound will be unjustified.[37]

Second, the right of self-defence does not extend to non-threats (i.e., people who pose no danger to society). Regarding Lemos's objection, then, social protection theorists can argue that it is important to keep the evidentiary bar high to ensure that we protect persons' liberty, rights, and dignity. The public health-quarantine model stresses the importance of balancing concerns about liberty and respect for persons against the need to protect the health and safety of society. Caruso, for instance, maintains that respect for autonomy needs to be weighed heavily against the use of state power.[38] He argues that 'the justificatory burden is always on those who want to limit one's liberty and autonomy by means of incarceration or incapacitation.'[39] Social protection theorists can therefore argue that the burden of proof should remain high in criminal cases and that the state should have to establish beyond a reasonable doubt that an individual has committed a crime and continues to pose a significant threat to society before it can justify restricting their liberty.

In response, Lemos objects that proponents of the public health-quarantine model cannot invoke the value of liberty to justify placing constraints on state power (including the abuse of neuroprediction). He points out that

37 Caruso (n 18).
38 Caruso (n 18), (2016) (n 24).
39 Caruso (n 18) 191.

dangerous criminals interfere with the liberty of victims. If infringing the liberty of a smaller number of potential offenders would protect the liberty of a larger number of potential victims, then overall liberty would be maximised. Thus, on Lemos's reasoning, the value of liberty cannot rule out preemptive detention based on neuroscientific risk prediction.

Lemos's argument, however, incorrectly assumes that our approach is consequentialist. The idea that good outcomes should be maximised is characteristic of consequentialist reasoning. In contrast, in our view, an individual's liberty is not something to be 'maximised'; it is to be respected. Actively interfering with an individual's liberty requires strong justification (with greater or more harmful infringements requiring correspondingly stronger justification). However, failing to prevent liberty infringements is significantly easier to justify. This approach relies on the doctrine of doing and allowing (DDA). There is no scope within this chapter to defend this doctrine, but it has the power to explain our intuitions in a wide range of cases.[40] For instance, it provides a rationale for criminal law's stance on omissions and human rights reasoning. Just as the scope of an individual's criminal liability for omissions is narrower than their criminal liability for actions, human rights law generally provides stronger protections against active violations of human rights by the state than against the state's omissions. It is also plausible that underlying the beyond a reasonable doubt requirement is the idea, based on the DDA, that it is worse to impose unjustified criminal sanctions than to refrain from imposing justified sanctions.

In relation to preemptive incapacitation, we similarly contend that social protection theorists could argue that the value of liberty precludes, in all but the most extreme circumstances, preemptive incapacitation based on neuropredictive risk assessments. Given that we cannot assess the likelihood of future violent behaviour, and given the potential for false positives, significant weight should be given to protecting individual liberty. Just as we adopt the presumption of innocence in criminal law, we should adopt the presumption of harmlessness in the context of neuroprediction.[41]

Furthermore, we contend that preemptive incapacitation should never be permitted when agents are competent, moderately reasons-responsive, and able to make rational and informed decisions. Consider, for instance, the following case:

> Imagine that someone has involuntarily been given a drug that makes it virtually certain that he will brutally murder at least one person during

40 F. Woollard, 'The Doctrine of Doing and Allowing II: The Moral Relevance of the Doing/Allowing Distinction' (2012) 7(7) *Philosophy Compass* 459.

41 J. Floud, W Young, *Dangerousness and Criminal Justice* (Heinemann, London, 1981); Caruso (n 198) 247; E. Shaw, 'Justice Without Moral Responsibility?' (2019) 28(1) *Journal of Information Ethics* 95 (referring to the 'presumption of non-dangerousness').

> the one-week period he is under its influence. There is no known antidote, and because he is especially strong, mere monitoring would be ineffective.[42]

In such a case, the public health-quarantine model may allow for preventative detention. However, this should not be a strong objection to the view since virtually everyone would agree that it would be at least *prima facie* permissible to preventatively detain this individual for the week. In fact, instead of being a weakness of the model, the possibility of exceptions in cases like this provides the model with additional advantages over retributivism. In this situation, retributivists would have difficulty justifying preemptive measures because the individual deserves punishment, since he has not yet done anything wrong. Yet, it also seems intuitive that we should detain the individual until the drug has worn off.

The case of the drugged man, however, points us in the direction of an important distinction that can be used to further clarify exceptional cases. In this case, the drug can be viewed as undermining the agent's reasons-responsiveness; in such cases, it is sometimes permissible to preemptively incapacitate non-reasons-responsive agents, as is currently permissible in cases of mental illness when an individual is involuntarily committed for being an imminent and serious threat of substantial harm to self or others. On the other hand, when agents are competent, moderately reasons-responsive, and able to make rational and informed decisions, the presumption of harmlessness and epistemic uncertainty count strongly, perhaps decisively, against preemptive legal coercion. Moderately reasons-responsive agents can conform their behaviour to their reasons for action. If we think that a reasons-responsive agent is going to harm another, perhaps on neuropredictive grounds, then we should reason with them or provide them with countervailing moral and/or legal considerations; yet they should not be subject to legal coercion unless they have broken or attempted to break the law (i.e., they should be afforded the presumption of harmlessness).

Two Neuropredictive Scenarios

So far, this chapter has discussed the worry that neuroprediction of criminal propensities may threaten individual rights. We cast doubt on the claim that, to protect these rights, we must invoke retributivism and the kind of 'free will' it depends on. Instead, we outlined a non-retributive, non-consequentialist approach, which we think can adequately constrain the use of neuroprediction. To test the strength of our approach, we will now apply it to two specific scenarios involving neuroprediction. For each scenario, we will compare our approach's results with the recommendations of retributivism

42 Pereboom and Caruso (n 18) 215.

(both compatibilist varieties and those relying on libertarian free will) and consequentialism.

Scenario A: Basing the Minimum Sentence Length of a Convicted Offender on Neuroprediction, With Release After That Period Conditional on a Satisfactory Neuroscientific Evaluation

Imagine the following futuristic neuropredictive sentencing scenario. Bertie is a 20-year-old man who has been convicted of robbery. He obtained the elderly victim's wallet using threats of violence, but he neither had a weapon nor inflicted physical harm. It is his first offence. He has undergone a risk evaluation prior to sentencing, based partly on the kind of highly accurate neuropredictive techniques that might be refined in the future. This could involve, for instance, measuring neural activity in his ACC while he performs an impulse-control task, like the experiment conducted by Aharoni et al.,[43] mentioned in the first section, but perhaps with an even higher probability of a true positive—say, 90% rather than the current <75% accuracy. Furthermore, he undergoes additional neuroscientific evaluations to determine his potential receptiveness to different methods of criminal rehabilitation. The risk assessors predict a 90% probability that Bertie would commit a similar offence if he were not detained and rehabilitated. They further predict that he will be resistant to rehabilitation (due to possessing neurological characteristics associated with psychopathic traits) and conclude that he will likely pose a risk of committing similar offences for at least the next 10 years. They cannot now be confident that even in 10 years he will be safe enough to be released. Would the judge be justified in imposing a minimum sentence of 10 years? Would the judge be justified in making Bertie's release after that minimum period conditional on a neuroscientific evaluation that declares him safe to be released?

Retributivists would reject both proposals. Instead, they would insist that the sentence should not exceed whatever fixed period would inflict the proportionate suffering he deserved for his original crime. We respond that retributivism cannot, by itself, rule out non-punitive preventive detention. According to retributivism, the guilty should not be punished. However, retributivism per se would not rule out releasing Bertie from prison, only for him to be transferred to a non-punitive preventive detention facility. In reply, retributivists might claim that free-will-based considerations weigh against Bertie's continued preventive detention (though we might wonder if such concerns could be outweighed). According to the free-will-based objection, if Bertie possesses free will, he could always choose to obey the law once released, whatever the neuroscientists predict, and our duty to respect his capacity for free choice entails that, once his retributively deserved prison term has expired, we should not preempt his future choices by continuing to detain

43 E. Aharoni et al. (n12).

him. Libertarian retributivists would insist that, however good the technology becomes, we could never be 100% sure that someone would reoffend, because such certainty would require determinism to be true, which libertarians deny. Compatibilist retributivists are committed to the view that, even if the neuro-predictive evaluation could make us 100% certain that Bertie will reoffend, he would retain the capacity for free choice/control.[44]

The libertarian version of this free-will-based objection to indefinite preventive detention might seem, in some ways, intuitively more plausible than the compatibilist version. The libertarian asks us to respect this spark of libertarian free will, this magical something unique in the universe, making Bertie so free that even God could not tell for sure what he will do. We should stand back, hoping Bertie makes the right choice, and showing respect for the value of his libertarian free will—as this kind of free will means that he actually might make the right choice, and making the right choice by exercising one's free will is intrinsically valuable. Now, for the reasons sketched earlier, there are empirical and conceptual reasons to doubt the existence of libertarian free will. But if, for the sake of the argument, we can suspend our disbelief in libertarian free will, then refraining from preemptive intervention out of respect for this kind of free will (sort of) makes sense. Or at least it (sort of) makes sense to say that this kind of free will could have some intrinsic value (although one would then ask whether its value might be outweighed by the value of protecting the potential victim). However, for the compatibilist, even if we are certain that factors beyond his control, such as neurological characteristics, will 100% guarantee that Bertie will choose to harm someone seriously, this would not undermine his compatibilist freedom. Intuitively, we might wonder why respect for Bertie's 'free will' would compel us to stand back in that situation and watch the inevitable unfolding. What exactly does our standing back show respect for? Despite its inevitability, the compatibilist insists that Bertie's wrongful action can be seen as an exercise of 'free will.' We disagree. But even if the compatibilist were right about this, it is hard to see why respect for his freely chosen immoral action should compel us to stand back (at the victim's expense). That could only make sense if freely committing a serious wrong were intrinsically morally valuable. However, that proposition is highly controversial.[45] Alternatively, are we meant to have such respect for the idea that there is some possible world in which Bertie refrained from harming his victim, that we should stand back in the actual world, even if we are 100% certain that Bertie will harm the victim in the actual world? This strikes us

44 S. Smilansky, 'Determinism and Prepunishment: The Radical Nature of Compatibilism' (2007) 67(4) *Analysis* 347.

45 M. Hauskeller, 'Is It Desirable to Be Able to Do the Undesirable? Moral Bioenhancement and the Little Alex Problem' (2017) 26(3) *Cambridge Quarterly of Healthcare Ethics* 365; J. Danaher, 'Moral Enhancement and Moral Freedom: A Critique of the Little Alex Problem' (2018) 83 *Royal Institute of Philosophy Supplements* 233.

as counterintuitive, and hardly a weighty consideration compared to the real harm to the victim.

Ultimately, we agree with many retributivists in rejecting indefinite detention, and we also reject the idea of lengthy minimum terms based largely/solely on neuroprediction. However, our objection to these practices does not depend on metaphysical free will. Our objection to indefinite detention is based on epistemic considerations and the value of liberty—in the sense of individuals acting by their own preferences without external compulsion. Liberty is valuable and worthy of respect, provided one's exercise of liberty does not violate others' fundamental rights. In the real world, the factors (deterministic or otherwise) that lead people to commit crimes are so numerous and complex that we will never be 100% certain that an individual will commit a serious crime unless they remain in detention. Even if neurotechnology advanced so much that we could be 90% certain, as Scenario A ambitiously stipulates, we would oppose indefinitely detaining Bertie based on this prediction. We maintain that a person's exercise of liberty (in non-rights-violating ways) is so valuable that a 10% epistemic possibility that he will exercise his liberty in this way should weigh heavily in the balance. Imagine that crime's social and neurological determinants are like individual dials in a vast combination lock. Even if 19 out of, say, 20 dials are in place, the lock will not open until the last dial (e.g., neurological trigger) is put in place. Of course, in real life, the number of variables responsible for violent behaviour is much greater. Because we are in a poor epistemic position to judge when (if ever) certain factors will trigger a violent episode, and because this will likely remain true for the foreseeable future, we should strongly safeguard individual liberty, especially with regard to risk assessed by brain scans or other statistical risk factors. When taken together with the following additional considerations, we think the scales tip firmly against indefinite detention.

There are at least three further non-retributive reasons to reject indefinite detention: mental cruelty, state inefficiency, and inequality of power between the state and citizens.[46] First, locking someone up with no clear endpoint in view arguably infringes a 'human right to hope' and is deeply demoralising even if offenders know they will be released sometime before they die.[47] Second, widespread use of indefinite detention would allow state inefficiency to go unchecked as the authorities would lack motivation to research and implement increasingly effective rehabilitation programmes if they may take as long as they please to rehabilitate people. Third, the power to routinely employ indefinite detention—leaving people to languish for as long as their

46 See E. Shaw, *Moral Uncertainty and Punishment: Seeking Convergence on Criminal Justice* (Cambridge University Press, New York, forthcoming).

47 S. Trotter, 'Hope's Relations: A Theory of the "Right to Hope" in European Human Rights Law' (2009) 22(2) *Human Rights Law Review* 1.

'jailors' see fit or until they 'die'—would vastly increase the inequality of power between citizens and the state.[48] For all these reasons, we oppose indefinite detention based on neuroprediction or other risk-predictive techniques in all real-world scenarios.

We further propose that social protection theorists should endorse a system of statutory determinate maximum sentences for each specific offence. The maximum sentence provides the state with a limited rehabilitation opportunity (LRO). This novel concept involves giving the state a time-limited chance to enable the offender to desist from crime via the most effective (and ethically acceptable) rehabilitation programmes.[49] The time-limited nature of LROs should incentivise the state to improve rehabilitation methods, to achieve results within the time frame. The LRO period should be based on the harmfulness of the offence and on evidence concerning the maximum period typically required to rehabilitate offenders who have committed that type of crime. A non-retributive proportionality principle should constrain the statutory maximum. The sentence should be proportionate to the impact that the harm to be prevented by the intervention would have on any particular victim.[50] So, a greater intervention, such as lengthy confinement, would be justified to prevent killing or a serious violent or sexual attack. In contrast, a much more minor intervention, such as counselling or supervision in the community, would be justified to avoid nuisances. This conception of proportionality rejects an aggregative approach (which could endorse lengthy sentences for minor nuisances if the number of victims inconvenienced was great enough). Non-aggregative proportionality is based on respect for the separateness of persons and an ideal of equality: it is *prima facie* wrong to create a situation where people suffer grossly unequal levels of distress.

Thus, while we agree with many retributivists in opposing indefinite detention (e.g., with the detainee's release conditional on neuropredictive findings), we reach that conclusion for non-retributive reasons. Furthermore, while our reasoning may sometimes invoke considerations about the consequences of different policies, our approach is not consequentialist. All of the considerations we invoked in this section must be understood within the rights-based framework informed by the DDA and involves a strong presumption against the active infliction of harm or infringement of fundamental rights by the state.

As well as opposing indefinite detention, we also oppose basing minimum terms on neuroprediction because we oppose fixed minimum terms generally for reasons explained in the next section.

48 M. Corrado, 'The Limits of the State's Power to Control Crime' (2021) 46(2) *Journal of Legal Philosophy* 126, 127.

49 Shaw (n 46) chapter 6.

50 Shaw (n 41); Caruso (n 18).

Scenario B: Using Neuroscientific Evidence for Early Release

We will now discuss how our approach would deal with a potentially controversial example of neuroprediction and early release and compare our recommendations with competing theories. Imagine that Carl has been convicted of robbery, after entering a store with other gang members and threatening the shopworker with an unloaded firearm. The shopworker handed over a substantial sum of money and was left very shaken. Carl has a history of low-level crime and delinquency during his adolescence and early twenties. However, he has recently started a family, and there is evidence that his enthusiasm about his criminal lifestyle has waned with age. He had participated in the robbery reluctantly, due to financial difficulties supporting his family. Before being apprehended, he had just acquired a new job and planned to leave the gang.

Imagine that accurate neuropredictive tools of the kind discussed previously have been developed. Imagine that if Carl participated in rehabilitation and training to succeed at a lawful occupation and underwent periodic neuro-evaluations while in detention, there is a strong possibility that after a relatively short time, he would be deemed safe to be transferred to a lower-security facility and ultimately released early. Should such periodic evaluations be undertaken and acted upon?

How would our social protection approach differ from current practice and alternative theories? In jurisdictions that impose mandatory minimum sentences for robbery, current practice would preclude releasing Carl before the expiration of the minimum sentence. Similarly, retributivists may object to releasing him before he has completed whatever sentence is 'deserved'. It's unclear exactly what a proportional punishment for armed robbery would be on the retributive theory. Currently, in the U.S., the sentence can vary depending on the state and circumstances of the crime. In many states, however, that sentence can be life in prison. First-degree robbery in Alabama, for instance, can result in a sentence of life or 10–99 years in prison. If a firearm was used, the sentence can be life or 20–99 years in prison. In other states, the sentence typically falls between 5 years and life, and the average sentence for robbery in the United States is nearly 10 years in prison.[51]

We reject the current approach, which is influenced by the retributive demand that the judge somehow finds the 'deserved' sentence despite dramatic disagreements about what desert entails. Instead, we contend that the maximum sentence should align with the non-retributive proportionality principle and with the idea of a 'limited rehabilitation opportunity.' Based on such considerations, the judge may determine that no more than 3 years is required. Our rejection of minimum sentences would allow for periodic evaluations to see if the individual can be released early or transferred to a lower security

51 https://www.ussc.gov/sites/default/files/pdf/research-and-publications/quick-facts/Robbery_FY15.pdf

regime—something we will argue is an advantage compared to retributivism. Imagine that after eight months, Carl undergoes a neuropredictive test that suggests that his risk is low and he is eligible to be transferred to a lower security facility. His 12-month evaluation suggests his risk level has dropped still further, and he is safe to be released. In such a situation, we would advocate releasing Carl early, since the right of self-defence and prevention of harm to others no longer justifies the state in restricting his liberty. However, we would also emphasise the importance of taking measures to support the victim, such as financial compensation and psychological support, and offering the possibility to engage in restorative justice measures that might promote healing and reconciliation. Restorative justice offers several key benefits that distinguish it from traditional punitive approaches to justice—including healing for victims, reduced recidivism, community involvement, empowerment for both victims and offenders, and a focus on rehabilitation over punitive measures. Free will sceptics can ground such restorative processes in forward-looking, non-desert-invoking desiderate such as safety, reconciliation, moral formation, and the recovery and restoration of victims.[52]

Furthermore, the resources that would, on a retributive approach, have been spent on detaining Carl beyond the period necessary for social protection would, on our approach, be diverted towards more effective, evidence-based ways of preventing future victimisation. A recent study by the RAND Corporation found, for instance, that prison education programs decrease recidivism rates by 43%, and for every dollar spent on prison education, taxpayers save between $4 and $5 U.S. dollars in the costs of re-incarceration.[53] Research also reveals that criminal behaviour is primarily driven by social determinants, such as poverty and low socioeconomic status, abuse and domestic violence, housing insecurity, mental illness, environmental health, nutrition, and lack of consistent access to healthcare.[54] By adopting a public health approach to criminal behaviour focused on prevention and social justice, a large portion of the money that would otherwise be spent on incarceration, which in the United States is between $80 billion and $1 trillion annually, would be redirected toward identifying, prioritizing, and addressing these social determinants.

Retributivists like Michael Moore might insist that Carl should serve his full sentence under conditions that are harsh enough to make him experience the suffering he deserves. One may wonder, though, which view better respects human dignity? We contend that our approach is more humane to offenders and helps victims in more practical, tangible ways than retributivism offers,

52 See G. D. Caruso, D. Pereboom, *Moral Responsibility Reconsidered* (Cambridge University Press, New York, 2022); Caruso (n 18).

53 Education and Vocational Training in Prisons Reduces Recidivism, Improves Job Outlook, Rand Corporation, August 22, 2013, <https://www.bja.gov/Publications/RAND_Correctional-Education-Meta-Analysis.pdf>.

54 Caruso (n 30); Caruso (n 18).

and it is the most defensible option given extant doubts about the existence of free will and basic desert moral responsibility.

We suggest that social protection theories have several distinct advantages over retributive theories. First, the use of neuroprediction has the potential to lead to less restrictive prison regimes for prisoners who are deemed less dangerous, even if their risk is not low enough to warrant early release. Strict retributivists, on the other hand, care little about rehabilitation and assessments of risk, since they hold that punishment should be distributed by desert. Hence, they are less likely to use neuroprediction to reduce restrictions on offenders that are assessed to be less dangerous. For the retributivist, if the person's original crime was quite severe, the prison conditions should not ease up just because neuropredictive technologies showed that their dangerousness has decreased over time. Retributivists would also oppose using limited rehabilitation opportunities to determine maximum sentences since determinations of non-dangerousness might result in lighter sentences than retributivists see as 'deserved.' Furthermore, retributivists who favour lengthy minimum sentences short of life prevent successfully rehabilitated offenders from contributing positively to society and greatly diminish the physical/mental/social well-being of the innocent children of these offenders, all at significant financial cost to society—finances that could have been directed toward vastly more effective ways of preventing people from being victimised.

Conclusion

Rapidly mounting research into neurotechnological criminal risk prediction promises more effective ways of preventing crime. However, there is a danger that states will misuse such technologies to provide a rationale for preemptive, indefinite, or excessively lengthy detention. Retributivists frequently claim to be in a better position than social protection theories to resist such misuses of state power. We have indicated how social protection theories can respond to this challenge without embracing either retributivism (or consequentialism). When applied to the emerging topic of neuroprediction, the core principles of the public health-quarantine model and the novel concept of the LRO[55] provide the conceptual resources to safeguard the interests and dignity of both victims and offenders. We have also argued that retributive grounds for opposing indefinite detention are shakier than retributivists typically assume.

Furthermore, unlike retributivism, we maintain that if someone is shown to be safe to be released, they should be released without serving a minimum term. Contra critics, then, social protection theories providwe more protections and opportunities for offenders to be released than does retributivism. Neuroscience does not just pose a threat to individual liberty. It can be a tool for safeguarding liberty. If new neuroscientific techniques enable successfully

55 Shaw (n 46).

rehabilitated offenders to be identified more reliably, this can provide grounds for releasing them early, allowing them to contribute positively to society, allowing their children to be better safeguarded, and allowing resources to be diverted towards more effective ways of preventing victimisation—potentially saving lives. In contrast, the current practice of mandatory minimums and the varieties of retributivism that support such practices will miss the opportunity to take advantage of liberty-enhancing neurotechnologies.

We have attempted to demonstrate how penal theory and debates about free will have the potential to inform how criminal justice policymakers deal with new neurotechnologies. Conversely, we believe that consideration of neuro-prediction has the potential to inform penal theory and the free will debate. For instance, critiques of compatibilism frequently focus on whether compatibilist responsibility judgments are counterintuitive. Still, we suggest that consideration of compatibilist objections to neuropredictive preemptive detention can also reveal that compatibilism has further counterintuitive implications.[56]

56 Cf Smilansky (n 44).

6 The Relevance of Trauma as a 'Mental Disorder or Abnormality' in Sentencing

An Australian Case Study

Katherine J. McLachlan

Introduction

Drawing from Australian case law and sentencing remarks, this chapter examines how neurophysiological and psychological trauma can impact the sentencing of defendants. Trauma may influence sentencing purposes, principles, factors, and non-legal considerations.[1] To examine how sentencing judges consider trauma in their decision-making, the concept of trauma is first explained. The chapter then explores how sentencing courts respond to neuroscientific evidence, particularly relating to neurophysiological and psychological trauma. Where courts consider trauma, in the minority of cases, a defendant may be found not guilty by reason of mental impairment. More often, people with neurophysiological and/or psychological trauma are found criminally responsible. In these cases, the potential relevance of trauma in the sentencing calculus will be explained by applying the seminal decision of *R v. Verdins*, in which the Victorian Court of Criminal Appeal determined that 'mental disorders or abnormalities' may be relevant in sentencing in six distinct ways. Overall, this chapter demonstrates how these principles may be applied to and benefit the sentencing of defendants with neurophysiological and psychological trauma. Considering the neuroscientific trauma evidence during sentencing can help reduce moral culpability and the relevance of deterrence, and inform effective sanctions. The issues raised in this chapter are of interest to jurisdictions such as Canada, the United States (U.S.), the United Kingdom (U.K.), and Aotearoa New Zealand, given the parallels in the sentencing calculus across countries with a Westminster system of law.

Manifestations of Trauma: Neurophysiological and Psychological Trauma

Trauma is 'a biopsychosocial response,'[2] specifically resulting:

1 McLachlan (n 1) 173–179.
2 P. Willmot, L. Jones (eds), *Trauma-Informed Forensic Practice* (1st ed., Routledge, 2022) 3.

DOI: 10.4324/9781003510246-7

> from an event, series of events, or set of circumstances that is experienced by an individual as physically or emotionally harmful or life threatening and that has lasting adverse effects on the individual's functioning and mental, physical, social, emotional, or spiritual well-being.[3]

Trauma is the product of adversity (i.e., overwhelming events or experiences that may be acute or chronic and involve actual or threatened harm or risk to life).[4] Complex trauma refers to 'the cumulative or compounded impact of multiple or prolonged traumatic stressors, leading to "underlying" dysfunction across a person's life.'[5] Complex trauma may be the product of adversity in adulthood (e.g., combat, chronic domestic abuse from an intimate partner) or adverse childhood experiences (ACEs), including childhood maltreatment (i.e., child abuse and neglect) and household dysfunction (e.g., household mental illness, substance abuse, parental absence, domestic abuse). The negative impact of chronic ACEs—developmental trauma—increases the prevalence of both affective and anxiety disorders across the life course, more so than adulthood-onset trauma. However, adversity in adulthood can also significantly impact an individual's functioning and well-being, often exacerbating developmental trauma.[6] Thus, this chapter discusses how psychological and neurophysiological trauma may affect the sentencing calculus for defendants with extensive adverse experiences.

Trauma can impact a person's functioning and well-being across various human domains, including psychological, emotional, neurophysiological, physical, and social. This chapter considers explicitly neurophysiological and psychological trauma evidence in sentencing. Neurophysiological trauma occurs when adverse events change the physical structure of a person's brain.[7] This is most likely to occur during key childhood development and growth periods,[8] with ACEs impacting the neurosequential development of the

3 Substance Abuse and Mental Health Services Administration, *SAMHSA'S Concept of Trauma and Guidance for a Trauma-Informed Approach* (U.S. Department of Health and Human Services, 2014) 7.

4 American Psychiatric Association, *Diagnostic and Statistical Manual of Mental Disorders* (American Psychiatric Association, 5th ed., text rev, 2022) F43.10(A); B. A. van der Kolk, 'The Psychological Consequences of Overwhelming Life Experiences' in B. A. van der Kolk (ed), *Psychological Trauma* (American Psychiatric Press, 1987) 1.

5 McLachlan (n 1) 18.

6 D. A. Chu et al., 'Early Life Trauma Predicts Self-Reported Levels of Depressive and Anxiety Symptoms in Nonclinical Community Adults: Relative Contributions of Early Life Stressor Types and Adult Trauma Exposure' (2013) 47 *Journal of Psychiatric Research* 23.

7 H. Peckham, 'Introducing the Neuroplastic Narrative: A Non-Pathologizing Biological Foundation for Trauma-Informed and Adverse Childhood Experience Aware Approaches' (2023) 14 *Frontiers in Psychiatry* 1.

8 M. H. Teicher et al., 'The Neurobiological Consequences of Early Stress and Childhood Maltreatment' (2003) 27 *Neuroscience and Biobehavioral Reviews* 33.

brain.[9] The human brain develops in a specific order: first, the brain stem develops before birth and in the first eight months of life, to regulate heart rate and breathing; second, the limbic system develops, controlling emotions and memories, with notable changes occurring from 10 to 13 years and continuing into early adulthood; and finally, the cerebral cortex continues to grow until the age of 25 years, which enables rational thinking and problem-solving.[10] As children enter adolescence and early adulthood, there is an increase in white matter (i.e., connecting axons or nerve fibres) and a decrease in grey matter (i.e., the neocortex and subcortical nuclei), resulting in improved brain functioning and connectivity, particularly in the prefrontal cortex.[11] During this time, decision-making shifts from being driven by the emotion-based amygdala, a part of the limbic system, to the prefrontal cortex, which enables more rational and evaluated decision-making, improved deductive reasoning, enhanced information processing, and better short- and long-term memory.[12] There are strong indications that developmental trauma can lead to structural abnormalities in the limbic system (i.e., prefrontal cortex, hippocampus, and amygdala), affecting an individual's ability to regulate stress, think rationally, and control impulses and emotions.[13] Thus, developmental trauma can have a significant impact on an individual's functioning and well-being, as well as the trajectory into offending.[14]

Neurophysiological trauma is not just developmental; it may occur at any time across the lifecycle via neuroplastic mechanisms and is not limited to adolescence. Neuroplasticity:

> refers to the capacity of neural systems to adapt and change in response to experience and injury. . . . [It] is greatest during development, but neuroplasticity is a property of living neural systems, a dynamic process that continues throughout life into aging.[15]

9 B. D. Perry, 'Examining Child Maltreatment through a Neurodevelopmental Lens: Clinical Applications of the Neurosequential Model of Therapeutics' (2009) 14 *Journal of Loss and Trauma* 240.

10 For a detailed understanding of adolescent brain development, see A. Galvan, *The Neuroscience of Adolescence* (Cambridge University Press, 2017).

11 C. Walsh, 'Youth Justice and Neuroscience: A Dual-Use Dilemma' (2011) 51(1) *The British Journal of Criminology* 21, 22.

12 P. Kambam et al., 'The Development of Decision-Making Capacities in Children and Adolescents: Psychological and Neurological Perspectives and Their Implications for Juvenile Defendants' (2009) 27(2) *Behavioral Sciences and the Law* 173.

13 C. Paquola, M. R. Bennett, J. Lagopoulos, 'Understanding Heterogeneity in Grey Matter Research of Adults with Childhood Maltreatment—A Meta-Analysis and Review' (2016) 69 *Neuroscience & Biobehavioral Reviews* 299.

14 C. G. Malvaso et al., 'Associations Between Adverse Childhood Experiences and Trauma Among Young People Who Offend: A Systematic Literature Review' (2022) 23(5) *Trauma, Violence & Abuse* 1677.

15 Peckham (n 8) 21.

Further, neurophysiological trauma may influence psychological trauma. Psychological trauma is a common outcome of exposure to adversity[16] and is understood to be 'an emotional state of discomfort and stress resulting from memories of an extraordinary catastrophic experience which shattered the survivor's sense of invulnerability to harm.'[17] Psychological trauma per se is not a recognised neurological condition or mental health diagnosis. Indeed, trauma is not found in the APA's *Diagnostic and Statistical Manual of Mental Disorders* (DSM-5) or the World Health Organisation's *International Classification of Diseases* (ICD-11).[18] However, there are several recognised mental health diagnoses associated with neurophysiological and psychological trauma, with the experience of an adverse event a diagnostic criterion. The most obvious of these are post-traumatic stress disorder (PTSD) and complex PTSD (CPTSD in the ICD-11). PTSD is a syndrome that lasts for several weeks or more in response to an adverse event or experience that is life-threatening or horrific, such as sexual violence, assault, war and combat, or disasters.[19] PTSD symptoms or manifestations include flashbacks and nightmares, avoidant behaviour, hypervigilance, and overwhelming emotions.[20] PTSD is not the same as CPTSD, as the former is more often in response to an acute stressor or one-off event. As explained by Cloitre:

> An individual can be diagnosed with either PTSD or CPTSD but not both. . . . [I]ndividuals who experienced chronic, repeated and prolonged traumas, such as childhood sexual abuse or domestic violence, tended to experience more complex reactions extending beyond those typically observed in PTSD and which included effects in three key domains: emotion regulation, self-identity and relational capacities.[21]

The diagnosis of CPTSD was excluded from the DSM because 'it does not fit neatly under the category of anxiety disorders. It might fit equally well under dissociative disorders, or somatization disorders, or even personality disorders.'[22] This highlights a core problem with the DSM[23] and diagnostic

16 M. Cloitre et al., 'A Developmental Approach to Complex PTSD: Childhood and Adult Cumulative Trauma as Predictors of Symptom Complexity' (2009) 22 *Journal of Traumatic Stress* 399.

17 C. R. Figley, 'Introduction' in Charles R Figley (ed), *Trauma and Its Wake: The Study and Treatment of Post-Traumatic Stress Disorder* (Brunner/Mazel, 1985) xvii, xviii.

18 World Health Organization, *International Classification of Diseases* (World Health Organization, 2024) 6B40.

19 World Health Organization, *Clinical Descriptions and Diagnostic Requirements for ICD-11 Mental, Behavioural and Neurodevelopmental Disorders* (World Health Organization, 2024) 339.

20 Ibid.

21 M. Cloitre, 'ICD-11 Complex Post-Traumatic Stress Disorder: Simplifying Diagnosis in Trauma Populations' (2020) 216 *The British Journal of Psychiatry* 129.

22 J. L. Herman, 'Foreword' in C. A. Courtois, J. D. Ford (eds), *Treating Complex Traumatic Stress Disorders: Scientific Foundations and Therapeutic Models* (Guilford Press, 2014), xiii.

23 APA (n 5).

labels: specifically, diagnostic labels lack a strong empirical evidence base, and there is a lack of inter-rater reliability,[24] with multiple symptomatic pathways resulting in the same diagnosis.[25] For these and other reasons, there have been criticisms of the validity and usefulness of diagnostic labels. Indeed, there is growing support to de-medicalise post-traumatic stress,[26] including the Clinical Branch of the British Psychological Society.[27] Practitioners relying on DSM diagnoses may identify what might otherwise be CPTSD, but (in the absence of the DSM recognising CPTSD), they may use other labels to diagnose individuals. Similarly, psychological trauma may also be associated with multiple diagnoses, including those relating to psychosis, such as schizophrenia and drug-induced psychosis; dissociation, anxiety, and depression; personality disorders (including borderline personality disorder); and bipolar disorder.[28]

There is also a crossover between diagnostic labels associated with neurophysiological trauma (i.e., associated with visible changes to brain structure) and symptoms or manifestations of psychological trauma (i.e., associated with changes to mood and behaviour), including dysfunctional coping and protective mechanisms, hypervigilance, and difficulty regulating emotions.[29] Studies have found that people diagnosed with PTSD have decreased activity in the medial prefrontal cortex and increased activity in the amygdala and hippocampus.[30] Changes associated with PTSD have also been found in the grey matter volume of the dorsal anterior cingulate cortex (involved in cognitive processing),[31] the prefrontal cortex (involved in higher cognitive functioning and emotional regulation), and the hippocampus.[32] Changes in the volume and functioning in areas of the brain associated with emotional regulation and problem-solving may result in neurophysiological trauma characterised by impulsive, unpredictable, or aggressive behaviours.[33] Although defendants with trauma commit a range of offences, research has found that crime victims who perpetrate offences are statistically more likely to commit an interpersonal offence, i.e., 'homicide (murder), other homicide, sexual offences, robbery, assault and other offences against the person' than people who were identified

24 B. van der Kolk with L. M. Najavits, 'Interview: What is PTSD Really? Surprises, Twists of History, and the Politics of Diagnosis and Treatment' (2013) 69(5) *Journal of Clinical Psychology: In Session* 516 at 516.

25 G. Young, C. Lareau, B. Pierre, 'One Quintillion Ways to Have PTSD Comorbidity: Recommendations for the Disordered DSM-5' (2014) 7(1) *Psychological Injury and Law* 61.

26 R. Tyson Smith, O. Whooley, 'Dropping the Disorder in PTSD' (2015) 14(4) *Contexts* 38.

27 See L. Johnstone et al., *The Power Threat Meaning Framework: Towards the Identification of Patterns in Emotional Distress, Unusual Experiences and Troubled or Troubling Behaviour, as an Alternative to Functional Psychiatric Diagnosis* (British Psychological Society, 2018).

28 McLachlan (n 1) 22.

29 C. Kezelman, P. Stavropoulos, *Practice Guidelines for Clinical Treatment of Complex Trauma* (Blue Knot Foundation, 2019) 81.

30 S. Boukezzi et al., 'Grey Matter Density Changes of Structures Involved in Posttraumatic Stress Disorder (PTSD) After Recovery Following Eye Movement Desensitization and Reprocessing (EMDR) Therapy' (2017) 266 *Psychiatry Research: Neuroimaging* 146.

31 M. A. Rinne-Albers et al., 'Anterior Cingulate Cortex Grey Matter Volume Abnormalities in Adolescents with PTSD after Childhood Sexual Abuse' (2017) 27 *European Neuropsychopharmacology* 1163.

32 Boukezzi et al. (n 31).

33 Rinne-Albers et al. (n 32).

as offenders only.[34] Thus, the offending behaviours of people with a history of adversity may be associated with psychological trauma and/or neurophysiological changes to the structure and function of the brain.

Mental Disorders and Criminal Law

The law has developed its own terminology for mental health issues. In Australia and the U.K., the concept is broad. For example, in Australia, *mental impairment* includes 'senility, intellectual disability, mental illness, brain damage and severe personality disorder,'[35] with mental illness referred to as 'underlying pathological infirmity of the mind.'[36] In South Australia, the legal concept of *cognitive impairment* includes developmental disabilities, acquired disabilities, and mental illness.[37] Similarly, U.K. and Canadian legislation refers to *mental disorders* as 'any disorder or disability of the mind' and 'disease of the mind' respectively,[38] with recent U.K. legislative amendments defining mental disorders as more than mental illness, to include personality disorders.[39] Conversely, the U.S. takes a more limited view, with legislation referring to *mental illness* as 'a diagnosable mental, behavioural, or emotional disorder . . . to meet diagnostic criteria within the . . . [DSM, and] that has resulted in functional impairment that substantially interferes with or limits 1 or more major life activities.'[40] The New Zealand Law Commission has identified the 'gulf' between the legal understanding of mental disorders and 'psychiatric concepts and practices.'[41] Thus, in all jurisdictions, the law accepts clinical mental health diagnoses, but Australia also considers intellectual disabilities, brain injuries, and personality disorders.

A defendant is presumed by law to be sane and accountable for their actions unless they can successfully raise a defence such as being not guilty by reason of mental impairment or, in some jurisdictions, the partial defence of diminished responsibility.[42] Jurisdictions such as the U.S., U.K., Canada, Aotearoa New Zealand, and Australia all have diversionary sentencing for defendants found not guilty by reason of mental impairment (sometimes referred to as 'the insanity defence'). These defences, which result in defendants being managed within secure health facilities rather than corrective services, are rarely used (see Table 6.1).[43]

34 Queensland Government Statistician's Office, *The Overlap between Offending and Victimisation in Queensland: Crime Research Report* (Queensland Treasury, 2023) 5.

35 *Criminal Code Act 1995* (Cth) s. 7.3(8).

36 Ibid. s. 7.3(9).

37 *Sentencing Act 2017* (SA), ss 5, 11(1)(f).

38 U.K.'s Mental Health Act 2007 s 1(2) and *Criminal Code, RSC 1985, c. C-46, s. 2.*

39 U.K.'s Mental Health Act 2007 s 1(2); see also *Mental Health Act 2007 Explanatory Notes* Section 1: Removal of Categories of Mental Disorder. This definition applies to the U.K.'s Sentencing Act 2020 s 232.

40 34 U.S. Code § 10472.

41 Law Commission, *Mental Impairment Decision-Making and the Insanity Defence NZLC R120* (New Zealand Law Commission, 2010) 5.

42 Diminished responsibility is a partial defence available in the U.K., the U.S. (as diminished capacity), and only some Australian jurisdictions. It is not formally available in Canada, Aotearoa New Zealand and is not explicitly discussed here.

43 Regarding Canada, see J. Latimer, A. Lawrence, *The Review Board Systems in Canada: An Overview of Results from the Mentally Disordered Accused Data Collection Study* (Government of Canada, 2006).

Table 6.1 Not Guilty by Reason of Mental Impairment Legislation and Use

Jurisdiction	*Known As*	*Legislative Authority*	*Frequency of Use*
Australia	Not guilty by reason of mental impairment/ illness; unfit to plead	e.g., *Criminal Code Act 1995* (Cth), s 7.3 *Criminal Code 2002* (ACT), ss 28, 29 *Mental Health and Cognitive Impairment Forensic Provisions Act 2020* (NSW) *Criminal Code Act 1983* (NT), s 43C *Criminal Code 1899* (Qld), s 27 *Criminal Law Consolidation Act 1935* (SA), s 269C *Criminal Code Act 1984* (Tas), ss. 15–16 *Crimes (Mental Impairment and Fitness to be Tried) Act 1997* (Vic), s 20 *Criminal Law (Mental Impairment) Act 2023* (WA)	Unknown but uncommon[44]
Canada	Not criminally responsible on account of mental disorder (NCRMD)	Criminal Code (RSC, 1985, c. C-46)	Less than 1% of adult criminal court cases processed annually[45]
Aotearoa New Zealand	The insanity defence	*Crimes Act 1961* and *the Criminal Procedure (Mentally Impaired Persons) Act 2003*	Run fewer than 50 times a year, rarely successfully[46] In 2020, 190 people were found 'unfit to stand trial' and 49 people were found 'not guilty by reason of insanity'—the highest number of annual insanity acquittals on record.[47]

44 A. Loughman, 'How the Insanity Defence against a Murder Charge Works', *The Conversation* (2015) <https://theconversation.com/how-the-insanity-defence-against-a-murder-charge-works-50188> accessed 29 March 2025.

45 Z. Miladinovic, J. Lukassen, 'Verdicts of Not Criminally Responsible on Account of Mental Disorder in Adult Criminal Courts, 2005/2006-2011/2012', *Juristat Bulletin* (Statistics Canada, 2014).

46 R. Tapsell, 'Forensic Psychiatry and the Law: A Judicial Update' (*Wellington*, Monday 7 November 2005), cited in Law Commission, *Mental Impairment Decision-Making and the Insanity Defence NZLC R120* (New Zealand Law Commission, 2010).

47 J. Skipworth, W. Brookbanks, 'New Justice System Responses to Mentally Impaired Defendants in New Zealand' (2022) 29(4) *Psychiatry, Psychology and Law* 549.

Table 6.1 (Continued)

Jurisdiction	*Known As*	*Legislative Authority*	*Frequency of Use*
United Kingdom	Not guilty by reason of insanity ("M'Naghten Rules")	*Criminal Procedure (Insanity) Act 1964*	Annually, approximately 100 people found unfit to plead and less than 25 found not guilty by reason of insanity.[48]
United States	The insanity defense Not guilty as a result of mental disease or defect In some states, Guilty but Insane	American Legal Institute Model Penal Code §4.01 The Comprehensive Crime Control Act (18 US Code § 17) The Durham Rule	Reportedly raised in about one percent of cases, but successful in about 30 cases a year.[49]

Beyond legal insanity, many more defendants have mental health issues and are found to have the capacity to plead or be found guilty. International research consistently finds high rates of serious mental illness in prison populations worldwide, with elevated levels of psychosis (3.6% of men and 3.9% of women) and major depression (10.2% of men and 14.1% of women).[50] In Australia, findings from the National Prisoner Health Data Collection found that more than half (51%) of people entering prison reported having been diagnosed with a mental health condition at some point during their lives.[51] Judicial officers often rely on diagnostic labels to understand how a mental disorder influences a defendant's functioning and behaviour and future risk of reoffending. Given that judges put considerable weight on expert reports, these provide opportunities for the courts to recognise the relevance of trauma.[52]

The Sentencing Calculus, Neuroscience, and Trauma

When a defendant has pleaded or been found guilty, a judicial officer will determine an appropriate sanction by applying the sentencing calculus, which

48 A. O'Loughlin, *Mental Disorder, Disability and Sentencing: A Review of Policy, Law and Research.* (Sentencing Academy, 2022).

49 This statistic is often cited, but it is difficult to determine the objective data on which it is based. Most sources refer back to Justia, *The Insanity Defence in Criminal Law Cases* (2025) <https://www.justia.com/criminal/defenses/insanity/> accessed 29 March 2025.

50 S. Fazel, K. Seewald, 'Severe Mental Illness in 33,588 Prisoners Worldwide: Systematic Review and Meta-Regression Analysis' (2012) 200(5) *The British Journal of Psychiatry* 364.

51 See Australian Institute of Health and Welfare, *Health of People in Prison* (AIHW, 2024).

52 See The Magnolia Project and Aboriginal Legal Rights Movement, *A Practice Guide for Preparing Mental Health Pre-Sentence Reports with Aboriginal People in the Criminal Justice System in South Australia* (The Magnolia Project, 2023).

involves calculating relevant sentencing purposes, principles, factors, and non-legal considerations.[53] Unlike the U.S. use of guidelines and formulas,[54] the U.K.'s guidelines and staged process of decision-making,[55] and Aotearoa New Zealand's staged process[56] to promote consistency and predictability in sentencing, Australian sentencing decisions balance the relevant elements on a case-by-case basis.[57] This 'instinctive synthesis' process is unstructured and individualised.[58] Judicial officers then present and publish factors and purposes on which they relied in reaching their decision in their sentencing remarks. Sentencing remarks 'summarise the information upon which the judicial officer has relied in making their decision (e.g., context of the offending behaviour, background information of the person who has offended and the victim, sentencing purposes, principles, and factors).'[59]

In Australia, sentencing aims to achieve several purposes: community safety, punishment and accountability, denunciation, harm recognition, general deterrence, specific deterrence, and rehabilitation. A single decision need not achieve all these purposes. To promote desistance from crime, defendants with mental health issues or trauma might receive intensive community-based sanctions that include conditions designed to promote community safety through risk management and mitigation strategies and desistance-based strategies that assist in reintegrating individuals. For example, for a traumatised defendant, an effective sanction might be an extended period of intensive community-based supervision, treatment, and intervention requirements, and stepped-down freedom-of-movement restrictions. The defendant would need to commit to engaging in intensive and long-term counselling. 'Indeed, surveys of offenders reveal that they are more likely to dread intensive and lengthy community-based punishments than shorter prison terms,'[60] with such sanctions representing rehabilitation and personal deterrence.

The four key sentencing principles are (1) parity (i.e., people who offend who are similarly situated are treated similarly); (2) totality (i.e., where people are being sentenced for more than one offence, the total sentence is just and appropriate regarding the offending behaviour); (3) parsimony (i.e., that a sanction of imprisonment is imposed as a last resort); and (4)

53 McLachlan (n 1) 172.

54 W. W. Schwarzer, 'Judicial Discretion in Sentencing' (1991) *Federal Sentencing Reporter* 399.

55 Sentencing Council (U.K.), *Imposition of Community and Custodial Sentences—Guideline Effective from: 01 April 2025* (2025) <https://www.sentencingcouncil.org.uk/overarching-guides/magistrates-court/item/imposition-of-community-and-custodial-sentences-overarching-guideline/>.

56 V. Kenworthy, 'Predicting Sentencing Decisions of the New Zealand Courts Using Support Vector Machines' (2023) 4 *New Zealand Law Students' Journal* 143.

57 McLachlan (n 1).

58 *Wong v. The Queen* (2001) 207 CLR 584, at 611 [75] per Gaudron, Gummow and Hayne JJ.

59 McLachlan (n 1) 200.

60 F. T. Cullen, C. Lero Jonson, D. S. Nagin, 'Prisons Do Not Reduce Recidivism the High Cost of Ignoring Science' (2011) 91(3, Suppl.) *Prison Journal* 48S, 52S.

proportionality, which dictates that the punishment imposed should be proportionate to the crime committed. A 'proportionate' approach for a defendant with trauma may be based on longer terms of community supervision rather than extensive incarceration, which would also enable cost savings and justice reinvestment, diverting funds from prisons to stable accommodation and evidence-informed, long-term therapeutic interventions. It would have the additional benefit of avoiding the criminogenic and re-traumatising impacts of prison.[61]

In Australia, sentencing factors include issues specific to the defendant and the offending behaviour and may consist of psychological and neurophysiological functioning. Sentencing factors are brought to the court's attention through submissions by the parties, expert reports, presentence reports, and victim impact statements. Where a defendant pleads guilty, a court may seek a presentence report about various issues, including the defendant's 'mental condition.'[62] Additionally, the defendant or their lawyer may seek to present expert evidence to the court, or the prosecution may request expert advice.

Instinctive synthesis requires that '[the sentencer takes] . . . all of the relevant factors and to arrive at a single result which takes due account of them all.'[63] This is a form of evidence-informed sentencing. Evidence-informed sentencing is not the same as the concept of 'evidence-based sentencing' in the U.S., which focuses explicitly on 'identifying offender risk factors, matching risk factors to supervision levels, and providing proven treatment services and programs tailored to an individual offender's specific characteristics, such as cognitive abilities and gender.'[64] In Australia, evidence-informed sentencing is broader, drawing from empirical evidence relating to risk, desistance research, and strengths-based practice.[65] True evidence-informed sentencing requires a shift from legal precedent and the excessive use of incarceration, which has been found to increase recidivism,[66] towards sentencing policy and practice that is driven by empirical evidence. Such an approach reserves imprisonment for the most serious offending, where individuals' risks and needs cannot be managed in the community.[67]

61 McLachlan (n 1).

62 e.g., Sentencing Act 2017 (SA) s. 17.

63 *Wong* (2001) 611 [75] per Gaudron, Gummow and Hayne JJ.

64 National Center for State Courts, *Evidence-Based Sentencing* (2014) 1.

65 T. Ward, S. Maruna, *Rehabilitation: Beyond the Risk Paradigm* (Routledge, 2007) 19. H. Graham, *Rehabilitation Work: Supporting Desistance and Recovery* (Routledge, 2016) 3; H. Blagg et al., *Understanding the Role of Law and Culture in Aboriginal and/or Torres Strait Islander Communities in Responding to and Preventing Family Violence* (ANROWS, 2020) 39.

66 K. Howells et al., *Correctional Offender Rehabilitation Programs: The National Picture in Australia* (Criminology Research Council, 2004) 11.

67 M. Bagaric, N. Fischer, G Wolf, 'Bringing Sentencing into the 21st Century: Closing the Gap Between Practice and Knowledge by Introducing Expertise into Sentencing Law' (2017) 45 *Hofstra Law Review* 785.

Neuroscience and Sentencing

International research focusing on neuroscience's influence on sentencing indicates that neuroscientific evidence may influence sentencing decisions in various ways.[68] The first systematic review of the use of neuroscience in Australian courts, published in 2023, considered which sentencing factors were commonly associated with neuroscience and whether neuroscientific evidence supported a harsher or a more lenient sentence.[69] Neuroscientific evidence includes neuroimaging evidence (such as functional Magnetic Resonance Imaging [fMRI] and Positron Emission Tomography [PET] scans) and the results of diagnostic tests conducted by medical professionals (e.g., neuropsychological assessments).[70] Based on the sentencing of 340 individuals over 40 years, the Australian study found that neuroscientific evidence may be used as an aggravating factor (associated with specific deterrence and community protection), an ambiguous factor (both aggravating and mitigating), but most often a mitigating factor, reducing moral culpability and general deterrence.[71]

Trauma, Crime, and Sentencing

Trauma-based neuroscientific evidence has previously been acknowledged in U.S. sentencing decisions.[72] South Australian research examining sentencing remarks has found that judges explicitly realise adversity in about half of their decisions. Judges sometimes also explicitly identify trauma, most often psychological trauma, using terms such as 'distress,' and relying on evidence from expert reports of psychologists and psychiatrists. Mental health reports may be beneficial in cases where a defendant has impaired mental functioning as a result of trauma to determine how best to promote community safety (e.g., through strategies to facilitate rehabilitation or incapacitation).[73]

The prevalence of adversity and trauma is higher in the lives of adults and children who are known to offend than it is in the general population.[74]

68 C. H. de Kogel, E. J. Westgeest, 'Neuroscientific and Behavioral Genetic Information in Criminal Cases in the Netherlands' (2015) 2(3) *Journal of Law and the Biosciences* 580; D. W. Denno, 'How Courts in Criminal Cases Respond to Childhood Trauma' (2019) 103(2) *Marquette Law Review* 301; A. Perricone, A. Baskin-Sommers, W. Ahn, 'The Effect of Neuroscientific Evidence on Sentencing Depends on How one Conceives of Reasons for Incarceration' (2022) 17(11) *PLoS One* e0276237; Z. Khalid, R. Lee, B. W. Wall, 'The Use of Neurobiological Evidence in Sentencing Mitigation' (2023) 42 *Behavioral Science & the Law* 65.

69 A. Alimardani, 'An Empirical Study of the Use of Neuroscience in Sentencing in New South Wales, Australia' (2023) 14(1228354) *Frontiers in Psychology* 1.

70 Ibid. 2. Dutch research has also recognised neuroscientific evidence 'referring to a certain neurobiological predisposition or damage of the brain', refer de Kogel and Westgeest (n 63) 583.

71 Ibid.

72 Khalid et al. (n 63).

73 McLachlan (n 1).

74 H. Edalati et al., 'Adverse Childhood Experiences and the Risk of Criminal Justice Involvement and Victimization among Homeless Adults with Mental Illness' (2017) 68 *Psychiatric Services* 1288; C. Malvaso et al., *Adverse Childhood Experiences and Trauma among Young People in the Youth Justice System* (Australian Institute of Criminology, 2021) 5–7.

Neurophysiological and psychological trauma may manifest as criminogenic risk factors of antisocial attitudes and behaviour,[75] associated with poor emotional regulation, impulsivity, hypervigilance, and inability to accurately read social cues.[76] These trauma manifestations translate as symptoms of medical diagnoses (e.g., PTSD, CPTSD, personality disorders, mood disorders), as well as substance use disorders, which are often associated with offending.[77] PTSD, for example, may be predictive of impulsive behaviour, aggression, and affect dysregulation.[78] A meta-analysis of 56 studies conducted across 20 countries found that adults in prison were more likely than non-incarcerated people to be diagnosed with PTSD.[79] Cuadra and colleagues, in their study of 338 men with child maltreatment histories, found that developmental trauma manifested as impaired cognitive processing, distorted self-image and social cues, as well as a belief in the appropriateness of aggressive or antisocial behaviours in certain situations.[80] This link between trauma, mental disorder, and criminality supports the argument that sentencing judges should consider defendants' neurophysiological and psychological trauma within the sentencing calculus.

Pre-sentence reports often explicitly linked exposure to traumatic stressors with complex trauma in terms of mental health diagnoses, behavioural and cognitive impairments or 'personality traits' such as poor coping skills, low tolerance for stress and frustration resulting in aggression (i.e., anger management issues), poor impulse control and impaired judgment, learned helplessness, poor emotional reasoning and social skills, and a 'corrupted . . . identity formation.'[81] Table 6.2 includes examples from sentencing remarks where sentencing judges have cited reports provided by clinicians about the relevance of trauma-related diagnostic labels. These two examples demonstrate how that information influenced the sanctions imposed.

Although these examples in Table 6.2 illustrate how sentencing judges consider the relevance of trauma-related diagnoses in influencing sentencing sanctions, the remainder of this chapter examines how the Victorian Court of Appeal case of *R v. Verdins* can be applied to demonstrate how trauma, as a neurophysiological mental impairment, may be relevant to the sentencing calculus: specifically considering sentencing purposes, principles, and factors.

75 K. Fritzon et al., 'Understanding the Relationships between Trauma and Criminogenic Risk Using the Risk-Need Responsivity Model' (2021) 30(3) *Journal of Aggression, Maltreatment & Trauma* 294.

76 McLachlan (n 1).

77 e.g., A. J. Barrett et al., 'PTSD, Panic Disorder and Alcohol Use Disorder as a Triple Threat for Violence among Male Jail Detainees' (2021) 11 *Journal of Criminal Psychology* 21.

78 V. Ardino, 'Offending Behaviour: The Role of Trauma and PTSD' (2012) 3 *European Journal of Psychotraumatology* 1.

79 G. Baranyi et al., 'Prevalence of Posttraumatic Stress Disorder in Prisoners' (2018) 40 *Epidemiologic Reviews* 134.

80 L. E. Cuadra et al., 'Child Maltreatment and Adult Criminal Behavior: Does Criminal Thinking Explain the Association?' (2014) 38(8) *Child Abuse & Neglect* 1399.

81 McLachlan (n 1) 206, references removed.

Table 6.2 How Sentencing Judges Use Information About Trauma-Related Diagnoses

South Australian Sentencing Remarks	*Extract Citing Trauma-Related Diagnoses and How These Influenced the Sentencing Sanction*
R v. B, M (District Court of SA, Judge #9, 4 June 2019)	*Dr [Forensic Psychologist] considers that you meet the diagnostic criteria for chronic PTSD arising from a violent incident you experienced at the age of 13, as well as from the domestic violence you experienced at the hands of your former partners. Dr [Forensic Psychologist] says you suffer from an attitude of learned helplessness and disempowerment, often adopted by victims of longstanding emotional, psychological and physical violence.* *Dr [Forensic Psychologist] says that you are currently at low risk of reoffending in a similar manner . . . however, it is difficult to gauge your prospects of rehabilitation given that you have never engaged in psychological treatment. . . . As individual psychotherapy is not currently on offer within the prison system, your PTSD symptoms are unlikely to be adequately treated during any period of imprisonment. Dr [Forensic Psychologist] also expresses some concern that if you are sentenced to an immediate term of imprisonment, you will not receive the counselling you require and you will continue to repeat the same dysfunctional patterns of behaviour and relationships.* *. . . For those reasons, I am satisfied that in your peculiar circumstances there is good reason to suspend your sentence.*
R v. MB (District Court of SA, Judge #10, August 2019)	*Dr [Forensic Psychiatrist] diagnosed you as suffering from borderline personality disorder which she described as a long-standing maladaptive pattern of behaving and feeling, with associated instability in moods, behaviour, self-image and functioning. Dr [Forensic Psychiatrist] recorded that these experiences often resulted in impulsive actions such as outbursts of anger, deliberate self-harm, unstable interpersonal relationships, extreme sensitivity to abandonment, depression and anxiety. In Dr [Forensic Psychiatrist] opinion this can be traced back to your childhood, where you were exposed to trauma such as neglect, abuse and domestic violence.* *Dr [Forensic Psychiatrist] is also of the opinion that you meet the diagnostic criteria for an antisocial personality disorder, which is demonstrated by evidence of a conduct disorder during childhood, repeated arrests during the duration of your life, hostility, anger and impulsivity.* *. . . In Dr [Forensic Psychiatrist]'s opinion, you manage stressful periods by using substances. This is perpetuated by the ready availability of those substances and the common nature of drug use in your family and friendship circles.* *. . . Your counsel submitted that a home detention order may be appropriate in the circumstances. I note that Dr [Forensic Psychiatrist] identifies that you will be at high risk of resuming heavy methamphetamine use, given your own admission that you have multiple family members, including siblings, aunts and uncles, who struggle with substance abuse and continue to use methamphetamines. As a result, your broader support system will be a contributing factor to your relapsing back into substance abuse.* *. . . In all of the circumstances, I do not consider you to be a suitable person to serve the sentence on home detention.* *. . . there is little prospect of rehabilitation until such time as you get your addiction under control and receive therapy designed specifically to assist you with your borderline personality disorder.*

R v. Verdins: The Relevance of 'Mental Disorders or Abnormalities' in Sentencing

In Australia, the Victorian Court of Appeal in *R v. Verdins*[82] ('Verdins') has been a leading authority outlining how mental impairment may be relevant in sentencing. Although decisions of the Court of Appeal in Victoria are only binding in the State of Victoria, they may be persuasive in other Australian jurisdictions. Decisions of the High Court are binding on other Australian courts. The High Court decision of *R v. Guode*[83] increases the likelihood that the *Verdins* principles will be applied across different Australian states and territories. Indeed, the Court of Appeal's decision in *Verdins* has been cited by Australian courts thousands of times.[84]

R v. Verdins*: Case Facts*

Mark Verdins and Leanne Elliott began dating in 1998 when he was in his final year of school. In 2002, he broke up with her to see other people, and when she started seeing someone else, he was 'devastated' and sought to rekindle the relationship, becoming 'controlling and demanding.'[85] In August 2003, she ended her relationship with him and began a new one. In early September 2003, Mr. Verdins called and texted Ms. Elliott hundreds of times. She encouraged him to move on from the breakup. Ms. Elliott and other family and friends were concerned that Mr. Verdins was suicidal. On September 17, 2003, Mr. Verdins asked Ms. Elliott to meet. She agreed. During that meeting, Mr. Verdins fatally shot her with a homemade firearm. Ms. Elliott was described as 'a beautiful young woman in the prime of her life.'[86] Mr. Verdins then drove with her in the car, shooting himself in the mouth while driving dangerously at speeds up to 200 kilometres an hour. While driving dangerously, he rear-ended the car of Kevin Bertram, causing it to 'burst into flames' and killing Mr. Bertram.[87] Mr. Verdins pleaded guilty to the manslaughter of Mr. Bertram. Mr. Bertram, a university lecturer, was described as 'a fine man, the father of a young son.'[88] At trial, Mr. Verdins pleaded guilty to the murder of Leanne Elliott and the manslaughter of Kevin Bertram.[89] He was sentenced to 23 years, with a non-parole period of 18 years. He appealed on the grounds that general deterrence was not afforded 'appropriate weight in light of evidence of depression' and the 'trial Judge failed to address the offender's moral culpability.'[90] The appeal decision has become pivotal in Australian case law

82 [2007] VSCA 102 per Maxwell P, Buchanan and Vincent JJA.

83 [2020] HCA 8.

84 BarNet's database Judgments and Decisions Enhanced (JADE) CaseTrace states that it has been cited 1220 times as of 15 November 2024. Refer: https://jade.io/article/72073

85 *R v. Verdins* [2005] VSC 479 at [8] per Williams J.

86 Ibid at [21] per Williams J.

87 [2007] VSCA 102 at [35] per Maxwell P, Buchanan and Vincent JJA.

88 *R v. Verdins* [2005] VSC 479 at [22] per Williams J.

89 Ibid.

90 [2007] VSCA 102.

R v. Tsiaras*: The Relevance of 'Serious Psychiatric Illness' in Sentencing*

The 2007 *Verdins* appeal considered the 1996 decision of *R v. Tsiaras*[91] ('Tsiaras') and its application. Mr. Tsiaras was convicted of trafficking cocaine and possessing cannabis contrary to sections 71 and 73 of the *Drugs, Poisons and Controlled Substances Act 1981* (Vic). He applied and was granted leave to appeal against the sentence but not the conviction. Evidence was presented at trial that Mr. Tsiaras had 'an ongoing psychiatric illness, namely schizophrenia,'[92] possibly with active symptoms at the time of offending. The full Victorian Court of Appeal held that 'serious psychiatric illness not amounting to insanity' was relevant to the sentence in the following ways:

> First, it may reduce the moral culpability of the offence, as distinct from the prisoner's legal responsibility. Where that is so, it affects the punishment that is just in all the circumstances and denunciation of the type of conduct in which the offender engaged is less likely to be a relevant sentencing objective. Second, the prisoner's illness may have a bearing on the kind of sentence that is imposed and the conditions in which it should be served. Third, a prisoner suffering from serious psychiatric illness is not an appropriate vehicle for general deterrence, whether or not the illness played a part in the commission of the offence. The illness may have supervened since that time. Fourth, specific deterrence may be more difficult to achieve and is often not worth pursuing as such. Finally, psychiatric illness may mean that a given sentence will weigh more heavily on the prisoner than it would on a person in normal health.[93]

As a result, Mr. Tsiaras's sentence was reduced from three years to 18 months. Because the *Tsiaras* decision focused on 'serious psychiatric illness,' it was unclear whether the broader application of the decision extended to other types of 'mental illness.'[94] This was a key focus of the Court of Appeal in *Verdins*.

Applying **Tsiaras** *to* **Verdins***: The* **Verdins** *Principles*

The *Verdins* appeal opened with a discussion of *Tsiaras*. The full Appeal Court (including Vincent JA, one of the appeal judges in *Tsiaras*) clarified that:

> The sentencing considerations identified in *R v Tsiaras* are not—and were not intended to be—applicable only to cases of 'serious psychiatric

91 *R v. Tsiaras* [1996] 1 VR 398.

92 Ibid at 399 per Charles, Callaway and Vincent JJA.

93 Ibid 400, emphasis added.

94 I. Freckelton, 'Sentencing Offenders with Impaired Mental Functioning R v Verdins, Buckley and Vo [2007] VSCA 102; (2007) 169 A Crim R 581; P. Maxwell, Vincent and Buchanan JJ' (2007) 14 *Psychiatry, Psychology and Law* 359, 361.

> illness.' One or more of those considerations may be applicable in any case where the offender is shown to have been suffering at the time of the offence (and/or to be suffering at the time of sentencing) from a mental disorder or abnormality or an impairment of mental function, whether or not the condition in question would properly be described as a (serious) mental illness.[95]

The Court highlighted that the focus should not be on the diagnosis, for '[w]hat matters is what the evidence shows about the nature, extent and effect of the mental impairment experienced by the offender at the relevant time,'[96] such that a diagnosis 'should be treated as the beginning, not the end, of the enquiry.'[97] The Court of Appeal then restated and reformulated the *Tsiaras* principles as follows:

> Impaired mental functioning, whether temporary or permanent ("the condition"), is relevant to sentencing in at least the following six ways:
>
> 1. The condition may reduce the moral culpability of the offending conduct, as distinct from the offender's legal responsibility. Where that is so, the condition affects the punishment that is just in all the circumstances; and denunciation is less likely to be a relevant sentencing objective.
> 2. The condition may have a bearing on the kind of sentence that is imposed and the conditions in which it should be served.
> 3. Whether general deterrence should be moderated or eliminated as a sentencing consideration depends upon the nature and severity of the symptoms exhibited by the offender, and the effect of the condition on the mental capacity of the offender, whether at the time of the offending or at the date of sentence or both.
> 4. Whether specific deterrence should be moderated or eliminated as a sentencing consideration likewise depends upon the nature and severity of the symptoms of the condition as exhibited by the offender, and the effect of the condition on the mental capacity of the offender, whether at the time of the offending or at the date of the sentence or both.
> 5. The existence of the condition at the date of sentencing (or its foreseeable recurrence) may mean that a given sentence will weigh more heavily on the offender than it would on a person in normal health.
> 6. Where there is a serious risk of imprisonment having a significant adverse effect on the offender's mental health, this will be a factor tending to mitigate punishment.[98]

95 [2007] VSCA 102 at [5].
96 Ibid [8] per Maxwell P, Buchanan and Vincent JJA.
97 Ibid [13] per Maxwell P, Buchanan and Vincent JJA.
98 [2007] VSCA 102 at [32].

The *Verdins* principles have been described as 'Australia's most sophisticated and subtle analysis of the relevance of psychiatric symptomatology to sentencing'[99] by acknowledging that mental impairment may be relevant both as a sentencing factor and when determining the weight to give to the sentencing purpose of deterrence and the sentencing principle of proportionality. Arguably, the *Verdins* principles may be applied to recognise trauma as a form of 'impaired mental functioning at the time of the offending.' Trauma is not a mental health diagnosis, nor is it necessarily visible as a structural abnormality in a brain scan. However, it is a cognitive and neurophysiological impairment, identifiable through neuropsychological assessments and associated with impaired functioning and criminogenic behaviour.

Applying the *Verdins* Principles to Trauma

The *Verdins* principles relate to the sentencing calculus: specifically, the relevance of mental impairment on sentencing purposes, principles, and factors. Forensic case formulation may assist the sentencing judiciary in developing a sanction that is likely to reduce future offences. Given the weight that judges place on expert mental health reports, forensic case formulation is key to incorporating the *Verdins* principles in an evidence-informed way.[100] Forensic case formulation can provide a structured approach to considering and presenting information about why someone has committed an offence and the factors that maintain that behaviour.[101]

> Case formulation has been described as a 'hypothesis about the causes, precipitants and maintaining influences of a person's psychological, interpersonal, and behavioural issues.' [Forensic] case formulation is therefore used to gain a psychological understanding of each offender's criminal behaviour, clinical problems, and criminogenic needs. [A] formulation concludes with a set of recommendations aimed at reducing and addressing the problems and needs identified.[102]

More specifically, forensic expert reports can and should include: (a) how trauma equates to 'a mental impairment'; (b) the relationship between trauma and the propensity to offend; (c) how trauma may 'reduce the moral culpability of the offending conduct'; (d) if trauma reduces the moral culpability, acknowledging

99 Freckelton (n 89) 362.

100 D. G. Gee, J. R. P. Ogloff, 'Sentencing Offenders with Impaired Mental Functioning: R v Verdins, Buckley and Vo [2007] at the Clinical Coalface' (2014) 21 *Psychiatry, Psychology and Law* 46.

101 V. Delle-Vergini, A. Day, 'Case Formulation in Forensic Practice: Challenges and Opportunities' (2016) 18 *Journal of Forensic Practice* 240.

102 V. Wheable, J. Davies and C. Lewis, 'Investigating the effectiveness of forensic case formulation recommendations' (2024) 30 *Psychology, Crime & Law* 823, 824 (references removed).

that denunciation (as a sentencing purpose) is less likely to be relevant; and (e) recommended sanctions likely to promote community safety by addressing the trauma symptoms associated with offending. In the next section, the *Verdins* principles will be specifically considered and applied to trauma in sentencing.

Verdins *Principle 1: Trauma May Reduce the Moral Culpability*

The Court's decision in *Verdins* clarified that:

> Impaired mental functioning at the time of the offending may reduce the offender's moral culpability if it had the effect of—
>
> (a) impairing the offender's ability to exercise appropriate judgment;
> (b) impairing the offender's ability to make calm and rational choices, or to think clearly;
> (c) making the offender disinhibited;
> (d) impairing the offender's ability to appreciate the wrongfulness of the conduct;
> (e) obscuring the intent to commit the offence; or
> (f) contributing (causally) to the commission of the offence.
>
> As we have said, this is not to be taken as an exhaustive list.[103]

Moral culpability influences the sentencing principle of proportionality.[104] The Victorian Court of Appeal in *DPP v. Herrmann*[105] explained that:

> In assessing an offender's 'moral culpability,' the sentencing court is making a moral judgment on behalf of the community about the degree of blameworthiness to be attached to the offender for the offending conduct . . . [which] often requires a close examination of the personal circumstances and background of the offender and an exploration of factors which may explain the offending conduct. To the extent that offending conduct can be seen to reflect the operation of factors which are beyond the offender's control, the harshness of the moral judgment is likely to be moderated.

Defendant trauma may reduce moral culpability while being perceived as increasing the risk of harm to the community. In her analysis of 37 South Australian sentencing remarks, Butrus found that judges recognised 'childhood adversity'

103 *R v. Verdins* [2007] VSCA 102 [26], references removed.

104 A. Ashworth, 'Desert' in A. von Hirsch, A. Ashworth, J. Roberts (eds), *Principled Sentencing: Readings on Theory and Policy* (3rd ed., Hart Publishing, Oxford, 2009) 102, 104; M. Bagaric, G. Wolf, P. Isham, 'Trauma and Sentencing: The Case for Mitigating Penalty for Childhood Physical and Sexual Abuse' (2019) 30 *Stanford Law and Policy Review* 1.

105 *DPP v. Herrmann* [2021] VSCA 160 [14].

as a mitigating factor in 17 cases (45.9%) when sentencing people for committing violent and sexual offences.[106] Jackson and colleagues, in their Victorian study, found 'trauma exposure' was most often treated as a mitigating factor (n = 23; 26.7%), rarely aggravating (n = 2; 2.3%) for people convicted of murder and manslaughter.[107] Thus, trauma may be a mitigating factor (i.e., 'a reason for the judge to impose a lower than average sentence'),[108] an aggravating factor (i.e., 'a reason for the judge to impose a higher than average sentence'),[109] or both.[110]

It follows that the first *Verdins* principle may be applied to trauma in cases where three elements exist: first, a defendant has experienced notable adversity, including ACEs and intergenerational trauma, and the traumatic impact of this adversity can be shown to result in impaired mental functioning; second, impaired cognitive functioning is associated with the crime or offending behaviour such that a 'realistic connection' or 'causal link' can exist;[111] and finally, mental health expert evidence must be provided to the court, demonstrating that trauma should reduce the moral culpability of the defendant.

Verdins *Principles 2 and 5: Trauma May Have a Bearing on the Kind of Sentence Imposed*

The *Verdins* Principle 2 states that 'the [mental] condition may have a bearing on the kind of sentence that is imposed and the conditions in which it should be served.' Combining Principle 2 with Principle 5, trauma may be a sentencing factor that influences whether a sentence of incarceration is appropriate, for such a sentence 'will weigh more heavily on the offender than it would on a person in normal health.'[112] In a South Australian study, trauma influenced judges' assessment of sanction appropriateness, with 'trauma-informed' sanctions being characterised by a shorter overall period of imprisonment or non-parole period, or a downgrading of a sentence of incarceration to a community-based sanction.[113] For example, in sentencing LSJ, Judge #24 said:

> I consider that a short prison sentence is justified. It will be much shorter than would normally be the case because of your chaotic and unstable

106 N. Butrus, 'Judicial Sentencing Considerations in Cases of Violent Offenders Versus Sexual Offenders' (2018) 25 *Psychiatry, Psychology and Law* 653.

107 V. Jackson et al., 'Trauma-Informed Sentencing of Serious Violent Offenders: An Exploration of Judicial Dispositions with a Gendered Perspective' (2021) 28 *Psychiatry, Psychology and Law* 748.

108 B. J. Grey, 'Neuroscience, PTSD, and Sentencing Mitigation' (2012) 34 *Cardozo Law Review* 53, 77.

109 Ibid.

110 See: *R v. Monks* [2019] SASCFC 47.

111 Ibid. [38].

112 Ibid. [32].

113 K. McLachlan, *"I Cannot Dismiss from My Mind Your Traumatic and Tragic Upbringing": Judges' Use of Defendant Trauma in Sentencing* (PhD thesis, University of South Australia, 2021) 193.

> childhood, disrupted education and all the mental health aspects which [your lawyer] has gone through, which I do not need to repeat. . . .[114]

Sanctions intended to be trauma-informed reflect judges' intentions to be merciful, yet sometimes are not evidence-informed strategies (i.e., by resolving trauma and reducing recidivism), for they have detrimental effects on accommodation, employment, and stable relationships.

Verdins *Principles 3 and 4: General and Specific Deterrence May be Moderated or Eliminated, Depending on the Nature, Severity, and Impact of the Trauma Symptoms*

The sentencing purpose of general deterrence is premised on the idea that crime is driven by free will, rational choice, and consequent moral responsibility.[115] For defendants whose neurophysiological functioning and well-being have been impacted by trauma, general deterrence is likely to be given less weight than other sentencing purposes, such as rehabilitation. For example, in the High Court case of *Bugmy v. The Queen*,[116] the Court accepted:

> The experience of growing up in an environment surrounded by alcohol abuse and violence may leave its mark on a person through life. Among other things, a background of that kind may compromise the person's capacity to mature and to learn from experience. It is a feature of the person's make-up and remains relevant to the determination of the appropriate sentence, notwithstanding that the person has a long history of offending.[117]

Thus, the traumatic impact of compounded ACEs may be relevant in sentencing, as it reduces the applicability of general deterrence. Conversely, in *Veen v. The Queen*, the defendant's history of trauma was used as an indicator of high risk, poor responsivity,[118] and a low likelihood of rehabilitation. Thus, when sentencing someone perceived as high risk who has trauma, a judge may moderate general deterrence in some (but not all) cases, specifically when

114 *R v. LSJ* (District Court of SA, Judge #24, 24 September 2019), cited in McLachlan (n 108) 193.

115 A. Ashworth, R. Kelly, *Sentencing and Criminal Justice* (7th ed., Hart Publishing, 2021) 69.

116 *Bugmy v. The Queen* (2013) 249 CLR 571.

117 Ibid [43], per French CJ, Hayne, Crennan, Kiefel, Bell, Keane JJ).

118 *Veen v. The Queen* (No 2) (1988) 164 CLR 465. Personal responsivity relates to individual characteristics, such as cognitive ability or learning style, that may impact an individual's ability to engage effectively in treatment. The impacts of trauma may undermine effective engagement in treatment, particularly group-based treatment (e.g., due to poor lateral thinking and problem-solving skills or an inability to regulate emotions effectively). See: D. A. Andrews, J. Bonta, *The Psychology of Criminal Conduct* (5th ed., Taylor & Francis, 2010) 309 for an overview of responsivity.

traumatised defendants are determined to be at low risk of serious or repeated future offending.

Verdins *Principle 6: Where Imprisonment May Have a Significant Adverse Effect, This May Mitigate Punishment*

Imprisonment may adversely affect either or both the incarcerated person and their dependents. Incarceration is both criminogenic and traumatic to most people, particularly those with preexisting trauma symptoms. For First Nations peoples in Australia, the most incarcerated population in the world,[119] as well as other First Nations people, including Aotearoa Māori, and North American First Nations peoples, intergenerational trauma is often compounded by the impact of incarceration—being away from country, community, and family in a small cell. Heffernan et al. have stated that:

> This nexus between social adversity, poor health and incarceration for Aboriginal people can at least in part be understood in terms of the impact of historical factors such as the colonisation of lands and the forced removal of children, discrimination, and associated experiences of unemployment, poverty, poor education and a lack of social capital.[120]

Canada has legislation that argues explicitly that, for Aboriginal defendants, 'all available sanctions, other than imprisonment, that are reasonable in the circumstances and consistent with the harm done to victims or the community should be considered for all offenders, with particular attention to the circumstances of Aboriginal offenders.'[121] In practice, '[i]t is remedial in nature and is designed to ameliorate the serious problem of overrepresentation of Aboriginal (sic) people in prisons, and to encourage sentencing judges to have recourse to a restorative approach to sentencing.'[122]

In the case of *R v. Gladue* ('Gladue'),[123] the interpretation and application of section 718.2(e) were reviewed by the Canadian Supreme Court, which suggested that courts consider:

> How has the offender who is being sentenced been affected by, for example, substance abuse in the community, or poverty, or overt racism, or

119 T. Anthony, 'FactCheck: Are First Australians the Most Imprisoned People on Earth?' *The Conversation* (6 June 2017) <https://theconversation.com/factcheck-are-first-australians-the-most-imprisoned-people-on-earth-78528>.

120 E. Heffernan et al., 'Mental Disorder and Cognitive Disability in the Criminal Justice System' in P. Dudgeon, H. Milroy, R. Walker (eds), *Working together: Aboriginal and Torres Strait Islander Mental Health and Wellbeing Principles and Practice* (2nd ed., Telethon Institute for Child Health Research & Australian Government Department of the Prime Minister and Cabinet, 2014) 87.

121 Canadian *Criminal Code*, s 718.2(e).

122 *R v. Gladue* [1999] 1 SCR 688, 690.

123 Ibid.

> family or community breakdown? Would imprisonment effectively serve to deter or denounce crime in a sense that would be significant to the offender and community, or are crime prevention and other goals better achieved through healing? What sentencing options present themselves in these circumstances?[124]

The Court reiterated that section 718.2(e) changed the weighting, such that Aboriginality was to be regarded as a key consideration and may make imprisonment 'a less appropriate or less useful sanction.'[125] Aboriginality, in *Gladue*, effectively referred to:

(A) The unique systemic or background factors which may have played a part in bringing the particular aboriginal (sic) offender before the courts; and
(B) The types of sentencing procedures and sanctions which may be appropriate in the circumstances for the offender because of his or her particular aboriginal heritage or connection.[126]

In addition to the weight of imprisonment that particularly impacts Aboriginal defendants, many criminalised adults have been traumatised by the absence of their parents during childhood due to incarceration.[127] This is a significant ACE. Thus, the sixth *Verdins* principle should also apply where imprisonment may result in secondary trauma on defendants' dependents, particularly 'children with serious disabilities or medical conditions.'[128] Judges may reduce developmental trauma in the next generation by offering alternatives to parental imprisonment (such as a suspended sentence or court-ordered home detention) or reducing time in custody through shorter-than-usual sentences.

Conclusion

Sentencing judges have sometimes been less inclined to acknowledge defendant neurophysiological or psychological trauma as a 'mental abnormality' because such examples are so commonplace in the population of criminalised people as to be unremarkable.[129] Judges appear to compare individual defendants' life experiences with those of other defendants rather than those of the general public.[130] Drawing from a neurolegal approach allows defendants to benefit from more individualised considerations in sentencing. Providing 'a

124 Ibid. [80].
125 Ibid. [37].
126 Ibid. [66].
127 McLachlan (n 108).
128 T. Walsh, H. Douglas, 'Sentencing Parents: The Consideration of Dependent Children' (2016) 37 *Adelaide Law Review* 135, 160.
129 McLachlan (n 108).
130 Ibid.

scientific foundation for understanding human behaviour'[131] may help achieve evidence-informed sentencing by focusing on trauma as an individualised 'mental impairment' that requires assessment and treatment by a mental health professional, rather than something that is perceived as common or 'normal' in the criminalised population.

To examine how sentencing judges use trauma evidence in their decision-making, this chapter has considered the relevance of trauma in offending behaviour and sentencing. For defendants with impaired functioning due to trauma, trauma is highly relevant to the sentencing calculus when balancing sentencing purposes, principles, factors, and non-legal considerations.[132] Specifically, the case of *Verdins* assists the judiciary in considering trauma in their decision-making and deliberations during sentencing to prevent future offending and maintain community safety. Trauma can reduce moral culpability and impact someone's capacity to cope with incarceration. Indeed, imprisonment can have adverse effects on both the person being incarcerated and their dependents. Finally, regarding sentencing purposes, trauma may reduce the applicability of general and personal deterrence in the sentencing calculus.

Overall, this chapter argues that neurophysiological and psychological trauma should be treated as a 'mental disorder or abnormality' in sentencing and that the *Verdins* principles can be applied when sentencing defendants to show how such considerations of trauma may be relevant in the sentencing calculus. In all Westminster systems, trauma-informed case formulations should be part of sentencing considerations to demonstrate where trauma equates to 'mental disorder or abnormality,' the relationship between trauma and criminality, how trauma may 'reduce the moral culpability of the offending conduct,' and, most all, how individualised sanctions based upon neurophysiological considerations of trauma likely promote community safety by addressing trauma symptoms associated with current and future offending behaviour.

131 G. D. Caruso, *Neurolaw* (Cambridge University Press, Cambridge, 2024) 1.
132 McLachlan (n 1) 172.

7 The Impact, and Lack of Impact, of Neurodiversity in the Criminal Justice System in Aotearoa, New Zealand

Mark Henaghan and Jean Grace Choi

Introduction

The knowledge of neurodiversity[1] by the judiciary in Aotearoa, New Zealand, varies a lot. It depends on the knowledge of counsel acting in cases where neurodiversity is either an evidentiary issue or a sentencing issue before the judge. For this chapter, we will focus on the impact, and lack of impact, of neuroscience in the criminal justice system in Aotearoa, New Zealand. By way of contrast, matters of insanity based on serious cases of schizophrenia and psychotic episodes will not be the primary focus because they are well established for the basis of establishing insanity.

This chapter will focus on neurodiversity matters, with a particular focus on Foetal Alcohol Syndrome Disorder (FASD). The best account of the dilemma that a judge faces when confronting a defendant with FASD is written by Judge Hastings in *New Zealand Police v. Morrison*.[2] Judge Hastings uses neuroscience to inform best practice guidelines to ensure defendants with FASD are treated fairly and appropriately: from arrest, bail conditions, fitness to plea, communication during trial, sentencing, and likely recidivism. This chapter explores other positive developments in the judiciary, like in *Maaka-Wanahi v. Police*, where the neuroscience of FASD was recognised as a factor in reducing the sentence due to the defendant's lack of moral culpability.[3] However, the impact of neuroscience on the criminal justice system has been limited due to practical issues like finding the right expertise on FASD to give evidence

1 Neurodiversity is recognition that people have a diverse range of cognitive, sensory, and social processing. However, neurodiverse people see the world and interact with others differently, not necessarily 'worse.' Due to the wide range of neurodiversity and the lack of a screening tool, the exact prevalence in Aotearoa, New Zealand is unknown. See I. Lambie, 'What were they thinking? A discussion paper on brain and behaviour in relation to the justice system in New Zealand' (Officer of the Prime Minister's Chief Science Advisor Kaitohutohu Mātanga Pūtaiao Matua ki te Pirimia, Janurary 2020) 6–7.

2 *New Zealand Police v. Morrison* [2019] NZDC 13977 2–7.

3 *Maaka-Wanahi v. Police* [2023] NZHC 3291 15.

DOI: 10.4324/9781003510246-8

at trial in *Gallacher v. R*,[4] *Platt v. R*,[5] and *Pora v. R*,[6] and the lack of community support available upon release when FASD is not recognised as a health disability by the state.[7] In addition, there is an emerging issue of defendants exposed to methamphetamine in utero, which is likely to pose similar challenges to defendants with FASD, which requires more research.[8]

This chapter finishes by looking at promising and positive developments in the Young Adult List (YAL), a specialist court developed by the lower courts, which includes a range of neurodiversity understandings for young defendants from 18 to 25 years old.[9] This is a positive development because everyone in the court, from the judge, counsel, advocates, and support workers, is alert to the special neurodiverse needs and characteristics of the defendants and is focused on neuroscience characteristics that could limit executive functions.[10] This enables procedural fairness, garnered positive feedback from both defendants and stakeholders, and the lower courts are to be congratulated for leading the way to ensure neurodiversity is not just a theory.[11]

The Neuroscience of Foetal Alcohol Syndrome Disorder (FASD)

FASD is described as a neurodevelopmental disorder caused by exposure to alcohol before birth.[12] Prenatal exposure to alcohol causes central nervous system damage, which produces a range of neurocognitive deficits.[13] There must be three or more deficits to the neurodevelopmental domains of a defendant's brain in the following areas: motor skills; neuroanatomy/neurophysiology; cognition; language; academic achievement; memory; attention; executive function (including impulse, control and hyperactivity); affect regulation; and adaptive behaviour, social skills, or social communication.[14] Defendants with FASD may not have reduced IQ, as each individual's presentation of FASD is

4 *Gallacher v. R* [2024] NZCA 335 3.

5 *Platt v. R* [2010] NZCA 43 9.

6 *Pora v. R* [2015] UKPC 9, [2016] 1 NZLR 277 11–15.

7 People with FASD are not eligible for the Disability Support Services in Aotearoa, New Zealand. See Disability Rights Commissioner and Children's Commissioner 'Fetal Alcohol Spectrum Disorder: A Call to Action' (Report to the Prime Minister, 2023) 6.

8 'Methamphetamine in utero' is the exposure of methamphetamine to a baby inside the womb before birth. Judge Jan-Marie Doogue, Judge John Walker, 'Proposal for a Trial of Young Adult List in Porirua District Court: Procedural Fairness for the Young and the Vulnerable' (2019) 3.

9 J. Paulin and others, 'Formative and Short-Term Outcome Evaluation of the Porirua District Court Young Adult List Court initiative: Iti rearea teitei kahikatea ka taea' (*Artemis Research*, 2021) 1.

10 Ibid.

11 Ibid. 4–11, 14–18.

12 *R v. Fawcett* [2021] NZHC 2406 7–9.

13 Ibid. 7.

14 Ibid.

unique.[15] It is only when a defendant in Aotearoa, New Zealand, has an IQ below 70 that they are diagnosed as Intellectually Disabled (ID) under section 7(3)(a) of the Intellectual Disability (Compulsory Care and Rehabilitation) Act 2003.[16] FASD is the most commonly occurring neurodiverse condition that has appeared in the courts of Aotearoa, New Zealand.

The Chief Science Advisor for the Justice Sector, Dr. Ian Lambie, wrote an important report that said people with brain and behaviour issues, such as FASD, are over-represented in the criminal justice system as both victims and offenders.[17] He goes on to say that the process of the criminal justice system itself may compound negative outcomes for both victims and offenders with brain and behaviour issues.[18] The emphasis was on early intervention, that even when brain damage is permanent as in FASD, its negative consequences and impacts do not have to be.[19] Dr. Lambie emphasised that the ways the judiciary react to issues of neurodiversity can be disabling to those who have neurodiversity.[20]

The Dilemma the Judiciary Faces With a Defendant With FASD

The best account of the dilemma that the judiciary faces when confronting a defendant who clearly has FASD is written by Judge Hastings.[21] When sentencing Mr. Morrison, in the case of *New Zealand Police v. Morrison*, Judge Hastings started by saying that the numerous challenges faced by a person with FASD cannot be easily overcome by a judge sitting alone at the end of a court process.[22] Judge Hastings goes on to say that individual and criminal justice outcomes are most likely to be improved by a more holistic wraparound approach involving health and social interventions that are put into place well before a defendant's criminal justice involvement.[23] This will reduce the risk of a defendant with FASD entering the criminal justice system.[24] Judge Hastings sums up that persons with FASD are likely to be suggestible, have difficulty organising memory, diminished capacity to foresee consequences, make reasoned decisions on the spot, and recognise and learn from mistakes.[25]

Judge Hastings sets out what he believes to be the best practice guidelines for ensuring that persons with FASD who encounter the criminal justice

15 Ibid. 7.
16 IQ refers to intelligence quotient, a score derived from psychometric tests to assess human intelligence.
17 Lambie (n 1) 5.
18 Ibid.
19 Ibid.
20 Ibid. 6.
21 *New Zealand Police v. Morrison* (n 2) 2.
22 Ibid.
23 Ibid.
24 Ibid.
25 Ibid. 4.

system are treated fairly and appropriately in terms of their condition. When arresting a person with FASD, it is unlikely that they will understand the consequences of what they have been alleged to have done.[26] They are more likely to want to please the interviewer, by agreeing with any leading and tagged questions asked of them.[27] This increases the risk of confabulation and false confessions.[28] The cure for this is to ensure that there are accurate notebook entries and visual recordings of the first encounter to assist in the subsequent admissibility of the evidence obtained at the first encounter.[29] Bail conditions create difficulty for people with FASD, as they may be more likely to not comply with them unless there are specific bail conditions to support them and ensure that they are able to get to the court when required.[30]

When making a plea, a person with FASD may have issues with fitness to plead.[31] Judge Hastings states that, at this stage, a comprehensive neuropsychological report should be recommended.[32] This report will help with reviewing the level of charge and the efficacy of a trial.[33] At the trial, to avoid issues of adverse credibility findings, consideration should be given to appointing a communication assistant to ensure the factfinder has the best evidence to reach a verdict.[34]

In sentencing, the fact that the defendant has FASD, in Judge Hastings' words, 'cannot be ignored in an assessment of the degree to which the defendant is responsible for the offending.'[35] The difficulty a judge faces when it comes to rehabilitation for a person with FASD is that they cannot be restored to a position that they would have been had they not been born with FASD.[36] FASD is a lifelong condition. Deterrence becomes a much less relevant consideration when sentencing a person with FASD, as such a person is less able to see the consequences of their actions.[37] In the words of Judge Hastings, 'reducing the risk of recidivism and reintegrating a defendant with FASD into the community becomes much more of a management issue than a punishment issue.'[38]

26 Ibid.
27 Ibid.
28 See J. Brown and others, 'Fetal Alcohol Spectrum Disorder and Confabulation in Psycholegal Settings: A Beginner's Guide for Criminal Justice, Forensic Mental Health, and Legal Interviewers' (2022) 40 *Behav Sci & Law* 46, 71.
29 *New Zealand Police v. Morrison* (n 25).
30 Ibid.
31 Ibid.
32 Ibid. 5.
33 Ibid.
34 Ibid. Communication assistance is provided through s 80 of the Evidence Act 2006.
35 Ibid.
36 Ibid (n 20).
37 Ibid.
38 Ibid.

Sentences that include release conditions will be difficult for defendants with FASD, as they are inherently less able to keep appointments or to remember what they are supposed to do between appointments.[39] Punishment again for such breaches will mean that people with FASD will be in the criminal justice system longer than what is necessary. In the words of Judge Hastings, the system 'effectively punishes them for having FASD rather than for criminal behaviour.'[40]

Mr. Morrison had been in and out of jail since he was 17 years old.[41] In total, he had spent 20 years in imprisonment.[42] The court expert, Dr. Valerie McGinn, who was trained in FASD in Canada, told the judge and the defendant that people in Canada with FASD received supported housing, employment, and an FASD worker who could help with problems when they arose.[43] Mr. Morrison said that he would like to receive all those things.[44] In Aotearoa, New Zealand, FASD is not recognised as a disability and, therefore, it is much harder for people with FASD to get state support for their condition.

Exploring the Reasons for the Lack of Impact of Neuroscience in the Criminal Justice System of Aotearoa, New Zealand

Lack of Support for FASD Offenders

In *R v. Tupoumalohi*, the offender had FASD and, according to the judge, probably Attention Deficit Hyperactivity Disorder (ADHD).[45] He was currently in prison, and the four assaults he was being sentenced for took place in prison.[46] The four assaults had a common pattern to them, and the defendant did not initiate any of them.[47] Each time, another prisoner came to punch the other prisoner, who the defendant had been happily talking to earlier, the defendant produced the shank, and stabbed the assaulted person multiple times.[48] Fortunately, the injuries were not serious enough to cause permanent damage.[49] The judge said the offender had an IQ of below 70 and also had anxiety and traumatic brain injury (TBI).[50] Edwards J went on to say, 'these disabilities mean you find it extremely hard to stop and think before acting' and 'other people influence you to do bad things, and you go along with

39 Ibid.
40 Ibid.
41 Ibid. 7.
42 Ibid.
43 Ibid. 7–8.
44 Ibid. 8.
45 *R v. Tupoumalohi* [2024] NZHC 3278 2.
46 Ibid.
47 Ibid. 2–3.
48 Ibid.
49 Ibid. 3.
50 Ibid. 6.

them.'[51] This is classically illustrated by the patterns of offending. Dr. McGinn, who was the same defence expert on the case, said that the overstimulation that the offender received in a prison setting made him less able to manage stress, which contributed to his offending.[52]

The Crown had asked for an increase in sentence, but based on the offender's background and disabilities, Edwards J refused an uplift.[53] Edwards J emphasised that a prison sentence, because of the FASD disability, would not act as a deterrent to the offender.[54] The judge went on to say that prison would not provide long-term protection for the community or others, particularly if the offender is not getting the support required.[55] The judge emphasised that the only way to protect the community was to ensure that the offender 'get[s] the correct support and medical assistance that you need.'[56] Unfortunately, such assistance is not available in prisons. In the end, the offender was sentenced to six years' imprisonment with no minimum period of imprisonment imposed.[57]

This is also illustrated in the case of *M v. R*, which involved the kidnapping and murder of a 17-year-old.[58] One of the offenders, who was a 16-year-old at the time of the offending and had been diagnosed with FASD and minor intellectual disability (ID), stood trial separately from the other two adult offenders.[59] She was charged with kidnapping and murder, and was found guilty on the kidnapping charge only.[60] The 16-year-old was given five years ten months' imprisonment and was ordered to be detained under section 34(1)(a)(ii) of the Criminal Procedure (Mentally Impaired Persons) Act 2003 in a secure facility as a special care recipient under the Intellectual Disability (Compulsory Care and Rehabilitation) Act 2003.[61] The 16-year-old appealed as her custodial sentence had expired, and she is now being held as a care recipient at a secure facility.[62] The Court of Appeal held that an allowance of 20% was given to recognise her personal circumstances, including FASD, ADHD, and ID, as well as an early life of deprivation and neglect.[63] The defendant also

51 Ibid.
52 Ibid. 7.
53 Ibid. 8.
54 Ibid. 9.
55 Ibid.
56 Ibid.
57 Ibid.
58 *M v. R* [2024] NZCA 451 1–2.
59 Ibid. 2.
60 Ibid.
61 Ibid. 2, 14–15. Under an order made under section 34(1)(a)(ii) of the Criminal Procedure (Mentally Impaired Persons) Act 2003 (commonly referred to as a "hybrid order"), the offender is sentenced and remains subject to the criminal justice system but is detained pursuant to the sentence in a secure facility as 'special care recipient' under the Intellectual Disability (Compulsory Care and Rehabilitation) Act 2003.
62 Ibid. (n 59).
63 Ibid. 10–11.

appealed the hybrid order.[64] The Court of Appeal affirmed the hybrid order with the care order attached to it on the basis that immediate release would place the 16-year-old in a precarious and unprepared situation without any support regime.[65]

The defendant also argued for her name to be suppressed based on the fact of expert evidence from Dr. McGinn that publication of her identity would likely significantly reduce rehabilitative options available to her.[66] Dr. McGinn stated that the defendant's 'mental state would deteriorate, and she may not be amenable to [the secure facility's] rehabilitation plan without name suppression' and that there had been concerns about depression and suicide in the future.[67] There was also concern that if her name was released, she would be vulnerable to predators and that identification would increase this risk.[68] Unfortunately, these submissions failed, as the threshold for permanent name suppression is extreme hardship on the basis that while the defendant's disability made life for her, and those caring for her difficult, there is nothing specific that emerges from the material to suggest her situation will be markedly worsened if her identity is known.[69] The Court of Appeal acted on the expectation that the offender would be held in a secure facility for some time and that the systems would keep her safe and manage her stresses.[70] This is a very disappointing decision, which ignores the clear evidence of Aotearoa, New Zealand's outstanding expert on FASD, Dr. McGinn.

The Difficulty in Getting the Right Expertise on FASD

One of the major problems of a small country, like Aotearoa, New Zealand, with a population of five million people, is that we have very few real experts on FASD.[71] In the Court of Appeal decision *Gallacher v. R*, one expert was available to undertake the FASD assessment but could not complete the report on time for it to have any real effect on the appeal.[72] By the time the expert's report would be available, the defendant would have already served six months of his sentence of imprisonment.[73]

An earlier Court of Appeal case where a medical expert gave evidence on FASD in *Platt v. R*, the court held that the expert had resorted to medical

64 Ibid. (n 59).
65 Ibid. 17.
66 Ibid. 25.
67 Ibid.
68 Ibid.
69 Ibid.
70 Ibid.
71 Aotearoa, New Zealand, has an estimated population of 5,308,500 people in the year ending December 2023. Stats NZ Tatauranga Aotearoa, *Statistics New Zealand* <https://www.stats.govt.nz/topics/population> accessed 20 December 2024.
72 *Gallacher v. R* (n 4).
73 Ibid.

literature by persons who are experts and applied it to the case 'from a distance as it were.'[74] Therefore, the medical expert could not be classified as an expert in FASD.[75]

In the case of *Pora v. R*, which went all the way to the Privy Council, the defendant, Mr. Pora, spent 21 years in jail for a case he clearly had not committed.[76] What was significant to winning the appeal was the evidence of the same expert Dr. McGinn, which is cited fully.[77] Dr. McGinn highlighted that Mr. Pora's developmental history was 'entirely consistent with a child with an undiagnosed FASD' and 'he was clearly alcohol exposed with a low birth weight' and 'described consistently as being slow and having difficulty with communicating from a very young age.'[78] Dr. McGinn gave evidence that having diagnosed and treated more than 200 children and young people with FASD, she was able to provide her opinion about the limitations that Mr. Pora would have shown at the age of 17 years old when interviewed by the police and charged.[79] In Dr. McGinn's opinion, 'at the age of 17 years Mr. Pora was thinking and acting like a much younger child of about eight to ten years of age.'[80] He was said to lack insight into his limitations and tended to respond as if he understood when he clearly did not.[81] The Privy Council concluded that 'the combination of [Mr.] Pora's frequently contradictory and often implausible confessions and the recent diagnosis of his FASD lead to only one possible conclusion that reliance on his confessions gave rise to a risk of a miscarriage of justice' and 'on that account, his convictions must be quashed.'[82] This case is a strong example of the crucial importance of having the right expert on FASD and the major impact that they can have on the outcome of a case.

The Positive Impact of Understanding Neuroscience in the Criminal Justice System of Aotearoa, New Zealand

Recognition of FASD as a Factor to Reduce Sentence Due to Lack of Moral Culpability

Mr. Kingi Maaka-Wanahi is 22 years old and has been diagnosed with FASD and ADHD in *Maaka-Wanahi v. Police*.[83] He was charged with burglary offences, use of an offensive weapon, and intentional damage charges, as well

74 *Platt v. R* (n 5).
75 Ibid.
76 *Pora v. R* (n 6) 278, 289, 295.
77 Ibid. 11–15.
78 Ibid.
79 Ibid.
80 Ibid.
81 Ibid.
82 Ibid. 21.
83 *Maaka-Wanahi v. Police* (n 3) 1, 4.

as assault with a weapon and assault on a police officer.[84] Dr. McGinn, the same expert in FASD, gave evidence to the court that the defendant was fit to plead.[85] She said that the defendant's level of understanding and communication was that of a 10-year-old, and that he was significantly delayed and immature in his thinking, with poorly regulated behaviour.[86] Dr. McGinn also said that Mr. Maaka-Wanahi's abstract reasoning, social understanding, and judgment are impaired, and that he is at risk of being easily misled.[87] Dr. McGinn summarised that Mr. Maaka-Wanahi was progressing well until he reached the age of 12 years old.[88] Since then, his development had been stalled by leaving school early and going into the criminal justice system.[89] Once he had 'aged out' at 18 years old of Oranga Tamariki care, he was not able to care for himself and was unable to abide by court-imposed conditions, particularly when he did not have his medication, was homeless, and under gang influence.[90]

Dr. McGinn also stated that the government denies disability support services to individuals with FASD, and they are left to fend for themselves in the community.[91] She says that they will inevitably enter the criminal justice system.[92] Dr. McGinn summed up Mr. Maaka-Wanahi that 'he contends with a form of brain damage not of his own making that makes him impulsive, reduces his capacity to moderate his actions and leads him into making poor decisions.'[93] His *whānau*, who were of Māori descent, had a history of alcohol and other harm due to colonisation and are not in a position to provide the defendant with the necessary structure, support, and supervision he requires.[94] Evidence was given that when the defendant was part of a START programme, which provided life and employment skills, he was doing well.[95] Once he left, he was described as falling through the gaps of the health system that is not FASD informed.[96] The expert concluded that people with FASD

84 Ibid. 3.

85 Ibid. 7–8.

86 Ibid. 7.

87 Ibid.

88 Ibid.

89 Ibid.

90 Ibid. *Oranga Tamariki* means Ministry for Children in Māori, the indigenous language of Aotearoa New Zealand. Oranga Tamariki is the social welfare care of children at risk of significant harm and young offenders. See 'Oranga Tamariki, Ministry for Children—About us, Mō mātau' (*New Zealand Government*, 2025) <https://www.orangatamariki.govt.nz/about-us/> accessed 29 April 2025.

91 Ibid.

92 Ibid.

93 Ibid.

94 Ibid. *Whānau* means 'family' in Māori. See 'whānau' (*Te Aka Māori Dictionary Online*, 2025) <https://maoridictionary.co.nz/word/10062> accessed 29 April 2025.

95 Ibid. The START Programme is a provider of a 20-week programme for young men in the youth justice system. *START Taranaki, Our Mission—Empower* <https://www.starttaranaki.co.nz> accessed 29 April 2025.

96 Ibid.

are not inherently dangerous, and support, not punishment, will keep them and the community safe.[97]

Dr. McGinn recommended that Mr. Maaka-Wanahi's FASD be accepted as a mitigating factor when applying sanctions.[98] The expert went on to say that a long period of incarceration 'will be crushing for a young disabled person like Kingi who is younger than his age developmentally' and recommended that if he were to go to prison, he would be more suitably placed in a youth unit or, if that was not available, he should be considered a vulnerable prisoner kept away from gang influences.[99]

In the District Court, Judge Grieg put a primary emphasis on protecting the community and also protecting the defendant and went on to say that 'a sentence that simply has you released in no better shape or in no better place . . . put[ting] you at greater risk of serious re-offending and you will simply suffer further, along with your victims.'[100] The High Court Judge, McQueen J, emphasised that when:

> there is a causative link between a lack of capacity or an impairment that reduces an offender's moral culpability, this must be taken into account when setting the starting point for the offending. The disability or impairment must have altered the character and gravity of the offending itself.[101]

This meant that Mr. Maaka-Wanahi's moral responsibility for his offending is reduced.[102] To reduce the sentence, McQueen J gave a six-month reduction of the overall starting point to account for totality and his reduced culpability, 25% discount for guilty plea, 15% discount for his mental health, and 10% discount for youth, which resulted in an end sentence of 15 months imprisonment.[103]

Calls for Transformative Change in Understanding Neuroscience: The Young Adult List (YAL) Court

The Chief District Court Judge, Heemi Taumaunu, has made a call for transformative change in the District Court.[104] The call is based on the fact that District Court judges who are on the front line of criminal justice have

97 Ibid.
98 Ibid. 8.
99 Ibid.
100 Ibid. 1, 9.
101 Ibid. 14.
102 Ibid. 15.
103 Ibid. 20–21.
104 Judge Heemi Taumaunu, 'Calls for Transformative Change and the District Court Response' (2021) *WkoLawRw* 29, 115–116. The 'Te Ao Mārama' transformative model called on by Chief Judge Taumaunu is a deliberate intention by the District Court to move 'towards a more enlightened world' for the benefit of all people who are affected by the justice system.

individually made calls for change within the existing legal framework inside the courtroom.[105] There has been a strong development in solution-based judging.[106] In basic terms, solutions-focused judging seeks to identify the drivers of offending and then address them by facilitating the provision of services and community support required.[107] The vehicle for this transformative change has been 'specialist courts.'[108] The Chief Justice said that they are a way of lighting the path ahead.[109] One of the first examples of a 'specialist court' was initiated by the then-Principal Youth Court Judge John Walker.[110] The Young Adult List (YAL) Court separates out 18- to 25-year-old defendants from the ordinary criminal list.[111]

The YAL Court focuses on engaging the young adult in the process and particularly making sure that there is procedural fairness, such as:[112]

1. Ensuring that the process is conducted in a way that the young adult can understand;
2. Ensuring that the young adult is aware of what the outcome of a hearing means for them such as what bail conditions have been imposed; and
3. Providing services at court so that the young adult can access the interventions necessary to address offending.

The YAL process is based on the idea that young adults bring disabilities, such as FASD, to the court that 'do not have an expiry date.'[113] It is based on the idea that the presence of disability, mental health conditions, neuro-disability, ID, acquired brain injury, in addition to the under-developed brain, require special considerations when it comes to court processes.[114] Whilst the targeted group is 17- to 24-year-olds, who account for 14% of the general population, they make up 40% of criminal justice apprehensions.[115] The underlying goal of taking into account any disability or neuro-disability that they have, because they are young, allows appropriate intervention and treatment.[116] This enables

105 Ibid. 123. The District Court covers a broad criminal jurisdiction, only excluding murder, manslaughter, and some other offences. The District Court disposed of 84,284 criminal cases, which was more than 95% of all criminal cases in the year ending June 2021. See District Court of New Zealand Te Kōti-ā-Rohe o Aotearoa, *Criminal Jurisdiction* <https://districtcourts.govt.nz/criminal-court/criminal-jurisdiction> accessed 29 April 2025.

106 Ibid. 124.

107 Ibid.

108 Ibid. 125.

109 Ibid.

110 Ibid.

111 Ibid. 129.

112 Ibid. 130.

113 Doogue and Walker (n 8) 1.

114 Ibid.

115 Ibid. 2.

116 Ibid.

the opportunity to redirect their lives by reducing the chance of becoming recidivist offenders and reducing the victims in our society.[117] At this inception, it was recognised that FASD and methamphetamine in utero were becoming increasingly prevalent in young offenders.[118]

One of the key procedures of the specialist court is to use a proposed screening tool.[119] The tool is to screen for any neuro-disability, mental health history, and alcohol and other drug issues.[120] The judge will be given this information, review it, identify the issues that need to be accommodated, and give both defence and prosecution this information.[121] An Adolescent Mental Health Worker, Alcohol and Other Drugs Clinician, iwi liaison, Work and Income New Zealand, Youth Specialist Probation Officer, a dedicated Police Prosecution, and defence counsel will also be present.[122]

Positive Impacts of Understanding Neurodiversity in the YAL Court

In 2021, a formative and short-term outcome evaluation of the Porirua District Court YAL Court initiative was carried out.[123] The review found that everyone in the court is alert to the special needs and characteristics of the defendants and is focused on special characteristics that could limit executive functions.[124] These characteristics include neuro-disabilities, such as dyslexia, FASD, and acquired brain injury.[125] As part of the review, 30 defendants from the YAL Court and 25 defendants from a comparison District Court of a comparable size were interviewed about their experiences.[126] Four of the ten defendants in the YAL Court had disabilities, and three out of ten in the comparison court.[127]

The YAL defendants were positive about having their names pronounced correctly.[128] In the comparison courts, the defendants would hear their name on the loudspeaker before they entered the courtroom, and the judge would be less likely to address them by name.[129] The YAL defendants were more likely to have a support person.[130] Two-thirds of them had a support person, and

117 Ibid. 13.
118 Ibid. 3.
119 Ibid. 14.
120 Ibid.
121 Ibid. 15.
122 Ibid. *Iwi* means 'tribe' in Māori. See 'iwi' (*Te Aka Māori Dictionary Online*, 2025) <https://maoridictionary.co.nz/search?keywords=iwi> accessed 29 April 2025.
123 Paulin (n 9). Porirua is a lower socio-economic area on the outskirts of the capital city, Wellington, with a diverse ethnic population. See Stats NZ Tatauranga Aotearoa, *Statistics New Zealand Porirua City* <https://www.stats.govt.nz/tools/2018-census-place-summaries/porirua-city> accessed 29 April 2025.
124 Ibid.
125 Ibid.
126 Ibid. 4.
127 Ibid.
128 Ibid.
129 Ibid.
130 Ibid.

that person was always acknowledged by the judge.[131] In comparison courts, the judge only acknowledged the support person half the time and even sent a support person's children out of the courtroom.[132] All YAL defendants said that they could hear the judge, compared to one-quarter of the comparison court.[133] Most YAL defendants said they could understand the judge.[134] One-fifth could not, which was much lower than the one-third of the comparison courts who could not understand the judge.[135] The YAL defendants were grateful for the opportunity to be referred for interventions.[136] The referrals they received were better suited to their needs.[137] They were referred to a wide range of services, such as counselling to focus on the underlying causes of offending, being tested for dyslexia, and psychiatric assessment, as well as restorative justice processes.[138] The YAL defendants were twice as likely to say that the court experiences made them think more deeply about their future and make some positive changes in their lives, particularly around stopping or reducing alcohol and drug consumption, managing anger, and attending self-improvement courses.[139] They also appreciated when their case came back for review, being asked directly by the judge about their progress, and being commended on any progress that was added.[140]

There were some negative comments by both the YAL and the comparison court defendants. Having to stand for the judge in the courtroom was a major concern; they said it was nerve-wracking, their dignity had diminished, and it made them anxious and nervous, and they coped by 'zoning out.'[141] The YAL defendants wanted fewer service groups in the actual courtroom because they found it scary standing in front of them when they did not know their roles.[142] The primary concern of all defendants, whether in the YAL or comparison court, was the waiting time before the court appearances. Some of them waited more than three hours, and others took a day of unpaid leave due to the uncertainty of how long they might have to wait.[143]

Eighteen stakeholders were also interviewed, including judges, police, corrections staff, defence lawyers, and other support providers.[144] The positive outcomes were that the stakeholders found defendants engaged and participated

131 Ibid. 4–5.
132 Ibid. 5.
133 Ibid. 6.
134 Ibid.
135 Ibid.
136 Ibid. 8.
137 Ibid.
138 Ibid. 9.
139 Ibid. 8–9.
140 Ibid. 7.
141 Ibid. (n 132).
142 Ibid.
143 Ibid.
144 Ibid. 28.

more in the YAL court than in comparable courts.[145] The YAL judges were less punitive because they understood the young defendants much more.[146] The YAL judges also addressed the young defendants directly and used plain language.[147] The YAL lawyers prepared defendants for what happened in the YAL courtroom.[148] The defendants' attitude toward the criminal justice system improved, and the defendants' families also had improved trust and confidence.[149] Despite not having developed an intended screening tool, the YAL judges and professionals had access to more extensive information, including disabilities and neurodiversity issues, than they otherwise would have had.[150]

Police worked differently to issue fewer warrants for non-appearances but stood the case down while the duty lawyer or *whānau* member reminded the young defendant who usually came to court voluntarily by the next Monday.[151] This was much better than keeping the young defendant in custody for the weekend, waiting for their court appearance.[152] The percentage of total events that needed warrants to arrest decreased from 12% to 8%, compared to the comparison court, which stayed the same at 14%.[153]

Success of the YAL Court Expanded to Other Regions of Aotearoa, New Zealand

As a result of the successful pilot in Porirua, the YAL approach has been expanded to three other parts of Aotearoa, New Zealand, including Gisborne and Hamilton.[154] One of the key guidelines for these courts is the clear definition of neurodiversity, which is defined as follows:[155]

> Neurodiversity is a term used to capture the natural diversity of human brains. It was coined to encourage the use of respectful, inclusive language

145 Ibid. 14.
146 Ibid.
147 Ibid.
148 Ibid 15.
149 Ibid 18.
150 Ibid. 19–20.
151 Ibid. 20, 23.
152 Ibid. 23. If a young adult is arrested in Porirua on a Friday night, they would ordinarily spend up to two nights in police custody to await their next court appearance.
153 Ibid. 13.
154 Ministry of Justice, 'Young Adult List National Operating Guidelines: Gisborne and Hamilton District Courts' (*New Zealand Government*, 2022) 1. Gisborne and Hamilton are cities in Aotearoa New Zealand with a high Māori population (56% and 26% respectively), well above the average (15%) for the total population. Māori have been very disadvantaged by traditional court system and often felt alienated by it. Sadly, the current prison population has 52% that are of Māori descent. See Ministry of Justice, *Key Initiatives—Hāpaitia te Oranga Tangata* <https://www.justice.govt.nz/justice-sector-policy/key-initiatives/key-initiatives-archive/hapaitia-te-oranga-tangata/> accessed 29 April 2025. Ibid. 9–10.
155 Ibid. 32–33.

when referring to neurological conditions. The underlying assumption is that neurological conditions are not 'disorders' to be cured and that language plays an important role in enabling neurodivergent individuals to fully participate in society.

The most recent expansion of a YAL has been to Whangārei, where the Executive Judge Greg Davis set up a pilot tackling unlicensed driving among young adults.[156] The primary reason for this is that many of the young adults, particularly boys, have an entry into the court system with driving type offences, such as driving while forbidden, driving while suspended, and driving without a licence.[157] The key link the court wants to make is with the Howard League, which was set up to avoid imprisonment for offenders, offering services and driver's licence training and being present in the YAL Court to directly link with offenders, book appointments, and get them on the road to be fully licenced to drive.[158] The Howard League pays for everything, including the driver's licence, training, and the vehicles for training.[159]

The Emerging Issue of Methamphetamine-Exposed Children in Aotearoa, New Zealand

Aotearoa, New Zealand, has a very high use of methamphetamine across all sectors of society.[160] The proposal for a trial of YAL Court recognised that methamphetamine in utero, like FASD, was becoming increasingly prevalent in young offenders.[161] However, there is a lack of research into how to detect, diagnose, and support methamphetamine-exposed defendants in Aotearoa, New Zealand's criminal justice system. Methamphetamine is difficult to detect compared to self-reporting.[162] For example, 210 methamphetamine-exposed infants in the

156 Whangārei is a city in Aotearoa, New Zealand, with a high Māori population (30%), well above the average for the total population. S. Pitman, 'Whangārei's New Court Tackles Unlicensed Driving among Young Adults' (*New Zealand Herald Whangārei*, 18 August 2024) 1.

157 Ibid.

158 Ibid. *New Zealand Howard League* <www.nzhowardleague.org.nz> accessed 20 December 2024.

159 Ibid.

160 25% of respondents indicating using methamphetamine during their lifetime in the New Zealand Drug Trends Survey in 2024. See C. Wilkins and others, 'What Drug Types Did NZDTS Survey Respondents Use in 2024?' (*Shore and Whāriki Research Centre, Massey University, Bulletin*, 2024) 2, 1 <https://nzdrugtrends.co.nz/> accessed 29 April 2025. Moreover, people in Aotearoa, New Zealand are consuming more methamphetamine. Wastewater testing indicated a 31% increase in the quantity of methamphetamine consumed in Aotearoa, New Zealand, compared to the previous four quarters of 2023. See C. Wilkins and others, 'Price of Meth Continues to Decline' (*Shore and Whāriki Research Centre, Massey University, Bulletin*, 2024) 4, 1 <https://nzdrugtrends.co.nz/> accessed 29 April 2025.

161 Doogue and Walker (n 8).

162 L. Smith and others, 'Developmental and Behavioural Consequences of Prenatal Methamphetamine Exposure: A Review of the Infant Development, Environment, and Lifestyle (IDEAL) Study' (2015) 51 *Neurotoxicology and Teratology* 39.

Infant Development and Lifestyle study (IDEAL study, the largest longest longitudinal study on prenatal methamphetamine exposure recruited from the U.S. and Aotearoa, New Zealand) had only 3.8% detected by meconium, compared to 71% maternal self-reporting.[163] The scientific effects on the prenatal child are neurotoxic effects such as reduced brain growth, low birth weight, disturbed adaptation, poor quality of movement, increased physiological stress, low arousal, and less excitability.[164] During childhood, the IDEAL study showed that children with methamphetamine exposure had reduced executive functions and signaled poor inhibitory control.[165] However, this study was not funded after the children reached their teenage years, and there is almost no information on adult outcomes after prenatal methamphetamine exposure.[166]

Other overseas research showed that by age 8 years old, such children had more problems relating to their peers, particularly with aggression.[167] At the age of 14 years old, they had poorer school performance, specifically in mathematics, language, and physical fitness.[168] Methamphetamine-exposed children were more likely to have lower scores on IQ and the individual indices of verbal comprehension, perceptual reasoning, working memory, and processing speed index.[169] Therefore, it is likely that methamphetamine-exposed defendants would face similar challenges in each stage of the criminal justice system, like defendants with FASD highlighted in *New Zealand Police v. Morrison*.[170] However, the future impacts of methamphetamine-exposed defendants on the Aotearoa, New Zealand criminal justice system are unknown.

Conclusion

This chapter has focused on a practical and realistic perspective of the impact of where, what, and how neuroscience has positively and concretely contributed to the criminal justice system in Aotearoa, New Zealand. It focused on defendants with FASD, the most commonly occurring neurodiverse condition that has appeared in the courts, and highlighted the emerging issue of methamphetamine-exposed defendants.

The neuroscience of FASD has impacted the judiciary, like Judge Hastings in *New Zealand Police v. Morrison*, to build best practice guidelines on dealing

163 Ibid. Meconium was used to detect methamphetamine from the first stool of an infant.

164 F. A. Perez and others, 'Prenatal Methamphetamine—Impact on the Mother and Child—A Review' (2021) 117 *Addiction* 251–254.

165 Perez (n 165) 254.

166 C. Reed, 'Fighting the Demon: The Children of the Meth Epidemic' (*New Zealand Herald*, New Zealand, 10 May 2019) 1. Dr. Trecia Wouldes from the IDEAL study said the research in Aotearoa New Zealand is 'dead in the water' without funding needed to continue research on prenatal methamphetamine exposure in children aged 9- to 13-years-old.

167 Ibid. Perez (n 166). This study was on amphetamine-exposed Swedish children followed to 14- to 15-years-old.

168 Ibid.

169 Ibid.

170 *New Zealand Police v. Morrison* (n 2).

with defendants with FASD to ensure they are treated fairly and appropriately.[171] Moreover, it has been optimistic that the neuroscience of FASD has been taken into account at sentencing, like in *Maaka-Wanahi v. Police*, as a factor to reduce sentence due to the defendant's lack of moral culpability.[172] However, the practical impact of neuroscience on the judiciary has been limited by the lack of expertise available on FASD in a small country.[173] Moreover, it is disappointing that FASD is not recognised as a disability by the state. Therefore, sentences of imprisonment have been imposed, like in *R v. Tupoumalohi*, despite a prison sentence not acting as a deterrent to an FASD offender,[174] and hybrid care orders upheld in *M v. R* due to the lack of community support available.[175] There have been promising and positive developments in the Youth Adult List, a specialist court, driven by the then-Principal Youth Court Judge Walker[176] and supported by the Chief Judge Taumaunu's transformative model.[177] The YAL Court recognises the neuroscience that defendants bring neuro-disabilities, such as FASD, which 'do not have an expiry date.'[178] Therefore, the court should use neuroscience to provide special considerations when it comes to court processes to ensure procedural fairness.[179] Once the defendant's neuroscience is understood, there is not only an emphasis on taking them into account in sentencing but also throughout the whole court process so that it is fully understood by those with neurodiverse conditions. There is also an emphasis on intervention and treatment once the diagnosis is recognised.

The court processes of recognising neuroscience depend very much on the lawyers and judges involved, who are aware of it, and who want to ensure that people with neurodiversity are treated fairly according to their condition during the court process. It is clear when the comparison is done between specialist courts, such as the YAL Court, and the general courts, that the specialist courts do a much better job in taking a fully therapeutic approach with those with neurodiversity than the general courts. Knowledge of neuroscience and neurodiversity in the court processes has made them much more human. Neurodiversity requires courts and those working in them to look at the world through the eyes of those with neurodiversity, so that there is a full understanding of the neuroscience behind the defendants' behaviors. The Youth and District Courts are to be congratulated for showing this respect to defendants and for leading the way and ensuring that neurodiversity is not just a theory.

171 Ibid.
172 *Maaka-Wanahi v. Police* (n 3).
173 See *Gallacher v. R* (n 4).
174 *R v. Tupoumalohi* (n 54).
175 *M v. R* (n 65).
176 Doogue and Walker (n 8).
177 Taumaunu (n 104).
178 Doogue and Walker (n 8).
179 Ibid.

8 Mental Health and Neuroscience

Future of Sentencing and Incarceration

Sandy S. Xie and Olivia Choy

Introduction

Rikers Island, home to New York's largest prison facility, is also the state's largest mental institution and one of the largest psychiatric care providers in the United States (U.S.), with the other two being the Los Angeles County Jail and the Cook County Jail in Chicago.[1] One man, who injured a woman by pushing her onto the train tracks, was found to have schizophrenia and spent more than eight years being transferred from facility to facility before his trial, until he ended up in Rikers, spending more time between facilities than he would have if convicted of a crime.[2] Similar stories of people with long histories of mental illness are common, either being shuffled to and from different facilities before landing in prison or staying in prison instead of receiving treatment.[3] Around half of the population at Rikers has a mental health diagnosis, mirroring a trend across the U.S. in which more than 70% of individuals in prisons and jails have one or more mental health diagnoses.[4] Because of this, current treatments in incarceration settings, although lacking and limited, include therapy, counselling, and medication.[5]

1 K. Adams, J. Ferrandino, 'Managing Mentally Ill Inmates in Prisons' (2008) 35 *Criminal Justice and Behavior* 911; A. McDonough, 'Mental Health Care on Rikers: New York's Largest Psychiatric Provider' (*City & State New York*, 30 September 2022) <https://www.cityandstateny.com/policy/2022/09/mental-health-care-rikers-new-yorks-largest-psychiatric-provider/377870/> accessed 1 October 2024.

2 J. Ransom, A. J. Harris, J. A. Alvarado Jr, 'How Rikers Island Became New York's Largest Mental Institution' (*The New York Times*, 29 December 2023) <https://www.nytimes.com/2023/12/29/nyregion/nyc-rikers-homeless-mental-illness.html> accessed 1 October 2024.

3 Ibid.; D. A. Pinals, 'For Too Many with Mental Illness, Incarceration Is the Default' (*Trend Magazine*, 2023) <https://pew.org/49FnDpG> accessed 1 October 2024.

4 Ransom, Harris and Alvarado Jr (n 2); P. Warth, 'Unjust Punishment: The Impact of Incarceration on Mental Health' (*New York State Bar Association*, 5 December 2022) <https://nysba.org/unjust-punishment-the-impact-of-incarceration-on-mental-health/> accessed 1 October 2024.

5 J. M. Reingle Gonzalez, N. M. Connell, 'Mental Health of Prisoners: Identifying Barriers to Mental Health Treatment and Medication Continuity' (2014) 104 *American Journal of Public Health* 2328.

DOI: 10.4324/9781003510246-9

However, because of the proliferation of individuals with mental illness who become incarcerated, some places in the U.S. have started to consider alternatives for mentally ill offenders. Various treatment approaches for offenders have been investigated, ranging from diversion to psychosocial interventions to those more biologically based; some of these approaches have been used as strategies to shorten a sentence or avoid traditional incarceration altogether.[6] Although these approaches seem to represent promising alternatives, ethical concerns surrounding them have emerged, including whether the decision to receive treatment is voluntary, due process questions, and possible stigmatisation.[7] Stemming from this background, the current chapter discusses possible ways that neuroscience can contribute to making mental health care more beneficial and lead to more positive outcomes for defendants diagnosed with mental illnesses.

History of Mental Health Treatment in Prisons

Mental health treatment in prisons today cannot be discussed without considering historical perspectives and trends of how mental illness has been addressed over time in criminal justice populations. In the past, mental illness 'was viewed not as a disease, but as a manifestation of evil spirits.'[8] This led to the inaccurate and inherently biased beliefs that mental illness is associated with moral depravity.[9] Internationally, France and the United Kingdom (U.K.) opened institutions in the 1600s and 1800s, respectively, housing those considered to be 'a threat to normality and progress.'[10] Early in the 1800s in the U.S., asylums were built following the ideal of 'moral treatment,' a therapeutic model emphasising kindness and character development, leading to recovery

6 J. S. Lamberti, 'Preventing Criminal Recidivism Through Mental Health—Criminal Justice Collaboration' (2016) 67 *Psychiatric Services* 1206; S. N. Thekkumkara and others, 'Psychosocial Interventions for Prisoners with Mental and Substance Use Disorders: A Systematic Review' (2022) 44 *Indian Journal of Psychological Medicine* 211.

7 A. Watson and others, 'Mental Health Courts and the Complex Issue of Mentally Ill Offenders' (2001) 52 *Psychiatric Services* 477; T. Seltzer, 'Mental Health Courts: A Misguided Attempt to Address the Criminal Justice System's Unfair Treatment of People with Mental Illnesses' (2005) 11 *Psychology, Public Policy, and Law* 570; U. Castellano, L. Anderson, 'Mental Health Courts in America: Promise and Challenges' (2012) 57 *American Behavioral Scientist* 163; E. M. Brank, J. A. Haby, 'The Intended and Unintended Consequences of Problem-Solving Courts' in R. L. Wiener and E. M. Brank (eds), *Problem Solving Courts: Social Science and Legal Perspectives* (Springer, 2013) 239–251 <https://doi.org/10.1007/978-1-4614-7403-6_13> accessed 15 November 2021.

8 J. A. Dvoskin, J. L. Knoll IV, M. Silva, 'A Brief History of the Criminalization of Mental Illness' (2020) 25 *CNS Spectrums* 638.

9 J. L. Knoll IV, 'The Recurrence of an Illusion: The Concept of "Evil" in Forensic Psychiatry' (2008) 36 *The Journal of the American Academy of Psychiatry and the Law* 105.

10 Dvoskin, Knoll IV and Silva (n 8).

and being cured.[11] However, individuals in asylums commonly stayed there for their entire lives.

Also, in the 1800s, Dorothea Dix played a significant role in shaping the treatment of the mentally ill, both during incarceration practices and in society more generally. During a visit to the East Cambridge Jail, she witnessed the horrific conditions that the inmates were subjected to, such as being denied clothes and being physically restrained.[12] This inspired her to investigate these conditions, eventually writing to the state legislature and supporting a 'moral treatment' model of care.[13] Eventually, Dix's efforts played a pivotal role in founding and expanding hospitals that could treat and help the mentally ill. By the end of the 1800s, public institutions and asylums were commonplace, with each state in the U.S. having at least one.[14]

However, as time passed, these public institutions became more and more crowded; the penal culture shifted from a rehabilitative model to a more retributive and punishment-oriented model, leading to another shift in the treatment of the mentally ill.[15] More individuals with mental health issues were being incarcerated for relatively low-level crimes.[16] One significant contributing factor to the growing criminalisation of the mentally ill was deinstitutionalisation.[17] Individuals with mental health diagnoses were transferred to out-of-state institutions that were soon closed. More than half a million individuals were occupied in state hospitals in 1960, with that number decreasing to less than 60,000 by 2000.[18] To compensate, community treatment programs were planned to handle the closing of state institutions, but not nearly enough were created to deal with those who exited state hospitals.[19] Closing state institutions and releasing these individuals left them with a lack of treatment, rehabilitative options, and services needed to help them successfully live and function in society.[20]

Once these individuals were released, other factors also increased the likelihood of their criminalisation and subsequent imprisonment. Many individuals suffering from mental health issues turned to substances to cope, which

11 M. S. Parry, 'Dorothea Dix (1802–1887)' (2006) 96 *American Journal of Public Health* 624; Dvoskin, Knoll IV and Silva (n 8).

12 Parry (n 11).

13 Ibid.; A. S. Luchins, 'Moral Treatment in Asylums and General Hospitals in 19th-Century America' (1989) 123 *The Journal of Psychology* 585.

14 Dvoskin, Knoll IV and Silva (n 8).

15 N. Bark, 'Prisoner Mental Health in the USA' (2014) 11 *International Psychiatry* 53.

16 Castellano and Anderson (n 7).

17 R. N. Slate, 'From the Jailhouse to Capitol Hill: Impacting Mental Health Court Legislation and Defining What Constitutes a Mental Health Court' (2003) 49 *Crime & Delinquency* 6.

18 Ibid.

19 Ibid.

20 E. F. Torrey, *Out of the Shadows: Confronting America's Mental Illness Crisis* (John Wiley & Sons, 1997) <https://www.pbs.org/wgbh/pages/frontline/shows/asylums/special/excerpt.html> accessed 1 November 2021.

led to substance abuse and addiction, and the increased enforcement of drug offences and quality-of-life crimes heavily prioritised criminal justice interventions.[21] Other factors included underfunded communities, inadequate re-entry support, limited mental health benefits, and a lack of consistent mental health services, all of which have continued to exacerbate the criminogenic and incarceration risks of mentally ill individuals.[22]

At the turn of the 20th century, more punitive and retributive societal attitudes completely dissolved the medical model of corrections, which saw the offender as 'sick' in some way, the offence as a symptom of the illness, and emphasised rehabilitation as the cure.[23] Being tough on crime and giving offenders their just deserts created mass incarceration and led to 'correctional facilities hous[ing] mentally ill persons in record numbers, becom[ing] the new asylums.'[24] This led to the present-day system, in which mental health is most often treated punitively via incarceration in the criminal justice system.

Mental Health and Incarceration Overlap

Individuals who are incarcerated often suffer from adverse mental health and neurological deficits as a result of social factors during childhood.[25] Many incarcerated individuals have a history of childhood trauma, which is correlated with antisocial behaviour in adulthood, drug and alcohol abuse, and mood and emotional disorders such as depression.[26] This trauma can include physical, emotional, and sexual abuse, as well as neglect—with this exposure linked to clinical symptoms and behavioural problems in adulthood.[27] Witnessing and being exposed to violence and victimisation also have negative consequences on health outcomes and future antisocial and violent behaviour.[28] Studies focusing on victimisation and exposure to violence found that between 43% and 80% of women and 13% and 55% of men incarcerated reported childhood trauma in their past, which in turn correlated to a higher frequency of mental health issues and increased violent behaviours while incarcerated.[29]

21 N. El-Guebaly, 'Substance Abuse and Mental Disorders: The Dual Diagnoses Concept' (1990) 35 *The Canadian Journal of Psychiatry* 261.

22 G. L. Wren, 'Mental Health Courts: Serving Justice and Promoting Recovery' (2010) 19 *Annals of Health Law* 18.

23 D. E. MacNamara, 'The Medical Model in Corrections Requiescat in Pace Requiescat in Pace' (1977) 14 *Criminology* 439.

24 Dvoskin, Knoll IV and Silva (n 8).

25 G. D. Caruso, *Public Health and Safety: The Social Determinants of Health and Criminal Behavior* (ResearcherLinks Books, 2017) 1–38.

26 N. Wolff, J. Shi, 'Childhood and Adult Trauma Experiences of Incarcerated Persons and Their Relationship to Adult Behavioral Health Problems and Treatment' (2012) 9 *International Journal of Environmental Research and Public Health* 1908.

27 Ibid.

28 Caruso (n 25).

29 M. S. Martin and others, 'Risk of Violence by Inmates with Childhood Trauma and Mental Health Needs' (2015) 39 *Law and Human Behavior* 614.

Another factor that can contribute to poor mental health and future incarceration is an individual's socioeconomic status. Previous studies found that not only was physical health affected negatively when an individual had a lower socioeconomic status, but mental illness was as well.[30] Children and adolescents who lived in poverty went through many stressful life situations, including financial burdens from illness, loss of employment of a parent, and problems in school, with this exposure increasing the risk of developing mental health problems.[31] Poverty can also lead to depressive symptoms and other forms of psychological distress, which is associated with a heightened risk of violent behaviour.[32] One biopsychosocial framework proposes that social factors, such as life events and family factors, lead to changes in biological functioning, such as autonomic arousal and brain alterations, which are associated with psychological factors predisposing to crime and delinquency.[33] Findings that link early social adversity and later antisocial behaviour are partly attributed to lower heart rates[34] and lower grey matter volume in brain regions associated with temporal discounting;[35] these findings support the notion that biological and psychological mechanisms may help explain why adverse social environments are related to criminal behaviour. Along with mental health impacts, low socioeconomic status was also associated with an increase in the number of self-reported crimes and violent victimisation.[36]

One more critical factor to note is the impact that structural racism and discrimination have on health and inequities. Experiencing discrimination and racism can have profound effects on an individual's psychology, leading to poor self-esteem, poor overall mental health, and specific outcomes such as depression, anxiety disorders, suicidal thoughts, and emotional irregularities.[37] Other

30 N. B. Anderson, C. A. Armstead, 'Toward Understanding the Association of Socioeconomic Status and Health: A New Challenge for the Biopsychosocial Approach' (1995) 57 *Biopsychosocial Science and Medicine* 213; Caruso (n 25).

31 F. Reiss and others, 'Socioeconomic Status, Stressful Life Situations and Mental Health Problems in Children and Adolescents: Results of the German BELLA Cohort-Study' (2019) 14 *PLoS One* e0213700

32 R. Yu and others, 'Depression and Violence in Adolescence and Young Adults: Findings from Three Longitudinal Cohorts' (2017) 56 *Journal of the American Academy of Child & Adolescent Psychiatry* 652.

33 O. Choy D. P. Farrington, A. Raine, 'The Need to Incorporate Autonomic Arousal in Developmental and Life-Course Research and Theories' (2015) 1 *Journal of Developmental and Life-Course Criminology* 189.

34 O. Choy and others, 'The Mediating Role of Heart Rate on the Social Adversity-Antisocial Behavior Relationship: A Social Neurocriminology Perspective' (2015) 52 *Journal of Research in Crime and Delinquency* 303.

35 S. Mackey and others, 'Brain Regions Related to Impulsivity Mediate the Effects of Early Adversity on Antisocial Behavior' (2017) 82 *Biological Psychiatry* 275.

36 Caruso (n 25); D. Fergusson, N. Swain-Campbell, J. Horwood, 'How Does Childhood Economic Disadvantage Lead to Crime?' (2004) 45 *Journal of Child Psychology and Psychiatry* 956.

37 S. Selvarajah and others, 'Racism, Xenophobia, and Discrimination: Mapping Pathways to Health Outcomes' (2022) 400 *The Lancet* 2109.

studies have also found increased associations between racial discrimination and poor mental health outcomes related to psychosis, such as schizophrenia.[38] Racial discrimination has also been found to have both neural and hormonal effects, often resulting in chronically higher cortisol levels, an uncontrolled hypothalamic-pituitary adrenal (HPA) axis, and impairments in prefrontal cortex (PFC) functioning.[39] As mental health symptoms and neurological deficits can contribute to the future likelihood of crime commission and subsequent incarceration, this suggests that understanding and involving neuroscience within the criminal justice and legal systems remains exceedingly crucial.

The Effect of Incarceration on Mental Health

Although many prisoners enter the criminal justice system and incarceration environments due to a history of mental illness, there is also evidence to show that being in prison and jail exacerbates symptoms or even contributes to the development of a mental illness. From a trauma perspective, trauma experienced in prison and its combined effect can cause severe mental illness, like post-traumatic stress disorder (PTSD), as well as worsening preexisting conditions.[40] Other factors of the prison itself can contribute to poorer mental health, including overcrowded prisons and larger prisons in general.[41] Overcrowding contributes to a lack of privacy, and being in close quarters with others who are suffering from mental health problems culminates in emotional and psychological disruptions.[42] The highly rigid structure and regime of a prison can also lead to issues such as depression, paranoia, suicidal thoughts, and other mood dysfunctions.[43]

One social factor within prisons that can affect a person's mental health negatively is isolation or solitary confinement, with more extended periods and a lack of mental stimulation and activity exacerbating mental health issues.[44] There is also strong evidence to suggest that solitary confinement affects the brain physiologically, leading to possibly permanent changes.[45] Some of these

38 E. A. Pascoe, L. Smart Richman, 'Perceived Discrimination and Health: A Meta-Analytic Review' (2009) 135 *Psychological Bulletin* 531; D. R. Williams, S. A. Mohammed, 'Discrimination and Racial Disparities in Health: Evidence and Needed Research' (2009) 32 *Journal of Behavioral Medicine* 20; M. Berger, Z. Sarnyai, '"More than Skin Deep": Stress Neurobiology and Mental Health Consequences of Racial Discrimination' (2015) 18 *Stress* 1.

39 Berger and Sarnyai (n 38).

40 C. Armour, 'Mental Health in Prison: A Trauma Perspective on Importation and Deprivation' (2012) 5 *International Journal of Criminology and Sociological Theory* 886.

41 J. Walker and others, 'Changes in Mental State Associated with Prison Environments: A Systematic Review' (2014) 129 *Acta Psychiatrica Scandinavica* 427.

42 A. Goomany, T. Dickinson, 'The Influence of Prison Climate on the Mental Health of Adult Prisoners: A Literature Review' (2015) 22 *Journal of Psychiatric and Mental Health Nursing* 413.

43 Ibid.

44 Ibid.

45 F. Coppola, 'The Brain in Solitude: An (Other) Eighth Amendment Challenge to Solitary Confinement' (2019) 6 *Journal of Law and the Biosciences* 184; V. Heng, M. Zigmond, R. J.

include hypersensitivity, cognitive deficits, and an increased risk of socially dysfunctional behaviours, such as aggression or panic.[46] In contrast, those in prison with a severe mental illness stressed how important routine, social interaction, and regular exercise are to maintain morale and regulate behaviour.[47] Another social factor that can lead to adverse mental health outcomes is the victimisation that some prisoners face. Violence is often used to uphold social hierarchy in prison, leading to the normalisation of bullying and other forms of victimisation.[48] Fear of victimisation can lead individuals to become isolated for their safety, resulting in higher loneliness levels, which directly correlate to worse mental health.[49]

An emotional factor that can lead to poorer mental health for those in prison is the forced disconnection and separation from family, such as children and spouses.[50] When visitation is allowed, it is heavily regulated and controlled, leading to some prisoners declining visits to lessen distress for their families.[51] Other conditions contributing to familial disconnection include being incarcerated far from home and not having consistent access to prison phones.[52] The psychological impact of this disconnection includes feelings of guilt, anxiety, fear, and worry, along with trauma and loss of purpose and identity.[53] Many of these factors not only increase the chances of mental health symptoms worsening, but they can also lead to the development and diagnosis of mental health conditions while incarcerated. This suggests a tremendous need for the development of mental health treatments and neuroscience-informed interventions for these populations moving forward.

Mental Health Treatments in the Criminal Justice System

Although access to mental health care for inmates has been sporadic, and a considerable portion of the prison population does not receive treatment for

---

Smeyne, 'Neuroanatomical and Neurochemical Effects of Prolonged Social Isolation in Adult Mice' (2023) 17 *Frontiers in Neuroanatomy* 1190291.

46 Coppola (n 45); Heng, Zigmond and Smeyne (n 45).

47 S. Yang and others, 'Doing Time: A Qualitative Study of Long-Term Incarceration and the Impact of Mental Illness' (2009) 32 *International Journal of Law and Psychiatry* 294.

48 See T. Newburn, E. A. Stanko, *Just Boys Doing Business?: Men, Masculinities and Crime* (Routledge, 1994).

49 J. L. Ireland, P. Qualter, 'Bullying and Social and Emotional Loneliness in a Sample of Adult Male Prisoners' (2008) 31 *International Journal of Law and Psychiatry* 19; Yang and others (n 47).

50 J. Nurse, P. Woodcock, J. Ormsby, 'Influence of Environmental Factors on Mental Health within Prisons: Focus Group Study' (2003) 327 *BMJ: British Medical Journal* 480; H. M. Harner, S. Riley, 'The Impact of Incarceration on Women's Mental Health: Responses from Women in a Maximum-Security Prison' (2013) 23 *Qualitative Health Research* 26.

51 Goomany and Dickinson (n 42); Harner and Riley (n 50).

52 Goomany and Dickinson (n 42); Harner and Riley (n 50); Nurse, Woodcock and Ormsby (n 50).

53 Goomany and Dickinson (n 42).

mental health conditions,[54] options are still sometimes provided. In the U.S., court mandates exist to ensure access to adequate healthcare in prisons.[55] The majority of state prisons have a screening process to assess mental health and determine if there are problems that require treatment.[56] Some of the treatment options include medication and cognitive behavioural therapy (CBT).[57] Non-invasive, biologically based interventions, such as nutritional supplementation, also show promise as forensic treatments.

One common approach used in forensic psychiatric settings involves pharmacological treatments. Psychotropic drugs have been prescribed to prisoners.[58] One type of psychotropic medication, antipsychotics, has been examined as a way to reduce aggressive behaviour, which is a diagnostic feature of various mental disorders, including antisocial personality disorder, intermittent explosive disorder, conduct disorder, and borderline personality disorder.[59] Randomised placebo-controlled trials (RCTs) have revealed an overall small but statistically significant effect of antipsychotic medications on reducing this symptom in adults.[60] Although this benefit was not found to differ significantly based on one's underlying psychiatric diagnosis, effect sizes were larger for the treatment of aggression in patients with schizophrenia and bipolar mood disorder, pointing to their effectiveness in reducing core symptoms of these disorders.[61]

Stimulants have also been proposed as a treatment for attention deficit hyperactivity disorder (ADHD) in correctional settings, where ADHD is more prevalent than in the general population.[62] However, RCTs on methylphenidate, a stimulant commonly used in ADHD treatment, have yielded mixed findings in studies on prisoners. One recent review showed that although improvements in self-reported ADHD symptoms have been documented in some experimental trials, one study reported a lack of significant effects on ADHD symptoms between treatment and placebo groups.[63] Conclusions are limited by the small body of research on such treatments in incarcerated

54 Reingle Gonzalez and Connell (n 5).

55 Ibid.

56 Adams and Ferrandino (n 1).

57 C. E. Samuels Jr., 'Treatment and Care of Inmates with Mental Illness' (*US Department of Justice*, 2014) Program Statement 5310.16.

58 E. V. Griffiths, J. Willis, M. J. Spark, 'A Systematic Review of Psychotropic Drug Prescribing for Prisoners' (2012) 46 *The Australian and New* Zealand *Journal of Psychiatry* 407.

59 American Psychiatric Association, *Diagnostic and Statistical Manual of Mental Disorders (DSM-5)* (American Psychiatric Publishing, 2013).

60 G. I. van Schalkwyk and others, 'Antipsychotics for Aggression in Adults: A Meta-Analysis' (2018) 81 *Progress in Neuro-Psychopharmacology and Biological Psychiatry* 452.

61 Ibid.

62 S. Baggio and others, 'Prevalence of Attention Deficit Hyperactivity Disorder in Detention Settings: A Systematic Review and Meta-Analysis' (2018) 9 *Frontiers in Psychiatry* 331.

63 C. Byrne, D. Guenter, 'Treatments for ADHD in Adults in Jails, Prisons and Correctional Settings: A Scoping Review of the Literature' (2023) 11 *Health & Justice* 36.

populations and suggest that medication may be viewed as a component of multimodal treatment that also includes non-pharmacological interventions.

In criminal justice settings, psychological treatments may also be used. When various psychological therapies are administered to individuals diagnosed with mental disorders in forensic mental health units or wards in prisons and jails, they have been found to have minor beneficial effects by improving patients' psychiatric symptoms, reducing pro-criminal and violent attitudes, and reducing problematic ward behaviour.[64] Of the psychological therapies that have been conducted in prisons to improve mental health outcomes, cognitive behavioural therapy (CBT) and mindfulness-based interventions have emerged as the treatment approaches with the most empirical evidence from experimental trials. CBT-based treatments address cognitions that contribute to the maintenance of emotional distress and behaviour problems, while mindfulness interventions help individuals attend to aversive stimuli, including cognitions and emotions, with non-reactive present-moment awareness.[65] Both treatments are modestly effective in reducing depressive and anxiety symptoms in prisoners.[66]

An alternative approach to treatment in criminal justice settings involves biologically based interventions for offenders that are safe and non-invasive.[67] One such intervention is nutritional supplementation. For example, fatty acid supplementation has been linked to a significant 42.7% reduction in conduct disorder problems.[68] This is notable because prisoners with conduct disorder carry a greater risk of further mental health problems.[69] As fatty acids such as omega-3 play a role in regulating the activity of membrane enzymes, protecting neurons from cell death, stimulating neurite outgrowth, and enhancing synaptic functioning and dendritic branching,[70] nutritional supplementation

64 L. G. McIntosh and others, 'Effectiveness of Psychological and Psychosocial Interventions for Forensic Mental Health Inpatients: A Meta-Analysis' (2021) 58 *Aggression and Violent Behavior* 101551.

65 N. Bouw and others, 'Mindfulness-Based Stress Reduction in Prison: Experiences of Inmates, Instructors, and Prison Staff' (2019) 63 *International Journal of Offender Therapy and Comparative Criminology* 2550; K. Saxena, A. Sahai, 'Understanding the Effectiveness of Cognitive Behavioural Therapy: A Study on Offenders' (2024) *Annals of Neurosciences* 09727531241288609.

66 I. A. Yoon, K. Slade, S. Fazel, 'Outcomes of Psychological Therapies for Prisoners with Mental Health Problems: A Systematic Review and Meta-Analysis' (2017) 85 *Journal of Consulting and Clinical Psychology* 783.

67 O. Choy, F. Focquaert, A. Raine, 'Benign Biological Interventions to Reduce Offending' (2020) 13 *Neuroethics* 29; T. F. Denson, O. Choy, 'Reconsidering Biological Treatments for Reducing Violent Offending' (2024) 14 *Psychology of Violence* 412.

68 L. Stevens and others, 'EFA Supplementation in Children with Inattention, Hyperactivity, and Other Disruptive Behaviors' (2003) 38 *Lipids* 1007.

69 B. Hofvander and others, 'Mental Health among Young Adults in Prison: The Importance of Childhood-Onset Conduct Disorder' (2017) 3 *BJPsych Open* 78.

70 S. Yehuda, S. Rabinovitz, D. I. Mostofsky, 'Essential Fatty Acids and the Brain: From Infancy to Aging' (2005) 26 *Neurobiology of Aging* 98; J. R. Hibbeln, T. A. Ferguson, T. L. Blasbalg, 'Omega-3 Fatty Acid Deficiencies in Neurodevelopment, Aggression and Autonomic

may help compensate for the structural and functional brain deficits observed in individuals who exhibit antisocial behaviour. Recent meta-analytic findings showing that omega-3 supplementation can reduce aggression in clinical samples and externalising-spectrum populations, such as prisoners,[71] also provide further support for its effectiveness in criminal justice settings. These options for treatment within incarceration settings can be beneficial, but neuroscience can also be utilised to either reduce the impact of incarceration or divert a defendant to an alternative outcome due to their mental health disorder.

Sentencing Mitigation for Mental Health Issues

Within the criminal justice system, neuroscience and mental health have been utilised as mitigating factors in court settings during sentencing. Neuropsychological testing has been increasingly used to examine an individual's cognitive functioning and to explain the link between mental health conditions or neurodevelopmental disorders and criminal behaviour.[72] Neuroimaging techniques, such as position emission tomography (PET), functional magnetic resonance imaging (fMRI), and computed tomography (CT) scans, have also been used to demonstrate activity in specific brain areas, particularly in relation to certain mental functions, including impulse control and moral judgment.[73] Neuroimages have been introduced in numerous ways to support mitigation claims, such as psychiatric disorders, developmental disorders, substance abuse, and other mental defects.[74] Behavioural genetics, which can be used as evidence for behavioural and medical histories of defendants, has also been admitted for mitigation purposes.[75] Finally, significant exposure to traumatic experiences, such as abuse, which affects areas of the brain such as the hippocampus and amygdala,[76] and can lead to a myriad of issues related to aspects such as emotional or affective regulation, threat perception, and memory, has been introduced as mitigating evidence surrounding adversity.[77]

Dysregulation: Opportunities for Intervention' (2006) 18 *International Review of Psychiatry* 107; P. M. Kidd, 'Omega-3 DHA and EPA for Cognition, Behavior, and Mood: Clinical Findings and Structural-' (2007) 12 *Alternative Medicine Review* 207.

71 A. Raine, L. Brodrick, 'Omega-3 Supplementation Reduces Aggressive Behavior: A Meta-Analytic Review of Randomized Controlled Trials' (2024) 78 *Aggression and Violent Behavior* 101956.

72 See K. J. Reddy, 'Mitigation and Sentencing in Criminal Cases', *Foundations of Criminal Forensic Neuropsychology* (Springer, Cham, 2025) <https://link.springer.com/chapter/10.1007/978-3-031-83771-5_13> accessed 28 April 2025.

73 Z. Khalid, R. Lee, B. W. Wall, 'The Use of Neurobiological Evidence in Sentencing Mitigation' (2024) 42 *Behavioral Sciences & the Law* 2.

74 Ibid.

75 Ibid.

76 K. C. Hughes, L. M. Shin, 'Functional Neuroimaging Studies of Post-Traumatic Stress Disorder' (2011) 11 *Expert Review of Neurotherapeutics* 275.

77 Khalid, Lee and Wall (n 73).

Although many of the successful mitigations to sentencing that have occurred because of neuroscience and mental health evidence relate to the death penalty and capital cases in the U.S.,[78] this evidence can be used to mitigate perceptions of establishing culpability in non-capital contexts as well. Indeed, mitigation can lead to many different sentencing outcomes. One possible outcome is that for those with severe mental health issues, sentences may better focus on providing treatment to address psychological problems.[79] Mitigation may also reduce the impact of incarceration on an individual's mental health, either through a reduced sentence or probation instead of prison in the case of nonviolent or first-time offences.[80] This can be especially helpful to prevent existing mental health symptoms from worsening in prison conditions. Neuroscience can also be used as a tool to recognise that certain defendants with mental health diagnoses do not have the cognitive capacity to be successfully 'punished' under the current punitive model.[81] Therefore, understanding that a defendant's mental health condition may have been a significant factor in their committed actions and may render them less responsive to current punishment practices may start to move the system towards a more rehabilitative model, involving outcomes outside of incarceration.

Alternatives to Incarceration

Recently, in the U.S., there has been a push towards alternatives to incarceration (ATI) programs for those suffering from mental health conditions and crises, both pre-booking and after successful mitigation during sentencing. Starting with prevention-based practices that occur before booking, crisis intervention teams (CITs) and co-responder teams have begun to emerge around the country, with the primary goal of connecting individuals with mental illnesses to treatment without arrest.[82] Crisis intervention teams consist of police officers who have specialised training to respond to mental health crisis calls.[83] Joint teams have a mental health crisis worker and a police officer responding to calls together; this requires a partnership between police and mental health providers in the community and takes a less forceful and stigmatising approach towards those with mental health problems that come into contact with the

78 Ibid.

79 Reddy (n 72); M. de Vel-Palumbo and others, 'Morally Excused but Socially Excluded: Denying Agency through the Defense of Mental Impairment' (2022) 17 *PLoS One* e0272061.

80 Reddy (n 72).

81 Ibid.

82 D. Cloud, C. Davis, 'Treatment Alternatives to Incarceration for People with Mental Health Needs in the Criminal Justice System: The Cost-Savings Implications' (*Vera Institute of Justice*, 2013) Research Summary.

83 F. Sirotich, 'The Criminal Justice Outcomes of Jail Diversion Programs for Persons with Mental Illness: A Review of the Evidence' (2009) 37 *The Journal of the American Academy of Psychiatry and the Law* 461–472.

criminal justice system.[84] Other prebooking strategies include hiring mental health professionals to consult and guide police officers in the field, as well as mental health mobile crisis teams that assist with police requests.[85]

Jail diversion programs are considered a form of post-booking diversion, where those in jail who are thought to have a mental illness are then evaluated, and those found eligible are linked with mental health services and treatment.[86] This process requires agreement and consent among the judge, prosecutor, and defence lawyer.[87] Court-based diversion programs are also categorised as post-booking diversion, where clinicians work inside the courthouse to assess and negotiate treatment plans for bail release or for defendants to receive probation with treatment conditions if convicted.[88]

The other central post-booking diversion process is the use of mental health courts. The first official mental health court was created in Florida following a grand jury recommendation during a case where someone suffering from a traumatic brain injury heard voices to push an older woman, fatally injuring her.[89] Mental health courts are considered problem-solving courts, going beyond criminal responsibility and focusing on reducing future criminal offending by using therapeutic and interdisciplinary methods to address the underlying issues contributing to offending.[90] Most mental health courts follow the same basic model. First, the offender must be deemed eligible based on a psychiatric diagnosis and a criminal charge, and once they qualify, they voluntarily participate in a community-based treatment program.[91] Successful completion of the program involves a determination by the court staff that the participant can live independently, has reached emotional wellness, and has stopped criminal activity. Those who are successful may have their sentences reduced or deferred.[92] Overall, these interventions have been argued as possible solutions to channel mentally ill individuals away from the criminal justice system and move the use of mental health services more into the realm of health care and community medical settings. Neuroscientific research is sure to improve these interventions in the future by providing insight into which treatments work and how individuals with specific diagnoses respond to them within diversionary services.

84 Cloud and Davis (n 81).
85 Sirotich (n 82).
86 K. J. Gill, A. A. Murphy, 'Jail Diversion for Persons with Serious Mental Illness Coordinated by a Prosecutor's Office' (2017) 2017 *BioMed Research International* 7917616.
87 Sirotich (n 82).
88 Ibid.
89 Castellano and Anderson (n 7); Slate (n 17).
90 P. Bowen, S. Whitehead, *Problem-Solving Courts: An Evidence Review* (Centre for Justice Innovation, 2015) 2.
91 Castellano and Anderson (n 7).
92 Ibid.

Ethical Issues With Mental Health Treatment in the Criminal Justice System

Although treatment and other alternatives for individuals with mental illness, especially diversion and other outcomes outside of incarceration, have been hailed as promising future directions, some ethical issues and questions have also emerged. Watson and other critics of mental health diversion courts have argued that individuals with mental illness lack due process when deciding to take part in a court that has the option of shortening a sentence or expunging it altogether.[93]

Individuals also typically have the option to either participate in voluntary treatment or remain incarcerated, which leads to the notions of 'constrained choice or 'coerced treatments.'[94] Having the threats of incarceration and the potential for dismissed charges can lead individuals to feel forced to participate in a mental health court.[95] This question of whether the decision was voluntary is also magnified when mentally ill individuals are involved because of issues with mental capacity, especially since many severe mental illnesses are linked with deficits in decision-making and executive functioning.[96] Individuals in diversion programs also have little say in the requirements they must follow, including interventions such as mandatory medications and treatment provisions chosen by psychiatrists or clinical staff.[97] Choosing not to follow rules set by the judge or a treatment team can result in a dismissal from the program and a return to incarceration; thus, mandatory requirements for medication may at times 'force' individuals to take part in pharmacological therapies when they otherwise would not.

Relatedly, those on medication, either as part of a diversion program or within prison, often have difficulties continuing care when they finish their programs or sentence. There is a lack of continuum-of-care resources during the re-entry process, especially regarding access to medication, overall monetary needs for medical expenses, and other services.[98] In a study of county jails in the state of Minnesota, 89% of facilities reported that the large majority of inmates are taking medications to treat mental illness at their release, but that pre-release planning was rarely conducted.[99] Another study found that,

93 Watson and others (n 7).

94 Castellano and Anderson (n 7); J. S. Goldkamp, C. Irons-Guynn, 'Emerging Judicial Strategies for the Mentally Ill in the Criminal Caseload: Mental Health Courts' (2000) *Crime and Justice Research Institutes* 1.

95 Brank and Haby (n 7); Castellano and Anderson (n 7).

96 S. L. Miller, A. M. Perelman, 'Mental Health Courts: An Overview and Redefinition of Tasks and Goals' (2009) 33 *Law & Psychology Review* 113.

97 Castellano and Anderson (n 7).

98 A. Steiner, 'Continuum-of-Care Programs Could Help Ex-Offenders Treat Their Mental Illness—and Stay out of Jail' (*MinnPost*, Minnesota, USA, 13 November 2017) <http://www.minnpost.com/mental-health-addiction/2017/11/continuum-care-programs-could-help-ex-offenders-treat-their-mental-i/> accessed 14 February 2025.

99 B. Rohrer, T. P. Stratton, 'Continuum of Care for Inmates Taking Psychiatric Medications While Incarcerated in Minnesota County Jails' (2017) 23 *Journal of Correctional Health Care.*

although almost 90% of a sample of inmates who had severe mental health needs had contact with a mental health professional during their incarceration, only 5% had a referral at release to a community team.[100] For this same sample, one-third had been charged with something new, and one-fifth had been reincarcerated, after a year—further contributing to the cycle of incarceration for those without resources.[101] Thus, serious ethical concerns can stem from providing treatment either in prison or as an alternative to incarceration if there are few to no resources to continue the same treatment on release.

One other potential ethical concern is the increased stigmatisation that someone may face if they are treated through a mental health diversion program. Individuals who come in contact with the criminal justice system already face social stigmatisation due to their criminal records, including issues with employment and housing, which may even occur if the charges are dismissed.[102] Because the separate docket of a diversion program like a mental health court clearly differentiates them as defendants with diagnosed mental illnesses, the societal stereotypes that those with mental health problems have a greater propensity to commit crimes can be intensified.[103] Having both the label of a person with mental illness *and* a criminal record can further contribute to their stigmatisation, leading to increased negative feelings and social experiences that may affect their lives after mental health court involvement.[104] Stigma remains a barrier for those within prison as well, with many individuals deciding to stop treatment or self-isolate to keep their symptoms and illness hidden from other inmates.[105] These ethical concerns can result in unintended negative consequences, which may detract from the positive outcomes that mental health treatment and diversion programs aim to achieve.

Conclusions and Future Directions for Mental Health Treatment and Neuroscience

To tackle the ethical concerns that may occur as the use of mental health treatment and diversion programs continues to grow, several factors may improve future practices. First, to tackle potential issues with due process, defence

100 C. C. Browne and others, 'Continuity of Mental Health Care during the Transition from Prison to the Community Following Brief Periods of Imprisonment' (2022) 13 *Frontiers in Psychiatry* 934837.

101 Ibid.

102 Seltzer (n 7).

103 G. L. Acquaviva, 'Mental Health Courts: No Longer Experimental' (2006) 36 *Seton Hall Law Review* 971; Castellano and Anderson (n 7).

104 B. Ray, C. B. Dollar, 'Exploring Stigmatization and Stigma Management in Mental Health Court: Assessing Modified Labeling Theory in a New Context' (2014) 29 *Sociological Forum* 720.

105 K. Canada and others, 'Multi-Level Barriers to Prison Mental Health and Physical Health Care for Individuals with Mental Illnesses' (2022) 13 *Frontiers in Psychiatry* 777124.

attorneys remain crucial, and they need to recognise that their duties extend past the typical responsibilities they may have in traditional court settings.[106] They are also critical because they are tasked with communicating and interacting with clients with mental illness, knowing how the local community healthcare systems function, and considering how to best defend their clients against due process concerns and other issues regarding coercion and voluntariness.[107] Second, judges in mental health courts must move away from the role of an 'authoritarian' to that of a more caring and understanding 'helper'; this may be a complete shift from their prior experiences and training in traditional court settings.[108] Judges also have increased discretionary power within these programs and may act in similar roles to social workers—interacting with participants on a more personal level, as well as being at the forefront of their treatment.[109] Therefore, specialised training for criminal justice actors working with clients in diversion programs may lead to more successful outcomes for defendants and less unintended consequences such as stigmatisation.

When it comes to the reintegration of defendants with mental health issues, continuum-of-care plans are essential to have in place for those who receive treatment, medication, and/or counselling. Indeed, continuum-of-care programs ensure that individuals receive housing and establish a transition of care.[110] A critical recommendation for the success of continuum-of-care programs is ensuring more collaboration between correctional facilities and community healthcare, such as sharing data and health information for individuals being released from incarceration or diversion programs.[111] Adopting a transition clinics model, which uses community health workers who have previously been incarcerated or have personal experiences with incarceration to connect with individuals who have just been released to improve health outcomes, may also lead to successful continuum-of-care plans.[112] Although only a small

106 M. Thompson, F. Osher, D. Tomasini-Joshi, 'Improving Responses to People with Mental Illnesses: The Essential Elements of a Mental Health Court' (2007) *Bureau of Justice Assistance* 1.

107 C. E. Keele, 'Criminalization of the Mentally Ill: The Challenging Role of the Defense Attorney in the Mental Health Court System' (2002) 71 *UMKC Law Review* 1; Seltzer (n 7); S. Stefan, B. J. Winnick, 'A Dialogue on Mental Health Courts' (2005) 11 *Psychology, Public Policy, and Law* 507.

108 Brank and Haby (n 7).

109 A. D. Redlich and others, 'Patterns of Practice in Mental Health Courts: A National Survey' (2006) 30 *Law and Human Behavior* 347; U. Castellano, 'The Politics of Benchcraft: The Role of Judges in Mental Health Courts' (2017) 42 *Law & Social Inquiry* 398.

110 Justice Center, 'Explainer: Building Effective Partnerships with Continuums of Care to Increase Housing Options for People Leaving Prisons and Jails' (*The Council of State Governments*, 2022) Explainer NCJ 304499; M. Frank and others, 'No Health without Access: Using a Retrospective Cohort to Model a Care Continuum for People Released from Prison at an Urban, Safety Net Health System' (2023) 11 *Health & Justice* 49.

111 B. Divakaran, S. Shavit, A. Steiner, 'Best Practices for Engaging the Reentry Population in Health Care'; Frank and others (n 110).

112 Frank and others (n 110).

number of these clinics presently exist in U.S. communities, they 'have been shown to improve engagement in primary care, reduce emergency department utilisation, minimise future criminal justice system involvement, and achieve cost savings.'[113] Ultimately, continuum-of-care models are important tools for criminal justice to 'identify major drop-offs in accessing care, reveal unexpected patterns of healthcare utilization, inform future interventions, and provide data for the evaluations for those intervention.'[114]

Directly considering and understanding the experiences and choices of those receiving treatment and/or participating in diversion/mental health courts, especially when it comes to forced coercion and stigmatisation, is also an area of future research that is profoundly needed. Prior work has shown that some participants in mental health courts have reported that they are 'too controlling,'[115] with some not even realising that they had a choice to participate.[116] In another study, more than 50% of those who chose to participate in two different diversion programs were unaware that the choice to participate was voluntary prior to their decision—and they were unsure of the full program's requirements and did not know they were able to quit at any time.[117] Also, other studies have found high levels of stigma toward African American individuals who chose to participate in mental health treatment and diversion programs.[118] Thus, better understanding the feelings and experiences of those directly involved in mental health courts and diversion programs, especially their motivations and reasoning for participation as well as the stigmatisation they may experience due to these choices, is both essential and necessary for their future successes.

113 Ibid.; E. A. Wang and others, 'Transitions Clinic: Creating a Community-Based Model of Health Care for Recently Released California Prisoners' (2010) 125 *Public Health Reports* 171; E. A. Wang and others, 'Engaging Individuals Recently Released From Prison Into Primary Care: A Randomized Trial' (2012) 102 *American Journal of Public Health* e22; E. A. Wang and others, 'Propensity-Matched Study of Enhanced Primary Care on Contact with the Criminal Justice System among Individuals Recently Released from Prison to New Haven' (2019) 9 *BMJ Open* e028097; T. D. Harvey and others, 'Cost Savings of a Primary Care Program for Individuals Recently Released from Prison: A Propensity-Matched Study' (2022) 22 *BMC Health Services Research* 585.

114 Frank and others (n 110).

115 K. E. Canada, K. R. Trawver, S. Barrenger, 'Deciding to Participate in Mental Health Court: Exploring Participant Perspectives' (2020) 72 *International Journal of Law and Psychiatry* 101628.

116 N. G. Poythress and others, 'Perceived Coercion and Procedural Justice in the Broward Mental Health Court' (2002) 25 *International Journal of Law and Psychiatry* 517.

117 A. D. Redlich and others, 'Enrollment in Mental Health Courts: Voluntariness, Knowingness, and Adjudicative Competence' (2010) 34 *Law and Human Behavior* 91.

118 P. A. Dirks-Linhorst and others, 'Factors Associated with Mental Health Court Nonparticipation and Negative Termination' (2013) 30 *Justice Quarterly* 681; B. G. Stare, D. M. Fernando, 'Black American Men's Treatment Experiences in Mental Health Court: A Phenomenological Analysis' (2019) 40 *Journal of Addictions & Offender Counseling* 17.

In conclusion, as the criminal justice system continues to tackle the issues faced by mentally ill individuals, neuroscience research can positively influence criminal justice policy and practice. Using the knowledge gained by neuroscientists on human behaviour, development, and decision-making, all of which can be affected by mental health diagnoses, the criminal justice system may evolve into a more rehabilitative system that can do the most good and the least harm.[119] Neuroscience research has already been utilised and applied in court rulings, primarily in juvenile sentencing reform, with cases protecting juveniles from execution[120] and mandatory life imprisonment sentences[121] based on evidence-based arguments about brain maturation and development. This could potentially extend to mental health diagnoses, with neuroscience informing the sentencing and treatment of offenders with mental illnesses and related criminal outcomes either within the system or through diversion.[122]

Further, this growing body of research on neuroscience and biologically based treatments for offenders can have profound positive impacts on the legal system. In sentencing considerations, knowledge about promising interventions to reduce aggressive behaviour can challenge a purely retributive perspective: consent and compliance with treatments may reduce the sentence given and influence decisions about release from prison.[123] Indeed, using neuroscience to inform mental health treatment in criminal justice settings should reduce additional, ongoing burdens on the legal system that arise from offender recidivism. Although larger-scale RCTs are still needed, findings from an experimental pilot study suggest that non-invasive health interventions in the form of omega-3 and vitamin D supplementation can reduce three-year recidivism in young offenders by 16.6%.[124] Lowered recidivism rates due to effective treatments can have longer-term impacts by decreasing financial and time constraints, most commonly placed on courts.[125] By acknowledging the challenges and concerns that arise from the overlap of mental health and the criminal justice system, neuroscience and other scientific research can be utilised to establish outcomes that are more conducive to mental health stability, personal growth, and crime reduction.

119 C. M. Altimus, 'Neuroscience Has the Power to Change the Criminal Justice System' (2017) 3 *eNeuro* ENEURO.0362.

120 *Roper v. Simmons* [2005] U.S. 551, 543 (1 March 2005).

121 *Miller v. Alabama* [2012] U.S. 460, 567 (25 June 2012).

122 A. R. Baskin-Sommers, K. Fonteneau, 'Correctional Change Through Neuroscience' (2016) 85 *Fordham Law Review* 423; D. L. Egbenya, S. Adjorlolo, 'Advancement of Neuroscience and the Assessment of Mental State at the Time of Offense' (2021) 2 *Forensic Science International: Mind and Law* 100046.

123 A. B. Shniderman, L. Solberg, 'Cosmetic Psychopharmacology for Prisoners: Reducing Crime and Recidivism Through Cognitive Intervention' (2015) 8 *Neuroethics* 315.

124 A. Raine and others, 'Omega-3 and Vitamin D Supplementation to Reduce Recidivism: A Pilot Study' (2024) 20 *Journal of Experimental Criminology* 683.

125 H. Yamatani, S. Spjeldnes, 'Saving Our Criminal Justice System: The Efficacy of a Collaborative Social Service' (2011) 56 *Social Work* 53.

9 The Impact of Neuroscience on Prison Litigation

The Case of Prolonged Solitary Confinement

Federica Coppola

Introduction

In the case of *Schmidt and Šmigol v. Estonia (2023)*,[1] the European Court of Human Rights (ECtHR) ruled that prolonged solitary confinement amounts to inhumane and degrading treatment under Article 3 of the European Convention of Human Rights (the Convention), regardless of its material conditions.[2] The case involved the legitimacy of repeated periods in isolation, albeit with intermittent breaks, contact with medical personnel, and access to rehabilitation programs. The Court found these measures exceeded acceptable punishment thresholds, emphasising the inherent mental harm of prolonged isolation. Thus, the Court stressed that solitary confinement must be a last resort, requiring compelling justification for exceptional circumstances to warrant extended isolation.

The ECtHR's reasoning and holding, grounded in the Convention's fundamental principle of human dignity, contrasts with the language employed by the U.S. Supreme Court and several lower federal courts in affirming the legitimacy of this controversial prison practice.[3] In the United States, incarcerated individuals can spend decades in solitary confinement, often allowed only one hour of solitary exercise per day, with no interaction with the general prison population, limited or nonexistent access to rehabilitation or recreational programs, and an overall lack of meaningful social contact.[4] Despite robust advocacy campaigns aimed at ending inhumane applications of this measure, as well as judicial and legislative efforts to (at least) restrict its use for vulnerable groups, solitary confinement remains widespread in the U.S. correctional system, with its harms persistently overlooked, concealed, and forgotten.[5]

1 App. no 3501/20 and two others (ECtHR, 28 November 2023).
2 Ibid. para. 140.
3 See the fourth and fifth sections of this chapter.
4 See Solitary Watch <https://solitarywatch.org/>
5 See Correctional Leaders Association & Arthur Liman Ctr., *Time-In-Cell: A 2021 Snapshot of Restrictive Housing Based on a Nationwide Survey of U.S. Prison Systems* (August 24, 2022) 60–1 <https://law.yale.edu/sites/default/files/area/center/liman/document/time_in_cell_2021.pdf>

DOI: 10.4324/9781003510246-10

In contrast, these harms are consistently documented in empirical research.[6] Behavioural studies have extensively documented the severe physical and mental health impacts of solitary confinement. More recently, neuroscience has begun to add compelling evidence, revealing that even short periods of isolation can cause significant structural and functional brain damage, leading to permanent psychopathological and behavioural conditions.[7] Significantly, neuroscientific evidence is increasingly cited in federal litigation against solitary confinement, supporting claims of its profound and lasting harms.[8] Although it may be too early to definitively assess the impact of such evidence on litigation outcomes, the growing incorporation of neuroscience in court opinions and briefs underscores the significant role this scientific discipline plays in providing additional and complementary support for challenges to solitary confinement.

Against this backdrop, this chapter seeks to provide an initial assessment of the place and role of neuroscience in solitary confinement litigation by examining selected case law that cites brain-based evidence on the detrimental effects of isolation. Beginning with *Ashker v. Governor of California* (2014),[9] the analysis will notably explore the type of use of neuroscientific evidence in solitary litigation, the claims it bolsters, the types of cases where it is cited, the challenges to its full consideration by courts, and its potential to fundamentally question the legitimacy of solitary confinement as a practice. The paper concludes by emphasising the indispensable role of scientific evidence in legal challenges and advocating for expanded interdisciplinary research to reassess the legitimacy of solitary confinement. Ultimately, it highlights the unique evidentiary power of neuroscience in contesting solitary confinement and its potential to support arguments for its abolition.

Solitary Confinement: International Definition and Standards

Solitary confinement is an extreme prison practice in which an incarcerated individual is isolated for extended periods, often for 22 to 24 hours a day, with minimal social interaction.[10] This practice is applied globally as either a disciplinary correctional measure, a pretrial detention regime, an administrative tool, or a court sentence. Despite being justified on utilitarian grounds, such as managing dangerous individuals and preventing prison violence, its severe psychological and physical harms have prompted international standards to restrict its use.

6 For an overview, see F. Coppola, 'The Brain in Solitude: An(other) Eighth Amendment Challenge to Solitary Confinement' (2019) 6 *Journal of Law and the Biosciences* 184.

7 Ibid.

8 See the fifth section of this chapter.

9 *Ashker v. Governor of California (2014)* No. C 09-5796 CW (N.D. Cal. Jun. 2, 2014).

10 United Nations General Assembly, 'United Nations Standard Minimum Rules for the Treatment of Prisoners', *Rule 44*, A/C.3/70/L.3 (2015).

The *Istanbul Statement*[11] (2007) and the *Mandela Rules* (2015)[12] are the primary international instruments setting limits on solitary confinement to reflect human rights principles and best practices. These instruments emphasise upholding human dignity through normalisation, meaningful human contact,[13] and access to rehabilitative activities. Importantly, these instruments establish a categorical maximum isolation period of 15 days, defining prolonged isolation beyond this time limit as a form of torture. Moreover, solitary confinement should be a last resort, prohibited for vulnerable groups, and subject to strict oversight.[14]

Despite these clear international standards, domestic prison systems often fail to comply with their requirements for respecting human dignity and safeguarding the psychological and physical well-being of incarcerated individuals. Solitary confinement is well-documented as being overused and abused globally, frequently accompanied by unreported or underreported inhumane and degrading conditions.[15] The United States is no exception. As the following analysis will highlight, the legal protections intended to guard against the harms of isolation are largely absent in the everyday application of solitary confinement in the U.S. prison system.

Solitary Confinement in the U.S.

Solitary confinement in the U.S. involves near-total isolation, typically in small, sparsely furnished cells with minimal natural light and constant artificial illumination. Individuals are confined for 22–23 hours daily, with limited or no access to rehabilitative activities or meaningful social contact. Communication is often restricted to brief exchanges with correctional staff or minimal interactions with other isolated individuals, like tapping on cell walls. Although international standards recommend a 15-day limit, solitary confinement in the U.S. can last months, years, or even indefinitely. Obtaining precise data on the prevalence of solitary confinement in the United States is inherently challenging. However, research and official reports estimate that approximately 60,000 to 80,000 individuals are held in solitary confinement each year. Notably, certain groups, including racial minorities and individuals from gender minorities, are disproportionately subjected to this measure.[16]

11 The Istanbul Statement on the Use and Effects of Solitary Confinement, adopted at the International Psychological Trauma Symposium, Istanbul (9 December 2007).

12 United Nations General Assembly (n 10).

13 See B. Naylor and S. Shalev, 'Solitary Confinement and the Meaning of 'Meaningful Human Contact' (2022) 12 *Human Rights behind Bars* 293.

14 United Nations General Assembly (n 10) Rule 45.

15 The Istanbul Statement on the Use and Effects of Solitary Confinement (n 11).

16 E.g., n 5; H. Pullen-Blasnik et al., 'The Population Prevalence of Solitary Confinement' (2021) 26 *Science Advances* eabj1928; G. Arkles, 'Safety and Solidarity across Gender Lines: Rethinking Segregation of Transgender People in Detention' (2009) 18 *Temple Political & Civil Rights Law Review* 515.

On paper, solitary confinement is meant to serve key penological functions, such as discipline, control, and protection, which are referred to as the 'legitimate interests' of the prison. Indeed, prison administrations normally invoke 'security arguments'[17] to justify the use of solitary confinement, particularly for managing individuals who are deemed exceptionally dangerous. In practice, however, solitary confinement is often imposed at the discretion of correctional officers for a broad range of punitive reasons that are unrelated to security concerns.[18]

Scholarly critiques vigorously challenge the official justifications for solitary confinement, often interpreting it as an institutional pretext to inflict additional suffering on incarcerated people. Some scholars[19] argue that solitary confinement is the extreme end of a prison system that perpetuates suffering, exclusion, and control over marginalised populations, reflecting broader systemic issues that prioritise punishment over rehabilitation or reintegration. In sum, if prison serves as a stark reflection of society, solitary confinement serves as a stark reflection of the prison system itself. In a society that incarcerates nearly two million people, often under excessively harsh conditions, one can (hardly) imagine the reality of life in solitary confinement.

Prolonged Solitary Confinement Under the Eighth Amendment

The increasing recognition of the profound harms associated with (prolonged) solitary confinement, along with the adoption of international standards intended to limit its use, has led many state jurisdictions to introduce policies aimed at reducing or altogether abolishing this practice.[20] According to Fettig,[21] 28 state legislatures introduced, and 12 successfully passed, bills to end or limit the use of solitary confinement in 2019. Similarly, between 2020 and 2022, additional states adopted measures to restrict or even prohibit its application. Despite these efforts, solitary confinement remains a pervasive practice in many facilities, and a coherent, nationwide pathway toward its meaningful reform—or outright abolition—has yet to emerge.

A significant barrier to a consistent reform of solitary confinement lies in the constitutional legitimacy afforded to this practice. Since the 1980s, constitutional challenges to solitary confinement, particularly when prolonged, have

17 J. Lobel, P. Scharff Smith, 'Solitary Confinement —From Extreme Isolation to Prison Reform' in J. Lobel, P. Scharff Smith (eds), *Solitary Confinement: Effects, Practices, and Pathways toward Reform* (Oxford University Press, New York, 2018) 10.

18 E.g., Solitary Watch, *Solitary Confinement in the United States: The Facts* <https://solitarywatch.org/facts/faq/>.

19 E.g., S. Dolovich, 'Exclusion and Control in the Carceral State' (2011) 16 *Berkley Journal of Criminal Law* 259; J. Reisnik, 'Not Isolating Isolation' in J. Lobel and Scharff Smith (2018) 89.

20 Reisnik (n 19) 101.

21 A. Fettig, '2019 Was a Watershed Year in the Movement to Stop Solitary Confinement' (*American Civil Liberties Union*, 16 December 2019) <https://perma.cc/DX2W-TDAZ>.

emerged periodically. Although the Supreme Court has established procedural safeguards for placing individuals in isolation,[22] prolonged solitary confinement retains substantial constitutional support. Although certain lower federal courts have demonstrated greater receptiveness to recognising the constitutional flaws of prolonged solitary confinement, others have declined to do so.[23] Consequently, a unified body of jurisprudence invalidating this practice remains elusive.

One reason for such constitutional inconsistency lies in the narrow interpretative framework frequently employed by courts to assess whether conditions of confinement, including solitary confinement, violate the Eighth Amendment's prohibition on cruel and unusual punishments.[24] To successfully claim Eighth Amendment violations, incarcerated individuals have to allege facts demonstrating that (1) they endured deprivations of basic human needs that were 'sufficiently serious,' and that (2) the prison officials inflicted such deprivations with 'a sufficiently culpable state of mind' amounting to deliberate indifference.[25] This subjective component requires individuals to sufficiently allege that prison officials knew, yet disregarded, that the prison conditions posed 'an excessive risk to an inmate's health and safety.'[26] Finally, although not explicitly required by constitutional standards, the justification for solitary confinement often hinges on its perceived penological legitimacy, particularly in addressing institutional needs for discipline, protection, and security. As noted earlier, prison administrations normally invoke these penological justifications to counter allegations of unnecessary or excessive infliction of pain through isolation. This argument often leads courts to defer decisions regarding the use of solitary confinement to prison authorities, at times uncritically abdicating their role in protecting individual rights against prison harms.

The (Neuro)Scientific Case Against 'Prolonged' Solitary Confinement

The experiences of individuals subjected to prolonged isolation reveal a complex blend of pain, horror, and resilience. Reactions to solitary confinement vary. Some people tragically take their own lives, others develop new or

22 *Wilkinson v. Austin*, 545 U.S. 209, 222 (2005); *Taylor v. Riojas*, 592 U.S. 7 (2020); *Davis v. Ayala*, 567 U.S. 257 (2015) (Kennedy J, concurring); *Apodaka et al. v. Raemish et al. / Lowe et al. v. Raemish et al.* 586 U. S. ____ (2018) (Sotomayor J, dissenting).

23 Federal circuit courts remain divided on whether prolonged solitary confinement constitutes a violation of the Eighth Amendment. See *Hope v. Harris*, U.S. 21 (2022) Petition for a Writ of Certiorari <https://www.macarthurjustice.org/wp-content/uploads/2020/08/Hope_CertPetition-final.pdf> This division makes it challenging to clearly establish the law governing prolonged solitary confinement. See *Toevs v. Reid*, 685 F.3d (2012) 903, 916.

24 U.S. Constitution, Eighth Amendment [1791].

25 *Thomas v. Tice*, 948 F.3d 133 (3d Cir. 2020); *Farmer v. Brennan*, 511 U.S. 825, 834 (1994).

26 *Beers-Capitol v. Whetzel*, 256 F.3d 120 (3d Cir. 2001).

intensified mental health issues, while others are hesitant to admit any psychological toll.[27]

The numerous testimonies of individuals who have endured solitary confinement too often fall short of making its full horrors visible and credible within legal settings. The reluctance of many courts to recognise the pervasive harms caused by solitary confinement underscores the pressing need for a more nuanced and comprehensive understanding of its impacts. Science has played a pivotal role in this effort, providing empirical validation of the harms of isolation and amplifying the voices of those whose endured suffering might otherwise be dismissed or overlooked.

The body of scientific literature on the damages of isolation is vast, with equally thorough documentation of its associated harms.[28] Solitary confinement is aptly defined as 'a special kind of social isolation,'[29] one that forces individuals into a state of physical solitude and exposes them to additional environmental stressors. These compounded conditions significantly deteriorate mental health, often resulting in lasting or permanent trauma. The root of these impairments lies in neurobiological disruptions to critical brain regions, including the hippocampus, amygdala, and prefrontal cortex—areas that are essential for cognitive functions such as spatial navigation, memory, emotional regulation, and impulse control. These neurobiological changes have been associated with heightened risks of mental health conditions, including PTSD, Alzheimer's, and major depression. Furthermore, behavioural dysfunctions, including increased aggression, self-harm, and hypersensitivity to external stimuli, are frequently observed as manifestations of the brain's adverse response to extended periods of isolation.[30]

In recent years, the neuroscience of isolation has played an increasingly pivotal role in solitary confinement litigation. A key case is the landmark federal class action *Ashker v. Governor of California* (2014),[31] in which thousands of individuals subjected to prolonged solitary confinement in California's Pelican Bay prison successfully challenged their conditions under the Eighth Amendment. The plaintiffs' claims were significantly strengthened by expert testimony presenting scientific evidence on the psychological and neurobiological harms of isolation. The expert testimony[32] highlighted three critical findings: (1) social interaction is a fundamental neurobiological need, essential for maintaining mental and physical health; (2) deprivation of this need results in

27 R. King et al., 'Sharing Experiences of Solitary Confinement—Prisoners and Staff' in Lobel and Scharff Smith (2018) 243.

28 See E. Tadros et al., 'Life in the Hole: The Impact of Solitary Confinement in the United States' (2023) *The Howard Journal of Crime and Justice* 374–390.

29 Lobel and Scharff Smith (n 17) 2.

30 See Coppola (n 6).

31 *Ashker v. Governor of California (2014)* (n. 9).

32 Ibid, Expert Report of Matthew Lieberman (filed on 11 March 2015) <https://ccrjustice.org/sites/default/files/attach/2015/07/Lieberman%20Expert%20Report.pdf>

measurable neurobiological and brain damage, often with irreversible effects; and (3) such deprivation causes social pain—distress arising from social exclusion, including isolation—which is physically manifested in the brain and underpins a wide range of psychological and physical problems. According to Jules Lobel, neuroscience played a vital role in this case by illustrating the profound harms of solitary confinement in ways that psychological testimony alone could not, thereby broadening the evidentiary foundation for the plaintiffs' claims.[33]

Three years after *Ashker*, the Third Circuit of Appeals in *Williams v. Sec'y Pa. Dept. Corr.* (2017)[34] explicitly referred to (neuro)scientific evidence on the mental and physical harms caused by prolonged solitary confinement. The case required the court to determine whether the state of Pennsylvania could continue to hold death-row prisoners in solitary confinement after their death sentences had been vacated while awaiting resentencing hearings. In its analysis, the court described the conditions of solitary confinement as atypical under '*any* plausible baseline'[35] and 'extremely hazardous to well-being.'[36] To support this observation, the court referenced extensive scientific evidence on the psychological and physical harms associated with isolation over both short and long durations. Notably, the court underscored two critical points. First, it acknowledged the dehumanising nature of solitary confinement, emphasising that its experience is 'psychologically painful, can be traumatic and harmful, and puts many of those who have been subjected to it at risk of long-term . . . damage.'[37] Second, the court cited neuroscientific data from EEG studies showing that 'even a short time in solitary confinement is associated with drastic cognitive changes'[38] to conclude that solitary confinement is 'strikingly toxic to mental functioning.'[39]

Following the landmark *Ashker and Williams* decisions, neuroscience has gained increased prominence in solitary confinement litigation. In *Clark v. Coupe* (2023),[40] the Third Circuit ruled in favour of Angelo Clark, a prisoner diagnosed with schizophrenia and bipolar disorder, who was subjected to near-total isolation for seven months. Despite being fully aware of Clark's severe mental illness, prison officials imposed conditions that exacerbated his psychiatric symptoms. Tragically, Clark's deteriorating mental state, marked by disruptive behaviours such as yelling and banging on his cell door, resulted in

33 J. Lobel, 'Litigation to End Solitary Confinement in California: The Role of Interdisciplinary and Comparative Experts' in Lobel and Scharff Smith (2018) 360.
34 848 F.3d 549 (3d Cir. 2017).
35 Ibid. 564 (quoting *Wilkinson* n 16 at 223).
36 Ibid. 563.
37 Ibid. 566.
38 Ibid.
39 Ibid.
40 No. 21-2310 (3d Cir. 2022).

prolonged isolation.[41] In its decision, the court drew on its prior judgement in *Palakovic v. Wetzel* (2017),[42] where it found that repeatedly placing mentally ill and intellectually disabled individuals in solitary confinement—while denying them mental health treatment—amounted to a severe violation of the Eighth Amendment. In *Palakovic*, the court recognised the life-threatening consequences of solitary confinement for individuals with preexisting mental vulnerabilities. It cited the 'robust body of legal and scientific authority'[43] documenting the devastating mental health effects of long-term isolation, which include disintegration of self-identity and a significantly heightened risk of self-harm or suicide. Importantly, the court noted 'a growing consensus' among legal and scientific communities that solitary confinement can cause 'severe and traumatic psychological damage,' particularly on vulnerable populations.[44]

Similarly, in *Finley v. Huss et al.*,[45] the Sixth Circuit ruled in favour of Finley, a person with a documented history of severe mental illness, who was placed in solitary confinement during a mental health crisis and held there for more than three months. During this period of isolation, Finley's condition deteriorated further, resulting in suicidal behaviour including cutting himself with razor blades and ingesting them. Although the court's opinion does not explicitly reference (neuro)scientific evidence, an amicus brief[46] submitted in the case highlighted the profound neurological impacts of solitary confinement. The brief explained that 'traumatic psychological harms associated with solitary confinement also often trigger detectable changes in neural pathways, the morphology and the neurochemistry of the brain.'[47] Crucially, the brief emphasised that 'these changes can be accurately characterized as a physical injury or illness because they adversely affect the nature and functioning of the sufferer's brain,'[48] underscoring the deep interconnection between mental and physical harm.

In *Sanders v. Melvin* (2022),[49] the Seventh Circuit ruled in favour of Sanders, a person diagnosed with schizophrenia who had been confined in isolation for ten years. During his segregation, Sanders repeatedly self-mutilated and attempted to challenge his conditions of confinement three times under § 1915(g) of the Prison Litigation Reform Act (PLRA).[50] However, he was

41 Ibid.

42 854 F. 3d 209 (3d Cir. 2017).

43 Ibid. 225.

44 Ibid.

45 No. 23-1083 (6th Cir. 2024).

46 Brief of Amici Curiae Professors and Practitioners of Psychology and Psychiatry in Support of Plaintiff-Appellant No. 23-1083 (6th Cir. 2024) (filed on August 2, 2017) <https://www.macarthurjustice.org/wp-content/uploads/2018/07/Finley_Amicus-Brief.pdf>.

47 Ibid. 10.

48 Ibid.

49 873 F.3d 957 (7th Cir. 2017); No. 20-3276 (7th Cir. 2022) (reversing the subsequent district court's dismissal of a lawsuit based on a finding of fraud for clear error).

50 Pub. L. No. 104–134, tit. VIII, 110 Stat. 1321–66 (1996) (codified as amended in scattered sections of the U.S. Code); see also 28 U.S.C. § 1915(g) (2012).

denied permission to proceed *in forma pauperis* without showing imminent danger of physical injury. The district court dismissed his claim, reasoning that Sanders' self-harm was volitional and therefore under his control, failing to meet the threshold for imminent danger under the PLRA. An amicus brief submitted by psychology and psychiatry experts highlighted the organic nature of the mental harm caused by solitary confinement, emphasising its severe impact on individuals with preexisting mental vulnerabilities.[51] Despite this evidence, the Seventh Circuit upheld the legal distinction that mental harm is qualitatively different from physical harm, concluding that evidence of mental harm alone does not satisfy the *in forma pauperis* requirement for showing an imminent risk to physical health. However, the court acknowledged the connection between Sanders' psychiatric condition and the risk of self-harm, citing his prior suicide attempts as evidence of an imminent physical threat. Based on this reasoning, the Seventh Circuit reversed the district court's decision, recognising that the conditions of confinement had sufficiently contributed to Sanders' self-harm to justify reconsideration of his claims.[52]

The case of *Crane v. Utah DOC* (2022)[53] affirmed the stringent threshold required to establish deliberate indifference to the harms of solitary confinement, even in cases involving vulnerable populations such as adolescents with preexisting mental conditions. The case concerned Brock Tucker, who was incarcerated at 17 years old with a history of abuse, traumatic brain injury that impaired his cognitive development, major depressive disorder, and unspecified psychosis. Before his incarceration at Utah Correctional Facility (CF), Tucker had experienced years of abuse in juvenile facilities. Shortly after arriving at Utah CF, he was placed in extreme solitary confinement for two years on punitive grounds, with restricted access to recreation, visitation, commissary privileges, and other basic amenities. Tragically, Tucker died by suicide two years into his confinement. Janet Crane, Tucker's grandmother who acted as the administrator of his estate, brought a lawsuit under 42 U.S.C. § 1983, alleging that the Utah Department of Corrections (DOC) violated Tucker's Eighth Amendment rights by exhibiting deliberate indifference to his medical needs, leading to his death. Amicus briefs submitted in support of the claim emphasised neuroscientific evidence about the unique vulnerability of adolescent brains to the harms of isolation. The briefs detailed how the immaturity of brain regions responsible for impulse control and risk assessment heightens adolescents' susceptibility to self-harm and suicide under conditions of extreme isolation.[54] Despite this evidence proving that DOC officials were

51 Brief of Amici Curiae Professors and Practitioners of Psychology and Psychiatry in Support of Plaintiff-Appellant No. 17-1938 (7th Cir. 2017), 33–34 <https://www.macarthurjustice.org/wp-content/uploads/2017/10/Sanders_Amicus.pdf.

52 See Pub. L. No. 104–134 (n. 50).

53 15 F.4th 1296 (2022).

54 Brief of Amici Curiae Professors and Practitioners of Psychology and Psychiatry in Support of Plaintiff-Appellant and Reversal No. 20-4032 (10th Cir. 2020) (filed on June 10 2020)

aware of Tucker's severe mental health challenges, the court granted qualified immunity to the defendants. Although the court acknowledged Tucker's serious medical needs, it found that Crane failed to provide sufficient evidence that officials consciously disregarded the risks posed by prolonged solitary confinement, thus falling short of the legal standard for deliberate indifference.[55]

Discussion

Since *Ashker*, neuroscientific evidence has assumed an increasingly prominent role in solitary confinement litigation. Although it remains too early to definitively gauge its impact on case outcomes, its growing presence in amicus briefs, complaints, and judicial opinions raises important questions about the trajectory and future implications of neuroscience in constitutional challenges to solitary confinement.

To provide an initial assessment of the role and relevance of neuroscientific evidence in this domain, the following subsections offer a structured exploration of its current and potential impact. Specifically, the analysis will address four key aspects: (1) the types of use made of neuroscientific evidence in solitary confinement litigation; (2) the nature of claims supported by this evidence; (3) the categories of cases in which such evidence is introduced; and (4) the normative hurdles that limit courts' full consideration of neuroscientific evidence.

Type of Use

The first significant aspect of the role of neuroscience in solitary confinement litigation concerns the type of evidence it provides to aid courts in more comprehensively assessing the systemic impacts of prolonged isolation. As discussed elsewhere, scientific evidence—including neuroscientific evidence—can be presented in legal contexts in two primary ways: as individualised evidence or as framework evidence.[56] Individualised evidence involves using neuroscientific data to substantiate specific claims about an individual. For example, brain scans or cognitive assessments can be introduced to a legal insanity defence by demonstrating functional or structural brain abnormalities present at the time of the crime. Although this approach remains prevalent, it is fraught with conceptual, evidentiary, and normative challenges. Chief among these challenges is the difficulty of deriving definitive conclusions about an individual from population-level neuroscientific data and the potential for

---

<https://a0c8672a-59c3-4f12-8764-cf2f7788522b.filesusr.com/ugd/b72ac6_ab881a79788d495cb26a0b562e7a8027.pdf>

55 Ibid.

56 F. Coppola, 'When the Brain Can Make a Difference: Individualized vs. Framework Uses of Neuroscience in Courtrooms' (2020) 1 *Diritto Penale e Uomo* 1.

normative judgments of responsibility to be based solely on the presence of brain dysfunctions.[57]

By contrast, the use of neuroscience as evidence shifts the focus away from individual claims to broader, systemic issues, lending empirical support to general theories or hypotheses relevant to legal arguments. The use of neuroscience as framework evidence aligns more accurately and reliably with the current capabilities of neuroscientific research, which primarily generates conclusions at the aggregate level and avoids problematic inferences about the brain and behaviour at the individual level.

As demonstrated in the cases analysed previously, framework neuroscientific evidence is employed to support claims that prolonged solitary confinement poses significant and irreversible risks of harm to *virtually anyone* subjected to it. This approach transcends the specifics of individual cases, aiming instead to bolster conclusions about the inherent dangers of solitary confinement for broader categories of individuals. By providing complementary evidence on the universally harmful effects of isolation on the brain, neuroscience strengthens empirical arguments regarding the generalisable impacts of solitary confinement. In so doing, neuroscience-based evidence contextualises individual cases within a broader scientific narrative. Importantly, this narrative carries legal relevance, offering a more informed foundation for judicial decision-making regarding the constitutionality and legitimacy of solitary confinement.

Type of Claims

Expanding on the type of claims supported by neuroscience in solitary confinement cases, it is essential to delve deeper into the convergence of these claims, as seen in amicus briefs, complaints, and judicial opinions. Collectively, neuroscience-based claims consistently emphasise the profound psychological and physical harms caused by prolonged isolation, distinguishing these harms from those typically endured by the general prison population. These harms are often irreversible and severe, resulting in debilitating or even fatal consequences. Notably, an analysis of solitary confinement cases highlights the following brain-based claims about the damages of isolation focused on the following aspects:

Social Interaction as a Neurobiological Need

A central claim emerging from the cases discussed is the fundamentally social nature of the human brain. Neuroscience evidence consistently underscores that the human brain 'is literally wired to connect with others.'[58] This assertion is grounded in extensive research demonstrating that meaningful social

57 See ibid.
58 Coppola (n. 56) 14.

interaction is vital for maintaining essential executive functions, emotional balance, and overall physical and mental health. For example, studies reveal that the absence of meaningful social engagement disrupts the brain's capacity to attain and sustain an 'adequate state of alertness and attention,'[59] a prerequisite for effective daily functioning. Social isolation, as imposed by solitary confinement, severely impairs this critical function, depriving individuals of the necessary stimuli to support fundamental neurological and psychological processes. As the case materials suggest, this claim serves as a cornerstone of the argument that solitary confinement poses a severe risk of inflicting objectively serious harm insofar as it deprives individuals of a minimal life necessity—meaningful social interaction—thereby undermining the very foundations of their mental and physical integrity.

Chronic Stress and Neurobiological Deterioration

A second, closely related critical aspect consistently emphasised in the cited neuroscientific evidence is the profound impact of extreme isolation on the brain's stress circuits and its resulting mental and physical repercussions. Research demonstrates that extreme isolation triggers an 'increased activation of the brain's stress systems,'[60] which initiates a cascade of physiological changes. Chronic stress leads to heightened cortisol levels which, in turn, adversely affect critical brain regions such as the hippocampus, amygdala, and prefrontal cortex.

The overactivation of stress systems creates a self-reinforcing cycle: as the brain becomes increasingly sensitive to stress, individuals subjected to prolonged isolation experience a progressive decline in psychological resilience. This decline not only heightens the risk of exacerbating psychological symptoms such as anxiety, depression, and paranoia but can also escalate to the development of major mental illnesses. Thus, the adverse effects of solitary confinement on the stress system are far from transient; such effects result in measurable neurobiological damage that can potentially have lasting, and even permanent, consequences.[61]

59 (n 47) 7.

60 Brief of Amici Curiae Professors and Practitioners of Psychology and Psychiatry in Support of Plaintiff-Appellant, Hope v. Harris No. 20-40379 (10th Cir. 2020) (filed on 28 September 2020) <https://www.macarthurjustice.org/wp-content/uploads/2020/08/2020-09-28-Amicus-Brief-of-Professors-Practitioners-2.pdf>; Amended Brief of Amici Curiae Professors and Practitioners of Psychiatry, Psychology, and Medicine in Support of Plaintiffs-Appellants No. 165A21 (10th Cir. 2021) (filed on 2 July 2021) <https://www.acluofnorthcarolina.org/sites/default/files/field_documents/sccoa.pdf>; see also n 47.

61 Ibid.; see also Brief of Amici Curiae Professors and Practitioners of Psychology and Psychiatry in Support of Plaintiff-Appellant (7th Cir. 2019) *Johnson v. Prentice et al. No. 18-3535* (filed on 8 May 2019) <https://www.macarthurjustice.org/wp-content/uploads/2020/07/Amicus-Brief-Professors-and-Practitioner.pdf>; *Thorpe et al. v. Virginia DOC*, Class Action Complaint (filed on 5 June 2019) <https://www.acluva.org/sites/default/files/

Rapid Onset and Irreversible Damage

A third key claim concerns the extent and rapid onset of neurological alterations caused by isolation. These alterations, as research reveals, 'have implications beyond the immediately visible behaviors,'[62] leading to a wide range of adverse psychological effects that may be long-lasting or even permanent. Notably, the neurological impact of solitary confinement can emerge swiftly, sometimes within just a few days. Although these effects may not be immediately apparent, they progressively manifest through psychological symptoms and behavioural dysfunctions, intensifying over time.

Prolonged isolation significantly amplifies these effects, often culminating in irreversible damage. Indeed, many individuals subjected to extended periods of solitary confinement find it exceedingly difficult—or even impossible—to reintegrate into normal social environments upon their release. In supporting this alarming data, neuroscientific evidence offers another layer of explanation for the profound and enduring harm inflicted by solitary confinement, which not only disfigures the brain but also leaves a lasting imprint on an individual's mental health and social well-being.[63]

Neurobiological Basis of Mental Harm (i.e., Mental Harm as Physical Harm)

Another critical claim pertains to the physical nature of mental harm. Neurological studies have consistently demonstrated that psychological damage associated with isolation—such as depression, anxiety, or post-traumatic stress—corresponds to observable and measurable changes in brain structure, function, and neurochemistry. A related aspect concerns the organic nature of social pain endured by isolation.[64] Contrary to common-sense-based understandings, neuroscientific research suggests that social pain has physical reality in the brain, thereby informing the critical insight that such pain should be qualified as 'real pain' rather than as a kind of 'metaphorical pain.' Importantly, the experience of social pain is not less serious or less deleterious than that of physical pain. Rather, its consequences for an individual may well be more distressful and harmful than those following forms of physical pain.

The claim on the physical nature of mental harm following isolation is particularly significant because it challenges traditional legal distinctions between mental and physical injury in prison, including solitary, litigation. By showing

---

field_documents/2019_05_06_001_complaint.pdf>; *Thorpe v. Clarke et al.* 37 F.4th 926 (2022) (acknowledging plaintiff's neuroscience-based complaint about the neurological damages of isolation).

62 E. Bennion, 'Banning the Bing: Why Extreme Solitary Confinement Is Cruel and Far Too Usual Punishment' (2015) 90 *Indiana Law Journal* 743, 763.

63 n 64; see also *Hammond v. Pennsylvania DOC (ongoing)*, Class Action Complaint (filed on March 3 2024) <https://abolitionistlawcenter.org/wp-content/uploads/2024/03/Hammond-v.-DOC-030424-Complaint.pdf>.

64 See, e.g., Expert Report of Matthew Lieberman (n 32).

that isolation-induced psychological harm has tangible, physical manifestations in the brain, neuroscientific research underscores that mental damage is not merely a subjective experience but a physiological condition. This claim has been employed to strengthen arguments that solitary confinement inflicts harm comparable to physical injury, demanding equal consideration in prison litigation.[65]

Particular Impact on Vulnerable Populations

Another current claim concerns the particularly detrimental impact of solitary confinement on vulnerable populations, including people with mental illness and adolescents. As for the former, research indicates that solitary confinement acts as a severe aggravator of mental diseases and disorders.[66] In fact, the absence of healthy socio-environmental interaction exacerbates neurobiological stress, rendering preexisting vulnerabilities even more fragile and susceptible to deterioration. Evidence indicates that symptoms such as depression, anxiety, or psychosis are often exacerbated, and individuals are more likely to engage in self-harm, experience episodes of psychotic breaks, or even attempt suicide.[67]

Likewise, adolescents are uniquely vulnerable to the detrimental effects of solitary confinement due to the critical developmental stages their brains are undergoing. Neuroscientific research demonstrates that adolescence is a period of significant brain maturation, particularly in regions governing impulse control, decision-making, and emotional regulation. Thus, prolonged isolation during these formative years disrupts these developmental processes, often resulting in lasting impairments.[68]

Type of Cases

The foregoing analysis indicates that neuroscientific evidence on the damages of isolation is predominantly introduced in cases involving prolonged solitary confinement, particularly when imposed on individuals with preexisting mental health conditions.[69] Although the use of prolonged solitary confinement,

65 (n 47) 10.

66 See S. Grassian, 'Psychiatric Effects of Solitary Confinement' (2006) 22 *Washington University Journal of Law & Policy* 325.

67 See, e.g., F. Kaba et al., 'Solitary Confinement and Risk of Self-Harm among Jail Inmates' (2014) 104(3) *American Journal of Public Health* 442.

68 Coppola (n 56); see also *G. H. et al. v. Florida Dept. of Juvenile Justice, Class Action Complaint* (filed on 9 May 2019), ongoing <https://www.splcenter.org/sites/default/files/doc._2_-_complaint.pdf>; *Harvard et al. v. Florida DOC,* Class Action Complaint (filed on August 5, 2019), ongoing <https://fji.law/wp-content/uploads/2019/05/Class-Action-Complaint-for-Declaratory-and-Injunctive-Relief-07205539xB3B17.pdf>.

69 See the fifth section of this chapter.

even when imposed on vulnerable individuals, does not automatically constitute an Eighth Amendment violation, some courts have demonstrated a greater willingness to recognise such breaches in cases involving these groups. This recognition stems from an acknowledgement of the heightened risk of 'objectively serious harm' faced by individuals with preexisting vulnerabilities, such as mental health conditions.[70]

The leading case in this area is *Madrid v. Gomez* (1995),[71] where the federal district court offered a compelling analogy, equating the placement of individuals with mental illness in solitary confinement to 'putting an asthmatic in a place with little air to breathe.'[72] Although the court recognised that prolonged isolation in scarce environments risks producing significant psychological traumas in incarcerated people with no history of mental illness as well, it held that 'for many inmates, it does not appear that the degree of mental injury suffered significantly exceeds the kind of generalized psychological pain that courts have found compatible with Eighth Amendment standards.'[73] By presuming the general prison population's resilience to the harms of extreme isolation, the court effectively differentiated between the impact of solitary confinement on individuals with mental illness and its effects on healthier populations. Alarmingly, the court deemed only the former as constitutionally relevant.

Following *Madrid*, other courts recognised the constitutional relevance of the substantial risk of serious harm for mentally ill prisoners in solitary confinement.[74] For instance, in *Scarver v. Litscher*,[75] the court held that placing a mentally ill inmate in solitary confinement marked by 'conditions so lacking in physical and social points of reference,' might reasonably lead to 'a kind of psychological torture and future acts of self-harm.'[76] Likewise, in *Coleman v. Brown*,[77] the court ordered prison officials in California not to place any mentally ill prisoner in solitary confinement 'unless that class member's treating physician certifies that . . . the inmate does not face a substantial risk of exacerbation of his or her mental illness or decompensation as a result of confinement in a SHU.'[78]

70 E.g., *Madrid v. Gomez*, 889 F. Supp. 1146 (N.D. Cal. 1995); *Jones' El v. Berge*, 164 F. Supp. 2d 1096 (W.D. Wis. 2001); *Palakovic v. Wetzel*, 854 F. 3d 209 (3d Cir. 2017); *United States v. D.W.* 198 F. Supp. 3d 18 (E.D.N.Y. 2016); *Peoples v. Annucci*, 180 F. Supp. 3d 294 (S.D.N.Y. 2016); *Wallace v. Baldwin*, 895 F.3d 481 (7th Cir. 2018)

71 889 F. Supp. 1146 (N.D. Cal. 1995).

72 Ibid.

73 Ibid.

74 Ibid.

75 371 F. Supp. 2d 986, 1003 (W.D. Wis. 2005), *aff'd*, 434 F.3d 972 (7th Cir. 2006).

76 Ibid.

77 28 F. Supp. 3d 1068, 1109 (E.D. Cal. 2014).

78 Ibid.

These cases signify important progress in the jurisprudence on solitary confinement conditions. However, they also underscore the persistent neglect of the widespread mental harm and psychological pain caused by extreme isolation among the general prison population. Courts frequently dismiss valid claims, often concluding that the evidence presented fails to establish an Eighth Amendment violation or that the conditions endured do not meet the requisite standard of severity.[79] Even more troubling though, the prior analysis reveals that courts sometimes fail to recognise Eighth Amendment violations also in cases involving individuals with mental illness, despite acknowledging the risks of harm for this vulnerable population. This failure often stems from the plaintiff's deemed inability to demonstrate the culpable state of mind—deliberate indifference—of prison officials responsible for inflicting excessively harmful conditions. As the next section clarifies, the deliberate indifference requirement remains the fundamental barrier to successful constitutional challenges to solitary confinement, even when its conditions are objectively intolerable.

Normative Hurdles

The prior analysis indicates that the primary limitation on the contribution of neuroscience to solitary confinement litigation lies with the overly restrictive standards for determining when a condition of confinement constitutes cruel and unusual punishment. As I argued elsewhere,[80] these criteria pose significant barriers to successful prison claims, especially in cases involving solitary confinement. At its core, this restrictive interpretation reflects a state-centered reading of the Eighth Amendment, one that prioritises the interests of the 'justice' system while often compromising, or even sacrificing, the rights and well-being of those who are under its protection.

Firstly, courts generally tend to minimise, or even disregard, the psychological impact of prolonged isolation under adverse conditions, assuming an implicit baseline of resilience among the general prison population. Although several appellate court decisions have recognised that serious psychological harm can trigger Eighth Amendment protections,[81] this perspective is not firmly established. For prison claims to succeed, courts often focus on primarily physical deprivations, such as hunger or thirst, and their resulting harms, if only because such harms are considered more verifiable and objective.

Notably, the prevailing judicial approach reflects a persistent failure to qualify mental harm as a form of physical harm. This stance is exemplified

79 Cf. S. Dolovich, 'The Coherence of Prison Law' (2022) 135 *Harvard Law Review* 302.

80 Coppola (n 6).

81 E.g., *Shakka v. Smith*, 71 F.3d 162, 166 (4th Cir. 1995); *Thomas v. Farley*, 31 F.3d 557, 559 (7th Cir. 1994); *Jordan v. Gardner*, 986 F.2d 1521, 1529 (9th Cir. 1993) (en banc); *Scher v. Engelke*, 943 F.2d 921, 924 (8th Cir. 1991).

in *Sanders*,[82] where, despite amicus briefs emphasising that isolation-induced mental harm constitutes organic, physical damage to the brain,[83] the court declined to recognise Sanders' severe psychological deterioration as indicative of impending physical harm, stating that '[m]ental deterioration . . . is a psychological rather than a physical problem.'[84] This approach not only reflects a still-common dichotomy between physical and psychological pain, but also the relegation of psychological pain to a secondary-class pain, or as 'metaphorical' rather than concrete pain, which deserves reduced legal protection.

A more important barrier to the full recognition of the objective (risk of) harms of solitary confinement lies in the stringent subjective criterion of deliberate indifference. Comparable to criminal recklessness, this requirement demands clear evidence—often challenging to obtain—that prison staff were aware of the risks posed by prolonged solitary confinement and consciously chose to expose the individual to such conditions.[85] Accordingly, conditions or treatments, however degrading and dangerous, that do not result from the reckless conduct of the prison administration (but instead arise from mere negligence or pathological prison dynamics) appear to fall beyond the scope of the Eighth Amendment clause and, therefore, are not subject to its protection.

The subjective knowledge of a substantial risk of harm can be inferred from the objective circumstances of a prison's conditions if such conditions pose an obvious danger to the individual.[86] Importantly, although courts have recognised that some risks of harm are so objectively clear that 'a fact finder may conclude that a prison official knew of a substantial risk from the very fact that the risk was obvious,'[87] this state of mind has to be assessed from the prison officials' point of view under the circumstances.

Prison officers can easily argue for a lack of knowledge to obtain qualified immunity.[88] Lacking any law establishing the scope of the lawfulness of the conditions of solitary confinement, even 'reasonable prison officials might regard long stints of solitary confinement as constitutional even for a mentally ill prisoner'[89] and obtain immunity as a consequence. However, in *Taylor v. Riojas* (2020),[90] the Supreme Court found that egregiously inhumane treatment cannot be shielded by qualified immunity. The case concerned Trent Taylor, who was forced to spend six days in cells covered in feces and raw sewage, followed by a frigid cell with overflowing water in which he was forced to sleep. The Fifth Circuit had found the conditions unconstitutional; however,

82 Pub. L. No. 104–134 (n. 50).
83 Pub. L. No. 104–134 (n. 52).
84 Pub. L. No. 104–134 (n. 50).
85 E.g., *Cox v. Glanz*, 800 F.3d 1231 (2015).
86 *Farmer*, 511 U.S., 825.
87 Ibid.
88 See *Peroza-Benitez v. Smith*, 994 F.3d 157, 165 (3d Cir. 2021).
89 Ibid. 1249.
90 592 U.S. 7 (2020).

it eventually granted qualified immunity to the officers, reasoning that no specific precedent had clearly established the unlawfulness of such conditions. Thus, the officers lacked fair notice that placing a person in such brutal conditions could constitute a constitutional violation. The Supreme Court disagreed, holding that any reasonable officer would know such treatment was unacceptable, regardless of precedent.

Finally, another relevant barrier to recognising Eighth Amendment violations in cases of prolonged solitary confinement is the frequent invocation of legitimate penological interests, particularly safety and protection (the so-called security argument),[91] to justify placing and maintaining individuals in solitary confinement, even in the face of risks to their health. These penological justifications are routinely asserted by prison administrations and often accepted by the courts, further complicating efforts to challenge the practice on constitutional grounds. In all, solitary jurisprudence manifests the acceptance of an implicit trade-off between the adverse impact of solitary confinement on incarcerated individuals and the penological benefits for the prison. Most often, the 'benefits' of solitary confinement prevail over the potential harms that this practice can inflict. Sadly, this balancing argument is implicitly supported by the Courts' attitude of judicial deference of solitary confinement management to prison administrators and officials,[92] indicating courts' predisposition to prioritising state interests over the integrity and dignity of incarcerated persons.

The Real Potential of Neuroscience Against Solitary Confinement

The prior analysis sought to shed light on the current role of neuroscientific evidence in solitary confinement litigation and the enduring barriers that prevent its full integration in supporting prison claims. Despite these legal obstacles, it is essential to consider the substantive potential of neuroscience to challenge the constitutionality of solitary confinement. As I and other scholars have highlighted,[93] neuroscience holds the capacity to present robust and novel challenges to solitary confinement, even within the constraints of existing constitutional frameworks. These challenges extend beyond addressing particular vulnerable groups or the prolonged duration of isolation. Instead, neuroscience has the potential to substantiate claims that challenge the practice of solitary confinement in its entirety, raising profound questions about its compatibility with constitutional thresholds.

91 Lobel and Scharff Smith (n. 17).

92 No. 21-2310 (3d Cir. 2022) (n. 41) 28; *Wilson v. Seiter*, 501 U.S. 294, 301–02 (1991) (approving state-of-mind inquiry to allow defense that prison officials lacked the subjective intent to punish).

93 Coppola (n 6); J. Lobel, H. Akil, 'Law and Neuroscience: The Case of Solitary Confinement' (2018) 147 *Deadalus* 61.

The first challenge that neuroscience exposes concerns the core component of solitary confinement—isolation—regardless of its duration or accompanying material conditions. As emphasised, social interaction and environmental stimulation are basic human physical needs that are essential to physiological brain function and mental health. Thus, extreme isolation is sufficient per se to deprive a person of his or her fundamental biological needs. The second and consequential claim concerns the 'objectively serious risk of [physical] harm' (i.e., brain damages) due to extreme isolation alone. As Bennion has noted,[94] even if physical (brain) damage following a period in solitary confinement never materialises, '[this] is not dispositive for . . . the test.'[95] Indeed, all that matters for the test is that the risk of undergoing serious brain deterioration following solitary confinement is objective—that is, it is universal. Neuroscientific findings suggest that *any* person who lives in extreme isolation—even for a short period—is vulnerable to such risk.

The second challenge concerns the deliberate indifference criterion. As noted earlier, this criterion can be met when the imposed condition of confinement is so objectively harmful that makes it obvious to any reasonable officer of the danger to the individual, regardless of their actual knowledge of the risked harm. Given the growing awareness of the risks of isolation environments for neurological health, proof that a prison official acted with 'deliberate indifference' would have to be inferred from the very act of placing someone in such environments. Imposing these conditions on an incarcerated person entails an objectively serious risk of harm; any further subjective inquiry is simply unnecessary.

This proposal is consistent with Dolovich's argument for adopting a 'modified strict liability' standard for prison administrations which, in this context, would entail 'an irrebuttable presumption of constructive knowledge in all cases of sufficiently serious state-created harm.'[96] The mere fact that an incarcerated person has been placed in depriving and dehumanising conditions and exposed to (a serious risk of) harm should be deemed as sufficient to make this condition cognisable under the Eighth Amendment, for the very reason that when prisoners suffer serious harm at the hands of the state, fault is necessarily present.

A serious acknowledgement of the objective risks of harm deriving from solitary confinement also upsets the purported 'balance' between the (objective risk of) harm accrued through placement in solitary confinement and the 'legitimate' penological prison interests of discipline, security, and safety. In fact, the serious harms accrued through the imposition of extreme isolation are too high compared to the safety or protection interests of prison administrations. As discussed earlier, the harms of isolation may not be limited to its

94 (n. 65) 776.

95 Ibid.

96 S. Dolovich, 'Cruelty, Prison Conditions, and the Eighth Amendment' (2009) 84 *New York University Law Review* 881, 964–972.

immediate implications, but they may well extend to long-lasting or even permanent consequences for the physical and psychological integrity of individuals. Thus, the harm risked to individuals is just too excessive compared to the legitimate penological needs of prison administrations. That is, the protection of others (both incarcerated people and prison officers) comes at too much of a cost for the individual.

Admittedly, the effectiveness of such claims largely hinges on a potential—though uncertain—interpretive shift by courts in their application of the Eighth Amendment. This shift would require a departure from prioritising the perspective of the state toward an interpretation that centres on recognising and valuing the perspective of individuals subjected to state-imposed conditions of confinement. Although this is not the forum to speculate on whether or when such a paradigm shift might occur, it is nonetheless crucial to underscore the aspects of solitary confinement that align with neuroscientific evidence, highlighting their objective relevance within the current constitutional framework. Ultimately, a neuroscientifically informed interpretation of the Eighth Amendment reveals solitary confinement as inherently constituting cruel and unusual punishment.

Concluding Remarks

Neuroscience has increasingly been introduced in solitary confinement litigation, providing empirical support for claims about the severe harms caused by isolation. Despite its growing use, neuroscientific evidence faces significant hurdles in achieving full recognition in court. Legal obstacles, including stringent Eighth Amendment criteria, limit the scope and impact of neuroscience in supporting prison claims. Nevertheless, neuroscientific evidence has the potential to substantiate unique claims that solitary confinement is inherently cruel and unusual punishment. Thus, further efforts are essential to identify new and innovative pathways for challenging solitary confinement from constitutional perspectives. Additionally, (neuro)scientific research should continue to support the adoption of alternative measures to solitary confinement, emphasising the positive effects of healthy social environments and connections on mental health and behavioural well-being.

However, any normative argument or scientific research on solitary confinement must consider the broader context in which this practice occurs. As emphasised herein,[97] solitary confinement cannot be understood in isolation from the larger prison system. The harms of solitary confinement are an extreme manifestation of the broader pains of punishment, rooted in systemic exclusion, rejection, indifference, and the dehumanisation of incarcerated individuals. The path toward ending solitary confinement should begin there.[98]

97 See Section 3 and n 19.

98 I would like to thank my research assistant, Dakota Green, for his valuable and dedicated assistance with this article.

10 How Neuroscience Can Improve the Sentencing of Defendants With Autism Spectrum Disorder

Colleen M. Berryessa and Carolina R. Caliman

Introduction

Defendants diagnosed with Autism Spectrum Disorder (ASD) face a range of difficulties with communication, comprehension, and interpersonal interactions at every stage of the criminal justice process; a vast body of works suggests that these difficulties can negatively affect their experiences in court and incarceration settings, including the utility and fairness of their outcomes at the sentencing stage.[1] Particularly, across jurisdictions, legal decision-makers have struggled to apply the forensic relevance of ASD to sentencing proceedings and how the diagnosis should be considered in decision-making, when weighing potential sentencing options, and also when evaluating how sentencing outcomes could be potentially harmful to defendants with ASD.[2]

At the same time, advances in and applications of neuroscience including related biological sciences have begun to positively impact sentencing and aftercare for a wide range of defendants; neuroscience has been thought to help contextualise and explicate offending, and even courtroom, behaviour for defendants with many mental disorder diagnoses, as well as inform legal decision-makers about modes of sentencing and aftercare that may be most efficacious for such defendants.[3] This may be especially impactful for

1 See C. R. Caliman, C. M. Berryessa, 'Legal Decision-Makers in Criminal Cases Involving Autism Spectrum Disorder: A Review of the Research and a Call for Action' in M. Miller, D. DeMatteo (eds), *Advances in Psychology and Law* (vol. 7, American Psychological Association, 2024) 104; C. S. Allely, *Autism Spectrum Disorder in the Criminal Justice System: A Guide to Understanding Suspects, Defendants and Offenders with Autism* (Routledge, London, 2022) 88; R. Slavny-Cross et al., 'Autism and the Criminal Justice System: An Analysis of 93 Cases' (2022) 15(5) *Autism Research* 904.

2 C. M. Berryessa, 'Brief Report: Judicial Attitudes Regarding the Sentencing of Offenders with High Functioning Autism' (2016) 46 *Journal of Autism and Developmental Disorders* 2770. C. M. Berryessa, 'Defendants with Autism Spectrum Disorder in Criminal Court: A Judges' Toolkit' (2021) 13 *Drexel Law Review* 841.

3 N. Gertner, 'Neuroscience and Sentencing' (2016) 85 *Fordham Law Review* 533; E. Shaw, 'Neuroscience, Criminal Sentencing, and Human Rights' (2022) 63(4) *William & Mary Law Review* 1409; H. Wishart, C. M. Berryessa, *Neurolaw in the Courtroom: Comparative Perspectives on Vulnerable Defendants* (Routledge, New York, 2023) 5.

DOI: 10.4324/9781003510246-11

defendants with limited or a lack of understanding of their diagnoses and how they should be considered or weighed during sentencing.[4] Given this backdrop, the current chapter examines the positive role of neuroscience in sentencing defendants with ASD, with a particular focus on how it can shape more just and prosocial legal decision-making during proceedings involving diagnosed defendants in the United States (U.S.).

Symptomology and Neuroscience of ASD

ASD is a complex neurodevelopmental condition characterised by significant variability in presentation and symptom severity. Two key features commonly associated with ASD are impairments in social communication, with restricted and repetitive patterns of behaviour, interests, or activities.[5] These core features typically manifest with other symptoms, such as flat facial affect or the inability to read others' emotions, and can significantly impact daily functioning. Lower-functioning ASD can also be associated with intellectual or language impairments, for example, being nonverbal or having an IQ below 70; however, individuals who have high-functioning ASD most often possess typical or above-average intellectual abilities and face challenges in social communication and interaction.[6]

For individuals with ASD, difficulties in social communication and interaction can manifest as issues of understanding social cues, maintaining eye contact, engaging in socioemotional reciprocity, or understanding others' actions and mental states.[7] For example, they may have difficulty interpreting nonverbal communication, such as facial expressions or body language, which can lead to misunderstandings or awkward social interactions.[8] Additionally, diagnosed individuals might exhibit unusual speech patterns, such as using overly formal language.[9] The restricted behaviours, interests, or activities characteristic of people with ASD also often involve repetitive movements,

4 D. Freedman, G. W. Woods, 'The Developing Significance of Context and Function: Neuroscience and Law' (2018) 36(4) *Behavioral Sciences & the Law* 411.

5 American Psychiatric Association, *Diagnostic and Statistical Manual of Mental Disorders* (5th-TR ed., American Psychiatric Publishing, 2022) 56.

6 C. P. Johnson, S. M. Myers, 'Identification and Evaluation of Children with Autism Spectrum Disorders' (2007) 120 *Pediatrics* 1183; S. Baldwin et al., 'Employment Activities and Experiences of Adults with High-Functioning Autism and Asperger's Disorder' (2014) 44 *Journal of Autism and Developmental Disorders* 2440.

7 T. Grant et al., 'Criminal Responsibility in Autism Spectrum Disorder: A Critical Review Examining Empathy and Moral Reasoning' (2018) 59 *Canadian Psychology* 65.

8 Johnson and Myers (n 6).

9 J. McCann, S. Peppé, 'Prosody in Autism Spectrum Disorders: A Critical Review' (2003) 38 *International Journal of Language & Communication Disorders* 325–350; I. Freckelton, 'Autism Spectrum Disorder: Forensic Issues and Challenges for Mental Health Professionals and Courts' (2013) 26 *Journal of Applied Research in Intellectual Disabilities* 420–434.

such as hand-flapping or rocking, or engaging in rigid routines and rituals.[10] Furthermore, individuals with ASD can have highly focused interests leading to exceptional knowledge or skills in a particular area (e.g., trains or computers), while interfering with daily functioning.[11]

Sensory processing difficulties are also frequently noted as a common ASD trait and can manifest as hypersensitivity or hyposensitivity to sensory stimuli, such as sounds, lights, or temperatures.[12] For example, some individuals may be unusually sensitive to loud noises or bright lights, leading to discomfort or distress, while others might seek out sensory input through behaviours like touching different surfaces.[13] These sensory sensitivities can significantly impact daily life, making certain environments overwhelming or uncomfortable.

Understanding the complex symptomatology of ASD requires an exploration of the underlying neurobiological mechanisms that contribute to the aforementioned behaviours and experiences of those diagnosed.[14] Neuroscience research suggests that ASD arises from an intricate interplay of genetic and environmental factors that disrupt normal brain development, including developmental trajectories as well as social, cognitive, and neural functioning.[15] These developmental abnormalities appear to underlie the core social and communicative challenges observed in individuals with ASD.

Research increasingly suggests that multiple etiologies disrupt the development of key brain regions involved in ASD.[16] Abnormalities can manifest as increased total brain volume and unusual connectivity of white matter tracts, which are thought to play roles in the cognitive and behavioural manifestations of ASD.[17] The frontal and temporal lobes, essential for higher cognitive functions and sensory processing, are often affected in individuals with ASD; these regions are crucial for tasks such as planning,

10 S. Gunasekaran, 'Assessment and Management of Risk in Autism' (2012) 6(6) *Advances in Mental Health and Intellectual Disabilities* 314.

11 M. Jiujias, E. Kelley, L. Hall, 'Restricted, Repetitive Behaviors in Autism Spectrum Disorder and Obsessive–Compulsive Disorder: A Comparative Review' (2017) 48 *Child Psychiatry Hum Dev* 944.

12 World Health Organization, *International Statistical Classification of Diseases and Related Health Problems* (11th ed., WHO, Geneva, 2019) 6A02.

13 O. Bogdashina, *Sensory Perceptual Issues in Autism and Asperger Syndrome: Different Sensory Experiences—Different Perceptual Worlds* (Jessica Kingsley Publishers, 2016) 97.

14 S. Yarnell-Mac Grory et al., 'Neuroscience of Autism in the Legal Context' in F. R. Volkmar et al. (eds), *Handbook of Autism Spectrum Disorder and the Law* (Springer Nature, Switzerland, 2021) 71.

15 Ibid.

16 H. Schroeder et al., 'The Neurobiology of Autism: Theoretical Applications' (2010) 4 *Research in Autism Spectrum Disorders* 555; B. S. Abrahams, D. H. Geschwind, 'Connecting Genes to Brain in the Autism Spectrum Disorders' (2010) 67 *Archives of Neurology* 395.

17 A. Koyama, 'A Review on the Cognitive Neuroscience of Autism' (2009) 51 *Activitas Nervosa Superior* 125.

decision-making, and regulating social behaviours.[18] Irregularities in these areas often lead to executive dysfunctions and sensory processing challenges—specifically, the frontal lobes show structural and functional deviations that correlate with difficulties in cognitive flexibility and social interactions faced by those with ASD, as well as decreased connectivity with other brain systems.[19] Simultaneously, the temporal lobes play a vital role in processing auditory and visual stimuli essential for language and social perception; dysfunctions in these regions contribute significantly to the difficulties of individuals with ASD in language processing and social communication and interactions.[20]

The amygdala, integral for emotional processing, has frequently exhibited atypical development in individuals with ASD. More specifically, a consistent increase in amygdala size, rather than a decrease, has been noted among individuals with ASD[21] and linked with the severity of social impairments.[22] Additionally, the cerebellum, traditionally associated with motor control, is also implicated in cognitive and affective processing for those with ASD.[23] Individuals exhibiting cerebellar cortical atrophy often experience deficits in executive function, visuospatial abilities, language, and affective processing—cognitive and behavioural traits that are commonly observed in ASD.[24]

Another significant aspect of the neural architecture in ASD is the corpus callosum, which facilitates interhemispheric communication. Structural and functional impairments in this brain structure, evidenced in reduced size and altered connectivity, are well-documented and contribute significantly to sensory integration challenges, sensitivities, and perceptual inconsistencies typical in ASD.[25] Studies using neuroimaging have shown that these anomalies in the corpus callosum affect its ability to efficiently transfer cognitive, sensory, and motor information between hemispheres, impacting various cognitive

18 Ibid.

19 E. Courchesne et al., 'Neuron Number and Size in Prefrontal Cortex of Children with Autism' (2011) 306 *JAMA* 2001; C. Ecker et al., 'Intrinsic Gray-Matter Connectivity of the Brain in Adults with Autism Spectrum Disorder' (2013) 110 *Proceedings of the National Academy of Sciences* 13222; D. H. Geschwind, P. Levitt, 'Autism Spectrum Disorders: Developmental Disconnection Syndromes' (2007) 17 *Current Opinion in Neurobiology* 103.

20 S. Baron-Cohen et al., 'Recognition of Faux Pas by Normally Developing Children and Children with Asperger Syndrome or High-Functioning Autism' (1999) 29 *Journal of Autism and Developmental Disorders* 407; N. Boddaert, M. Zilbovicius, 'Functional Neuroimaging and Childhood Autism' (2002) 32 *Pediatric Radiology* 1.

21 Koyama (n 18).

22 C. M. Schumann et al., 'Amygdala Enlargement in Toddlers with Autism Related to Severity of Social and Communication Impairments' (2009) 66 *Biological Psychiatry* 942.

23 Courchesne et al. (n 19); B. F. Sparks et al., 'Brain Structural Abnormalities in Young Children with Autism Spectrum Disorder' (2002) 59 *Neurology* 184.

24 Koyama (n 17).

25 Yarnell-Mac Grory et al. (n 14).

processes and exacerbating the sensory processing difficulties observed in individuals with ASD.[26]

ASD and Sentencing in the Criminal Justice System

Although most individuals with ASD are thought to be law-abiding and at a higher risk of being victimised rather than being perpetrators of a crime,[27] some find themselves entangled in the criminal justice system. Yet the unique characteristics of an individual's ASD symptomatology commonly contribute to vulnerabilities that can lead to their engagement in offending behaviour that will later be sentenced in a legal setting.[28] Significant challenges in social communication characteristics of ASD can lead to behaviours that conflict with societal or legal norms, such as difficulty interpreting social cues, understanding others' intentions, and engaging in reciprocal social interactions.[29] Individuals with ASD might misinterpret nonverbal communication, such as facial expressions or body language, in social situations that precipitate offending behavior; for example, individuals with ASD can struggle to maintain appropriate boundaries in relationships, which can result in behaviours like stalking when conventional social niceties, like smiling, may be taken as romantic interest.[30] For example, in one case study, a man named Andrew stalked a fellow secondary school student whom he barely knew for 10 years after she showed him casual friendly behavior at a school event.[31]

Another common trait associated with ASD symptomatology—the presence of restricted interests and repetitive behaviours—can also lead to involvement in the criminal justice system.[32] Although these behaviours may serve as self-coping mechanisms, they can also result in conflicts with social or legal

26 A. L. Alexander et al., 'Diffusion Tensor Imaging of the Corpus Callosum in Autism' (2007) 34 *Neuroimage* 61; M. A. Just et al., 'Functional and Anatomical Cortical Underconnectivity in Autism: Evidence from an FMRI Study of an Executive Function Task and Corpus Callosum Morphometry' (2007) 17 *Cerebral Cortex* 951; C. N. Vidal et al., 'Mapping Corpus Callosum Deficits in Autism: An Index of Aberrant Cortical Connectivity' (2006) 60 *Biological Psychiatry* 218.

27 J. Beadle-Brown et al., *Living in Fear: Better outcomes for people with learning disabilities and autism* (Project report, Tizard Centre, Canterbury, 2014) 7.

28 E. Woodhouse et al., 'Identification and Support of Autistic Individuals within the UK Criminal Justice System: A Practical Approach Based upon Professional Consensus with Input from Lived Experience' (2024) 22 *BMC Medicine* 157.

29 S. E. Mouridsen et al., 'Pervasive Developmental Disorders and Criminal Behaviour' (2007) 52(2) *International Journal of Offender Therapy and Comparative Criminology* 196; Grant et al. (n 8).

30 I. Freckelton, D. List, 'Asperger's Disorder, Criminal Responsibility and Criminal Culpability' (2009) 16(1) *Psychiatry, Psychology and Law* 16, 33.

31 N. Rawdon et al., 'Exploring the Experiences of an Autistic Male Convicted of Stalking' (2024) 35 *The Journal of Forensic Psychiatry & Psychology* 461.

32 Gunasekaran (n 10).

norms,[33] particularly since disrupting an anticipated routine or compulsion can potentially provoke distress and trigger violent reactions.[34] Furthermore, the social naivete commonly associated with ASD can lead to misunderstandings regarding others' intentions and consequent involvement in offending.[35] For example, individuals with ASD often struggle to recognise when others are attempting to exploit them due to their social impairments, which could result in interactions with individuals involved in criminal activities who harbor malicious intentions; for example, in one case, a man named Berty was used by a local criminal group to house stolen goods in exchange for their friendship.[36]

Common characteristics associated with ASD also may significantly complicate the courtroom and sentencing experiences for diagnosed individuals across jurisdictions. Features of ASD can affect how defendants with ASD interact with legal proceedings and how they are perceived by legal decision-makers.[37] Due to their impaired social communication, defendants with ASD may struggle with understanding and appropriately responding to social cues, as well as interpreting the body language or tone of voice of judges, attorneys, or witnesses; this can lead to miscommunications or confusion during sentencing.[38] Defendants with ASD may also avoid eye contact, which might be seen as evasive or disrespectful, fail to respond to direct questions or provide responses that seem off-topic or unrelated, which can be perceived as uncooperative or insolent, and engage in behaviours such as speaking out of turn or interrupting others, which can be interpreted as disruptive.[39] For example, in one case, a man with ASD spoke with a robotic cadence and appeared disinterested and evasive during the prosecutor's questioning, which his attorney feared would prejudice the court and lead them to believe he was guilty.[40] Misinterpretations of these common ASD traits can negatively impact how a defendant is perceived by the court, potentially influencing key outcomes during sentencing.[41] For example, a defendant who avoids eye contact might be perceived as deceptive or dishonest, while one who speaks out of turn might

33 Ibid.

34 A. Westphal, R. Loftin, 'Violence Risk Assessment in Autism Spectrum Disorder (ASD)' in F. R. Volkmar et al. (eds), *Handbook of Autism Spectrum Disorder and the Law* (1st ed., Springer, 2021) 307.

35 D. C. Murrie et al., 'Asperger's Syndrome in Forensic Settings' (2002) 1(1) *International Journal of Forensic Mental Health* 59.

36 P. Howlin, *Autism and Asperger Syndrome: Preparing for Adulthood* (2nd ed., Routledge, London, 2004) 306.

37 Caliman and Berryessa (n 1).

38 C. S. Allely, P. Cooper, 'Jurors' and Judges' Evaluation of Defendants with Autism and the Impact on Sentencing: A Systematic Preferred Reporting Items for Systematic Reviews and Meta-analyses (PRISMA) Review of Autism Spectrum Disorder in the Courtroom' (2017) 25(1) *Journal of Law and Medicine* 105.

39 Ibid.

40 *W. Austl. v. Mack* [2012] WASC 127, 41 (17 April 2012).

41 Freckelton (n 9).

be viewed as disrespectful. Such perceptions can lead to prejudicial impressions among legal decision-makers, which can result in harsher or inappropriate sentences for individuals with ASD.[42] Further, as discussed later in more detail, legal jargon and specialised terminology can be confusing for defendants with ASD, who may struggle with nuanced or abstract language, which can hinder their understanding of legal proceedings and their ability to participate effectively in their defence.[43]

Studies have shown that, both in the U.S. and elsewhere, legal decision-makers often lack a clear understanding of how to interpret and handle cases involving defendants with ASD during sentencing.[44] These misinterpretations can lead to prejudicial impressions and punitive outcomes, as decision-makers may not understand that offending or courtroom behaviours are symptomatic of ASD rather than indicators of character flaws or criminal intent.[45] Even when judges are sympathetic to defendants with ASD, their lack of understanding of the disorder can lead to uncertainty in how to factor the diagnosis into sentencing processes.[46]

For example, while some judges in the U.S. have reported considering ASD as a potential mitigating factor in sentencing determinations, others have indicated that they might view it as an aggravating factor.[47] Indeed, some participants in a study involving judges from the state of California believed that a defendant's ASD could make him more dangerous or less amenable to rehabilitation.[48] When seen as a mitigating factor, judges often raise doubts about whether a defendant's blameworthiness may be reduced if their offending behaviour was meaningfully influenced by their symptomatic presentation and prioritise alternatives to incarceration to address a defendant's behaviour.[49] Conversely, some judges appear to perceive an ASD diagnosis as a potential aggravating factor to sentencing—stemming from beliefs that it might heighten the risk of future offending (given challenges in impulse control associated with the condition) and, thus, raising concerns about public safety.[50]

42 C. M. Berryessa, 'Educator of the Court: The Role of the Expert Witness in Cases Involving Autism Spectrum Disorder' (2017) 23(6) *Psychology, Crime & Law* 575.

43 Berryessa (n 1).

44 See C. M. Berryessa, 'Judiciary Views on Criminal Behaviour and Intention of Offenders with High-Functioning Autism' (2014) 5 *Journal of Intellectual Disabilities and Offending Behaviour* 97; Berryessa (n 2); C. M. Berryessa, 'Judicial Perceptions of Media Portrayals of Offenders with High Functioning Autistic Spectrum Disorders' (2014) 3 *International Journal of Criminology and Sociology* 46.

45 Freckelton (n 9).

46 C. M. Berryessa, 'Brief Report: Judicial Attitudes Regarding the Sentencing of Offenders with High Functioning Autism' (n 2); C. M. Berryessa, 'Judiciary Views on Criminal Behaviour and Intention of Offenders with High-Functioning Autism' (n 44).

47 Ibid.

48 Ibid.

49 Ibid.

50 Ibid.

Overall, legal decision-makers often struggle to determine the relevance of an ASD diagnosis to legal issues, as well as overestimate or underestimate the impact of ASD on the defendant's offending or courtroom behaviour.[51] Although potentially exerting less influence on determinations of guilt, a limited yet expanding body of research indicates that information regarding a defendant's ASD diagnosis and symptomatology meaningfully affects considerations of their intent, blameworthiness, and concerns about the manner and appropriateness of their sentence.[52] The challenges surrounding the integration of an ASD diagnosis into legal and particularly sentencing processes highlight the critical need for a greater understanding of the disorder, its symptoms, and its impact on the sentencing process among legal decision-makers. In this sense, the use of neuroscience presents an opportunity for legal decision-makers to gain a deeper understanding of the underlying mechanisms and behavioral patterns associated with ASD, thereby facilitating more equitable and just outcomes in the sentencing phase for diagnosed individuals.

The Impact of Neuroscience on Sentencing Defendants With ASD

As we detail as follows across three main areas, neuroscience represents a promising tool for the sentencing of defendants with ASD, especially about informing members of the court on the more appropriate and considerate treatment of such defendants in sentencing. First, we discuss how neuroscience may aid legal decision-makers in better contextualising ASD diagnoses and neurodiversity during sentencing proceedings. Then, we explore how neuroscience can be used to cultivate better models of care and service innovations when developing and implementing sentencing accommodations for defendants with ASD. Finally, we describe how neuroscience is being used to increase the education, awareness, and training of legal decision-makers, including judges, attorneys, and court personnel, on ASD and its forensic relevance to sentencing and other legal processes.

Using Neuroscience to Contextualize ASD and Neurodiversity During Sentencing

As ASD encompasses a complex set of behaviours and symptoms, there is no singular test to determine whether a person has ASD; instead, diagnosis stems from examining a person's history, including the age at which the person attained developmental milestones, observing levels of social and intellectual functioning, and scores on different screening instruments.[53] However, the

51 Ibid.

52 Caliman and Berryessa (n 1).

53 D. P. Gallo, *Diagnosing Autism Spectrum Disorders: A Lifespan Perspective* (Wiley-Blackwell, West Sussex, 2015) 17.

neuroscience of ASD has represented a new way of helping to contextualise the diagnosis within court settings in two main ways.

First, neuroscience can help contextualise diagnoses and symptoms of ASD during sentencing. However, at the outset, it is essential to discuss what neuroscience does *not* bring to ASD in sentencing contexts: the potential for a definitive diagnosis of specific defendants. Akin to other mental disorders, neuroscience research on ASD has focused on group-level analysis—with the brain scans of individuals with ASD being pooled and compared to pooled scans of those without ASD, findings such as these have allowed scientists to advance their knowledge on the neurodevelopment leading to ASD and how it diverges from an average 'neurotypical brain.'[54]

However, neuroscience—both in the lab and in the courtroom—is not yet able to discern if specific neuroscience findings published in academic research are characteristic of or apply to any one individual with ASD. Experts cannot yet conclusively show that a person has ASD by using neuroimaging, as many neuroimaging findings for ASD are not unique and are shared by other conditions such as Attention Deficit Hyperactivity Disorder and Obsessive Compulsive Disorder.[55] Further, brain findings for ASD can differ based on a person's age or sex.[56] Thus, there is no objective evidence to support that individual neuroimaging evidence is robust enough to support a diagnosis of ASD for specific defendants during sentencing—limiting their application in legal settings.[57] Indeed, sentencing proceedings and legal processes more generally focus on evaluating a single person's behaviour on a case-by-case basis, while neuroscience research assesses what we know about the brains of groups and applies that to individual people; this has been called the group-to-individual (G2i) issue.[58] Although the U.S. Model Penal Code is drafted in a way that accommodates advances in neuroscience and the knowledge it provides on understanding different types of 'mental disease,' it remains challenging for legal systems to use neuroscience on a case-by-case basis for defendants with ASD or to better determine the mental state of a particular defendant.[59]

Yet, instead of providing definitive diagnoses for specific defendants, neuroscience may be more informative in helping members of the court more

54 Yarnell-Mac Grory et al. (n 14).

55 C. O. Carlisi, 'Comparative Multimodal Meta-Analysis of Structural and Functional Brain Abnormalities in Autism Spectrum Disorder and Obsessive-Compulsive Disorder' (2017) 82(2) *Biological Psychiatry* 83; M. H. Johnson et al., 'Annual Research Review: Infant Development, Autism, and Adhd—Early Pathways to Emerging Disorders' (2014) 56(3) *Journal of Child Psychology and Psychiatry* 228.

56 M. Lai et al., 'Imaging Sex/Gender and Autism in the Brain: Etiological Implications' (2016) 95(1–2) *Journal of Neuroscience Research* 380.

57 Yarnell-Mac Grory et al. (n 14) 84–89.

58 D. L. Faigman et al., 'Group to Individual (G2i) Inference in Scientific Expert Testimony' (2013) 81(2) *University of Chicago Law Review* 417.

59 D. Caruso, 'Autism in the U.S.: Social Movement and Legal Change' (2010) 36 *American Journal of Law & Medicine* 483.

fully understand the general context and nature of an ASD diagnosis during sentencing and how it can impact behaviour. For example, Caruso argues that ASD's 'frontal attack on the notion of moral responsibility might prompt welcome reflections on the general ethics of retribution and punishment' in the U.S.[60] In the same vein, expert witnesses in the U.S. who give testimony and evidence in trials involving defendants with ASD have similarly expressed how they commonly draw from neuroscience and genetics in their testimonies to positively affect perceptions of fact finders in court about the origins and nature of the disorder.[61] In a study of these experts, they said that using biological science allows them to craft a 'medical model [of ASD] instead of a definition' of ASD so that the court better understands it and to illuminate the intricacies of a disorder that may, at first, appear 'invisible' but bear heavily on the situation at hand.[62] One expert said,

> I think when you can present something in terms of a medical model and show that there's a neurobiological basis for something, especially for something that's a disability that can be an 'invisible' disability so to speak, especially the less severe folks, that I think that can only help serve to work in the benefit of folks who are charged with crimes or are in contact with the justice system.[63]

Other experts talked about using neuroscience to help contextualise impairments of ASD:

> If there's known genetic causes, there's brain development, there's medical issues like prematurity that may result in developmental disabilities . . . so all of these things magnify and make a stronger statement of how the brain is impaired in autism and how that could be responsible for them not understanding and becoming involved in the legal system.[64]

Furthermore, several experts said they also use neuroscience information in an attempt to influence legal decision-makers to consider their testimony on ASD and its symptoms as potentially more serious than without its presentation:

> In my experience judges and juries and lay persons are extremely interested in the origins of these types of things, where they might not have been interested in all the intricacies of it an all that. When you can begin to show that there's a genetic component from within their family and

60 Berryessa (n 50) 538.
61 Ibid.
62 Ibid. 592.
63 Ibid.
64 Ibid.

you point to other people in the family that have this, they are much more likely to consider it a significant aspect in the trial, whatever the trial is.[65]

Caruso argues that U.S. judges now feel more public scrutiny in cases involving defendants with ASD, including during sentencing, and may be expected to consider evidence provided by experts on the more general brain deficits characteristic of ASD.[66] In 2008, the New Jersey Supreme Court ruled that expert evidence on the diagnosis of a defendant with ASD, including neuroscience information, should have been admitted in his original trial as it was relevant to his defence and understanding his behaviour.[67]

Second, neuroscience has begun to help contextualise ASD as a form of *neurodiversity* in the legal system and during sentencing. Neurodiversity suggests that the human brain has variations that result in differences—not disabilities—in intellect, learning, social skills, attention, and other mental abilities; this promotes a novel shift in how we think about disabilities and human differences in cognition.[68] Akin to cultural, gender, or sexual diversity, neurodiversity applies the same kinds of societal thinking about the brain: variations in the brain should be respected as crucial parts of people's identities and senses of self.[69] Armstrong argues that neuroscientific origins of non-neurotypical behaviours, including ASD, are natural human differences that, if viewed more appropriately and in context, can lead to significantly more prosocial and effective interactions between those exhibiting such behaviours and 'neurotypical' people, including within the legal system.[70]

In recent years, these views have become progressively more adopted in legal settings and particularly in sentencing contexts for defendants coming from neurodiverse backgrounds, including those diagnosed with ASD. Legal actors are beginning to rely more on neuroscience to holistically learn more about ASD and broaden their understanding of human differences to integrate the benefits of neurodivergent conditions into their legal decision-making.[71] Aligned with the Social Model of Disability, restrictions or hindrances that are faced by those with neurodiverse backgrounds in legal systems often stem from physical layouts of or structures associated with the legal process (e.g., how courtrooms are laid out), social conventions used in court settings

65 Ibid.

66 Caruso et al. (n 59) 510.

67 *State v. Burr* [2008] N.J. 948 A.2d 627, 634.

68 T. Armstrong, *Neurodiversity: Discovering the Extraordinary Gifts of Autism, ADHD, Dyslexia, and Other Brain Differences* (Da Capo Lifelong, 2010) 3.

69 D. B. Pickar, 'Considerations Regarding Child and Parent Neurodiversity in Family Court' (2022) 60(3) *Family Court Review* 492.

70 Armstrong (n 68).

71 D. L. Baker, *The Politics of Neurodiversity: Why Public Policy Matters* (Lynne Rienner Publishers, Boulder, 2011) 3.

(e.g., eye contact, the use of non-literal language), or the reliance on standard processes, procedures, or criminal sentences that are commonplace for and standard in 'neurotypical' cases in criminal justice systems.[72] As such, reconceptualising how legal decision-makers understand these factors, and how they can incorporate varying levels of neurodiversity into cases involving ASD and especially in the sentencing of defendants with ASD, is essential.

For example, individuals with ASD may show their brain differences as disabilities in some contexts, such as in social or unpredictable environments, while in other contexts, the 'disabilities' of ASD can be curtailed and allow such differences to 'blossom as talents.'[73] In her toolkit for U.S. judges, Berryessa argues that judges should consider how both the court environment during sentencing, as well as the choices they make concerning what sentences they give to defendants with ASD, may minimise or maximise the social, communication, and brain differences experienced by those with ASD.[74] The difficulties of defendants with ASD with understanding and foreseeing the feelings, emotions, and needs of others have been especially critical for judges to consider during sentencing proceedings—as sentencing centers around perspective-taking concepts such as remorse, blameworthiness, and the feelings and experiences of victims.[75] Drapela argues that 'strong working-knowledge of neurodivergence—[ASD] in particular—enriches judicial capacities to deliver procedural due process, as judicial awareness of neurodivergent offenders' needs can enhance the courts' communication with and understandings of defendants actions,' especially during sentencing contexts.[76] Such working knowledge can be instilled via training now available in certain jurisdictions in the U.S., as discussed later.

Neuroscience and Accommodations in Sentencing

Stemming from more holistic and neurodiverse ways of thinking about ASD during sentencing, neuroscience has also begun to contribute to the development and consideration of different accommodations for defendants with ASD in the sentencing process. In the U.S., Larson and colleagues recently used a statement from the International Society of Autism Research[77] as a framework to outline how legal decision-makers can use language accommodations

72 L. A. Drapela, 'Incorporating Neurodiversity into Therapeutic Jurisprudence: Exploring the Policy Diffusion Potential of Pennsylvania's Autism Training Law for Juvenile Court Judges' (2022) 19 *Justice Policy Journal* 1.

73 S. Baron-Cohen, 'The Concept of Neurodiversity Is Dividing the Autism Community' (2019) *Scientific American* 2.

74 Berryessa (n 2).

75 Ibid.

76 Drapela (n 72) 3.

77 INSAR, 'Autism and the Criminal Justice System: Policy Opportunities and Challenges' (*International Society of Autism Research*, 2022) <https://www.autism-insar.org/resource/resmgr/docs/2022_CJ_INSAR_Policy_Brief.pdf>

during sentencing and other legal processes to minimise brain differences and difficulties of those with ASD.[78]

For example, legal language and language used to communicate legal issues are highly complicated and inaccessible to those with ASD, who commonly have structural language deficits and difficulties with syntax and multi-part sentences due to their brain differences.[79] Complex linguistic expectations are perhaps most apparent during questioning, testimonies, or statements made in trial and sentencing contexts when individuals with ASD are asked to detail a narrative account of their feelings surrounding events, which can be difficult for defendants with ASD, who commonly struggle with telling timelines of events, their feelings during and perspectives of such events, and becoming anxious during the retelling of events.[80] Larson outlines accommodations for judges and attorneys in the U.S. to use modified questioning strategies when interacting with defendants with ASD, such as using more straightforward and literal language; this would allow sufficient time for responses and the provision of questioning approaches that may not wholly rely on narrative accounts.[81]

Neuroscience has also begun to contribute to the increased use of the Sequential Intercept Model (SIM) in sentencing decisions for defendants with ASD in the U.S. SIM relies on the use of interventions that limit and prevent the participation of defendants with mental disorders in traditional legal processes—stemming from the idea that different cognitive abilities and brain differences can lead to issues with formulating criminal intent or difficulties controlling behavior that should potentially preclude their arrest, incarceration, or total involvement in the legal system.[82] There are several 'interception' stages in which the SIM model can be applied, including at the sentencing stage.[83] Indeed, a defendant's brain deficits may help dictate the nature of their disposition during sentencing processes when using the SIM model.[84]

In 2022, the International Society for Autism Research released a policy brief on developing and disseminating a specific SIM framework and model for defendants with ASD in the U.S., so that both community and criminal justice services can specifically address the treatment, social, and communication needs of defendants with ASD based on their known brain and developmental

78 C. Larson et al., 'Language Is a Critical Mediator of Autistic Experiences within the Criminal Justice System' (2023) 16(12) *Autism Research* 2240.

79 Ibid.

80 Ibid.

81 Ibid.

82 N. Bonfine et al., 'Meeting the Needs of Justice-Involved People with Serious Mental Illness within Community Behavioral Health Systems' (2020) 71(4) *Psychiatric Services* 355.

83 M. R. Munetz and P. A. Griffin, 'Use of the Sequential Intercept Model as an Approach to Decriminalization of People with Serious Mental Illness' (2006) 57(4) *Psychiatric Services* 544.

84 E. Gansel, 'Military Service-Related PTSD and the Criminal Justice System: Treatment as an Alternative to Incarceration' (2014) 23 *Southern California Interdisciplinary Law Journal* 147.

differences.[85] For sentencing, the model involves legal decision-makers prioritising and using alternative or community correctional strategies, if possible, to prevent reoffending; especially in cases in which defendants with ASD may demonstrate inappropriate empathetic reactions, incarceration may not achieve the anticipated goals of sentencing.[86] Alternative sentencing programs for individuals with ASD, such as inpatient rehabilitation, community programs, or private organisational services in which staff are specialists in ASD, may be much better-tailored environments for defendants with characteristic brain and perspective-taking deficits.[87] Community correctional strategies may involve adapting probation services to include more individualised stipulations, routine assessments to evaluate support needs and provide stability, and the use of social workers—so probation interfaces with community-based supports and services that aid in providing employment, housing, medical care, and mental health care.[88]

For defendants with ASD who end up being sentenced to incarceration, judges should also ensure that facilities are prepared to care for a defendant with a neurodiverse background *before* the defendant arrives at the correctional institution. The policy brief explicitly recommends specialised intake and transfer tools to assess social, communication, executive functioning, and sensory considerations for corrections officers and staff; this will help them to determine the potential accommodations needed for a defendant with ASD due to their brain and developmental differences, as well as whether alternate or sensory-friendly environments should be utilised while the defendant is incarcerated.[89]

Neuroscience and Educating Legal Decision-Makers in Cases Involving ASD

In some jurisdictions in the U.S., neuroscience is now being used to increase legal decision-makers' education, awareness, and training on ASD and its forensic relevance to sentencing and other legal processes. One leading jurisdiction is the U.S. state of Pennsylvania, which has devoted significant resources to research, education, and support for understanding ASD, particularly in the legal system. The Pennsylvania Department of Human Services' Office of Developmental Programs houses the Autism Services, Education, Resources, and Training Collaborative (ASERT), which specialises in assisting legal decision-makers working with defendants with ASD by providing training on interacting with these populations given their brain and developmental

85 INSAR (n 77) 1.
86 Ibid.
87 L. L. Shea et al., 'Preventing and Improving Interactions between Autistic Individuals and the Criminal Justice System: A Roadmap for Research' (2021) 14(10) *Autism Research* 2053.
88 INSAR (n 77) 2.
89 Ibid.

deficits.[90] In November 2020, led by Justice Kevin Daugherty, the Pennsylvania Supreme Court worked with ASERT to unveil a state-level initiative to help judges better recognise and communicate with individuals with ASD; the Pennsylvania court system has now also created archives on topics and educational materials on ASD and the courts, allowing for open access to knowledge and training on these issues.[91]

Most significantly, however, Pennsylvania passed a law that mandates that Magisterial District Judges receive ASD training, so they are better aware and equipped to communicate and interact with defendants with ASD.[92] Pennsylvania Democratic Representative Thomas Caltagirone sponsored the legislation after hearing about an episode in another state in which a person with mental illness was fatally shot by law enforcement who were very poorly trained in working with those with brain, developmental, and other mental disabilities.[93] In the Pennsylvania Judicial Code, Magisterial District Judges must complete ASD training within their Continuing Legal Education credits at least once every six years, and the training explicitly highlights the use of diversionary options before and at the sentencing stage for diagnosed defendants:

> Continuing Education Requirement: Magisterial District Judges Every magisterial district judge shall complete a continuing education program each year equivalent to not less than 32 hours per year in such courses or programs as are approved by the board. At least every six years, the program shall include the identification of mental illness, intellectual disabilities and autism and the availability of diversionary options for individuals with mental illness, intellectual disabilities or autism.[94]

The U.S. state of Alabama has also engaged in similar educational services for legal decision-makers. The Alabama Forensic Assessment Research and Evaluation Project is a partnership between the University of Alabama and the Alabama Department of Mental Health's Office of Forensic Mental Health Services.[95] In 2020, a training curriculum consisting of two components was developed under this partnership for both mental health staff and legal decision-makers in Alabama: (1) training and problem-solving activities on

90 Drapela (n 72).

91 Ibid.

92 Pennsylvania Judicial Code [2017] Title 42, Section 3118.

93 J. Smydo, 'Becoming Aware of Mental Illness: Pa. Law Requires Training for Police, Judges' (*Pittsburgh Post-Gazette*, 2015) <https://www.hmpglobal.earningnetwork.com/site/emsworld/news/14043681/becoming-aware-of-mental-illness-pa-law-requires-training-for-police-judges>

94 Pennsylvania Judicial Code (n 117) Subsection 1.

95 L. E. Kois et al., 'University-Community Mental Health Training Collaboration: Teaching Criminal Legal Stakeholders about Autism' (2023) 74(12) *Psychiatric Services* 1311.

the etiology of ASD, experiences of people with ASD, and trajectories leading to individuals' involvement in the criminal legal system; (2) training on evidence-based strategies for addressing behavioural and executive deficits of ASD, issues with social and emotional communication and regulation, and characteristic social and language deficits—to decrease 'conflict' in legal processes involving those with ASD and improving their care in the legal system, including the use of diversion and sentencing alternatives.[96] Thus far, those who have undergone training in the Alabama legal system have reported having increased confidence in their ASD knowledge and beliefs in their capacity to work with defendants with ASD and expressed high satisfaction with the training.[97]

Conclusions

Overall, this chapter has shown how neuroscience may aid legal decision-makers to better contextualise ASD diagnoses and neurodiversity during sentencing, cultivate better models of care when developing and implementing sentencing accommodations for defendants with ASD, and how neuroscience is being used in awareness and training of legal decision-makers on ASD and its forensic relevance to sentencing and other legal processes. To date, the applications and the use of neuroscience within these avenues and in specific jurisdictions have been limited. Different legal systems should explore these applications, and future research should also assess how they may extend internationally. For example, the two training programs discussed here are U.S.-based but would likely be successful and applicable to other countries. As neuroscience represents a valuable tool to inform members of the court on the more appropriate and considerate treatment of defendants with ASD during sentencing and in court more generally, legal systems across the globe should begin to focus more on its utility in justice processes and how they can adopt such principles in their jurisdictions.

96 Ibid.
97 Ibid.

11 Drug Policy

Neuroscience-Informed Responses to Substance Use

Amanda V. Chen and Stephanie Tabashneck

Introduction to Substance Use Disorder and Public Policy

Neuroscience has long demonstrated that substance use disorders (SUDs) are chronic, brain-based illnesses that have a profound effect on the brain, decision-making, and self-control.[1] This contrasts with the perception of addiction as a moral failing; for example, the idea that people with SUD continue to use substances because they are unmotivated, self-indulgent, or lacking in willpower. Like other chronic diseases, such as asthma, arthritis, or heart disease, the process of addiction recovery includes periods of remission followed by relapse or return to use, even when appropriate treatment is provided and even when the individual follows the plan recommended by healthcare professionals.[2]

Public policy is an important consideration for the management and treatment of SUDs. The use and misuse of drugs and alcohol have an array of effects on public health. These effects include transmission of blood-borne illnesses, such as HIV or hepatitis B and C, when using or sharing contaminated needles.[3] Public safety is also impacted by unsafe behaviours that occur during substance use, such as driving under the influence or violence that occurs while under the influence of a substance.[4]

However, questions remain as to how societies should regulate drug and alcohol use, and what role the criminal justice system should play in this regulation. For example, for someone who struggles with alcohol use disorder, how should society respond if the person drives while intoxicated? How would

1 N. D. Volkow, M. Boyle, 'Neuroscience of Addiction: Relevance to Prevention and Treatment' (2018) 175 *American Journal of Psychiatry* 729.

2 C. C. DiClemente, M. A. Crisafulli, 'Relapse on the Road to Recovery: Learning the Lessons of Failure on the Way to Successful Behavior Change' (2022) 48 *Journal of Health Service Psychology* 59.

3 B. P. Kolla, T. Oesterle, M. Gold, F. Southwick, T. Rummans, 'Infectious Diseases Occurring in the Context of Substance Use Disorders: A Concise Review' (2020) 411 *Journal of the Neurological Sciences* 116719.

4 S. Zhong, R. Yu, S. Fazel, 'Drug Use Disorders and Violence: Associations with Individual Drug Categories' (2020) 42(1) *Epidemiologic Reviews* 103–116.

DOI: 10.4324/9781003510246-12

these responses change, if at all, if the person does so multiple times, or injures someone else while driving under the influence? What if someone provides fentanyl to a friend struggling with withdrawal symptoms and the friend subsequently overdoses? Frequent issues of debate center around how law and public policy should balance rehabilitating the person using substances with the retribution that is expected when a crime is committed.

Neuroscience-informed approaches to SUD involve medication and psychosocial management; in contrast, the legal approaches to people with SUDs center around punishment.[5] Many countries have begun to take the neuroscience of SUD into account when drafting and implementing public policy regarding substance use.[6] However, those with SUD continue to face inequities that would be mitigated if a neuroscience-based approach to SUD was more thoroughly integrated into legislation and the criminal justice system.

Neuroscientific research and its findings on SUDs, as well as their impact on the brain, play an important role in informing these decisions. This chapter will describe the current understanding of SUD as a brain-based illness, the application of this understanding to public policy, and the lessons that can be learned from countries to inform the implementation of a more neuroscience-based approach to SUD in legislation.

Neurobiology of Addiction

The neuroscience behind addiction can help elucidate the behaviours that society sees as related to addiction, including behaviours related to withdrawal and cravings. The primary neurotransmitter implicated in addiction is dopamine, which is active in the reward system in the brain. When an individual is intoxicated with a drug, large bursts of dopamine are released in the mesolimbic pathway, also known as the 'reward' pathway.[7] This pathway spans parts of the brain involved in more basic functions, such as movement and sensation, as well as those involved in higher-level cognitive functioning. These large bursts of dopamine reinforce drug-taking behaviour and lead the individual to learn to associate certain stimuli with the 'reward' feeling, or 'high.' For example, in the future, an individual may see a needle, which primes their brain to expect a 'high,' which motivates the individual to consume substances. Of note, dopamine receptors are present in the prefrontal cortex, the part of the brain that is responsible for decision-making and emotional regulation.

5 L. A. Ray and others, 'Combined Pharmacotherapy and Cognitive Behavioral Therapy for Adults with Alcohol or Substance Use Disorders' (2020) 3 *JAMA Network Open* 1–15.

6 I. Benfer and others, 'The Impact of Drug Policy Liberalisation on Willingness to Seek Help for Problem Drug Use: A Comparison of 20 Countries' (2018) 56 *International Journal of Drug Policy* 162.

7 Volkow and Boyle (n 1) 729.

Tolerance, Withdrawal, and Cravings

Over time, individuals with a substance use disorder begin to develop tolerance. Prolonged exposure to a substance causes a decrease in receptors in the brain, and thus a decreased response to the substance.[8] The individual then requires an increased use of the drug to achieve the same effect or 'high.'

Withdrawal occurs when the effect of the substance wears off, leading to a decrease in activity in the reward system in the brain. Withdrawal tends to affect individuals who have used the substance regularly. Withdrawal symptoms can vary depending on the substance, but they usually involve several uncomfortable side effects, including negative mood, anxiety, sleep problems, and irritability.[9] Individuals with SUD may use substances as a way of avoiding these unpleasant symptoms of withdrawal.

Cravings occur when certain stimuli that the person associates with the drug, such as environmental stimuli, motivate the addicted individual to seek out the drug. Stimuli that trigger cravings can include seeing the substance, a friend who has used substances with the individual, or a street or building where the individual had previously used or bought substances. In the brain, cravings are associated with (a) the prefrontal cortex, which is involved in decision-making; (b) the amygdala, which processes emotions; and (c) the hippocampus, which is associated with learning and memory.[10]

Impact of Addiction on Executive Functioning

Repeated drug use can cause the prefrontal cortex to lose some of its function, making it difficult for someone to consider the long-term consequences of using drugs or to engage in rational decision-making. Due to profound changes in the brain, conditioned response, and cravings, individuals with SUD continue to be motivated to seek out the substance even when they are no longer experiencing the drug's positive effects.[11] They 'want' the substance, but they may no longer enjoy it or feel pleasure from it.

Chronic drug use can have long-lasting effects on the brain, contributing to vulnerability to a return to use (relapse) even if an individual has not used the substance for years.[12] At the same time, stopping use of substances can lead to recovery of brain function, as demonstrated by multiple studies using brain imaging.[13] Thus, someone who struggles with SUD is not a 'lost cause';

8 Ibid. 729.

9 Ibid.

10 Ibid.

11 Ibid.

12 National Institute on Drug Abuse, 'Principles of Drug Abuse Treatment for Criminal Justice Populations: A Research-Based Guide' (*U.S Department of Health and Human Services*, 2018) 1.

13 M. A. Parvaz and others, 'Structural and Functional Brain Recovery in Individuals with Substance Use Disorders during Abstinence: A Review of Longitudinal Neuroimaging Studies' (2022) 232 *Drug and Alcohol Dependence* 109319.

the brain holds potential for recovery, and as such, the availability of treatment and support is all the more important.

Symptomology and Risk Factors

Symptoms and Diagnosis

The American Psychiatric Association's *Diagnostic and Statistical Manual of Mental Disorders*, Fifth Edition Text Revision (DSM-5-TR) is the gold standard for diagnosing and treating mental illness. The *DSM-5* uses 11 symptom criteria to diagnose Substance Use Disorder (SUD). SUD is diagnosed on a spectrum, with two or three symptoms triggering a mild SUD, four or five denoting a moderate SUD, and six or more symptoms denoting a severe SUD. The 11 symptom criteria fall under four categories: impaired control with substance use, physical dependence, social problems, and risky use. Impaired control includes being unsuccessful in trying to decrease or control substance use, cravings, and spending time obtaining, using, and recovering substances. Physical dependence includes tolerance—or needing more of the substance to feel the same effect—and withdrawal. Social problems include failure to fulfil work, school, or home obligations, or withdrawing from activities due to substance use. Risky use includes using in dangerous environments and continuing to use a substance despite knowing that the substance is impacting physical and mental health.[14]

Risk Factors for Addiction

Many factors can increase the likelihood of addiction, including biological, genetic, behavioural, and environmental factors. Approximately half of the risk for addiction involves genetic factors encoded in an individual's DNA. Such differences in genes profoundly impact how an individual responds to or metabolises substances, which can lead someone to respond more strongly to substances or increase the amount of time the substance is active in the body.

Adolescents, in particular, are more predisposed to experiment with drugs and subsequently develop substance use disorders. Compared to the adult brain, the adolescent brain is more neuroplastic, meaning that it has a greater ability to change and adapt, and is more susceptible to developing addiction.[15] Another reason why adolescents are particularly vulnerable to substance use disorder is due to the fact that different parts of the brain undergo different rates of development. The human brain is not fully developed until the individual reaches their mid-twenties. The reward-seeking and emotional circuits

14 American Psychiatric Association, *Diagnostic and Statistical Manual of Mental Disorders: DSM-5* (5th ed., American Psychiatric Publishing, 2013) 481–590.

15 Volkow and Boyle (n 1) 729.

of the brain develop earlier. As a result, adolescents are more emotionally reactive to stressful situations, particularly when peers are involved, and engage in more reward-seeking behaviour, such as substance use. Additionally, the prefrontal cortex, which is responsible for decision-making, planning, and controlling impulses, is not yet fully developed, making it more difficult for adolescents to regulate their emotions and increasing their vulnerability to risky behaviours. This increased impulsivity can be adaptive, as risk-taking can lead to growth. For example, this neurobiologically based inclination towards risk-taking can include exploring different academic interests, making new friendships, or learning different skills.[16] However, impulsivity also applies in other contexts, such as trying substances. Additionally, once exposed to substances, the development of the prefrontal cortex can be blunted, resulting in a cycle where the adolescent is at further risk for substance use and, consequently, addiction.

Behaviour traits such as impulsivity, increased sensation seeking, and increased reactivity to stress all increase the likelihood of addiction. Thus, factors that impact these behavioural traits also impact the likelihood of addiction. For example, social stressors during early childhood, such as social deprivation, have also led to impaired development in the brain, leading to increased impulsivity and consequently increased risk for addiction.[17]

There is a high comorbidity of SUD and other mental illnesses such as depression, anxiety, and ADHD. Almost 20% of people with mental illness simultaneously have a SUD, which is more than three times the base rate of SUD in the general population.[18] Addiction often occurs with mental illness at least partly because these psychiatric illnesses share brain circuits, neurotransmitter systems (dopamine, serotonin, GABA, glutamate, norepinephrine), as well as genetic and environmental risk factors.[19]

Neuroscience-Informed Treatment Approaches

Effective treatment of SUD involves a multidisciplinary approach, often including medication, therapy, and social services such as case management. Given the chronic nature of addiction, and the fact that return to use (relapse) is a common part of the recovery process, individuals generally require multiple episodes of treatment. The National Institute on Drug Abuse recommends that treatment is long enough that the individual is stable and able to learn and

16 C. Insel, S. Tabashneck, F. X. Shen and others, 'White Paper on the Science of Late Adolescence: A Guide for Judges, Attorneys, and Policy Makers' (*Center for Law, Brain & Behavior*, 2 February 2022) <https://clbb.mgh.harvard.edu/white-paper-on-the-science-of-late-adolescence/> 11.

17 Volkow and Boyle (n 1) 729.

18 M. N. Iqbal, C. J. Levin, F. R. Levin, 'Treatment for Substance Use Disorder with Co-Occurring Mental Illness' (2019) 17 *Focus* 88.

19 Volkow and Boyle (n 1) 729.

sustain behavioural changes. Such behavioural changes include breaking cognitive patterns around drugs and learning new skills to cope with withdrawal and cravings.[20]

Due to the high comorbidity between mental illness and addiction, it is also important that any comorbid mental illness be adequately treated, as substance use is often a coping mechanism for depression, anxiety, or psychotic disorder. It is a myth that SUD and mental health disorders should be treated sequentially. Best practices for SUD and co-occurring mental health disorders indicate that both treatments should be integrated and provided in the same time period.[21]

Medications

Medications for addiction differ depending on the substance, as well as factors such as when the substance was last used and accessibility of the medication. For example, methadone, buprenorphine, and naltrexone are all options for treating opioid use disorder, but methadone must be provided in a supervised setting, and naltrexone should only be administered after an individual has withdrawn from opioids.[22] These differences illustrate the parameters of treatment that can shape the experience of someone in recovery, particularly if they are under-resourced and cannot easily access special facilities.

Many medications used to treat SUD affect dopamine. For example, bupropion, an antidepressant that also treats tobacco use disorder, increases dopamine and norepinephrine.[23] This increase in dopamine can help individuals who are abstaining from the drug to cope with the effects of dopamine depletion, including anxiety and depression. Providing dopamine through medication enables people to regain function, allowing them to return to activities such as academics, work, or caring for their families.

Psychosocial Intervention Programs

Due to the psychosocial factors contributing to the development and sustaining of substance use disorder, non-medical treatment–based intervention programs should be incorporated as well. Cognitive behavioural therapy (CBT), for example, is considered a first-line behavioural treatment and focuses on changing cognitions and behaviours around SUDs, such as learning behavioural skills that help an individual abstain from using. Examples of cognitions that an individual might work on changing include redefining what it means

20 National Institute on Drug Abuse (n 12) 1.

21 Ibid. 4.

22 American Academy of Family Physicians, 'Opioid Use Disorder: Medical Treatment Options' (2019) 100(7) *American Family Physician* 416–423.

23 K. Guo and others, 'The Effect of Varenicline and Bupropion on Smoking Cessation: A Network Meta-Analysis of 20 Randomized Controlled Trials' (2022) 131 *Addictive Behaviors* 107329.

to 'relax' and reframing setbacks.[24] CBT utilises the concept of neuroplasticity, or the brain's ability to make new neural pathways. As someone repeatedly practices reframing or new behaviour skills, the brain forms and strengthens these new pathways, allowing for these coping mechanisms to be more available in the future. A combination of CBT and medication has been shown to be more effective in treating SUDs compared to medication alone.[25]

Another important evidence-based therapy is relapse prevention, which helps individuals recognise warning signs for returns to use and help them develop the appropriate coping skills. Relapse prevention can be conceptualised in three stages: emotional, mental, and physical. Emotional relapse occurs when individuals are not taking care of themselves emotionally or physically, which can lead to mental relapse, where individuals begin to think of using substances again. Relapse prevention therapy helps individuals plan and rehearse strategies for when they find themselves in a situation where physical relapse occurs and they begin using again.[26]

Community Reinforcement Approach and Family Training (CRAFT) has also been effective in increasing treatment engagement. CRAFT is an approach where therapists engage with loved ones or concerned significant others of the person with the SUD. Concerned significant others are educated about the nature of SUD and ways to communicate with the person with SUD. These concerned significant others also learn ways to reinforce positive behaviour and encourage the person with SUD to seek help.[27]

Neuroscience research has also shown that strategies not exclusive to substance use can be beneficial for people with SUDs. For example, mindfulness programs and other interventions targeting stress have been shown to be helpful because chronic stress has been shown to make the brain susceptible to drug-seeking and other risky behaviours. Additionally, programs that promote executive function can be preventative. Early Risers for homeless youth and Head Start for kindergarten children are interventions that improve neural circuits early in life and decrease susceptibility to addiction later in life.[28]

Criminal Justice and Substance Use

Mental health, substance use, and the criminal justice system are inextricably intertwined because countries default to the criminal justice system when they are unable to treat patients. In 1939, British psychiatrist Lionel Penrose

24 S. M. Melemis, 'Relapse Prevention and the Five Rules of Recovery' (2015) 88 *Yale Journal of Biology and Medicine* 325.

25 L. A. Ray and others, 'Combined Pharmacotherapy and Cognitive Behavioral Therapy for Adults with Alcohol or Substance Use Disorders' (2020) 3 *JAMA Network Open* 1–15.

26 Melemis (n 24).

27 M. Archer and others, 'Community Reinforcement and Family Training and Rates of Treatment Entry: A Systematic Review' (2020) 115 *Addiction* 1024.

28 G. R. Uhl, G. F. Koob, J. Cable, 'The Neurobiology of Addiction' (2019) *1451 Annals of the New York Academy of Sciences* 5.

coined the term, 'The Penrose Effect,' which detailed the inverse relationship between mental health treatment infrastructure and criminal incarcerations. He analysed 18 European countries and found that when treatment beds for psychiatric disorders decreased, the number of people incarcerated increased. In the decades since, the Penrose Effect has been validated in multiple studies. For example, when psychiatric hospitals closed in the United States in the 1960s, patients were left unhoused and without the outpatient treatment that was originally promised. Many were then diverted to the criminal justice system, and patients effectively became prisoners. One study found that as of 2012, in almost all states, there were more people incarcerated with mental health illnesses than there are patients in the largest state psychiatric hospital.[29]

Although the United States is notable for incarcerating more people than any other country, both in total number and per capita, the Penrose Effect has not been limited to the United States and has been seen in countries in Europe and South America.

Effects of Incarceration on the Brain

Given that environmental factors have substantial impacts on the pathways in the brain, it is critical to acknowledge the effects of incarceration on the brain. Incarceration settings are considered 'impoverished' settings, given the sedentary lifestyle, lack of cognitive and physical stimuli, lack of autonomy, and increased stress levels.

Incarceration settings are especially harmful to those with SUDs for several reasons. First, behavioural control interventions often involve isolation, which has been shown to be harmful to the brain on a neuronal level and to increase the risk of developing further mental illness. There is also a negative cycle where patients with mental illness experience higher rates of solitary confinement and symptom worsening in prison.

Incarceration settings can contribute to a decrease in prefrontal cortex functioning, which is already affected by SUDs. Sleep disturbances and stress, such as stress arising from feelings of unsafety, both negatively impact the prefrontal cortex. Moreover, because many decisions are taken away from people who are incarcerated, they are unable to practice self-regulation, an important skill in coping with SUDs.[30]

Policy Recommendations for the Criminal Justice Population

Given the effects of incarceration on the brain, and the brain-based nature of SUDs, several treatment considerations are particularly critical for the criminal

29 E. Fuller Torrey et al., 'The Treatment of Persons with Mental Illness in Prisons and Jails: A State Survey' (*Treatment Advocacy Center*, 8 April 2014) 6 <https://www.tac.org/reports_publications/the-treatment-of-persons-with-mental-ilnnes-in-prisons-and-jails-a-state-survey/>

30 J. Meijers, J. M. Harte, E. J. A. Scherder, 'Prison and the Brain' (2023) *Handbook of Clinical Neurology* 55.

justice population. Treatment should include access to medicines for SUD and targeting cognitive patterns that contribute to drug use and criminal behaviour. Such cognitive skills include recognising judgment errors and anticipating the consequences of one's behaviour. Given that the criminal justice population generally experiences more socioeconomic hardships, treatment should also include providing social support services, such as stable housing, childcare, and employment assistance.

As stated in the National Institute on Drug Abuse's *Principles of Drug Abuse Treatment for the Criminal Justice Population*, 'Treatment offers the best alternative for interrupting the drug abuse/criminal justice cycle.'[31] Given how often people with SUDs interface with the criminal justice system, the criminal justice system should serve as a contact point for treatment for those with SUDs. For example, treatment can be incorporated as an alternative to conviction or punishment and imposed as a condition of probation.[32] Additionally, treatment should be provided in prison and continued after release. Continuity of care is crucial during re-entry into the community, as the transition from prison into the community can be a stressful experience with drastic changes in the individual's environment. This is also a period where there is an increase in overdoses. Treatment should also include access to medications for SUD, strengthening healthy interpersonal relationships and finding constructive activities to replace drug-seeking behaviours.

Given that infectious diseases such as HIV and hepatitis are more prevalent in the criminal justice population compared to the general population, people who are incarcerated should be offered infectious disease testing and education on harm reduction practices.[33] Harm reduction focuses on reducing risks associated with using substances, such as providing clean needles for people who engage in intravenous drug use to reduce the transmission of bloodborne illnesses like HIV or hepatitis C. Probation and parole officers should also provide support in healthcare matters such as providing information for health services and interacting in a non-stigmatizing, nonjudgemental way that centers SUD as a medical condition.[34]

Special attention should be paid to juveniles, given that one-half to two-thirds of detained juveniles may have a SUD.[35] Additionally, the increased neuroplasticity of adolescents allows them to have an increased susceptibility to rehabilitation, making it even more critical for minors to have access to

31 2014 (Principles of drug abuse treatment) (n 12) 13.

32 United Nations, 'Treatment of Drug Use Disorders for People with Drug Use Disorders in Contact with the Criminal Justice System' (*Office on Drugs and Crime, United Nations*) <https://www.unodc.org/unodc/en/treatment-and-care/webstories/2021/july/treatment-of-drug-use-disorders-for-people-with-drug-use-disorders-in-contact-with-the-criminal-justice-system.html> accessed 3 February 2025.

33 2014 Principles of drug abuse treatment (n 12) 5.

34 Ibid.

35 Ibid. 13.

treatment.[36] For minors who use substances, family-based therapy and environmental changes should also be considered for treatment options.

War on Drugs and Outcomes

The War on Drugs illustrates the consequences of adhering to a non-neuroscience-based drug policy. The War on Drugs originated in the United States but had a significant impact on an international level. The War on Drugs refers to a set of legal policies that address SUDs with attempts to resolve addiction through punitive measures via the criminal justice system. These punitive policies originated in the United States in the 1970s and expanded in the 1980s, resulting in an estimated annual cost of approximately $51 billion as of 2017.[37] The War on Drugs drastically increased the incarceration rate, with the number of arrests for drug possession in the United States increasing from 500,000 in 1982 to approximately 1.5 million in 2007.[38] Notably, the punitive approach to the War on Drugs is almost completely opposite of a neuroscience-based approach.

Despite its 'tough on crimes' approach, this set of policies did not reduce drug-related crime or drug supply, nor did it reduce rates of SUD. In fact, the War on Drugs contributed to an increase in drug-related violence on an international level. This prohibitionist approach to substance use has led to drug markets run by criminal networks. Violence occurs both because of the criminal organisations seeking to protect their markets and because of police or military forces pursuing these organisations, contributing to violence in the community.[39]

Moreover, the War on Drugs has been shown to increase barriers to treatment, and the propaganda of addiction as exclusively a criminal behaviour has been shown to increase overdoses and infectious disease rates such as HIV and hepatitis. Other significant consequences include increasing racial inequity, such as increased police violence in Black communities, increased racial profiling, and increased racialised mass incarceration.[40]

The War on Drugs in the United States has accelerated the Penrose Effect on a national and international level, as those with mental illness and SUD were disproportionately penalised by criminalisation of addiction; simultaneously,

36 Insel (n 16) 36.

37 See, for example, C. J. Coyne, A. R. Hall, 'Four Decades and Counting: The Continued Failure of the War on Drugs' (*Policy Analysis No 811, Cato Institute*, 2017) <https://www.cato.org/policy-analysis/four-decades-counting-continued-failure-war-drugs>

38 Bureau of Justice Statistics, *Drug Arrests for Sales or Possession* (2021) <https://bjs.ojp.gov/drugs-and-crime-facts/enforcement/salespos-table>

39 Coyne and Hall, (n 37).

40 M. L. Rosin, M. W. Hughey, 'The War on Drugs, Racial Meanings, and Structural Racism: A Holistic and Reproductive Approach' (2018) 77 *The American Journal of Economics and Sociology* 849.

funding for treatment and intervention was diverted into the criminal justice system. One analysis showed that for every one treatment bed lost, five more individuals end up in prison.[41]

Case Studies by Country

This section discusses national drug policies from several countries. Many of these policies are centred around decriminalisation, which refers to decreasing or eliminating penalties for drug law violations, typically in reference to drug possession or use. Decriminalisation policies are often aligned with the neuroscience-based practices detailed earlier because they consider that people with SUDs need treatment to help them rewire their brains; such treatment is not found in punitive policies. According to the European Union Drugs Agency (EUDA), previously known as the European Monitoring Centre for Drugs and Drug Addiction (EMCDDA), drug decriminalisation is a movement toward 'an approach that distinguishes between the drug trafficker, who is viewed as a criminal, and the drug user, who is seen more as a sick person who is in need of treatment.'[42]

Over the last few decades, the decriminalisation movement has gained increasing popularity in Europe, with notable examples being Portugal and the Netherlands. Several international human rights and health-related organisations, such as Human Rights Watch, Amnesty International, the World Health Organisation, and the International Federation of Red Cross and Red Crescent Societies,[43] recommend decriminalisation, citing reasons including health and children's rights.[44]

One analysis of 20 countries indicated that people are more likely to seek help when their country adopts policies oriented towards drug liberalisation, such as decriminalisation. Countries that decriminalise drug use tend to invest resources in treatment and harm reduction. Harm reduction aims to reduce risks associated with using substances, such as providing clean needles to reduce transmission of blood-borne illnesses, or providing take-home naloxone, a medication that reverses opioid overdose. On a social level, such

41 A. P. Mundt and others, 'Psychiatric Hospital Beds and Prison Populations in South America since 1990' (2015) 72 *JAMA Psychiatry* 112.

42 European Monitoring Centre for Drugs and Drug Addiction, 'Annual Report 2008: The State of the Drugs Problem in Europe' (*Office for Official Publications of the European Communities*, 2008) <https://www.drugsandalcohol.ie/11593/1/EMCDDA_Annual_report_2008.pdf> 22.

43 Drug Policy Alliance, 'Approaches to Decriminalizing Drug Use & Possession' (*Drug Policy Alliance, New York*) 3 <https://www.unodc.org/documents/ungass2016/Contributions/Civil/DrugPolicyAlliance/DPA_Fact_Sheet_Approaches_to_Decriminalization_Feb2015_1.pdf> accessed 3 February 2025.

44 Norwegian Human Rights Institution, 'Drug Use and Human Rights' Report' (*Norwegian Human Rights Institution*, 10 March 2023) <https://www.nhri.no/en/2023/drug-use-and-human-rights/> accessed 3 February 2025

decriminalisation policies aim to remove stigma and fear of arrest, thus making it more likely for those who use substances to seek help, such as counselling services, emergency services following an overdose, and needle exchange programs.[45]

Portugal

Portugal's drug policy has been one of the most notable in recent decades, after it decriminalised the personal use and possession of all substances in 2001. Portugal had previously participated in the War on Drugs in the 1970s, but it began decriminalisation with the intention of destigmatising addiction and encouraging treatment. In 2001, Portugal implemented the Portuguese Drug Policy Model (PDPM), which stated that possession or use of drugs is an administrative violation and not a criminal offence; drug trafficking remained a criminal offence. Unlike other decriminalisation policies, the Portuguese Drug Policy Model did not distinguish between 'soft' and 'hard' drugs, nor did it distinguish between private and public use. Those who are found using or possessing drugs at a certain threshold are referred to commissions that incorporate officials from the legal, health, and social services fields.[46] The commission provides education about the risks and effects of drugs, as well as harm reduction strategies. The commission determines the appropriate sanction or treatment and is advised to suspend proceedings if the individual is considered to have a SUD and is willing to undergo treatment. Notably, the commission cannot mandate treatment or imprison the individual, although it may impose fines[47] or nonpecuniary sanctions, such as revoking their driver's license or mandating community service.[48] Commissions cannot incarcerate someone for continuing to use drugs, failing to enter treatment, or failing a drug test.

In addition to the legal changes, Portugal invested significantly in harm reduction, treatment, and prevention. For example, by 2008, needle exchange programs had expanded to cover 50% of the country.[49] Kits that include clean

45 I. Benfer and others, 'The Impact of Drug Policy Liberalisation on Willingness to Seek Help for Problem Drug Use: A Comparison of 20 Countries' (2018) 56 *International Journal of Drug Policy* 162.

46 Drug Policy Alliance, 'Drug Decriminalization in Portugal Learning from a Health and Human-Centered Approach' (*Drug Policy Alliance*, New York, 2018) 4 <https://drugpolicy.org/wp-content/uploads/2023/08/dpa-drug-decriminalization-portugal-health-human-centered-approach_0.pdf> accessed 3 February 2025.

47 H. Laqueur, 'Uses and Abuses of Drug Decriminalization in Portugal' (2015) 40 *Law & Social Inquiry* 746.

48 Drug Policy Alliance (n 46).

49 K. Russoniello, 'The Devil (and Drugs) in the Details: Portugal's Focus on Public Health as a Model for Decriminalization of Drugs in Mexico' (*Yale Law School Legal Scholarship Repository*, 25 November 2021) 392 <https://openyls.law.yale.edu/handle/20.500.13051/5897> accessed 3 February 2025.

syringes and needles, distilled water, gauze, and a condom are distributed by social workers to common places where people use drugs.[50]

Overall, Portugal's decriminalisation policy has generally resulted in positive outcomes in health, costs, and the criminal justice system. With increased investment in treatment, Portugal has seen a rise in the number of people receiving treatment. Between 1998 and 2010, the number of outpatient treatment centres in Portugal increased from 53 to 79. The number of people treated also increased. Data analysis shows that this increase is due to an increase in an ageing population of users who are ready to seek treatment, as opposed to an increase in the number of people using substances.[51] Treatment has extended into prisons, with Portugal's national health service providing medications for SUD to people who are incarcerated.[52]

From an infectious disease standpoint, in Portugal, new HIV diagnoses fell from 1,287 diagnoses attributable to injecting drug use in 2001 to 16 new diagnoses in 2019, with a drastic decrease compared to the rest of the European Union population. Additionally, annual reports on hepatitis B and C have been in a consistent decline over the past 20 years. These results are in line with what would be expected from harm reduction policy.

In terms of crime, there was a decrease in incarceration for all drug-related offences, including drug trafficking.[53] From 2001 to 2010, the number of individuals convicted and incarcerated for drug trafficking decreased by almost half.[54]

Decriminalisation in Portugal led to a decrease in the social costs of substances. For example, one policy analysis showed that the social cost of drugs, including both health and non-health-related costs, decreased by 12% in the first five years and by 18% in the first eleven years. This decrease in costs was primarily driven by decreases in overdose-related deaths, legal proceedings, and lost income and productivity by people who were imprisoned for drug-related offences.[55]

From a social and cultural perspective, Portugal's emphasis on decriminalisation has led to less stigma for people who use drugs. The Portuguese police have been a significant element of the decrease in stigma, and have

50 A. Domoslawski, H. Siemaszko, *Drug Policy in Portugal: The Benefits of Decriminalizing Drug Use* (Open Society Institute, 2011) 33.

51 C. E. Hughes, A. Stevens, 'What Can We Learn from the Portuguese Decriminalization of Illicit Drugs?' (2010) 50 *British Journal of Criminology* 999.

52 C. Moury, M. Escada, 'Understanding Successful Policy Innovation: The Case of Portuguese Drug Policy' (2022) 118 *Addiction* 967.

53 Drug Policy Alliance (n 46) 7.

54 Laqueur (n 48) 757.

55 R. Gonçalves, A. Lourenço, S. N. Silva, 'A Social Cost Perspective in the Wake of the Portuguese Strategy for the Fight Against Drugs' (2015) 26 *International Journal of Drug Policy* 199.

been crucial to referring people who use drugs to treatment.[56] However, some stigma remains, affecting the implementation of harm reduction policy. For example, Portugal had intended to provide free syringes in prisons to provide clean needles for people who are incarcerated. Although several pilot programs were implemented in 2007, they were never widely adopted, largely due to the stigma. Prison guards disapproved of such a policy, and individuals who were incarcerated had to ask for clean needles, thus putting them at risk of losing access to their substances.[57]

Although the Portuguese Drug Policy Model has been generally accepted as a successful model for decriminalisation, there has been some pushback in recent years. *The Washington Post* reported that overdose rates have hit 12-year highs in Portugal. Additionally, the number of users being directed into drug treatment peaked in 2015 at 1,150 and declined to 352 in 2021. Part of the setback has been attributed to the economic crisis that led to a funding drop from $82.7 million to $17.4 million for the country's drug oversight operation.[58]

The Netherlands

The Netherlands has a history of implementing coordinated and integrated harm reduction interventions. The Netherlands Opium Act is the Netherlands' core national drug law. The Opium Act distinguishes between a person who uses drugs and a person who traffics or produces drugs. Substance use is not a criminal act, although for public health reasons, people are prohibited from using substances in certain public areas, such as on public transport. Possession of small quantities of substances is technically a crime, but it is rarely prosecuted in practice, except when there is a potential referral to a care agency. The Netherlands Opium Act also distinguishes between Schedule I drugs ('hard drugs'), such as cocaine, heroin, and amphetamines, and Schedule II drugs ('soft drugs'), such as cannabis and hallucinogens. Dutch drug policy oversight is coordinated between several ministries, including the Ministry of Health, Welfare and Sport, the Ministry of Justice and Security, and the Ministry of Foreign Affairs.[59]

The Netherlands has invested significantly in harm reduction and treatment for decades. For example, needle exchange programs began in the

56 B. Mann, 'How Portugal Eased Its Opioid Epidemic, While U.S. Drug Deaths Skyrocketed' (*NPR*, 24 February 2024) <https://www.npr.org/2024/02/24/1230188789/portugal-drug-overdose-opioid-treatment> accessed 16 February 2025.

57 Moury (n 52) 975.

58 A. Faiola, C. F. Martins, 'Once Hailed for Decriminalizing Drugs, Portugal Is Now Having Doubts' (*The Washington Post*, 7 July 2023) <https://www.washingtonpost.com/world/2023/07/07/portugal-drugs-decriminalization-heroin-crack/>

59 European Monitoring Centre for Drugs and Drug Addiction, 'Netherlands Country Drug Report 2019' (*European Union Drugs Agency EUDA*, 2019) 3 <https://www.euda.europa.eu/publications/country-drug-reports/2019/netherlands_en> accessed 3 February 2025.

1970s[60] as a pilot project and were subsequently adopted as official government programs; by 2012, there were 150 needle exchange programs in the Netherlands.[61] These programs are run by addiction care services and the municipality.[62] The Netherlands also has supervised injection facilities, where there is an official agreement with public prosecution that drug possession at an official drug-testing service will not be prosecuted.[63] Heroin-assisted treatment, which is typically for people with an opioid use disorder who have not had success with other treatments, has also been a legal medical treatment since 2006.[64]

The criminal justice system in the Netherlands emphasises continuity of care and treatment in prisons. Mental health services and medications, such as continuation of methadone maintenance treatment, are provided in prisons. Additionally, referral to treatment services outside of prison can be offered as an alternative to imprisonment.[65]

The Dutch government has made substantial investments in the social determinants of health for people who use substances, the unhoused population, and psychiatric patients since 2006. Such investments include homeless shelters, services for the homeless,[66] public mental health care, and criminal justice interventions such as treatment or other psychiatric interventions.[67]

Cannabis has been decriminalised for personal use since 1971, and a subsequent piece of legislation in 1977 led to law enforcement not prosecuting small-scale cannabis offences. This led to the rise of cannabis 'coffee shops' in the Netherlands, where the small amounts sold in the shop are considered legal, and the coffee shop provides a safe environment for customers to use.[68] Interestingly, the supply to these cannabis 'coffee shops' is not legal and not

60 G. Blok, 'Pampering "Needle Freaks" or Caring for Chronic Addicts? Early Debates on Harm Reduction in Amsterdam, 1972–82' (2008) 22 *The Social History of Alcohol and Drugs* 243.

61 J. P. Grund and others, 'Reaching the Unreached: Targeting Hidden IDU Populations with Clean Needles via Known User Groups' (1992) 24 *Journal of Psychoactive Drugs* 41.

62 EUDA (n 59) 16.

63 (*European Drug Report 2017*, June 2017) <https://www.euda.europa.eu/publications/edr/trends-developments/2017/html_en> accessed 3 February 2025.

64 P. Blanken and others, 'Heroin-Assisted Treatment in the Netherlands: History, Findings, and International Context' (2010) 20 *European Neuropsychopharmacology* 113.

65 EUDA (n 59) 20.

66 E. Schatz, K. Schiffer, J. P. Kools, 'The Dutch Treatment and Social Support System for Drug Users: Recent Developments and the Example of Amsterdam' (International Drug Policy Consortium, IDPC Briefing Paper, January 2011) 9.

67 M. van Laar and others, *Report to the EMCDDA by the REITOX National Focal* (Netherlands Institute of Mental Health and Addiction, *THE NETHERLANDS DRUG SITUATION 2014*, 2015) 27. <https://www.trimbos.nl/wp-content/uploads/sites/31/2021/09/af1367-the-netherlands-drug-situation-2014.pdf> accessed 3 February 2025.

68 The Scottish Government, *International Approaches to Drug Law Reform: Research* (Justice Directorate Scottish Government, 1 July 2021) <https://www.gov.scot/publications/international-approaches-drug-law-reform/> accessed 3 February 2025.

regulated, leading to the involvement of organised crime and no quality control.[69] Despite the prevalence of cannabis 'coffee shops,' cannabis use in the Netherlands is on par with that of its neighbours in the European Union.[70]

In terms of health outcomes, the Netherlands has one of the lowest rates of injecting use amongst people who use opioids. These low rates decrease the risks of overdose and HIV, thus contributing to a higher life expectancy for people who use heroin.[71]

Due to the investment in social services and housing, many people in the Netherlands who used to use substances on the street are now in sheltered or supported housing, where they receive integrated harm reduction: welfare, medical care, drug treatment, and on-site drug consumption rooms.[72] Such a multidisciplinary approach to substance use follows evidence-based treatment.

The State of Oregon in the U.S.

In November 2020, Oregon passed Measure 110 (M110) and became the first state to decriminalise possession of all personal use of nonprescribed drugs. Measure 110 also diverted hundreds of millions of dollars towards harm reduction interventions, treatment, and recovery programs. However, post-decriminalisation, there was not sufficient treatment available for the individuals who would require treatment, and public drug use increased. Additionally, between 2020 and 2021, there was approximately a 50% increase in fatal overdoses. Subsequently, in March 2024, Oregon recriminalised drug possession. A later 2024 analysis noted that the increase in fatal overdoses coincided with an increase in the supply and potency of fentanyl, a highly potent and dangerous opioid, in Oregon's unregulated drug supply. After accounting for the increase in fentanyl, the analysis found no association between M110 and fatal overdose rates.[73]

In terms of the criminal justice system, one study found that after M110, there was a decrease in arrests for possession of controlled substances; however, there was an increase in arrests for crimes such as loitering. One study showed that M110 decreased racial disparity in arrests, with arrest rates for Black individuals declining by 77% compared to 67% for white individuals. However, overall, Black individuals continued to be four times more likely to face arrest compared to white individuals. There was no change in violent crimes after M110 was passed.[74]

69 J. P. C. Grund, J. J. Breeksema, 'Drug Policy in the Netherlands 1' (2017) *European Drug Policies* 128.

70 Grund (n 69).

71 Ibid.

72 Schatz (n 66).

73 M. J. Zoorob and others, 'Drug Decriminalization, Fentanyl, and Fatal Overdoses in Oregon' (2024) 7 *JAMA Network Open* 8.

74 C. S. Davis and others, 'Changes in Arrests Following Decriminalization of Low-Level Drug Possession in Oregon and Washington' (2023) 119 *International Journal of Drug Policy* 104155.

At the same time, Oregon studies found that police perceived an increase in lawlessness after M110, and there was continued heavy policing of people who use substances even after passing M110. Studies showed that police continued to seize substances and drug paraphernalia even when individuals were not engaged in any criminal behaviour and were only using substances.[75] One 2023 study found that nearly three-quarters of people who used substances reported involvement in the criminal justice system in the past year.[76]

The State of Washington in the U.S.

Washington state decriminalised drug possession beginning in 2021 by court order after the Washington Supreme Court found that Washington's drug possession statute was unconstitutional in *State v. Blake* (2021).[77] This decision legalised the possession of small amounts of drugs. In July 2021, the state legislature recriminalised drug possession but reclassified it as a misdemeanour instead of a felony. Moreover, law enforcement was required to offer a referral to health services at least twice before arresting someone for possession of small amounts of drugs. The new law also established funding for treatment and related services, and law enforcement was required to undergo training in interacting with people with SUDs.[78]

One study found that after the policy change, there were almost 5 fewer drug possession arrests per 100,000 people every month, a statistically significant difference, although there continued to be significant racial disparities in arrest rates.[79]

The State of Massachusetts in the U.S.

Most states in the United States heavily criminalise most drug use and have explicitly rejected decriminalisation or efforts to curtail the criminal justice system's role in regulating substance use. For example, in *Commonwealth v. Eldred* (2005), the Massachusetts Supreme Judicial Court (SJC) held that a judge could require an individual on probation to remain drug-free, even if that individual had a SUD.[80] In recent cases, the Massachusetts Supreme Judicial Court

75 H. M. Smiley-McDonald and others, '"All Carrots and No Stick": Perceived Impacts, Changes in Practices, and Attitudes among Law Enforcement Following Drug Decriminalization in Oregon State, USA' (2023) 118 *International Journal of Drug Policy* 104100.

76 Smiley-McDonald (n 75).

77 *State v. Blake* (Wash Sup Ct, No 96873-0, 25 February 2021).

78 CERTIFICATION OF ENROLLMENT, ENGROSSED SENATE BILL 5476 (67th Legislature, 2021 Regular Session, State of Washington) <https://lawfilesext.leg.wa.gov/biennium/2021-22/Pdf/Bills/Senate%20Passed%20Legislature/5476.PL.pdf?q=20210425125304> accessed 18 February 2025

79 Davis (n 74).

80 *Commonwealth v. Eldred* (Mass SJC, No SJC-12279, 9 July 2018).

(SJC) has held that probation violations may not be sanctioned if they are due to an involuntary condition. However, in *Eldred*, the SJC did not say whether drug use is voluntary when an individual has a substance use disorder.[81] This decision is at odds with the medical understanding that relapse, or returning to substance use, is a part of recovery, and that addiction creates a neurobiological state where drug-seeking behaviour can overwhelm more rational decision-making.

Conclusion

Substantial neuroscience research demonstrates that SUDs are a chronic, brain-based condition that benefits from treatment, as opposed to the view that addiction is a moral failure. Given that SUDs have biological, cognitive, and social consequences for the person using substances, effective treatment utilises a multidisciplinary approach, including medications, therapy, and social services as needed.

In greater alignment with this neuroscientific framework of SUDs, an increasing number of countries have endeavoured to decriminalise drug use through legislation, court cases, and implementing harm reduction policies. As seen in this chapter, such harm reduction policies have included needle exchange programs, supervised injection sites, and offering referrals to treatment as an alternative to incarceration.

The overall movement of decriminalisation has aligned drug policy more with neuroscience, with the emphasis placed more on support than punishment. Neuroscience has demonstrated that treatment methods work, but policymakers still have several strides to make to integrate evidence-based treatments comprehensively with the justice system. Comparing and contrasting the outcomes of several countries demonstrates the importance of several factors in countries endeavouring to implement harm reduction policies. For example, coordination between the criminal justice system and health agencies helped the Netherlands achieve success in providing consistent harm reduction efforts. Another important factor is adequate funding; for example, a decrease of the financing for Portugal's harm reduction efforts contributed to the decline in the number of people directed to treatment.

SUDs have enormous consequences for individuals and society at large. National and international drug policy must reflect the neuroscience underlying SUDs to provide adequate treatment. The case studies of different countries' approaches demonstrate that an understanding of neuroscience is not enough; sufficient resources must be devoted to the treatment and management of SUDs on a systemic level. Looking to the future, policies that endeavour to incorporate effective, neuroscience-based treatments should ensure sufficient funding and consistent coordination and messaging among the legislature, courts, medical system, and social services.

81 Ibid.

12 Neuroscience Education in the Criminal Justice System

Mia A. Thomaidou

Introduction

Continuous advances in neuroscience offer a window into the neurobiological and environmental factors that shape human behaviour, shedding light on the complexities of cognitive development, mental health, and criminal behaviour. This growing body of knowledge holds promise for transforming how legal professionals comprehend criminal responsibility and how the criminal justice system addresses punishment and rehabilitation.[1] Central to this transformation is the education of legal professionals in neuroscience, a crucial step in ensuring this complex evidence is properly understood, interpreted, and utilised. This chapter aims to explore the increasing relevance of neuroscience education in the criminal-legal system and for legal professionals.

The use of scientific evidence in the courtroom is not a novel concept. For centuries, courts have incorporated forensic evidence, medical diagnoses, and psychological evaluations into criminal cases, to help juries and judges determine guilt, competency, and appropriate sentences.[2] However, neuroscience is a relatively recent entrant to this domain, gaining traction in the latter part of the 20th century as advances in neuroimaging research and cognitive science not only revealed new insights into human cognition and behaviour but also made it possible to more accurately quantify and examine the neural and physiological correlates of behaviour.[3] Technological advancements, such as

1 D. Aono, G. Yaffe, H. Kober, 'Neuroscientific Evidence in the Courtroom: A Review' (2019) 4 *Cognitive Research: Principles and Implications* 40.

2 D. W. Shuman, 'Psychiatric and Psychological Evidence' (*Office of Justice Programs*, 1986) <https://www.ojp.gov/ncjrs/virtual-library/abstracts/psychiatric-and-psychological-evidence> accessed 25 September 2024; W. W. Schwarzer, 'Judicial Discretion in Sentencing' (1991) *Federal Sentencing Reporter* 399.

3 C. Yen, C-L. Lin, M-C. Chiang, 'Exploring the Frontiers of Neuroimaging: A Review of Recent Advances in Understanding Brain Functioning and Disorders' (2023) 13 *Life* 1472; M. J. Zielinski and others, 'Making Change Happen in Criminal Justice Settings: Leveraging Implementation Science to Improve Mental Health Care' (2020) 8 *Health & Justice* 21; T. Morita, M. Asada, E. Naito, 'Contribution of Neuroimaging Studies to Understanding Development of Human Cognitive Brain Functions' (2016) 10 *Frontiers in Human Neuroscience*

DOI: 10.4324/9781003510246-13

the advent of functional Magnetic Resonance Imaging (fMRI), as well as molecular and genetic studies of brain function, allowed researchers to explore the neurobiological underpinnings of cognition, decision-making, and behaviour with greater precision and reliability, offering a deeper understanding of the factors that drive human behaviour. Neuroscience thus offers a framework for understanding how brain factors, such as injury, illness, psychological trauma, and natural variation in brain development, can contribute to criminal behaviour. At the same time, this understanding can also inform the design of rehabilitation programs that may better target the root causes of criminality.[4]

Developmental neuroscience was among the aid fields to highlight the potential for neuroscience to influence legal decision-making. In the United States, landmark cases such as *Roper v. Simmons* (2005)[5] and *Miller v. Alabama* (2012)[6] cemented the influence of neuroscience in sentencing. These rulings determined that juveniles could not be sentenced to death or mandatory life without parole, with the Supreme Court relying on developmental neuroscience to argue that adolescents' brains, particularly areas responsible for impulse control and decision-making, are not fully developed. These cases opened the door to broader acceptance of neuroscience in courtrooms. Notably, a growing understanding of the neurobiological underpinnings of psychiatric disorders has also begun informing legal decisions. In the U.K., for example, the Sentencing Council has, in recent years, placed greater emphasis on mental health mitigation, introducing initiatives like the Mental Health Treatment Requirements (MHTR), which allow judges to integrate mental health support into community sentencing. These shifts illustrate the evolving role of neuroscientific and psychological evidence in criminal justice systems.

Given the increasing reliance on neuroscientific evidence in legal proceedings, a fundamental question arises: how well-equipped are legal professionals to understand and evaluate such evidence? Historically, defence attorneys, prosecutors, judges, and other criminal justice actors have not received formal training in neuroscience or psychology as part of their foundational legal

<https://www.frontiersin.org/journals/human-neuroscience/articles/10.3389/fnhum.2016.00464/full> accessed 25 September 2024; R. Plomin and others, 'Top 10 Replicated Findings from Behavioral Genetics' (2016) 11 *Perspectives on Psychological Science: A Journal of the Association for Psychological Science* 3.

4 S. Xie, C. M. Berryessa, F. Focquaert, 'The Impact of Neuromorality on Punishment: Retribution or Rehabilitation?' in M. C. Altman (ed), *The Palgrave Handbook on the Philosophy of Punishment* (Palgrave MacMillan, 2023) 441–464; A. R. Baskin-Sommers, K. Fonteneau, 'Correctional Change Through Neuroscience' (2016) 85 *Fordham Law Review* 423; See, generally, E. Martin, 'Emerging Relevance of Neuroscience in Corrections' (*Corrections Today / National Institute of Justice*, 2023) NCJ Number: 306049 <https://nij.ojp.gov/library/publications/emerging-relevance-neuroscience-corrections> accessed 25 September 2024.

5 *Roper v. Simmons* [2005] USSC 03-633.

6 *Miller v. Alabama* [2012] USSC 10-9646.

training.[7] As a result, legal actors may be underprepared to critically assess the validity, relevance, and limitations of neuroscientific evidence presented in court. As legal systems worldwide grapple with this reality, courts often rely on independent neuroscience or clinical experts to present and explain neuroscience evidence.[8] Some legal systems, particularly in Europe, have developed frameworks that require scientific experts to be appointed by the court. However, as will be discussed in this chapter, the reliance on scientific experts—who generally lack legal expertise in determining admissibility, guilt, and punishment—highlights a crucial gap. Legal professionals need a basic understanding of neuroscience and scientific methods to effectively engage with expert testimony and ensure that it is properly considered in the context of justice.

As neuroscience continues to evolve and its implications for criminal justice become clearer, the need for a scientifically informed legal system becomes increasingly apparent. Neuroscience education for legal professionals is critical for ensuring that justice is served in cases involving complex scientific evidence. Integrating neuroscience into the criminal justice system represents both a challenge and an opportunity: a challenge to legal professionals to engage with a rapidly advancing field outside of their home discipline and an opportunity to create a more humane and scientifically informed system of justice.

Chapter Roadmap

This chapter starts by providing a brief historical context for the use of neuroscience and psychology in the criminal legal system, before describing its growing relevance and application in contemporary criminal justice. The relevance of neuroscience in the various stages of the criminal justice process is described, beginning at a conceptual level and ending with a discussion on how neuroscience can inform custodial and community-based sentences. The admissibility of neuroscience evidence, as well as relevant case law, are also discussed. Thereafter, current standards in neuroscience education are described, including early and continuing professional education for attorneys and judges, as well as the training standards and use of scientific experts during criminal proceedings. Finally, the gaps, challenges, and opportunities created by a growing neuroscientific understanding of human behaviour are discussed.

7 M. L. Merlino and others, 'Science Education for Judges: What, Where, and by Whom' (2002) 86 *Judicature* 210; D. W. Shuman, 'Expertise in Law, Medicine, and Health Care' (2001) 26 *Journal of Health Politics, Policy and Law* 267.

8 D. L. Shapiro and others, 'Psychological Expert Witness Testimony and Judicial Decision Making Trends' (2015) 42–43 *International Journal of Law and Psychiatry* 149; O. D. Jones and others, 'Neuroscientists in Court' (2013) 14 *Nature Reviews Neuroscience* 730; M. L. Henneberg, 'Admissibility Frameworks and Scientific Evidence: Controversies in Relation to Shaken Baby Syndrome / Abusive Head Trauma' (2015) 4 *British Journal of American Legal Studies* 555.

Policy recommendations and future directions for criminal justice systems are also provided, before summarising and concluding this chapter.

The Growing Relevance of Neuroscience in Criminal Justice

Stemming from the English Common Law system, the American criminal justice system was originally focused on flexible, case-by-case decision-making.[9] By the early 1900s, a shift in the understanding of criminality introduced rehabilitation as a main goal of sentencing—a movement often termed the 'rehabilitative ideal.'[10] At that time, systems of indeterminate sentencing placed increased discretionary powers on correctional staff, such as parole board members and correctional officers, to decide when defendants were reformed and could be released from prison.[11] As a result of a decision-making system that focused on carceral rehabilitation, enforced by corrections staff with limited education in neuroscientific and related scientific fields, widespread disparities in punishment emerged over the next 50 years, and rehabilitation began to be viewed as generally ineffective.[12] In response to unfavourable justice outcomes and a growing consensus that 'nothing works' in rehabilitating offenders, the Sentencing Reform Act of 1984 established the U.S. Sentencing Commission, marking a pivotal shift towards creating guidelines and formulas aimed at increasing consistency and predictability in criminal sentencing.[13] Although mandatory sentencing standards were short-lived, advisory guidelines continue to serve as a critical sentencing tool, and today, U.S. judges can consider a range of aggravating and mitigating factors to weigh individual circumstances in their sentencing decision-making.[14] Similar practices exist in other countries, such as in the U.K. and across Europe, where judicial guidelines provide a framework for sentencing that still allows judges to account for individual factors in each case.[15] These factors include neuroscience and psychiatric evidence, with their influence shaped by sentencing standards and guidelines, as well as judicial discretion, which is contingent on judges' individual evaluation and comprehension of neuroscientific information pertaining to defendants' behaviour.

9 J. R. Fuller, *Introduction to Criminal Justice: A Brief Edition* (2nd ed., Oxford University Press, New York, USA, 2019) <https://www.alibris.com/search/books/isbn/9780197504048> accessed 17 January 2023.

10 M. S. Phelps, 'Rehabilitation in the Punitive Era: The Gap between Rhetoric and Reality in U.S. Prison Programs' (2011) 45 *Law & Society Review* 33.

11 Fuller (n 9).

12 Phelps (n 10).

13 Schwarzer (n 2).

14 United States Sentencing Commission, *Federal Sentencing Guidelines 2018* (Chapter 5—Determining the Sentence) 406. <https://www.ussc.gov/guidelines/2018-guidelines-manual/2018-chapter-5> accessed 6 June 2025.

15 Sentencing Council, *Sentencing Council for England and Wales* <https://www.sentencing-council.org.uk/> accessed 27 September 2024.

Law Enforcement and Policing

Because the criminal justice system fundamentally deals with human behaviour that deviates from societal norms, insights from neuroscience and psychology influence every stage of the criminal-legal process. At the earliest stage of criminal justice involvement, policing practices are increasingly informed by neuroscience, particularly in their approaches to handling individuals in crisis. Crisis Intervention Training (CIT) programmes, for instance, have been designed to educate police officers about mental health issues, enabling them to respond more effectively to situations involving individuals experiencing mental health crises.[16] These programmes incorporate knowledge derived from neuroscience to help officers recognise symptoms of psychiatric disorders, understand altered brain states, and employ de-escalation techniques grounded in the science of stress and emotional regulation. This type of training helps law enforcement officers make distinctions based on an individual's neurological state, such as distinguishing between intentional aggression and behaviours resulting from a mental health crisis. By equipping law enforcement with the tools to assess and respond to individuals whose brain states may affect their behaviour, CIT programs also gradually change officers' perceptions of psychiatric disorders, providing a valuable education at the intersection of neuroscience, behaviour, and criminality.[17]

Adjudicating Criminal Responsibility

Neuroscience evidence is reshaping how courts assess a defendant's state of mind, particularly in cases where mental capacity and criminal responsibility are scrutinised. In criminal trials, a central question often revolves around a person's intent (*mens rea*), which is a requisite for a defendant to be held fully accountable for their actions. As neuroscience is gradually providing more precise tools to evaluate brain function and behaviour, it is also generating knowledge relevant to criminal intent by allowing for a deeper understanding of how various neurobiological factors—such as traumatic brain injury, psychiatric disorders, life experiences, or developmental conditions—can impair judgment, impulse control, and decision-making. However, introducing such evidence into legal proceedings raises questions requiring a nuanced understanding of neuroscience and legal standards, posing challenges for legal professionals who may lack a scientific background.

16 M. T. Compton and others, 'A Comprehensive Review of Extant Research on Crisis Intervention Team (CIT) Programs' (2008) 36 *Journal of the American Academy of Psychiatry and the Law Online* 47.

17 C. Ritter and others, 'Crisis Intervention Team (CIT) Training: Selection Effects and Long-Term Changes in Perceptions of Mental Illness and Community Preparedness' (2010) 10 *Journal of Police Crisis Negotiations* 133.

Despite educational barriers, defence and prosecution teams frequently rely on neuroscience to strengthen their arguments in court.[18] Research shows that it is far more common for defence attorneys to present neuroscience evidence and use it as a mitigating factor,[19] arguing that a client has a disorder that impairs their judgement or that their mental state at the time of the crime was impaired, thereby reducing their culpability or supporting an insanity plea. For example, in cases where a defendant suffers from conditions such as psychosis or Post-Traumatic Stress Disorder (PTSD), neuroscientific evidence might be used to show how these conditions disrupted normal cognitive processes, impaired the ability to form intent or control behaviour. On the other hand, the prosecution may use the same body of evidence to argue that while a defendant might have a neurological or psychiatric condition, they could still understand the wrongfulness of their actions. Additionally, neuroscience is often invoked to argue that a defendant is dangerous because of their inability to control or change their behaviour.[20] Thus, neuroscience evidence has been described as a double-edged sword, with both sides leveraging it to support their interpretation of criminal responsibility. Critically, however, research indicates that neuroscience evidence serves more consistently as a mitigating factor when assessed by decision-makers with a sufficient understanding of the underlying science or the availability of therapeutic interventions for neurological or psychiatric conditions.[21]

Informing Custodial and Community-Based Programs

To some extent, neuroscience also informs the development and implementation of custodial and community-based programmes, providing new insights that can help improve behavioural rehabilitation and address psychiatric problems. For example, neuroarchitecture research has shown that the traditional prison environment does not promote psychological health or well-being[22]

18 C. M. Berryessa, J. A. Chandler, 'The Role of the Defense Attorney in Relation to Biological Interventions as Rehabilitative Strategies' (2020) 59 *Journal of Offender Rehabilitation* 389; D. W. Denno, 'The Myth of the Double-Edged Sword: An Empirical Study of Neuroscience Evidence in Criminal Cases' (2015) 56 *Boston College Law Review* 493.

19 Denno (n 18).

20 M. L. Davidson and J. W. Rosky, 'Dangerousness or Diminished Capacity? Exploring the Association of Gender and Mental Illness with Violent Offense Sentence Length' (2015) 40 *American Journal of Criminal Justice* 353.

21 Denno (n 19); N. Gertner and others, 'Supporting Responsive Federal Drug Sentencing through Education in the Workshop on Science-Informed Decisionmaking' (2021) 34 *Federal Sentencing Reporter* 12; M. A. Thomaidou, C. M. Berryessa, 'A Jury of Scientists: Formal Education in Biobehavioral Sciences Reduces the Odds of Punitive Criminal Sentencing' (2022) 40 *Behavioral Sciences & the Law* 787.

22 R. Karthaus, L. Block, A. Hu, 'Redesigning Prison: The Architecture and Ethics of Rehabilitation' (2019) 24 *The Journal of Architecture* 193; J. Farbstein, M. Farling, 'Neuroscience and Correctional Facility Design Workshop: Understanding Cognitive Processes in

and is generally ill-suited to host individuals with psychiatric and neurological conditions or treatment programs for those experiencing psychiatric disorders,[23] and this insight may be motivating a shift away from traditional carceral sentences.[24] Moreover, specific neuroscience-informed evaluations can play a role in determining whether an offender may benefit from specialised therapeutic support rather than traditional incarceration,[25] and these insights have influenced the design of rehabilitation programs in corrections. For example, the Mendota Juvenile Treatment Center in Wisconsin uses a treatment model for juvenile offenders focused on emotional and social deficits, informed by research in psychology and neuroscience, and has achieved significant reductions in recidivism among participants.[26] Comparable reductions in reoffending have been achieved through the U.K.'s Thinking Skills Programme, a prison-based intervention based on cognitive neuroscience principles linking problematic cognitive patterns to behaviour.[27]

Neuroscientific knowledge also plays a role in shaping the design of community-based rehabilitation programmes, particularly for individuals with psychiatric disorders. Community sentences offer an environment better suited for rehabilitation for individuals whose offences may have been driven by impaired cognitive functioning.[28] Several international examples demonstrate the impact of neuroscientific evidence on policy decisions. For instance, based on neuroscience evidence that increasingly sheds light on the behavioural correlates of addiction, many U.S. jurisdictions now divert defendants with addictions to specialised courts that incorporate evidence-based treatment approaches that allow individuals to remain within their communities. This shift of focus from personal blame to treatment efficacy highlights how neuroscience knowledge can reshape a criminal justice system's response to offending. In the U.K., the Sentencing Council has implemented measures like the

---

Correctional Settings' (*Office of Justice Programs*, 2007) NCJ Number: 240143 <https://www.ojp.gov/ncjrs/virtual-library/abstracts/neuroscience-and-correctional-facility-design-workshop> accessed 30 September 2024.

23 S. Abramsky, *Ill-Equipped: U.S. Prisons and Offenders with Mental Illness* (Human Rights Watch, 2003); E. F. J. C. Van Ginneken and others, 'The Life in Custody Study: The Quality of Prison Life in Dutch Prison Regimes' (2018) 4 *Journal of Criminological Research, Policy and Practice* 253.

24 See M. Tonry, 'Community Punishments' in E. Luna (ed), *Reforming Criminal Justice* (vol. 4, The Academy for Justice, 2017) <https://law.asu.edu/sites/default/files/pdf/academy_for_justice/10_Criminal_Justice_Reform_Vol_4_Community-Punishments.pdf>

25 C. M. Altimus, 'Neuroscience Has the Power to Change the Criminal Justice System' (2017) 3 *eNeuro* ENEURO.0362; Baskin-Sommers and Fonteneau (n 4).

26 National Gang Center, *Mendota Juvenile Treatment Center (Intervention Program)*. <https://nationalgangcenter.ojp.gov/spt/Programs/3586> accessed 1 October 2024.

27 A. Brinn and others, *An Impact Evaluation of the Prison-Based Thinking Skills Programme (TSP) on Reoffending* (Ministry of Justice, 2023) <https://assets.publishing.service.gov.uk/media/64c10e4a90b54500143e8376/TSP_Reoffending_Report.pdf>.

28 Phelps (n 10).

Mental Health Treatment Requirements (MHTR), a program designed to provide targeted mental health support for offenders as part of a community sentence.[29] At the same time, in some European countries, rehabilitative programs that incorporate neuroscientific understanding of youth delinquency, substance abuse, or impulse control disorders are offered as alternatives to imprisonment for low-risk offenders.[30]

Admissibility Standards for Neuroscientific Information

Scholars and legal practitioners have debated the admissibility of neuroscientific evidence and expertise in courtrooms. Neuroscience has the potential to elucidate the mechanisms underlying cognitive and behavioural functioning, yet its application in the legal context presents numerous challenges related to scientific education, particularly in evaluating its credibility and relevance, a task currently assigned to professionals with limited scientific education. Neuro-law scholars have highlighted the positive impact and challenges presented using neuroscience evidence in the courtroom, noting that current criteria for evaluating its admissibility remain inadequate and need reform.[31]

In the U.S., the two major standards used to determine the admissibility of expert scientific testimony are the Daubert and Frye standards. The Daubert standard, established by *Daubert v. Merrell Dow Pharmaceuticals, Inc.* (1993),[32] requires scientific evidence be relevant, reliable, and based on valid methodology to be admitted in court. This standard provides judges with greater discretion in determining the admissibility of expert evidence. On the other hand, the Frye standard, originating from *Frye v. United States* (1923),[33] requires that the scientific principle must be generally accepted in the relevant field to be admissible. Other countries follow comparable standards based on case law involving neuroscience. In Australia, for example, the equivalent test

29 Sentencing Council, *Sentencing Offenders with Mental Disorders, Developmental Disorders, or Neurological Impairments* <https://www.sentencingcouncil.org.uk/overarching-guides/magistrates-court/item/sentencing-offenders-with-mental-disorders-developmental-disorders-or-neurological-impairments/>.

30 H. Linderborg, M. J. Tolvanen, P. Andersson, 'Probation in Europe: Finland' (*Confederation of European Probation*,2020) <https://www.cep-probation.org/wp-content/uploads/2021/07/Probation-in-Europe-chapter-Finland-2020.pdf>; S. Young, B. Greer, R. Church, 'Juvenile Delinquency, Welfare, Justice and Therapeutic Interventions: A Global Perspective' (2017) 41 *BJPsych Bulletin* 21; See, generally, D. L. MacKenzie, *What Works in Corrections: Reducing the Criminal Activities of Offenders and Deliquents* (Cambridge University Press, 2006) <https://www.cambridge.org/core/books/what-works-in-corrections/D10E55C780D3BBF78FB0EDA19D6D1AD3> accessed 27 September 2024.

31 E. Baron, J. Sullivan, 'Judging Mechanistic Neuroscience: A Preliminary Conceptual-Analytic Framework for Evaluating Scientific Evidence in the Courtroom' (2018) 24 *Psychology, Crime & Law* 334.

32 *Daubert v. Merrell Dow Pharmaceuticals, Inc, 509* [1993] US Supreme Court U.S. 579.

33 *Frye v. United States*, 293 F 1013 (DC Cir).

is the Bonython test, which examines the reliability and acceptance of the scientific expertise or evidence presented.[34]

Influential Case Law Involving Neuroscience

Neuroscientific evidence has played a critical role in several landmark U.S. cases, shaping judicial attitudes towards issues such as the death penalty and sentencing for juveniles. In *Roper v. Simmons* (2005),[35] the U.S. Supreme Court relied on developmental neuroscience to rule that sentencing juveniles to death was unconstitutional. The Court recognised that adolescent brains are not fully developed, which impairs their decision-making abilities and behavioural control, making the death penalty a disproportionate and unjust punishment for juveniles. This decision integrated knowledge on the neurological limitations of adolescent brain development into the legal doctrine, providing a valuable lesson for criminal justice actors on the neuroscientific basis of diminished criminal responsibility for juveniles. Another valuable educational moment came in 2012, when the *Miller v. Alabama* case[36] ruled against mandatory life without parole for juveniles, accepting that the brains of juveniles are inherently different from those of adults in terms of their ability to consider the consequences of their actions. This ruling further influenced courts across the U.S. to consider the unique neurological characteristics of adolescents, which may encourage criminal justice decision-makers to apply similar neuroscientific insights to other individuals.

Neuroscience and mental health evidence have also influenced case law related to psychiatric defences and sentencing mitigation. In *Porter v. McCollum* (2009),[37] the U.S. Supreme Court ruled that George Porter Jr. received ineffective assistance of counsel when his attorney failed to present crucial mitigating evidence of his mental health history during the sentencing phase. Porter, a Korean War veteran, had untreated PTSD, and the Court emphasised that evidence of his mental health condition could have influenced the outcome of his sentencing, highlighting the importance of considering such evidence when determining punishment. This decision paved the way for greater acceptance of neuroscientific evidence in courts and underscores the need to educate legal professionals on how neuroscience can inform criminal responsibility assessments and appropriate sentencing.

Mitigating neuroscience evidence has, in some cases, also contributed to courts opting for community-based rather than custodial sentences. In a notable example from the U.K. known as the case of Caroline, the defendant's history of trauma, untreated mental health issues, and addiction contributed

34 *R v. Bonython* 38 SASR [1984] Supreme Court of South Australia 45 to 47.

35 *Roper v. Simmons* (n 5).

36 *Miller v. Alabama* (n 6).

37 *Porter v. McCollum*, 558 US 30 [2009] United States Supreme Court 08-10537.

to her offending behaviour. After serving six months in custody, Caroline was placed in a community-based structured mental health treatment program, based on the assessment that addressing her underlying mental health needs through a community sentence would more effectively prevent recidivism. Relatedly, the 2010 case of *U.S. v. Bannister*[38] involved several gang-related cases in which scientific evidence was presented to show how defendants' neurological development and exposure to trauma had impaired their decision-making abilities. Based on this evidence, the judge opted for reduced sentences and community-based alternatives to incarceration for some defendants, emphasising the importance of addressing the root causes of criminal behaviour rather than relying solely on punitive measures. These landmark cases set important precedents for neuroscientific understandings of behaviour to be considered in adjudicating legal responsibility, thereby also increasingly requiring all actors involved in the criminal justice process to develop an understanding of neuroscience information.

Current Standards in Neuroscience Education

Integrating legal practices and criminal justice standards with a holistic understanding of behaviour, including an appreciation of brain development and neuroscientific factors influencing criminal behaviour and rehabilitation, can lead to positive outcomes for defendants and communities. However, achieving an adequate level of scientific education among criminal justice actors is essential for integrating neuroscience effectively and avoiding the shortcomings experienced during the 'rehabilitative ideal' era. By addressing these educational gaps using an interdisciplinary approach, the legal system can better integrate scientific insights into its processes, ultimately benefiting both individuals and society.

Education for Criminal Justice Professionals

Neuroscience and psychology education for criminal justice professionals, including law enforcement and correctional officers, prosecutors and defence attorneys, as well as juries and judges, is crucial for effectively integrating neuroscience into the legal system. In police academies, curricula often cover various aspects of psychology, including crisis intervention strategies that incorporate principles of mental health and neurobehavioral responses. In the United States, organisations like the National Center for Police Training offer specialised courses that integrate psychological principles into law enforcement training. Additionally, programs focusing on mental health, crisis intervention, and the psychology of crime have gained traction over the past decade. CIT programs are a major example of this shift towards de-escalation

38 *US v. Bannister*, 786 F Supp 2d 617 United States District Court, ED New York 10-CR-0053.

of mental health crises, specifically designed to equip law enforcement with knowledge about mental health issues, helping officers recognise and appropriately respond to situations involving individuals whose acute mental states may influence their responses[39] and behaviour.[40] However, these programs only provide the most basic training and often focus on dealing with mental health problems among officers themselves.[41]

In Europe, law enforcement officer training often includes psychological components. For example, the European Police College (CEPOL) organises courses that emphasise the importance of scientific research in law enforcement,[42] and forensic psychology is part of standard training programs developed by the agency.[43] Psychological principles relevant to forensics are included in police training across various countries, but they often constitute a minor component of the curriculum. Furthermore, educational programs lack an in-depth exploration of broader scientific concepts and neuroscientific foundations that intersect with notions of individual agency, criminal responsibility, and justice. One exception is Iceland, which serves as an exemplary case of integrated police education that combines practical training with scientific education, requiring officers to obtain a police science diploma—a opportunity that remains optional in the United States.[44]

Attorneys are responsible for presenting the most convincing case for their clients or the prosecution, which requires a solid understanding of the scientific evidence related to a defendant's conduct. Despite this crucial responsibility, law schools have only begun to incorporate courses on psychology or neuroscience, and these remain limited in scope. For example, New York University's Law School only offers one elective seminar on the topic of psychological dimensions in criminal law and includes no courses in the domains of neuroscience, human behaviour, or scientific methodology.[45] At the same time, the American Bar Association has recognised the need for continuing legal education (CLE) related to emerging scientific developments, including

39 Ritter and others (n 17).

40 Mental Health First Aid, *Mental Health First Aid for Corrections Professionals.* <https://www.mentalhealthfirstaid.org/population-focused-modules/adults/corrections/> accessed 1 October 2024.

41 Ibid.

42 European Union Agency for Law Enforcement Training, 'CEPOL Higher Education and Research' (*CEPOL—European Union Agency for Law Enforcement Training*, 2024) <https://www.cepol.europa.eu/thematic-areas/higher-education-and-research> accessed 1 October 2024.

43 See, generally, M. Pagon (ed), *Policing in Central and Eastern Europe: Comparing Firsthand Knowledge with Experience from the West* (College of Police and Security Studies, Ljubljana, Slovenia, 1996).

44 World Population Review, *Police Training Requirements by Country* <https://worldpopulationreview.com/country-rankings/police-training-requirements-by-country>.

45 NYU Law, *Course Descriptions, NYU School of Law* <https://its.law.nyu.edu/courses/index.cfm#searchResults2> accessed 15 October 2024.

neuroscience.[46] However, while participation in these CLE programs is often mandatory the specific content can vary significantly from one jurisdiction to another, and many attorneys may not prioritise neuroscience or other scientific topics in their professional development. For example, California, a state with strict CLE requirements, mandates training in specific domains, including competency issues and implicit bias, but not in neuroscience, psychology, or other related sciences.[47] This inconsistency in education, and the optional nature of neuroscience and psychology education, can lead to a lack of understanding of how neuroscientific evidence relates to legal standards and the defence or prosecution of defendants.

Continuous professional education also applies to the judiciary, with specialised CLE curricula mainly designed to keep judges informed of evolving legal standards and practices.[48] Similarly to attorneys, judges are mostly free to select the topics of the seminars and training they attend.[49] Except for mandatory specialised science education for those presiding over speciality courts, most judges seem to opt for subjects they find more immediately relevant, potentially sidelining crucial neuroscience education.[50] Judges presiding over speciality and treatment courts, such as mental health or addiction courts, undergo specific training to understand substance abuse, psychiatric disorders, or evidence-based intervention strategies. The Office of Justice Programs offers training and technical assistance for treatment courts, incorporating a neuroscience-informed approach and ensuring that judges know the current science and best practices for addressing psychiatric and psychological issues.[51] Similar training standards are applied for judges presiding over cases in Treatment Courts in other countries worldwide, such as Ireland,[52] Chile,[53]

46 American Bar Association, *Mandatory CLE* <https://www.americanbar.org/events-cle/mcle/> accessed 15 October 2024.

47 American Bar Association, *California CLE Requirements and Courses* <https://www.americanbar.org/events-cle/mcle/jurisdiction/california/> accessed 15 October 2024.

48 American Bar Association, *Judicial Division—Events and CLE* <https://www.americanbar.org/groups/judicial/events_cle/> accessed 15 October 2024.

49 M. A. Thomaidou, C. Berryessa, 'A Mixed-Methods Analysis of the Influence of Bio-Behavioral Scientific Evidence on U.S. Judges' Reasoning and Sentencing Decision-Making' (2025) 102 *International Journal of Law and Psychiatry* [in press]; 'Judicial Division—Events and CLE'.

50 Thomaidou and Berryessa (n 49).

51 Office of Justice Programs, *Treatment Courts: Training & Technical Assistance* <https://www.ojp.gov/feature/treatment-courts/training-technical-assistance> accessed 2 October 2024.

52 The Court Services of Ireland, *The Drug Treatment Court* <https://www.courts.ie/drug-treatment-court> accessed 5 October 2024.

53 Ministry of the Interior and Public Security, 'Tribunales de Tratamiento de Drogas' (*Ministry of the Interior and Public Security; Chilean The National Service for the Prevention and Rehabilitation of Drug and Alcohol Consumption (SENDA)*, 2022) <https://www.senda.gob.cl/tratamiento/programas/tribunales-de-tratamiento-de-drogas/> accessed 15 October 2024.

and Jamaica.[54] What non-specialised criminal courts tend to rely on in place of their own in-depth understanding of neuroscience, psychology, or psychiatry is the testimony of experts in these domains.

Expert Testimony

Generally, experts who provide testimony on neuroscientific and psychological evidence are required to possess advanced degrees in their respective fields along with relevant practical experience. Professional boards, such as state medical boards, the American Board of Professional Psychology, and the American Board of Clinical Neuropsychology, are tasked with the certification of professionals; however, there is no standard determining the educational requirements for expert witnesses.[55] In the U.S., the level of training and suitability of these experts is often assessed during trial, where their qualifications may be scrutinised to determine the credibility of their testimony. Some European countries have more consistent and stricter standards for scientific experts, their training, boundaries of expertise, and continuous education.[56] Expert witness testimony, however, is a less common feature of criminal trials, as compared to the work of clinical and forensic psychologists who work in pretrial services or compile presentencing reports and conduct psychological assessments of defendants. Training standards for individuals employed in these positions are often low, typically requiring only an undergraduate degree in one of several relevant disciplines.[57]

Ultimately, judges, juries, and attorneys are tasked with understanding and assessing expert testimonies and psychological reports relating to a defendant's background and behaviour. As such, adequate scientific comprehension among criminal justice actors is crucial. During trials, judges and juries must follow, understand, and critically evaluate the relevance and reliability of expert testimony, especially in cases involving conflicting assessments on behalf of the prosecution and defence. One criminal justice institution that could serve as an archetype for bridging this gap between science and law is the International Criminal Court (ICC), which is tasked with investigating and trying crimes of concern to the global international community. The ICC has addressed the issue of evaluating scientific evidence and testimonies by employing specialised, highly experienced experts who serve as non-partisan

54 Justice Speakers International, 'Treatment Courts: Jamaica' (*Justice Speakers International*, 2017) <https://www.justicespeakersinternational.com/drug-treatment-courts-around-world/jamaica/> accessed 2 October 2024.

55 Shapiro and others (n 8).

56 N. R. G. Deskundigen, *The Netherlands Register of Court Experts*. <https://english.nrgd.nl/find-an-expert/the-experts> accessed 2 October 2024.

57 United States Courts, *U.S. Probation & Pretrial Services Careers* <https://www.uscourts.gov/careers/who-works-judiciary/us-probation-pretrial-services-careers> accessed 2 October 2024.

court consultants.[58] One example of this approach being implemented was in the prosecution of Dominic Ongwen, where the ICC heard expert testimony about contested and complex matters surrounding psychological trauma and related impacts on the brain relevant to Ongwen's abduction and abuse as a child soldier, mitigating his responsibility for later war crimes.[59] This integration of expert knowledge within legal proceedings, exemplified by the ICC's approach, underscores the necessity of interdisciplinary education for criminal justice actors to ensure just outcomes in cases involving complex scientific evidence.

Educational Gaps, Challenges, and Opportunities

Despite developments in using neuroscience evidence, most criminal justice systems globally rely on a minimum amount of neuroscience education and scientific training to interpret neuroscience evidence and apply relevant standards. Neuroscience and psychology are currently not a compulsory part of undergraduate law programs, juris doctorates, or continuous professional development programs for legal practitioners. However, a recent shift towards specialised courts that deal with cases involving neuroscience evidence may serve as a model for how neuroscience education can be integrated into criminal justice.

Education and Resource Gaps

There are currently no requirements for legal professionals to study neuroscience, psychology, or the principles of scientific research methods, creating a gap in the education needed to properly interpret and evaluate neuroscience information presented in criminal cases. Legal professionals, especially those who handle cases involving psychiatric or neurological disorders, should have a foundational understanding of how the brain functions and can give rise to cognition, decision-making, and behaviour. Moreover, a solid grasp of scientific epistemology and methodology, including understanding how scientific knowledge is created and validated, as well as concepts such as correlation versus causation, statistical significance, and standards for the reliability and generalizability of scientific evidence, is crucial. Such knowledge allows professionals to critically assess expert testimonies, differentiate between reliable and unreliable research findings, and ultimately make decisions that rely more on solid evidence rather than intuition or false generalisations.

58 International Criminal Court, *International Criminal Court: Experts* <https://www.icc-cpi.int/get-involved/experts> accessed 2 October 2024.

59 A. Branch, 'Dominic Ongwen on Trial: The ICC's African Dilemmas' (2017) 11 *International Journal of Transitional Justice* 30.

The continuing education provided to legal professionals is equally lacking. In many countries, including the United States,[60] judges are allowed to select the topics of their continuing education, often opting out of neuroscience or science-related subjects.[61] This autonomy in choosing topics leaves critical gaps in the neuroscientific understanding of human behaviour, as no mandates require a focus on scientific literacy. To bridge these gaps, continuing professional education curricula for judges and attorneys should be enriched to cover behavioural neuroscience and cognitive psychology, as well as the key principles of research methods and evidence interpretation. At least some of this neuroscience content ought to be part of a standard or mandatory basic and/or continuing education for legal professionals. Such an interdisciplinary education would better equip judges to understand critical issues like the effects of psychiatric disorders, addiction, and other brain conditions on behaviour, agency, and intent, thus enhancing their ability to understand the relevance of neuroscience evidence and to apply appropriate standards of justice.

Speciality courts, such as Drug Treatment Courts and Mental Health Courts, have seen significant investment in many countries around the world,[62] equipping staff and legal processes with a more in-depth understanding of the brain processes and limitations that affect defendants with psychiatric disorders, as well as knowledge regarding effective, targeted interventions. These specialised courts, however, have strict eligibility criteria and do not typically deal with cases involving serious offences or individuals considered high-risk in terms of dangerousness or reoffending.[63] Speciality courts are tailored to severe psychiatric disorders, cognitive impairments, or adverse childhood experiences and complex trauma histories, which could address this need more directly. Such courts would allow judges with specialised training in neuroscience and psychology to apply their expertise in cases that require a deeper understanding of brain function and behavioural control.[64]

60 American Bar Association, *Judicial Division—Events and CLE* <https://www.americanbar.org/groups/judicial/events_cle/> accessed 1 October 2024.

61 Thomaidou and Berryessa (n 49).

62 'Treatment Courts: Jamaica' (n 54); Ministry of the Interior and Public Security, *Tribunales de Tratamiento de Drogas* <https://www.senda.gob.cl/tratamiento/programas/tribunales-de-tratamiento-de-drogas/> accessed 15 October 2024; U.S Department Office of Justice Programs, *Treatment Courts: Training & Technical Assistance* <https://www.ojp.gov/feature/treatment-courts/training-technical-assistance> accessed 2 October 2024; The Court Service of Ireland, *The Drug Treatment Court* <https://www.courts.ie/drug-treatment-court> accessed 5 October 2024; E. M. Lowder, C. B. Rade, S. L. Desmarais, 'Effectiveness of Mental Health Courts in Reducing Recidivism: A Meta-Analysis' (2018) 69 *Psychiatric Services* 15.

63 T. Kaplan, M. Miller, E. Wood, 'Looking Backward, Looking Forward: How the Evolution of Specialty Courts Can Inform the Courts of Tomorrow' (2018) 54 *Court Review: The Journal of the American Judges Association* 14.

64 M. L. Perlin, H. Cucolo, D. A. Dorfman, '"I Saw Guns and Sharp Swords in the Hands of Young Children": Why Mental Health Courts for Juveniles with Autism Spectrum Disorder and Fetal Alcohol Spectrum/Disorder Are Needed' (2023) *SSRN Electronic Journal* 229–263 <https://www.ssrn.com/abstract=4515470> accessed 9 July 2024; Kaplan, Miller and Wood (n 63).

The reliance on expert testimony further highlights the inadequacies of current educational standards for experts and legal professionals. Although experts possess advanced degrees in the neurosciences or psychiatry, they are not required to obtain a legal education that would familiarise them with the standards for guilt determination, sentencing mitigation, and admissibility criteria. This gap in legal literacy potentially limits their ability to effectively communicate their findings within a legal context. Therefore, addressing these gaps in education and communication using an interdisciplinary approach is essential.

Policy Recommendations

In addressing the gaps in neuroscience education in the criminal justice system, a key focus should be fostering interdisciplinary approaches that integrate neuroscience and legal knowledge at every stage. Policy should focus on reforming legal education and ongoing professional development to incorporate scientific disciplines more effectively. Interdisciplinary learning would not only enhance decision-making but also provide the necessary foundation for understanding complex evidence presented in court, benefiting both the legal process and society.

A foundational recommendation is to reform legal education to include neuroscience and scientific methodology courses. This is crucial for equipping future legal professionals with a scientific understanding of behaviour and cognition. Law schools should embed neuroscience education into their curricula, with mandatory courses teaching the core principles of brain function, cognition, and behavioural outcomes. By doing so, law students can develop the skills to critically evaluate expert testimonies, understand the implications of neuroscience evidence, and make informed decisions based on reliable data rather than intuition or popular understandings of science.[65]

Judicial training should also be restructured to mandate ongoing professional education in neuroscience. As judges often have discretion in choosing the topics they study for continuing education, there is a risk of avoiding areas perceived as complex or unrelated, especially those in scientific fields. Implementing a requirement for all judges to undertake education in neuroscience would lead to a better understanding of human behaviour and ultimately to making more informed judicial decisions.

Moreover, all professionals involved in the criminal justice process should possess a fundamental understanding of scientific epistemology, which encompasses the principles and methods used to assess and evaluate scientific research. Criminal justice professionals ought to grasp concepts such as statistical significance, correlation versus causation, and the standards for the reliability, validity, and generalisability of scientific evidence. Such an educational

65 Thomaidou and Berryessa (n 21).

foundation in epistemology would enhance professionals' ability to critically evaluate scientific evidence and forensic or clinical assessment tools, while also cultivating essential critical thinking skills and awareness of the generalisations and biases that may arise from misinterpreting scientific data.

Building on the recommendation to enhance education for criminal justice professionals, it is essential for policymakers to explore how new educational requirements can be integrated into their existing workload. Although these professionals are receptive to neuroscience education,[66] any policy shift should include solutions that prevent additional burdens on their workload, such as offering online training modules or reexamining prosecutorial and defence workloads as well as the ratio of judges to cases heard. Ultimately, equipping criminal justice professionals with a solid grounding in scientific epistemology is crucial for informed decision-making and ensuring justice is served based on sound, evidence-based practices.

Finally, a crucial aspect of policy reform is addressing resistance to integrating neuroscience into the criminal justice system. Misconceptions about the applicability of neuroscience, such as overestimating its potential influence on legal norms or misunderstanding its relevance to issues of legal and moral responsibility,[67] contribute to the reluctance to adopt these reforms. Therefore, educational initiatives should cover the fundamentals of neuroscience and address these misconceptions, providing legal professionals with an accurate understanding of what neuroscience can—and cannot–tell us about human behaviour. This approach would help mitigate scepticism and promote a more balanced perspective on how scientific evidence should inform legal outcomes.

Conclusion

Ultimately, the criminal justice system is tasked with enforcing ethical standards intrinsically linked to evolving understanding of human nature and behaviour.[68] Establishing interdisciplinary educational programs across the system—from law schools to the Supreme Court—would ensure key actors are better prepared to understand, interpret, and apply scientific evidence in their work. Neuroscience education lies at the heart of meaningful reform in the criminal justice system. Understanding human behaviour through the lens of neuroscience will support legal professionals in making decisions that are fair and rooted in scientific knowledge. By promoting cross-disciplinary education, we can shape justice systems that are equipped to undertake the great responsibility of enforcing societies' ethical principles and the rule of law.

66 Thomaidou and Berryessa (n 49).

67 A. Bigenwald, V. Chambon, 'Criminal Responsibility and Neuroscience: No Revolution Yet' (2019) 10 *Frontiers in Psychology* 1–19 <https://www.frontiersin org/articles/10.3389/fpsyg.2019.01406/full> accessed 27 May 2021.

68 R. M. Sapolsky, 'Neuroscience and the Law' (2021) 15 *University of St. Thomas Journal of Law and Public Policy (Minnesota)* 138.

Bibliography

Abrahams, B. S., D. H. Geschwind, 'Connecting Genes to Brain in the Autism Spectrum Disorders' (2010) 67 *Archives of Neurology* 395–399.

Abramsky, S., 'Ill-Equipped: U.S. Prisons and Offenders with Mental Illness' (*Human Rights Watch*, 2003).

Acquaviva, G. L., 'Mental Health Courts: No Longer Experimental' (2006) 36 *Seton Hall Law Review* 971–1013.

Adams, K., J. Ferrandino, 'Managing Mentally Ill Inmates in Prisons' (2008) 35 *Criminal Justice and Behavior* 913–927.

Aharoni, E. et al., 'Neuroprediction of Future Rearrest' (2013) 110(15) *Proceedings of the National Academy of Sciences of the United States of America* 6223–6228.

Aharoni, E. et al., 'Predictive Accuracy in the Neuroprediction of Rearrest' (2014) 9(4) *Social Neuroscience* 332–336.

Alexander, A. L. et al., *Crime and Culpability: A Theory of Criminal Law* (Cambridge University Press, New York, 2009).

Alexander, A. L. et al., 'Diffusion Tensor Imaging of the Corpus Callosum in Autism' (2007) 34 *Neuroimage* 61–73.

Alimardani, A., 'An Empirical Study of the Use of Neuroscience in Sentencing in New South Wales, Australia' (2023) 14(1228354) *Frontiers in Psychology* 1–19.

Allely, C. S., *Autism Spectrum Disorder in the Criminal Justice System: A Guide to Understanding Suspects, Defendants and Offenders with Autism* (Routledge, New York, 2022).

Allely, C. S., P. Cooper, 'Jurors' and Judges' Evaluation of Defendants with Autism and the Impact on Sentencing: A Systematic Preferred Reporting Items for Systematic Reviews and Meta-Analyses (PRISMA) Review of Autism Spectrum Disorder in the Courtroom' (2017) 25(1) *Journal of Law and Medicine* 105–123.

Altimus, C. M., 'Neuroscience Has the Power to Change the Criminal Justice System' (2017) 3 *eNeuro* ENEURO362, 369.

Altman, M. C., *The Palgrave Handbook on the Philosophy of Punishment* (Palgrave Macmillan, 2023).

Amended Brief of Amici Curiae Professors and Practitioners of Psychiatry, Psychology, and Medicine in Support of Plaintiffs-Appellants No. 165A21 (10th Cir. 2021) (filed on 2 July 2021) <https://www.acluofnorthcarolina.org/sites/default/files/field_documents/sccoa.pdf>

American Academy of Emergency Medicine, 'AAEM Excited Delirium Statement' <https://apps.aaem.org/UserFiles/RevisedAAEMExcitedDelirium9.21.22.pdf> accessed July 2025.

American Bar Association, 'California CLE Requirements and Courses' (*American Bar Association*, 2023) <https://www.americanbar.org/events-cle/mcle/jurisdiction/california/> accessed 1 October 2024.

American Bar Association, 'Judicial Division—Events and CLE' (*American Bar Association*, 2024) <https://www.americanbar.org/groups/judicial/events_cle/> accessed 1 October 2024.

American Bar Association, 'Mandatory CLE' (*American Bar Association*, 2024) <https://www.americanbar.org/events-cle/mcle/>

American Medical Association, 'New AMA Policy Opposes "Excited Delirium" Diagnosis' (*American Medical Association*, 14 June 2021) <https://www.ama-assn.org/press-center/press-releases/new-ama-policy-opposes-excited-delirium-diagnosis> accessed 2 December 2024.

American Psychiatric Association, *Diagnostic and Statistical Manual of Mental Disorders* (5th-TR ed, American Psychiatric Publishing, 2022).

American Psychiatric Association, *Diagnostic and Statistical Manual of Mental Disorders (DSM-5)* (American Psychiatric Publishing, 2013).

Anderson, J., K. Kiehl, 'Psychopathy: Developmental Perspectives and Their Implications for Treatment' (2014) 32(1) *Restorative Neurology Neuroscience* 103–117.

Anderson, N. B., C.A. Armstead, 'Toward Understanding the Association of Socioeconomic Status and Health: A New Challenge for the Biopsychosocial Approach' (1995) 57 *Biopsychosocial Science and Medicine* 213–225.

Anderson, N. E., K. A. Kiehl, 'Psychopathy: Developmental Perspectives and Implications for Treatment' (2014) 32 (1) *Restorative Neurology Neuroscience* 103–107.

Andrews, D. A., J. Bonta, *The Psychology of Criminal Conduct* (5th ed, Taylor & Francis, New Providence, 2010).

Anthony, T., 'FactCheck: Are First Australians the Most Imprisoned People on Earth?' (*The Conversation,* 6 June 2017) <https://theconversation.com/factcheck-are-first-australians-the-most-imprisoned-people-on-earth-78528>

Aono, D., G. Yaffe, H. Kober, 'Neuroscientific Evidence in the Courtroom: A Review' (2019) 4(40) *Cognitive Research* 40–60.

Archer, M. and others, 'Community Reinforcement and Family Training and Rates of Treatment Entry: A Systematic Review' (2020) 115 *Addiction* 1024–1037.

Ardino, V., 'Offending Behaviour: The Role of Trauma and PTSD' (2012) 3 *European Journal of Psychotraumatology* 1–4.

Arkles, G., 'Safety and Solidarity across Gender Lines: Rethinking Segregation of Transgender People in Detention' (2009) 18 *Temple Political & Civil Rights Law Review* 515–560.

Armour, C., 'Mental Health in Prison: A Trauma Perspective on Importation and Deprivation' (2012) 5 *International Journal of Criminology and Sociological Theory* 886–894.

Armstrong, T., *Neurodiversity: Discovering the Extraordinary Gifts of Autism, ADHD, Dyslexia, and Other Brain Differences* (Da Capo Lifelong, 2010).

Ashworth, A., R. Kelly, *Sentencing and Criminal Justice* (7th ed., Hart Publishing, Oxford, 2021).

Associated Press News, 'Family Rallies for Man Killed in 2017 Omaha Police Struggle' (*Associated Press News*, 6 June 2021) <https://apnews.com/article/ne-state-wire-omaha-28d4820fecb111234d641f609db031f3> accessed 29 November 2024.

Australian Institute of Health and Welfare, *Health of People in Prison* (AIHW, Canberra, 2024).

'Autism and the Criminal Justice System: Policy Opportunities and Challenges' (*International Society of Autism Research*, 2022) <https://cdn.ymaws.com/www.autism-insar.org/resource/resmgr/docs/2022_CJ_INSAR_Policy_Brief.pdf>

Bagaric, M., N. Fischer, G. Wolf, 'Bringing Sentencing into the 21st Century: Closing the Gap between Practice and Knowledge by Introducing Expertise into Sentencing Law' (2017) 45 *Hofstra Law Review* 785–850.

Bagaric, M., G. Wolf, P. Isham, 'Trauma and Sentencing: The Case for Mitigating Penalty for Childhood Physical and Sexual Abuse' (2019) 30 *Stanford Law and Policy Review* 1–59.

Baggio, S. and others, 'Prevalence of Attention Deficit Hyperactivity Disorder in Detention Settings: A Systematic Review and Meta-Analysis' (2018) 9 *Frontiers in Psychiatry* 1–10.

Baker, D. L., *The Politics of Neurodiversity: Why Public Policy Matters* (Lynne Rienner Publishers, 2011).

Baldwin, S. et al., 'Employment Activities and Experiences of Adults with High-Functioning Autism and Asperger's Disorder' (2014) 44 *Journal of Autism and Developmental Disorders* 2440–2449.

Baranyi, G., M. Cassidy, S. Fazel, S. Priebe, A. P. Mundt, 'Prevalence of Posttraumatic Stress Disorder in Prisoners' (2018) 40 *Epidemiologic Reviews* 134–145.

Bark, N., 'Prisoner Mental Health in the USA' (2014) 11 *International Psychiatry* 53–55.

Baron, E., J. Sullivan, 'Judging Mechanistic Neuroscience: A Preliminary Conceptual-Analytic Framework for Evaluating Scientific Evidence in the Courtroom' (2018) 24 *Psychology* 334–352.

Baron-Cohen, S., 'The Concept of Neurodiversity Is Dividing the Autism Community' (2019) 30(4) *Scientific American* 30–32.

Baron-Cohen, S. et al., 'Recognition of Faux Pas by Normally Developing Children and Children with Asperger Syndrome or High-Functioning Autism' (1999) 29 *Journal of Autism and Developmental Disorders* 407–418.

Baroness Bennett of Manor Castle, 'After Clause 138, Police, Crime, Sentencing and Courts Act 2022' (Report Stage, Amendment) at 90 <https://bills.parliament.uk/bills/2839/stages/15878/amendments/89993> accessed February 2025.

Barrett, J., S. L. Taylor, A. M. Kopak, N. G. Hoffmann, 'PTSD, Panic Disorder and Alcohol Use Disorder as a Triple Threat for Violence among Male Jail Detainees' (2021) 11 *Journal of Criminal Psychology* 21–29.

Baskin-Sommers, A. R., K. Fonteneau, 'Correctional Change through Neuroscience' (2016) 85 *Fordham Law Review* 423–453.

Bay Area Rapid Transit, '"Excited Delirium" Removed from BART Police Department Policy Manual and Will No Longer Be Used in Written Reports' (*Bay Area Rapid Transit*, 18 August 2022) <https://www.bart.gov/news/articles/2022/news20220818> accessed 2 December 2024.

Beadle-Brown, J. et al., 'Living in Fear: Better Outcomes for People with Learning Disabilities and Autism' (Project Report, Tizard Centre, Canterbury, 2014).

Bearak, B., 'Eerie Deaths of 17 Women Baffle Miami' (*Los Angeles Times*, 14 May 1989) <https://www.latimes.com/archives/la-xpm-1989-05-14-mn-413-story.html> accessed 2 December 2024.

Benfer, I. and others, 'The Impact of Drug Policy Liberalisation on Willingness to Seek Help for Problem Drug Use: A Comparison of 20 Countries' (2018) 56 *International Journal of Drug Policy* 162–175.

Bennion, E., 'Banning the Bing: Why Extreme Solitary Confinement Is Cruel and Far Too Usual Punishment' (2015) 90 *Indiana Law Journal* 742–789.

Berger, M., Z. Sarnyai, '"More Than Skin Deep": Stress Neurobiology and Mental Health Consequences of Racial Discrimination' (2015) 18 *Stress* 1–10.

Berryessa, C. M., 'Brief Report: Judicial Attitudes Regarding the Sentencing of Offenders with High Functioning Autism' (2016) 46 *Journal of Autism and Developmental Disorders* 2770–2773.

Berryessa, C. M., 'Defendants with Autism Spectrum Disorder in Criminal Court: A Judges' Toolkit' (2021) 13 *Drexel Law Review* 841–868.

Berryessa, C. M., 'Educator of the Court: The Role of the Expert Witness in Cases Involving Autism Spectrum Disorder' (2017) 23(6) *Psychology, Crime & Law* 575–600.

Berryessa, C. M., 'Impact of Psychiatric Information on Potential Jurors in Evaluating High-Functioning Autism Spectrum Disorder (hfASD)' (2015) 8 *Journal of Mental Health Research in Intellectual Disabilities* 140–167.

Berryessa, C. M., 'Judicial Perceptions of Media Portrayals of Offenders with High Functioning Autistic Spectrum Disorders' (2014) 3 *International Journal of Criminology and Sociology* 46–60.

Berryessa, C. M., 'Judiciary Views on Criminal Behaviour and Intention of Offenders with High-Functioning Autism' (2014) 5 *Journal of Intellectual Disabilities and Offending Behaviour* 97–106.

Berryessa, C. M., J. A. Chandler, 'The Role of the Defense Attorney in Relation to Biological Interventions as Rehabilitative Strategies' (2020) 59 *Journal of Offender Rehabilitation* 389–415.

Bidesi, N. and others, 'The Role of Neuroimaging in Parkinson's Disease' (2021) 159 *Journal of Neurochemistry* 660–689.

Bigenwald, A., V. Chambon, 'Criminal Responsibility and Neuroscience: No Revolution Yet' (2019) 10 *Frontiers in Psychology* 1406, 1–19.

Blagg, H., T. Tulich, V. Hovane, D. Raye, T. Worrigal, S. May, *Understanding the Role of Law and Culture in Aboriginal and/or Torres Strait Islander Communities in Responding to and Preventing Family Violence* (ANROWS, Melbourne, 2020).

Blakemore, S. J., T. Robbins 'Decision-Making in the Adolescent Brain' (2012) 15(9) *Nature Neuroscience* 1184–1191.

Blanken, P. and others, 'Heroin-Assisted Treatment in the Netherlands: History, Findings, and International Context' (2010) 20 *European Neuropsychopharmacology* S105–S158.

Blitz, M. J., J. C. Bublitz (eds), *The Law and Ethics of Freedom of Thought* (vol. 1, Palgrave Studies in Law, Neuroscience, and Human Behavior, Palgrave McMillan, 2021).

Blitz, M. J., J. C. Bublitz (eds), *The Law and Ethics of Freedom of Thought*, (vol. 2, Cognitive Liberty and Privacy, Palgrave McMillan, 2025).

Blok, G., 'Pampering "Needle Freaks" or Caring for Chronic Addicts? Early Debates on Harm Reduction in Amsterdam, 1972–82' (2008) 22 *The Social History of Alcohol and Drugs* 243–261.

Boddaert, N., M. Zilbovicius, 'Functional Neuroimaging and Childhood Autism' (2002) 32 *Pediatric Radiology* 1–7.

Bogdashina, O., *Sensory Perceptual Issues in Autism and Asperger Syndrome: Different Sensory Experiences—Different Perceptual Worlds* (Jessica Kingsley Publishers, 2016).

Boire, R. G., 'On Cognitive Liberty, Part I' (2000) *Journal of Cognitive Liberties* 7–13.

Bonfine, N. et al., 'Meeting the Needs of Justice-Involved People with Serious Mental Illness within Community Behavioral Health Systems' (2020) 71(4) *Psychiatric Services* 355–363.

Boukezzi, S., M. El Khoury-Malhame, G. Auzias, E. Reynaud, P. F. Rousseau, E. Richard, X. Zendjidjian, J. Roques, N. Castelli, N. Correard, V. Guyon, C. Gellato, J. C. Samuelian, A. Cancel, M. Comte, M. Latinus, E. Guedj, S. Khalfa, 'Grey Matter Density Changes of Structures Involved in Posttraumatic Stress Disorder (PTSD) after Recovery Following Eye Movement Desensitization and Reprocessing (EMDR) Therapy' (2017) 266 *Psychiatry Research: Neuroimaging* 146–152.

Bouma, K., 'Het criminele brein: Pieter Baan centrum duikt in neuropoli in de hersenen van verdachten' (*De Volkskrant*, 23 June 2023) <https://www.volkskrant.nl/wetenschap/het-criminele-brein-pieter-baan-centrum-duikt-in-neuropoli-in-de-hersenen-van-verdachten~bda3c47b/> accessed 26 August 2024.

Bouw, N. and others, 'Mindfulness-Based Stress Reduction in Prison: Experiences of Inmates, Instructors, and Prison Staff' (2019) 63 *International Journal of Offender Therapy and Comparative Criminology* 2550–2571.

Bowen, P., S. Whitehead, *Problem-Solving Courts: An Evidence Review* (Centre for Justice Innovation, 2015).

Branch, A., 'Dominic Ongwen on Trial: The ICC's African Dilemmas' (2017) 11 *International Journal of Transitional Justice* 30–49.

Brank, E. M., J. A. Haby, 'The Intended and Unintended Consequences of Problem-Solving Courts' in R. L. Wiener, E. M. Brank (eds), *Problem Solving Courts: Social Science and Legal Perspectives* (Springer, 2013).

Brief of Amici Curiae Professors and Practitioners of Psychology and Psychiatry in Support of Plaintiff-Appellant (7th Cir. 2019) Johnson v. Prentice et al. No. 18-3535 (filed on 8 May 2019) <https://www.macarthurjustice.org/wp-content/uploads/2020/07/Amicus-Brief-Professors-and-Practitioner.pdf>

Brief of Amici Curiae Professors and Practitioners of Psychology and Psychiatry in Support of Plaintiff-Appellant, Hope v. Harris No. 20-40379 (10th Cir. 2020) (filed on 28 September 2020) <https://www.macarthurjustice.org/wp-content/uploads/2020/08/2020-09-28-Amicus-Brief-of-Professors-Practitioners-2.pdf>

Brief of Amici Curiae Professors and Practitioners of Psychology and Psychiatry in Support of Plaintiff-Appellant No. 17-1938 (7th Cir. 2017), 33–34 <https://www.macarthurjustice.org/wp-content/uploads/2017/10/Sanders_Amicus.pdf>

Brief of Amici Curiae Professors and Practitioners of Psychology and Psychiatry in Support of Plaintiff-Appellant No. 23-1083 (6th Cir. 2024) (filed on 2 August 2017) <https://www.macarthurjustice.org/wp-content/uploads/2018/07/Finley_Amicus-Brief.pdf>

Brief of Amici Curiae Professors and Practitioners of Psychology and Psychiatry in Support of Plaintiff-Appellant and Reversal No. 20-4032 (10th Cir. 2020) (filed on 10 June 2020) <https://a0c8672a-59c3-4f12-8764-cf2f7788522b.filesusr.com/ugd/b72ac6_ab881a79788d495cb26a0b562e7a8027.pdf>

Brinn, A., J. Preston, R. Costello, T. Opoku, I. Elliott, A. Sorbie, 'An Impact Evaluation of the Prison-Based Thinking Skills Programme (TSP) on Reoffending' (*Ministry of Justice of the United Kingdom*, 2023) <https://assets.publishing.service.gov.uk/media/64c10e4a90b54500143e8376/TSP_Reoffending_Report.pdf>

Brown, A., A. Charles, 'The Minimum Age of Criminal Responsibility: The Need for a Holistic Approach' (2019) 21 *Youth Justice* 153–171.

Browne, C. C. and others, 'Continuity of Mental Health Care during the Transition from Prison to the Community Following Brief Periods of Imprisonment' (2022) 13 *Frontiers in Psychiatry* 1–13.

Bryan, K., G. Garvani, J. Gregory, K. Kilner, 'Language Difficulties and Criminal Justice: The Need for Earlier Identification' (2015) 50(6) *International Journal of Language and Communication Disorders* 763–775.

Bublitz, J. C., 'Neurotechnologies and Human Rights: Restating and Reaffirming the Multi-Layered Protection of the Person' (2024) 28 *The International Journal of Human Rights* 782–807.

Bublitz, J. C., R. Merkel, 'Crimes against Minds: On Mental Manipulations, Harms and a Human Right to Mental Self-Determination' (2014) 8 *Criminal Law and Philosophy* 51–77.

Buelens, W., C. Herijgers, S. Illegems, 'The View of the European Court of Human Rights on Competent Patients' Right of Informed Consent. Research in the Light of Articles 3 and 8 of the European Convention on Human Rights' (2016) 23 *European Journal of Health Law* 481–509.

Butrus, N., 'Judicial Sentencing Considerations in Cases of Violent Offenders Versus Sexual Offenders' (2018) 25 *Psychiatry, Psychology and Law* 653–674.

Byard, R. W., 'Ongoing Issues with the Diagnosis of Excited Delirium' (2018) 14 *Forensic Science, Medicine, and Pathology* 149–151.

Byju, A. S., 'Excited Delirium: How Cops Invented a Disease' (*Current Affairs*, 2021) <https://www.currentaffairs.org/news/2021/04/excited-delirium-how-cops-invented-a-disease> accessed 2 December 2024.

Byrne, C., D. Guenter, 'Treatments for ADHD in Adults in Jails, Prisons and Correctional Settings: A Scoping Review of the Literature' (2023) 11 *Health & Justice* 1–10.

Canada, K. and others, 'Multi-Level Barriers to Prison Mental Health and Physical Health Care for Individuals with Mental Illnesses' (2022) 13 *Frontiers in Psychiatry* 1–11.

Canada, K. E., K. R. Trawver, S. Barrenger, 'Deciding to Participate in Mental Health Court: Exploring Participant Perspectives' (2020) 72 *International Journal of Law and Psychiatry* 1–11.

Carlisi, C. O., 'Comparative Multimodal Meta-Analysis of Structural and Functional Brain Abnormalities in Autism Spectrum Disorder and Obsessive-Compulsive Disorder' (2017) 82(2) *Biological Psychiatry* 82–103.

Caruso, G. D., 'Autism in the U.S.: Social Movement and Legal Change' (2010) 36 *American Journal of Law & Medicine* 483–539.

Caruso, G. D., *Free Will and Consciousness: A Determinist Account of the Illusion of Free Will* (Lexington Books, Lanham, MD, 2012).

Caruso, G. D., 'Free Will Skepticism and Criminal Behavior: A Public Health-Quarantine Model' (2016) 32(1) *Philosophical Review* 25–48.

Caruso, G. D., 'Justice without Retribution: An Epistemic Argument against Retributive Criminal Punishment' (2020) 13(1) *Neuroethics* 13–28.

Caruso, G. D., *Neurolaw* (Cambridge University Press, Cambridge, 2024).

Caruso, G. D., 'Preemptive Incapacitation, Victim's Rights, Desert, and Respect for Persons: Replies to McCormick and Donelson' (2023) 10(3) *Journal of Practical Ethics* 29–56.

Caruso, G. D., *Public Health and Safety: The Social Determinants of Health and Criminal Behavior* (Research Links Books, London, 2017).

Caruso, G. D., *Rejecting Retributivism: Free Will, Punishment, and Criminal Justice* (Cambridge University Press, New York, 2021a).

Caruso, G. D., 'Retributivism, Free Will Skepticism, and the Public Health-Quarantine Model: Replies to Kennedy, Walen, Corrado, Sifferd, Pereboom, and Shaw' (2021b) 46(2) *Journal of Legal Philosophy* 161.

Caruso, G. D., O. Flanagan (eds), *Neuroexistentialism: Meaning, Morals, and Purpose in the Age of Neuroscience* (Oxford University Press, New York, 2018).

Caruso, G. D., D. Pereboom, *Moral Responsibility Reconsidered* (Cambridge University Press, New York, 2022).

Castellano, U., 'The Politics of Benchcraft: The Role of Judges in Mental Health Courts' (2017) 42 *Law & Social Inquiry* 398–422.

Castellano, U., L. Anderson, 'Mental Health Courts in America: Promise and Challenges' (2012) 57 *American Behavioral Scientist* 163–173.

Catley, P., L. Claydon, 'The Use of Neuroscientific Evidence in the Courtroom by Those Accused of Criminal Offenses in England and Wales' (2015) 2(3) *Journal of Law and Biosciences* 510–549.

CBS News Colorado, '"Excited Delirium": Elijah McClain's Mother Talks to "60 Minutes" about Use of Ketamine to Sedate Suspects—CBS Colorado' (14 December 2020) <https://www.cbsnews.com/colorado/news/excited-delirium-elijah-mcclain-60-minutes-ketamine-sedate-suspects/> accessed 29 November 2024.

Chandler, J. A., 'The Use of Neuroscientific Evidence in Canadian Criminal Proceedings' (2015) 2(3) *Journal of Law and Biosciences* 550–579.

Chang, A., 'Police Repeatedly Cite "Excited Delirium" in Killings, But It Has No Real Definition' (*NPR*, 7 April 2021) <https://www.npr.org/2021/04/07/985128452/

police-repeatedly-cite-excited-delirium-in-kilings-but-it-has-no-real-definitio> accessed 2 December 2024.

Child, J. J., R. A. Duff, *Criminal Law Reform Now* (Hart Publishing, Oxford, 2021).

Choy, O. and others, 'The Mediating Role of Heart Rate on the Social Adversity-Antisocial Behavior Relationship: A Social Neurocriminology Perspective' (2015) 52 *Journal of Research in Crime and Delinquency* 303–341.

Choy, O., D. P. Farrington, A. Raine, 'The Need to Incorporate Autonomic Arousal in Developmental and Life-Course Research and Theories' (2015) 1 *Journal of Developmental and Life-Course Criminology* 189–207.

Choy, O., F. Focquaert, A. Raine, 'Benign Biological Interventions to Reduce Offending' (2020) 13 *Neuroethics* 29–41.

Chu, D. A., L. M. Williams, A. W. F. Harris, R. A. Bryant, J. M. Gatt, 'Early Life Trauma Predicts Self-Reported Levels of Depressive and Anxiety Symptoms in Nonclinical Community Adults: Relative Contributions of Early Life Stressor Types and Adult Trauma Exposure' (2013) 47 *Journal of Psychiatric Research* 23–32.

Clausen, J., N. Levy (eds), *Handbook of Neuroethics* (Springer Science, 2015).

Cloitre, M., 'ICD-11 Complex Post-Traumatic Stress Disorder: Simplifying Diagnosis in Trauma Populations' (2020) 216 *British Journal of Psychiatry* 129–131.

Cloitre, M., B. C. Stolbach, J. L. Herman, B. van der Kolk, R. Pynoos, J. Wang, E. Petkova, 'A Developmental Approach to Complex PTSD: Childhood and Adult Cumulative Trauma as Predictors of Symptom Complexity' (2009) 22 *Journal of Traumatic Stress* 399–408.

Cloud, D., C. Davis, 'Treatment Alternatives to Incarceration for People with Mental Health Needs in the Criminal Justice System: The Cost-Savings Implications' (*Vera Institute of Justice*, 2013) Research Summary.

The College of American Pathologists, 'CAP Supports Discontinuing Term "Excited Delirium" as Cause of Death' (*The News Market*, 13 October 2023) <https://newsroom.cap.org/latest-news/cap-supports-discontinuing-term-excited-delirium-as-cause-of-death/s/c29dd694-6877-428a-95b4-d5fc5c0d82cc> accessed 2 December 2024.

Collins, P., B. McPhail, 'Seventeen Dead So Far' (*New Times*, 3 May 1989).

Compton, M. T., M. Bahora, A. C. Watson, J. R. Oliva, 'A Comprehensive Review of Extant Research on Crisis Intervention Team (CIT) Programs' (2008) 36 *Journal of the American Academy of Psychiatry and the Law Online* 47–60.

Connor, J. P. and others, 'Cannabis Use and Cannabis Use Disorder' (2021) 7 *Nature Reviews Disease Primers* 1–24.

Coppola, F., 'The Brain in Solitude: An (Other) Eighth Amendment Challenge to Solitary Confinement' (2019) 6 *Journal of Law and the Biosciences* 184–225.

Coppola, F., *The Emotional Brain and the Guilty Mind: Novel Paradigms of Culpability and Punishment* (Hart Publishing, Oxford, 2020).

Coppola, F., 'When the Brain Can Make a Difference: Individualized vs Framework Uses of Neuroscience in Courtrooms' (2020) 1 *Diritto Penale e Uomo* 1–24.

Corrado, M., 'The Limits of the State's Power to Control Crime' (2021) 46(2) *Journal of Legal Philosophy* 126–131.

Council on Psychiatry and Law, *Position Statement on Concerns about Use of the Term "Excited Delirium" and Appropriate Medical Management in Out-of-Hospital Contexts* (American Psychiatric Association, APA Official Actions, 2020).

Courchesne, E. et al., 'Neuron Number and Size in Prefrontal Cortex of Children with Autism' (2011) 306 *Journal of the American Medical Association* 2001–2010.

Courtois, A., J. D. Ford (eds), *Treating Complex Traumatic Stress Disorders: Scientific Foundations and Therapeutic Models* (Guilford, New York, 2014).

The Courts Service of Ireland, 'The Drug Treatment Court' (*The Courts Service of Ireland*, 2023) <https://www.courts.ie/drug-treatment-court>

Crenshaw, K. W., A. J. Ritchie, R. Anspach and others, 'Say Her Name: Resisting Police Brutality Against Black Women' (July 2015) *Columbia Center for Intersectionality and Social Policy Studies* 1–48.
Crofts, T., 'Will Australia Raise the Minimum Age of Criminal Responsibility' (2019) 43 *Criminal Law Journal* 26–40.
Cuadra, L. E., A. E. Jaffe, R. Thomas, D. DiLillo, 'Child Maltreatment and Adult Criminal Behavior: Does Criminal Thinking Explain the Association?' (2014) 38(8) *Child Abuse & Neglect* 1399–1408.
Cullen, F. T., C. L. Jonson, D. S. Nagin, 'Prisons Do Not Reduce Recidivism the High Cost of Ignoring Science' (2011) 91(3, Suppl.) *Prison Journal* 48S–65S.
da Silva Bhatia, B. et al., *Excited Delirium and Deaths in Police Custody March 2022 the Deadly Impact of a Baseless Diagnosis* (Physicians for Human Rights, March 2022).
Danaher, J., 'Moral Enhancement and Moral Freedom: A Critique of the Little Alex Problem' (2018) 83 *Royal Institute of Philosophy Supplements* 233–250.
Davidson, M. L., J. W. Rosky, 'Dangerousness or Diminished Capacity? Exploring the Association of Gender and Mental Illness with Violent Offense Sentence Length' (2015) 40 *American Journal of Criminal Justice* 353–376.
Davis, C. S. and others, 'Changes in Arrests Following Decriminalization of Low-Level Drug Possession in Oregon and Washington' (2023) 119 *International Journal of Drug Policy* 104155, 1–11.
De Brigard, F., W. Sinnott-Armstrong (eds), *Neuroscience and Philosophy* (MIT Press, Cambridge, MA, 2022).
de Kogel, H., E. J. Westgeest, 'Neuroscientific and Behavioral Genetic Information in Criminal Cases in the Netherlands' (2015) 2(3) *Journal of Law and the Biosciences* 580–605.
De Kogel, K., L. Westgeest, 'Neuroscientific and Behavioral Genetic Information in Criminal Cases in the Netherlands' (2015) 2 *Journal of Law and the Biosciences* 580–605.
De Oliveira-Souza, R. et al., 'Psychopathy as a Disorder of the Moral Brain: Fronto Temporo-Limbic Grey Matter Reductions Demonstrated by Vox-Based Morphometry' (2008) 40(3) *NeuroImage* 1202–1213.
Delfin, C. et al., 'Prediction of Recidivism in a Long-Term Follow-up of Forensic Psychiatric Patients: Incremental Effects of Neuroimaging Data' (2019) 14(5) *PLoS One* e0217127.
Delle-Vergini, V., A. Day, 'Case Formulation in Forensic Practice: Challenges and Opportunities' (2016) 18 *Journal of Forensic Practice* 240–250.
Dennis, M. L. and others, 'The Duration and Correlates of Addiction and Treatment Careers' (2005) 28 *Journal of Substance Abuse Treatment* S51–S62.
Denno, D. W., 'How Courts in Criminal Cases Respond to Childhood Trauma' (2019) 103(2) *Marquette Law Review* 301–363.
Denno, D. W., 'The Myth of the Double-Edged Sword: An Empirical Study of Neuroscience Evidence in Criminal Cases' (2015) 56 *Boston College Law Review* 493–551.
Denson, T. F., O. Choy, 'Reconsidering Biological Treatments for Reducing Violent Offending' (2024) 14 *Psychology of Violence* 412–421.
Department of Health, *The Children Act 1989 Guidance and Regulations Volume 2 Family Support, Day Care and Educational Provision for Young Children* (HMSO, London, 1991).
Deskundigen, N. R. G., 'The Netherlands Register of Court Experts' (*NRGD*, 30 April 2022) <https://english.nrgd.nl/find-an-expert/the-experts>
DiaMaio, T. G., V. J. M. DiMaio, *Excited Delirium Syndrome Causes of Death and Prevention* (CRC Press, Boca Raton, 2005).
DiClemente, C. C., M. A. Crisafulli, 'Relapse on the Road to Recovery: Learning the Lessons of Failure on the Way to Successful Behavior Change' (2022) 48 *Journal of Health Service* Psychology 5–68.

DiMaio, T. G., V. J. M. DiMaio, *Excited Delirium Syndrome: Cause of Death and Prevention* (CRC Press, Taylor & Francis Group, Boca Raton, 2005).

Dirks-Linhorst, P. A. and others, 'Factors Associated with Mental Health Court Non-participation and Negative Termination' (2013) 30 *Justice Quarterly* 681–710.

Divakaran, B., S. Shavit, A. Steiner, 'Best Practices for Engaging the Reentry Population in Health Care' (2022) *Transitions Clinic Network* 1–11.

Dolovich, S., 'The Coherence of Prison Law' (2022) 135 *Harvard Law Review* 302–342.

Dolovich, S., 'Cruelty, Prison Conditions, and the Eighth Amendment' (2009) 84 *New York University Law Review* 881–979.

Dolovich, S., 'Exclusion and Control in the Carceral State' (2011) 16 *Berkley Journal of Criminal Law* 259–339.

Domoslawski, A., H. Siemaszko, *Drug Policy in Portugal: The Benefits of Decriminalizing Drug Use* (Open Society Institute, 2011).

Donnelly, M., *Healthcare Decision-Making and the Law: Autonomy, Capacity and the Limits of Liberalism* (Cambridge University Press, 2011).

Doogue, J., J. Walker, 'Proposal for a Trial of Young Adult List in Porirua District Court: Procedural Fairness for the Young and the Vulnerable' (2019) <https://www.districtcourts.govt.nz/reports-publications-and-statistics/publications/trial-of-young-adult-list-proposal>

Dore-Horgan, E., 'Do Criminal Offenders Have a Right to Neurorehabilitation?' (2023) 17(2) *Criminal Law Philosophy* 429–451.

Douglas, T. and others, 'Coercion, Incarceration and Chemical Castration: An Argument from Autonomy' (2013) 10 *Bioethical Inquiry* 393–405.

Drapela, L. A., 'Incorporating Neurodiversity into Therapeutic Jurisprudence: Exploring the Policy Diffusion Potential of Pennsylvania's Autism Training Law for Juvenile Court Judges' (2022) 19 *Justice Policy Journal* 1–23.

Drug Policy Alliance, 'Approaches to Decriminalizing Drug Use & Possession' (*Drug Policy Alliance*, New York, February 2015) <https://www.unodc.org/documents/ungass2016/Contributions/Civil/DrugPolicyAlliance/DPA_Fact_Sheet_Approaches_to_Decriminalization_Feb2015_1.pdf> accessed 3 February 2025.

Drug Policy Alliance, 'Drug Decriminalization in Portugal Learning from a Health and Human-Centered Approach' (*Durg Policy Alliance*, New York, 2018) <https://drugpolicy.org/wp-content/uploads/2023/08/dpa-drug-decriminalization-portugal-health-human-centered-approach_0.pdf> accessed 3 February 2025.

Dudgeon, P., H. Milroy, R. Walker (eds), *Working Together: Aboriginal and Torres Strait Islander Mental Health and Wellbeing Principles and Practice* (2nd ed., Telethon Institute for Child Health Research & Australian Government Department of the Prime Minister and Cabinet, Canberra, 2014).

Durand, E., M. Chevignard, A. Ruet, A. Dereix, C. Jourdan, P. Pradat-Diehl, 'History of Traumatic Brain Injury in Prison Populations: A Systematic Review' (2017) 60(2) *Annals of Physical and Rehabilitation Medicine* 95–101.

Dvoskin, J. A., J. L. Knoll IV, M. Silva, 'A Brief History of the Criminalization of Mental Illness' (2020) 25 *CNS Spectrums* 638–650.

Ecker, C. et al., 'Intrinsic Gray-Matter Connectivity of the Brain in Adults with Autism Spectrum Disorder' (2013) 110 *Proceedings of the National Academy of Sciences* 13222–13227.

Edalati, H., T. L. Nicholls, A. G. Crocker, L. Roy, J. M. Somers, M. L. Patterson, 'Adverse Childhood Experiences and the Risk of Criminal Justice Involvement and Victimization among Homeless Adults with Mental Illness' (2017) 68 *Psychiatric Services* 1288–1295.

Edwards-Grossi, È., C. D. E. Willoughby, 'Slavery and Its Afterlives in US Psychiatry' (2024) 114 *American Journal of Public Health* S250–S257.

Eisler, P., T. Reid, J. Szep, 'Shock Tactics: Taser Inserts Itself in Probes Involving Its Stun Guns' (*Reuters*, 24 August 2017) <https://www.reuters.com/investigates/special-report/usa-taser-experts/> accessed 3 December 2024.

El Akkad, O., J. Leeder, 'How Taser International Wins in the Courtroom' (*The Globe and Mail*, 28 November 2007) <https://www.theglobeandmail.com/news/national/how-taser-international-wins-in-the-courtroom/article20406364/> accessed 2 December 2024.

El-Guebaly, N., 'Substance Abuse and Mental Disorders: The Dual Diagnoses Concept' (1990) 35 *The Canadian Journal of Psychiatry* 261–267.

European Monitoring Centre for Drugs and Drug Addiction, *European Drug Report 2017* (European Union Drugs Agency, June 2017) <https://www.euda.europa.eu/publications/edr/trends-developments/2017/html_en> accessed 3 February 2025.

European Monitoring Centre for Drugs and Drug Addiction, *Netherlands Country Drug Report 2019* (European Union Drugs Agency, 2019) <https://www.euda.europa.eu/publications/country-drug-reports/2019/netherlands_en> accessed 3 February 2025.

European Union Agency for Law Enforcement Training, 'CEPOL Higher Education and Research' (*CEPOL—European Union Agency for Law Enforcement Training*, 2024) <https://www.cepol.europa.eu/thematic-areas/higher-education-and-research>

The Excited Delirium (ExDS) Task Force, *White Paper Report on Excited Delirium Syndrome Office of Justice Programs* (American College of Emergency Physicians, 238235, 2009) <https://www.ojp.gov/ncjrs/virtual-library/abstracts/white-paper-report-excited-delirium-syndrome> accessed 2 December 2024.

Expert Report of Matthew Lieberman (filed on 11 March 2015) <https://ccrjustice.org/sites/default/files/attach/2015/07/Lieberman%20Expert%20Report.pdf>

Faigman, D. L. et al., 'Group to Individual (G2i) Inference in Scientific Expert Testimony' (2013) 81(2) *University of Chicago Law Review* 417–480.

Faiola, A., C. F. Martins, 'Once Hailed for Decriminalizing Drugs, Portugal Is Now Having Doubts' (*The Washington Post*, 7 July 2023) <https://www.washingtonpost.com/world/2023/07/07/portugal-drugs-decriminalization-heroin-crack/>

Farahani, N. A., *The Battle for Your Brain: Defending the Right to Think Freely in the Age of Neurotechnology* (St. Martin's Press, 2023).

Farahani, N. A., 'The Costs of Changing Our Minds'(2019) 69 *Emory Law Journal* 75–100.

Farahani, N. A., 'Neuroscience and Behavioral Genetics in US Criminal Law: An Empirical Analysis' (2015) 2 *Journal of Law and Biosciences* 485–509.

Farahany, N. A., *The Impact of Behavioral Sciences on Criminal Law* (Oxford University Press, 2009) (Accessed via Oxford Scholarship Online).

Farbstein, J., M. Farling, 'Neuroscience and Correctional Facility Design Workshop: Understanding Cognitive Processes in Correctional Settings' (*Office of Justice Programs*, 2007) NCJ Number: 240143 <https://www.ojp.gov/ncjrs/virtual-library/abstracts/neuroscience-and-correctional-facility-design-workshop>

Fazel, S., K. Seewald, 'Severe Mental Illness in 33,588 Prisoners Worldwide: Systematic Review and Meta-Regression Analysis' (2012) 200(5) *The British Journal of Psychiatry* 364–373.

Fergusson, D., N. Swain-Campbell, J. Horwood, 'How Does Childhood Economic Disadvantage Lead to Crime?' (2004) 45 *Journal of Child Psychology and Psychiatry* 956–966.

Fettig, A., '2019 Was a Watershed Year in the Movement to Stop Solitary Confinement' (*American Civil Liberties Union*, 16 December 2019) <https://perma.cc/DX2W-TDAZ>

Figley, R., 'Introduction' in C. R. Figley (ed), *Trauma and Its Wake: The Study and Treatment of Post-Traumatic Stress Disorder* (Brunner/Mazel, 1985).
Fishbain, D. A., C. V. Wetli, 'Cocaine Intoxication, Delirium, and Death in a Body Packer' (1981) 10 *Annals of Emergency Medicine* 531–532.
Floud, J., W. Young, *Dangerousness and Criminal Justice* (Heinemann, London, 1981).
Focquaert, F et al. (eds), *Routledge Handbook of the Philosophy of Science of Punishment* (Routledge, New York, 2020).
Fodor, J., 'Review of Freedom Evolves' (2003) 5 *London Review of Books* <https://www.lrb.co.uk/the-paper/v25/n05/jerry-fodor/why-would-mother-nature-bother>
Fogelson, N. M. Shah et al., 'Prefrontal Cortex is Critical for Contextual Processing: Evidence from Brain Lessons' (2009) 132(11) *Brain* 3002–3010.
Francis, C., J Hayashi, 'Explainer: Building Effective Partnerships with Continuums of Care to Increase Housing Options for People Leaving Prisons and Jails' (2022) *Explainer NCJ* 1–3.
Frank, M. and others, 'No Health without Access: Using a Retrospective Cohort to Model a Care Continuum for People Released from Prison at an Urban, Safety Net Health System' (2023) 11 *Health & Justice* 1–9.
Freckelton, I., 'Autism Spectrum Disorder: Forensic Issues and Challenges for Mental Health Professionals and Courts' (2013) 26 *Journal of Applied Research in Intellectual Disabilities* 420–434.
Freckelton, I., 'Sentencing Offenders with Impaired Mental Functioning R v Verdins, Buckley and Vo [2007] VSCA 102; (2007) 169 A Crim R 581 Maxwell P, Vincent and Buchanan JJ' (2007) 14 *Psychiatry, Psychology and Law* 359–363.
Freckelton, I., D. List, 'Asperger's Disorder, Criminal Responsibility and Criminal Culpability' (2009) 16(1) *Psychiatry, Psychology and Law* 16–40.
Freedman, D., G. W. Woods, 'The Developing Significance of Context and Function: Neuroscience and Law' (2018) 36(4) *Behavioral Sciences & the Law* 411–425.
Friedrich, M., 'Medical Groups Disavow Discredited Excuse for Deaths in the Criminal Justice System' (*Arnold Ventures*, 26 January 2024) <https://www.arnoldventures.org/stories/medical-groups-disavow-discredited-excuse-for-deaths-in-the-criminal-justice-system>
Fritzon, K., S. Miller, D. Bargh, K. Hollows, A. Osborne, A. Howlett, 'Understanding the Relationships between Trauma and Criminogenic Risk Using the Risk-Need Responsivity Model' (2021) 30(3) *Journal of Aggression, Maltreatment & Trauma* 294–323.
Fuller, J. R., *Introduction to Criminal Justice: A Brief Edition* (2nd ed., Oxford University Press, New York, USA, 2019) <https://www.alibris.com/search/books/isbn/9780197504048> accessed 17 January 2023.
Fuller Torrey, E. et al., 'The Treatment of Persons with Mental Illness in Prisons and Jails: A State Survey' (*Treatment Advocacy Center*, 8 April 2014) <https://www.tac.org/reports_publications/the-treatment-of-persons-with-mental-ilnnes-in-prisons-and-jails-a-state-survey/>
Gallo, D. P., *Diagnosing Autism Spectrum Disorders: A Lifespan Perspective* (Wiley-Blackwell, 2015).
Galvan, A., *The Neuroscience of Adolescence* (Cambridge University Press, Cambridge, 2017).
Gansel, E., 'Military Service-Related PTSD and the Criminal Justice System: Treatment as an Alternative to Incarceration' (2014) 23 *Southern: California. Interdisciplinary Law Journal* 147–184.
Garcia-Roberts, G., 'Is Excited Delirium Killing Coked-up, Stun-Gunned Miamians?' (*Miami New Times*, 15 July 2010) <https://www.miaminewtimes.com/news/is-excited-delirium-killing-coked-up-stun-gunned-miamians-6367399> accessed 2 December 2024.

Gee, G., J. R. P. Ogloff, 'Sentencing Offenders with Impaired Mental Functioning: R v Verdins, Buckley and Vo [2007] at the Clinical Coalface' (2014) 21 *Psychiatry, Psychology and Law* 46–66.

Gehrke, D., '18 Killings Leave Families Struggling with Uncertainty' (*Miami Herald*, 18 June 1989).

Gehrke, D., 'Missed Calls, Close Calls Mar Serial Killings Case' (*Miami Herald*, 26 April 1990).

Gertner, N., 'Neuroscience and Sentencing.' (2016) 85 *Fordham Law Review* 533–546.

Gertner, N. and others, 'Supporting Responsive Federal Drug Sentencing through Education in the Workshop on Science-Informed Decision Making' (2021) 34 *Federal Sentencing Reporter* 12–30.

Geschwind, D. H., P. Levitt, 'Autism Spectrum Disorders: Developmental Disconnection Syndromes' (2007) 17 *Current Opinion in Neurobiology* 103–111.

Geukes, S. H. and others, 'Neurotechnology in Criminal Justice: Key Points for Neuroscientists and Engineers'(2024) 21(1) *Journal of Neural Engineering* 013001.

Gilbert, C., A. Caputo, G. Hing 'Tasers Are Less Reliable Than Their Maker Has Claimed: The Results Can Be Deadly' (*APM Reports*, 9 May 2019) <https://www.apmreports.org/episode/2019/05/09/when-tasers-fail> accessed 2 December 2024.

Gill, K. J., A. A. Murphy, 'Jail Diversion for Persons with Serious Mental Illness Coordinated by a Prosecutor's Office' (2017) 2017 *BioMed Research International* 1–7.

Gilling McIntosh, L. and others, 'Effectiveness of Psychological and Psychosocial Interventions for Forensic Mental Health Inpatients: A Meta-Analysis' (2021) 58 *Aggression and Violent Behavior* 1–17.

Glannon, W. (ed), *Free Will and the Brain: Neuroscientific, Philosophical, and Legal Perspectives* (Cambridge University Press, Cambridge, 2015).

Glen, A. et al., 'Increased Volume of the Striatum in Psychopathic Individuals' (2010) 67 *Biological Psychiatry* 52–58.

Glenn, S., '"Can't Breathe": Tacoma Police Restraint of Manuel Ellis Caused His Death, Medical Examiner Reports' (*The Seattle Times*, 3 June 2020) <https://www.seattletimes.com/seattle-news/cant-breathe-tacoma-police-restraint-of-manuel-ellis-caused-his-death-medical-examiner-reports/> accessed 29 November 2024.

Goldkamp, J. S., C. Irons-Guynn, 'Emerging Judicial Strategies for the Mentally Ill in the Criminal Caseload: Mental Health Courts' (2000) *Crime and Justice Research Institutes* 1–83.

Goldsmith, L. S. (2024) '§39.18 Traumatic Brain Injury, Listing 11.18' in 5 Social Security Practice Guide §39.18, Matthew Bender & Company, Inc. (2024).

Goldsmith, L. S. (2024) '§73.06 Management of Head Injury: Overview' in 4 Medical Malpractice: Guide to Medical Issues §73.06, Matthew Bender & Company, Inc. (2024).

Gonçalve, R., A. Lourenço, S. N. Silva, 'A Social Cost Perspective in the Wake of the Portuguese Strategy for the Fight against Drugs' (2015) 26 *International Journal of Drug Policy* 199–209.

Goomany, A., T. Dickinson, 'The Influence of Prison Climate on the Mental Health of Adult Prisoners: A Literature Review' (2015) 22 *Journal of Psychiatric and Mental Health Nursing* 413–422.

Goudreau, R., 'Somebody Killed 19 Women' (*Miami Herald*, 31 May 1989).

Government of the Netherlands, 'Penalties for Juvenile Offenders' (*Government of the Netherlands*) <https://www.government.nl/topics/sentences-and-non-punitive-orders/penalties-juvenile-offenders> accessed 16 August 2024.

Grabenwarter, C., *The European Convention on Human Rights: A Commentary* (Hart Publishing, 2014).

Graham, H., *Rehabilitation Work: Supporting Desistance and Recovery* (Routledge, Abingdon, 2016).

Grant, T. et al., 'Criminal Responsibility in Autism Spectrum Disorder: A Critical Review Examining Empathy and Moral Reasoning' (2018) 59 *Canadian Psychology* 65–75.

Grassian, S., 'Psychiatric Effects of Solitary Confinement' (2006), 22 *Washington University Journal of Law & Policy* 325–385.

Green, L., P. Dass-Brailsford, A. Hurtado De Mendoza, M. Mete, S. M. Lynch, D. D. Dehart et al., 'Trauma Experiences and Mental Health among Incarcerated Women' (2016) 8(4) *Psychological Trauma: Theory, Research, Practice, and Policy*, 455–463.

Greenberg, G., *The Book of Woe: The DSM and the Unmaking of Psychiatry* (Scribe, London, 2013).

Greene, J., J. Cohen, 'For the Law, Neuroscience Changes Nothing and Everything' (2004) 359 *Philosophical Transactions of the Royal Society of London B: Biological Sciences* 1775–1785.

Grey, J., 'Neuroscience, PTSD, and Sentencing Mitigation' (2012) 34 *Cardozo Law Review* 53–106.

Griffiths, E. V., J. Willis, M. J. Spark, 'A Systematic Review of Psychotropic Drug Prescribing for Prisoners' (2012) 46 *The Australian and New Zealand Journal of Psychiatry* 407–421.

Grove, L. J., J. Kukucka, 'Do Laypeople Recognize Youth as a Risk Factor for False Confession? A Test of the 'Common Sense Hypothesis' (2021) 28(2) *Psychiatry, Psychology and Law*, 185–205.

Grund, J.-P. C. and others, 'Reaching the Unreached: Targeting Hidden Idu Populations with Clean Needles via Known User Groups' (1992) 24 *Journal of Psychoactive Drugs* 41–47.

Grund, J.-P. C., J. J. Breeksema, 'Drug Policy in the Netherlands 1' (2017) *European Drug Policies* 128–148.

Gunasekaran, S., 'Assessment and Management of Risk in Autism' (2012) 6(6) *Advances in Mental Health and Intellectual Disabilities* 314–320.

Guo, K. and others, 'The Effect of Varenicline and Bupropion on Smoking Cessation: A Network Meta-Analysis of 20 Randomized Controlled Trials' (2022) 131 *Addictive Behaviors* 107329.

Hafner, M., 'Judging Homicide Defendants by Their Brains: An Empirical Study on the Use of Neuroscience in Homicide Trials in Slovenia' (2019) 6(1) *Journal of Law and Biosciences* 226–254.

Hamilton, M., 'Evaluating Algorithmic Risk Assessment' (2021b) 24(2) *New Criminal Law Review* 156–211.

Hamilton, M., 'Investigating Algorithmic Risk and Race' (2021a) 5(1) *UCLA Criminal Justice Law Review* 53–102.

Harner, H. M., S. Riley, 'The Impact of Incarceration on Women's Mental Health: Responses from Women in a Maximum-Security Prison' (2013) 23 *Qualitative Health Research* 26–42.

Harrington, R., S. Bailey, *Mental Health Needs and Effectiveness of Provision for Young Offenders in Custody and in the Community* (Youth Justice Board, London, 2005).

Harris, D. and others, *Harris, O'Boyle and Warbrick: Law of the European Convention on Human Rights* (5th ed., Oxford University Press, Oxford, 2023).

Harvey, T. D. and others, 'Cost Savings of a Primary Care Program for Individuals Recently Released from Prison: A Propensity-Matched Study' (2022) 22 *BMC Health Services Research* 1–11.

Hauskeller, M., 'Is It Desirable to Be Able to Do the Undesirable? Moral Bioenhancement and the Little Alex Problem' (2017) 26(3) *Cambridge Quarterly of Healthcare Ethics* 365–376.

Hawryluk, M., R. Rayasam, 'Doctors Abandon a Diagnosis Used to Justify Police Custody Deaths: It Might Live on, Anyway' (*KFF Health News*, 16 October 2023) <https://kffhealthnews.org/news/article/excited-delirium-diagnosis-police-custody-deaths-emergency-doctors-renounce>

Hawryluk, M., R. Rayasam, 'Police Blame Some Deaths on "Excited Delirium": ER Docs Consider Pulling the Plug on the Term' (*KFF Health News*, 2 October2023)<https://kffhealthnews.org/news/article/police-blame-some-deaths-on-excited-delirium-er-docs-consider-pulling-the-plug-on-the-term>

Heng, V., M. Zigmond, R. J. Smeyne, 'Neuroanatomical and Neurochemical Effects of Prolonged Social Isolation in Adult Mice' (2023) 17 *Frontiers in Neuroanatomy* 1–14.

Henneberg, M. L., 'Admissibility Frameworks and Scientific Evidence: Controversies in Relation to Shaken Baby Syndrome/Abusive Head Trauma' (2015) 4 *British Journal of American Legal Studies* 555–584.

Hertz, N., 'Neurorights—Do We Need New Human Rights? A Reconsideration of the Right to Freedom of Thought' (2023) 16(1) *Neuroethics* 1–15.

Hibbeln, J. R., T. A. Ferguson, T. L. Blasbalg, 'Omega-3 Fatty Acid Deficiencies in Neurodevelopment, Aggression and Autonomic Dysregulation: Opportunities for Intervention' (2006) 18 *International Review of Psychiatry* 107–118.

Hildt, E., A. G. Franke (eds), *Cognitive Enhancement: Trends in Augmentation of Human Performance* (vol. 1, Springer, 2013).

Hofvander, B. and others, 'Mental Health among Young Adults in Prison: The Importance of Childhood-Onset Conduct Disorder' (2017) 3 *BJPsych Open* 78–84.

Home Office, *No More Excuses: A New Approach to Tackling Youth Crime in England and Wales* (The Stationery Office, London, 1997).

Home Office, *Youth Justice: Preventing Offending* (HMSO, London, 1998).

House of Commons Debate, vol. 294 col 390 (19 May 1997), per Jack Straw <https://hansard.parliament.uk/Commons/1997-05-14>

House of Lords Debate, *Age of Criminal Responsibility Bill*, vol. 749 (8 November 2013) <https://hansard.parliament.uk/lords/2013-11-08/debates/13110858000393/AgeOfCriminalResponsibilityBill(HL)>

House of Lords Debate, *Age of Criminal Responsibility Bill*, vol. 783, Col 2211, Baroness Vere of Norbiton (Con) (8 September 2017) <https://hansard.parliament.uk/Lords/2017-09-08/debates/D3E4D198-45BB-4B60-9FF0-CFF5B0EA1CB6/AgeOfCriminalResponsibilityBill#:~:text=Volume%20783%3A%20debated%20on%20Friday%208%20September%202017&text=That%20the%20Bill%20be%20now%20read%20a%20second%20time.&text=school%20can%20be%20prosecuted%20and,in%20the%20adult%20Crown%20Court>

House of Lords Debate, *Age of Criminal Responsibility Bill [HL]*, Second Reading, col 1553–54 (Lord Dholakia, 29 January 2016) <https://hansard.parliament.uk/Lords/2016-01-29/debates/16012936000411/AgeOfCriminalResponsibilityBill>

House of Lords Debate, vol. 585, col 1323 (12 February 1998), per Lord Williams of Mostyn <https://hansard.parliament.uk/Lords/1998-02-12/debates/7ab3c6d3-228b-47a9-a098-c66fa85a6e52/LordsChamber>

Howells, K., K. Heseltine, R. Sarre, L. Davey, A. Day, *Correctional Offender Rehabilitation Programs: The National Picture in Australia* (Criminology Research Council, Adelaide, 2004).

Howlin, P., *Autism and Asperger Syndrome: Preparing for Adulthood* (2nd ed., Routledge, London, 2004).

Hughes, C. E., A. Stevens, 'What Can We Learn from the Portuguese Decriminalization of Illicit Drugs?' (2010) 50 *British Journal of Criminology* 999–1022.

Hunter, S., L. E. Kois, A. T. Peck, E. B. Elbogen, C. LaDuke, 'The Prevalence of Traumatic Brain Injury (TBI) among People Impacted by the Criminal Legal System: An Updated Meta Analysis and Subgroup Analyses' (2023) 47(5) *Law and Human Behavior*, 539–565 <https://doi.org/10.1037/lhb0000543>.

Ienca, M., R. Andorno, 'Towards New Human Rights in the Age of Neuroscience and Neurotechnology' (2017) 13 *Life Sciences, Society and Policy* 1–27.

Insel, C., S. Tabashneck, F. X. Shen and others, 'White Paper on the Science of Late Adolescence: A Guide for Judges, Attorneys, and Policy Makers' (*Center for Law, Brain & Behavior*, 2 February 2022) <https://clbb.mgh.harvard.edu/white-paper-on-the-science-of-late-adolescence/> accessed 3 February 2025.

International Criminal Court, 'International Criminal Court: Experts' (*ICC*, 2024) <https://www.icc-cpi.int/get-involved/experts> accessed 2 October 2024.

'Investigation Report (Antoinette Burns. M.E. Case No. 7703575)' (Metropolitan Dade County Medical Examiner Department 1988) Medical Examiner Department Report 7703575. (Accessed provided courtesy of Julia Sherwin).

Iqbal, M. N., C. J. Levin, F. R. Levin, 'Treatment for Substance Use Disorder with Co-Occurring Mental Illness' (2019) 17 *Focus* 88–97.

Ireland, J. L., P. Qualter, 'Bullying and Social and Emotional Loneliness in a Sample of Adult Male Prisoners' (2008) 31 *International Journal of Law and Psychiatry* 19–29.

The Istanbul Statement on the Use and Effects of Solitary Confinement, adopted at the International Psychological Trauma Symposium, Istanbul (9 December 2007).

Jackson, V., D. H. Sullivan, D. Mawren, A. Freiberg, J. Kulkarni, R. Darjee, 'Trauma-Informed Sentencing of Serious Violent Offenders: An Exploration of Judicial Dispositions with a Gendered Perspective' (2021) 28 *Psychiatry, Psychology and Law* 748–773.

Jiujias, M. et al., 'Restricted, Repetitive Behaviors in Autism Spectrum Disorder and Obsessive–Compulsive Disorder: A Comparative Review' (2017) 48 *Child Psychiatry & Human Development* 944–959.

Johnson, C. P., S. M. Myers, 'Identification and Evaluation of Children with Autism Spectrum Disorders' (2007) 120 *Pediatrics* 1183–1125.

Johnson, M. H. et al., 'Annual Research Review: Infant Development, Autism, and ADHD—Early Pathways to Emerging Disorders' (2014) 56(3) *Journal of Child Psychology and Psychiatry* 228–247.

Johnson, M. M. and others, 'Increased Heat Shock Protein 70 Gene Expression in the Brains of Cocaine-Related Fatalities May Be Reflective of Postdrug Survival and Intervention Rather Than Excited Delirium' (2012) 57 *Journal of Forensic Sciences* 1519–1523.

Johnstone, L. and others, *The Power Threat Meaning Framework: Towards the Identification of Patterns in Emotional Distress, Unusual Experiences and Troubled or Troubling Behaviour, as an Alternative to Functional Psychiatric Diagnosis* (British Psychological Society, Leicester, 2018).

Joint Committee on Human Rights, *Legislative Scrutiny: Police, Crime, Sentencing and Courts Bill (Parts 7 and 8): Sentencing and Remand of Children and Young People* (Parliament Publications, 23 September 2021).

Joint Committee on Human Rights, 'Oral Evidence: Legislative Scrutiny of the Police, Crime, Sentencing and Courts Bill, and Youth Justice' (HC 451, 30 June 2021, published 6 June 2021) <https://committees.parliament.uk/oralevidence/2491/html/>

Jones, O. D., J. D. Schall, F. X. Shen, *Law and Neuroscience* (2nd ed., Aspen Publishing, 2020).

Jones, O. D., A. Wagner, D. L. Faigman, M. Raichle, 'Neuroscientists in Court' (2013) 14 *Nature Reviews Neuroscience* 730–736.

Jouvenal, J., '"Excited Delirium" Cited in Dozens of Deaths in Police Custody: Is It Real or a Cover for Brutality?' (*Washington Post*, 7 May 2015) <https://www.washingtonpost.com/local/crime/existence-of-excited-delirium-ruling-in-va-womans-death-has-experts-split/2015/05/06/b1cc9499-ddaa-474c-9e8a-9ae89a9ae679_story.html> accessed 29 November 2024.

Just, M. A. et al., 'Functional and Anatomical Cortical Underconnectivity in Autism: Evidence from an FMRI Study of an Executive Function Task and Corpus Callosum Morphometry' (2007) 17 *Cerebral Cortex* 951–961.

Justice Committee, *Sentencing Guideline: Overarching Principles-Sentencing Youths, Memorandum Submitted by Sainsbury Centre for Mental Health* (April 2009).

Justice Speakers International, 'Treatment Courts: Jamaica' (*Justice Speakers International*, 2017) <https://www.justicespeakersinternational.com/drug-treatment-courts-around-world/jamaica/>

Kaba, F. et al., 'Solitary Confinement and Risk of Self-Harm among Jail Inmates' (2014) 104(3) *American Journal of Public Health* 442–447.

Kambam, P., C. Thompson, 'The Development of Decision-Making Capacities in Children and Adolescents: Psychological and Neurological Perspectives and Their Implications for Juvenile Defendants' (2009) 27(2) *Behavioral Sciences and the Law* 173–190.

Kaplan, T., M. Miller, E. Wood, 'Looking Backward, Looking Forward: How the Evolution of Specialty Courts Can Inform the Courts of Tomorrow' (2018) 54 *Court Review* 14–25.

Karthaus, R., L. Block, A. Hu, 'Redesigning Prison: The Architecture and Ethics of Rehabilitation' (2019) 24 *The Journal of Architecture* 193–222.

Keele, C. E., 'Criminalization of the Mentally Ill: The Challenging Role of the Defense Attorney in the Mental Health Court System' (2002) 71 *University of Missouri Kansas City Law Review* 193–210.

Keller, A. et al., 'Hierarchical Functional Systems Development Supports Executive Function' (2023) 27(2) *Trends in Cognitive Sciences* 160–174.

Kellmeyer, P. and others, 'The Effects of Closed-Loop Medical Devices on the Autonomy and Accountability of Persons and Systems' (2016) 25 *Cambridge Quarterly of Healthcare Ethics* 623–633.

Kempes, M. and others, 'Neurobiological Information and Consideration in Dutch Pre-Trial Forensic Reports of Juvenile Criminal Offenders' (2019) 18(3) *International Journal of Forensic Mental Health* 212–219.

Kenworthy, V., 'Predicting Sentencing Decisions of the New Zealand Courts Using Support Vector Machines' (2023) 4 *New Zealand Law Students' Journal* 143–172.

Kezelman, C., P. Stavropoulos, *Practice Guidelines for Clinical Treatment of Complex Trauma* (Blue Knot Foundation, Sydney, 2019).

Khalid, Z., R. Lee, B.W. Wall, 'The Use of Neurobiological Evidence in Sentencing Mitigation' (2023) 42 *Behavioral Science & the Law* 65–78.

Kidd, P. M., 'Omega-3 DHA and EPA for Cognition, Behavior, and Mood: Clinical Findings and Structural-' (2007) 12 *Alternative Medicine Review* 207–227.

Kiedrowski, J., R.-F. Melchers, 'An Independent Review of the Adoption and Use of Conducted Energy Weapons by the Royal Canadian Mounted Police' (*Royal Canadian Mounted Police*, 5 June 2008) <https://web.archive.org/web/20091231091631/http:/www.rcmp-grc.gc.ca/ccaps-spcca/cew-ai/kiedrowski-report-rapport-eng.htm> accessed 2 December 2024.

Kiehl, K. et al. 'Age of Gray Matters: Neuroprediction of Recidivism' (2018) 19 *NeuroImage: Clinical* 813–823.

Knehans, R. and others, 'Modulating Behavioural and Self-Reported Aggression with Non-Invasive Brain Stimulation: A Literature Review' (2022) 12(2) *Brain Sciences* 200.

Knoll IV, J. L., 'The Recurrence of an Illusion: The Concept of "Evil" in Forensic Psychiatry' (2008) 36 *The Journal of the American Academy of Psychiatry and the Law* 105–116.

Kois, L. E. et al., 'University-Community Mental Health Training Collaboration: Teaching Criminal Legal Stakeholders about Autism' (2023) 74(12) *Psychiatric Services* 1311–1314.

Koyama, A., 'A Review on the Cognitive Neuroscience of Autism' (2009) 51 *Activitas Nervosa Superior* 125–139.

Kurmelovs, R., '"Excited Delirium": How a Disputed US Term Found Its Way to Australian Deaths-in-Custody Inquests' (*The Guardian*, 3 July 2021) <https://www.theguardian.com/australia-news/2021/jul/04/excited-delirium-how-a-disputed-us-term-found-its-way-to-australian-deaths-in-custody-inquests> accessed 2 December 2024.

Lacey, N., 'Space, Time and Function: Intersecting Principles of Responsibility across the Terrain of Criminal Justice' (2007) 1 *Criminal Law and Philosophy* 233–250.

Lai, M. et al., 'Imaging Sex/Gender and Autism in the Brain: Etiological Implications' (2016) 95(1–2) *Journal of Neuroscience Research* 380–397.

Lamberti, J. S., 'Preventing Criminal Recidivism through Mental Health and Criminal Justice Collaboration' (2016) 67 *Psychiatric Services* 1206–1212.

Lambie, I., 'What Were They Thinking? A Discussion Paper on Brain and Behaviour in Relation to the Justice System in New Zealand' (Officer of the Prime Minister's Chief Science Advisor Kaitohutohu Mātanga Pūtaiao Matua ki te Pirimia, 2020).

Laqueur, H., 'Uses and Abuses of Drug Decriminalization in Portugal' (2015) *Law & Social Inquiry* 746–781.

Larsen, B., B. Luna, 'Adolescence as a Neurobiological Critical Period for the Development of High-Order Cognition' (2018) 94 *Neuroscience & Biobehavioral Reviews* 94–195.

Larson, C. et al., 'Language Is a Critical Mediator of Autistic Experiences within the Criminal Justice System' (2023) 16(12) *Autism Research* 2240–2246.

Latimer, J., A. Lawrence, *The Review Board Systems in Canada: An Overview of Results from the Mentally Disordered Accused Data Collection Study* (Government of Canada, Ottawa, 2006).

Law Commission, *Criminal Liability: Insanity and Automatism* (Discussion Paper, July 2013).

Law Commission, *Mental Impairment Decision-Making and the Insanity Defence NZLC R120* (New Zealand Law Commission, Wellington, 2010).

Lemos, J., *Free Will's Value: Criminal Justice, Pride, and Love* (Routledge, New York, 2023).

Lemos, J., *Freedom, Responsibility, and Determinism: A Philosophical Dialogue* (Hackett, Indianapolis, Indiana, 2013).

Lemos, J., 'Moral Concerns about Responsibility Denial and the Quarantine of Violent Criminals' (2016) 35 *Law and Philosophy* 461–483.

Lemos, J., *A Pragmatic Approach to Libertarian Free Will* (Routledge, New York, 2018).

Lennings, N. J., C. J. Lennings, 'Assessing Serious Harm under the Doctrine of Doli Incapax: A Case Study' (2014) 21 *Psychiatry, Psychology and Law* 791–800.

Leutgeb, V. et al., 'Brain Abnormalities in High-Risk Violent Offenders and Their Association with Psychopathic Traits and Criminal Recidivism' (2015) 12 (308) *Neuroscience* 194–201.

Lexipol Team, 'Understanding Excited Delirium: 4 Takeaways for Law Enforcement' (*Lexipol*, 3 November 2023) <https://www.lexipol.com/resources/blog/understanding-excited-delirium-4-takeaways-for-law-enforcement-officers-2/> accessed 2 December 2024.

Ligthart, S., *Coercive Brain-Reading in Criminal Justice: An Analysis of European Human Rights Law* (Cambridge University Press, 2022).

Ligthart, S. and others, 'Closed-Loop Brain Devices in Offender Rehabilitation: Autonomy, Human Rights, and Accountability' (2021) 30 *Cambridge Quarterly of Healthcare Ethics* 669–680.

Ligthart, S. and others, 'Minding Rights: Mapping Ethical and Legal Foundations of "Neurorights"' (2023) 32(4) *Cambridge Quarterly of Healthcare Ethics* 461–481.

Ligthart, S., E. Dore-Horgan, G. Meynen, *Minds, Freedoms and Rights: On Neurorehabilitation in Criminal Justice* (Cambridge University Press, 2025).

Linderborg, H., M. J. Tolvanen, P. Andersson, 'Probation in Europe: Finland' (*Confederation of European Probation*, 2020) <https://www.cep-probation.org/wp-content/uploads/2021/07/Probation-in-Europe-chapter-Finland-2020.pdf>

Lindsay, B., 'Canadian Coroners Starting to Reject Excited Delirium as Cause of Police-Related Deaths' (*CBC News*, 17 April 2023) <https://www.cbc.ca/news/health/coroners-excited-delirium-1.6811083> accessed 3 December 2024.

Livings, B., A. Reed, N. Wake, *Mental Condition Defences and the Criminal Justice System: Perspectives from Law and Medicine* (UK Cambridge Scholars Press, 2015).

Lobel, J., H. Akil, 'Law and Neuroscience: The Case of Solitary Confinement' (2018) 147 *Deadalus* 61–75.

Lobel, J., P. Scharff Smith (eds), *Solitary Confinement: Effects, Practices, and Pathways toward Reform* (Oxford University Press, New York, 2018).

Lõhmus, K., *Caring Autonomy: European Human Rights Law and the Challenges of Individualism* (Cambridge University Press, 2015).

Lord Dholakia, 'Age of Criminal Responsibility Bill [HL]' (*Hansard*, Volume 783, 8 September 2017) <https://hansard.parliament.uk/Lords/2017-09-08/debates/D3E4D198-43BB-4B60-9FF0-CFF5B0EA1CB6/AgeOfCriminalResponsibilityBill>

Loughman, 'How the Insanity Defence against a Murder Charge Works' (*The Conversation*, 2015) <https://theconversation.com/how-the-insanity-defence-against-a-murder-charge-works-50188> accessed 29 March 2025.

Lowder, E. M., C. B. Rade, S. L. Desmarais, 'Effectiveness of Mental Health Courts in Reducing Recidivism: A Meta-Analysis' (2018) 69 *Psychiatric Services* 15–22.

Luchins, A. S., 'Moral Treatment in Asylums and General Hospitals in 19th-Century America' (1989) 123 *The Journal of Psychology* 585–607.

MacKenzie, D. L., *What Works in Corrections: Reducing the Criminal Activities of Offenders and Delinquents* (Cambridge University Press, 2006) <https://www.cambridge.org/core/books/what-works-in-corrections/D10E55C780D8BB-F78FB0EDA19D6D1AD3> accessed 27 September 2024.

Mackey, S. and others, 'Brain Regions Related to Impulsivity Mediate the Effects of Early Adversity on Antisocial Behavior' (2017) 82 *Biological Psychiatry* 275–282.

MacNamara, D. E. J., 'The Medical Model in Corrections Requiescat in Pace Requiescat in Pace' (1977) 14 *Criminology* 439–448.

The Magnolia Project and Aboriginal Legal Rights Movement, *A Practice Guide for Preparing Mental Health Pre-Sentence Reports with Aboriginal People in the Criminal Justice System in South Australia* (The Magnolia Project, Adelaide, 2023)

Mallory, L. C., E. P. Shulman & E. Cauffman, 'Interrogations, Confessions, and Guilty Pleas among Serious Adolescent Offenders' (2014) 38(3) *Law and Human Behavior* 181–193.

Malvaso, C., A. Day, P. Delfabbro, J. Cale, L. Hackett, S. Ross, *Adverse Childhood Experiences and Trauma among Young People in the Youth Justice System* (Australian Institute of Criminology, Canberra, 2021).

Malvaso, C. G., J. Cale, T. Whitten, A. Day, S. Singh, L. Hackett, P. H. Delfabbro, S. Ross, 'Associations between Adverse Childhood Experiences and Trauma among Young People Who Offend: A Systematic Literature Review' (2022) 23(5) *Trauma, Violence & Abuse* 1677–1694.

Mann, B., 'How Portugal Eased Its Opioid Epidemic, While U.S. Drug Deaths Skyrocketed' (*NPR*, 24 February 2024) <https://www.npr.org/2024/02/24/1230188789/portugal-drug-overdose-opioid-treatment> accessed 16 February 2025.

Mannix, A., 'After Conflict-of-Interest Concerns, HCMC Ends Deal with Taser Manufacturer' (*The Minnesota Star Tribune*, 19 June 2019) <https://www.startribune.com/after-conflict-of-interest-concerns-hcmc-ends-deal-with-taser-manufacturer/511528142> accessed 2 December 2024.

Mannix, A., 'Minnesota Gov. Walz Signs Law Banning "Excited Delirium" for Police' (*Star Tribune*, 5 June 2024) <https://www.startribune.com/minnesota-

gov-walz-signs-law-banning-excited-delirium-for-police/600371297> accessed 2 December 2024.

Marshall, J., *Personal Freedom through Human Rights Law?: Autonomy, Identity and Integrity under the European Convention on Human Rights* (Brill Nijhoff, 2008).

Marshall, J. (ed), *Personal Identity and the European Court of Human Rights* (Routledge, Oxon, 2022).

Martin, E., 'Emerging Relevance of Neuroscience in Corrections' (*Corrections Today / National Institute of Justice*, 2023) NCJ Number: 306049 <https://nij.ojp.gov/library/publications/emerging-relevance-neuroscience-corrections>

Martin, M. S. and others, 'Risk of Violence by Inmates with Childhood Trauma and Mental Health Needs.' (2015) 39 *Law and Human Behavior* 614–623.

Mash, D. C. and others, 'Brain Biomarkers for Identifying Excited Delirium as a Cause of Sudden Death' (2009) 190 *Forensic Science International* e13–e19.

Mash, D. C. and others, 'Cocaine Abusers Have an Overexpression of α-Synuclein in Dopamine Neurons' (2003) 23 *The Journal of Neuroscience* 2564–2571.

Mash, D. C., J. K. Staley, 'D3 Dopamine and Kappa Opioid Receptor Alterations in Human Brain of Cocaine-Overdose Victims' (1999) 877 *Annals of the New York Academy of Sciences* 507–522.

McCann, J., S. Peppé, 'Prosody in Autism Spectrum Disorders: A Critical Review' (2003) 38 *International Journal of Language & Communication Disorders* 325–350.

McDiarmid, C., 'After the Age of Criminal Responsibility: A Defence for Children Who Offend' (2016) 67(3) *Northern Ireland Legal Quarterly* 327–341.

McDiarmid, C., 'An Age of Complexity: Children and Criminal Responsibility in Law' (2013) 13(2) *Youth Justice* 145–160.

McDonough, A., 'Mental Health Care on Rikers: New York's Largest Psychiatric Provider' (*City & State NY*, 30 September 2022) <https://www.cityandstateny.com/policy/2022/09/mental-health-care-rikers-new-yorks-largest-psychiatric-provider/377870/> accessed 1 October 2024.

McLachlan, K. J., *'I Cannot Dismiss from My Mind Your Traumatic and Tragic Upbringing': Judges' Use of Defendant Trauma in Sentencing*, PhD thesis (University of South Australia, 2021).

McLachlan, K. J., *Trauma-Informed Criminal Justice: Towards a More Compassionate Criminal Justice System* (Springer Macmillan, Cham, 2024).

Meijers, J., J. M. Harte, E. J. A. Scherder, 'Prison and the Brain' (2023) *Handbook of Clinical Neurology* 55–63.

Mele, A., *Aspects of Agency: Decisions, Abilities, Explanations, and Free Will* (Oxford University Press, New York, 2017).

Melemis, S. M., 'Relapse Prevention and the Five Rules of Recovery' (2015) 88 *Yale Journal of Biology and Medicine* 325–332.

Mental Health First Aid, 'Mental Health First Aid for Corrections Professionals' (*Mental Health First Aid*, 2023) <https://www.mentalhealthfirstaid.org/population-focused-modules/adults/corrections/>

Merlino, M. L., R. C Dillehay, V. Dahir, D. Maxwell, 'Science Education for Judges: What, Where, and by Whom' (2002) 86 *Judicature* 210–212.

Metzl, J. M., *The Protest Psychosis: How Schizophrenia Became a Black Disease* (Beacon Press, Boston, 2009).

Meynen, G., 'Forensic Psychiatry and Neurolaw: Description, Developments, and Debates' (2019) 65 *International Journal of Law and Psychiatry* 101345, 1–6.

Meynen, G., *Legal Insanity: Explorations in Psychiatry, Law, and Ethics* (Springer International Publishing, 2016).

Meynen, G., 'Neurolaw: Neuroscience, Ethics, and Law: Review Essay' (2014) 17 *Ethical Theory and Moral Practice* 819–829.

Michalowski, S., 'Critical Reflections on the Need for a Right to Mental Self-Determination' in A. von Arnauld, K. von der Decken, M. Susi (eds), *Cambridge*

Handbook of New Human Rights: Recognition, Novelty, Rhetoric (Cambridge University Press, Cambridge, 2020).

Miladinovic, Z., J. Lukassen, 'Verdicts of Not Criminally Responsible on Account of Mental Disorder in Adult Criminal Courts, 2005/2006–2011/2012' in *Juristat Bulletin* (Statistics Canada, Ottawa, 2014).

Miller, M., D. DeMatteo (eds), *Advances in Psychology and Law* (vol. 7, American Psychological Association, 2024).

Miller, S. L., A. M. Perelman, 'Mental Health Courts: An Overview and Redefinition of Tasks and Goals' (2009) 33 *Law & Psychology Review* 113–124.

Ministry of the Interior and Public Security, 'Tribunales de Tratamiento de Drogas' (*Ministry of the Interior and Public Security; Chilean the National Service for the Prevention and Rehabilitation of Drug and Alcohol Consumption (SENDA)*, 2022) <https://www.senda.gob.cl/tratamiento/programas/tribunales-de-tratamiento-de-drogas/>

Ministry of Justice, 'A Smarter Approach to Sentencing' (Consultation Paper 292, HMSO, London, September 2020).

Ministry of Justice, *Young Adult List National Operating Guidelines: Gisborne and Hamilton District Courts* (New Zealand Government, 2022).

Ministry of Justice Submission to House of Commons Justice Committee, *Children and Young People in Custody (Part 1): Entry into the Youth Justice System Twelfth Report of Session 2019–21*, (HC 306, 2020)

Modecki, K. L., 'Addressing Gaps in the Maturity and Judgment Literature: Age Differences and Delinquency' (2008) 32 *Law and Human Behaviour* 78–91.

Moore, M., *Placing Blame* (Oxford University Press, New York, 1997).

Morita, T., M. Asada, E. Naito, 'Contribution of Neuroimaging Studies to Understanding Development of Human Cognitive Brain Functions' (2016) 10 *Frontiers in Human Neuroscience* 464–478.

Mouridsen, S. E. et al., 'Pervasive Developmental Disorders and Criminal Behaviour' (2007) 52(2) *International Journal of Offender Therapy and Comparative Criminology* 196–205.

Moury, C., M. Escada, 'Understanding Successful Policy Innovation: The Case of Portuguese Drug Policy' (2022) 118 *Addiction* 967–978.

Mundt, A. P. and others, 'Psychiatric Hospital Beds and Prison Populations in South America since 1990' (2015) 72 *JAMA Psychiatry* 112–118.

Munetz, M. R., P. A. Griffin, 'Use of the Sequential Intercept Model as an Approach to Decriminalization of People with Serious Mental Illness' (2006) 57(4) *Psychiatric Services* 544–549.

Murdoch, J., *Freedom of Thought, Conscience and Religion: A Guide to the Implementation of Article 9 of the European Convention on Human Rights* (Human Rights Handbooks No. 9, Council of Europe, 2007).

Murrie, D. C. et al., 'Asperger's Syndrome in Forensic Settings' (2002) 1(1) *International Journal of Forensic Mental Health* 59–70.

Myrick Walsh, B., I. K. Agboola and others et al., 'Revisiting "Excited Delirium": Does the Diagnosis Reflect and Promote Racial Bias?' (2023) 24 *Western Journal of Emergency Medicine* 152–159.

Nadelhoffer, T. et al., 'Neuroprediction, Violence, and the Law: Setting the Stage' (2012) 5(1) *Neuroethics* 67–99.

Nasiripour, S., 'Zapping Taser' (*Reveal*, 1 December 2008) <http://revealnews.org/article/zapping-taser/> accessed 2 December 2024.

National Center for State Courts, *Evidence-Based Sentencing* (NCSC, Williamsburg, 2014).

National Gang Center, 'Mendota Juvenile Treatment Center (Intervention Program)' (*National Gang Center*, 1995) <https://nationalgangcenter.ojp.gov/spt/Programs/3586>

National Institute of Neurological Disorders and Stroke, 'Traumatic Brain Injury: Hope through Research' (2020) <https://catalog.ninds.nih.gov/sites/default/

files/publications/traumatic-brain-injury-hope-through-research_1.pdf> accessed 22 November 2024.
National Institute on Drug Abuse, *Principles of Drug Abuse Treatment for Criminal Justice Populations: A Research-Based Guide* (U.S Department of Health and Human Services, 2018).
Naylor, B., S. Shalev, 'Solitary Confinement and the Meaning of "Meaningful Human Contact"' (2022) 12 *Human Rights behind Bars* 293–318.
New Zealand Howard League, 'New Zealand Howard League' <www.nzhowardleague.org.nz> accessed 20 December 2024.
Newburn, T., E A. Stanko (eds), *Just Boys Doing Business?: Men, Masculinities and Crime* (Routledge, 1994).
Norwegian Human Rights Institution, *Drug Use and Human Rights* (Norwegian Human Rights Institution, Oslo, 10 March 2023) <https://www.nhri.no/en/2023/drug-use-and-human-rights/> accessed 3 February 2025
Nowak, M., *U.N. Covenant on Civil and Political Rights: CCPR Commentary* (2nd rev. ed., Engel, Rhein, 2005).
Nurse, J., P. Woodcock, J. Ormsby, 'Influence of Environmental Factors on Mental Health within Prisons: Focus Group Study' (2003) 327 *British Medical Journal* 480–485.
NYU Law, 'Course Descriptions, NYU School of Law' (*NYU Law*, 2024) <https://its.law.nyu.edu/courses/index.cfm#searchResults2> accessed 15 October 2024
Obasogie, O. K., 'Excited Delirium and Police Use of Force' (*Virginia Law Review*, 28 December 2021) <https://virginialawreview.org/articles/excited-delirium-and-police-use-of-force/> accessed 29 November 2024.
O'Callaghan, P., B. Shiner, 'The Right to Freedom of Thought in the European Convention on Human Rights' (2021) 8 *European Journal of Comparative Law and Governance* 112–145.
Office of Justice Programs, 'Treatment Courts: Training & Technical Assistance' (U.S. Department of Justice—Office of Justice Programs, 2022) <https://www.ojp.gov/feature/treatment-courts/training-technical-assistance>
O'Hare, M., J. Budhu, A. Saadi, 'Perspective | Police Keep Using "Excited Delirium" to Justify Brutality: It's Junk Science' (*The Washington Post*, 17 July 2020) <https://www.washingtonpost.com/outlook/chokehold-police-excited-delirium/2020/07/17/fe907ec8-c6bc-11ea-b037-f9711f89ee46_story.html> accessed 4 December 2024.
O'Loughlin, A., *Mental Disorder, Disability and Sentencing: A Review of Policy, Law and Research* (Sentencing Academy, York, 2022).
Ondruschka, B. and others, 'Drug- and/or Trauma-Induced Hyperthermia? Characterization of HSP70 and Myoglobin Expression' (2018) 13 *PLoS One* e0194442.
Pagon, M., *Policing in Central and Eastern Europe: Comparing Firsthand Knowledge with Experience from the West* (College of Police and Security Studies, 1996).
Panel of Mental Health and Medical Experts Review of Excited Delirium, *Report of the Panel of Mental Health and Medical Experts Review of Excited Delirium* (Government of Nova Scotia, 30 June 2009).
Paquola, C., M. R. Bennett, J. Lagopoulos 'Understanding Heterogeneity in Grey Matter Research of Adults with Childhood Maltreatment—a Meta-Analysis and Review' (2016) 69 *Neuroscience & Biobehavioral Reviews* 299–312.
Parry, M. S., 'Dorothea Dix (1802–1887)' (2006) 96 *American Journal of Public Health* 624–625.
Parvaz, M. A. and others, 'Structural and Functional Brain Recovery in Individuals with Substance Use Disorders during Abstinence: A Review of Longitudinal Neuroimaging Studies' (2022) 232 *Drug and Alcohol Dependence* 109319.
Pascoe, E. A., L. S. Richman, 'Perceived Discrimination and Health: A Meta-Analytic Review' (2009) 135 *Psychological Bulletin* 531–554.

Paulin, J. and others, 'Formative and Short-Term Outcome Evaluation of the Porirua District Court Young Adult List Court Initiative: Iti rearea teitei kahikatea ka taea' (*Artemis Research*, 2021).

Peckham, H., 'Introducing the Neuroplastic Narrative: A Non-Pathologizing Biological Foundation for Trauma-Informed and Adverse Childhood Experience Aware Approaches' (2023) 14 *Frontiers in Psychiatry* 1–21.

Per Lord Faulks, 'Hansard House of Lords Debate vol. 768' (29 January 2016) <https://hansard.parliament.uk/Lords/2016-01-29/debates/16012936000411/AgeOfCriminalResponsibilityBill>

Pereboom, D., *Free Will, Agency, and Meaning in Life* (Oxford University Press, New York, 2014).

Pereboom, D., *Living without Free Will* (Cambridge University Press, New York, 2001).

Perez, F. A. and others, 'Prenatal Methamphetamine—Impact on the Mother and Child—a Review' (2021) 117(1) *Addiction* 250–260.

Perlin, M. L., H. Cucolo, D. A. Dorfman, '"I Saw Guns and Sharp Swords in the Hands of Young Children": Why Mental Health Courts for Juveniles with Autism Spectrum Disorder and Fetal Alcohol Spectrum/Disorder Are Needed' (NYLS Legal Studies Research Paper No. 4515470, 2023) <https://www.ssrn.com/abstract=4515470>

Perricone, A., A. Baskin-Sommers, W. Ahn, 'The Effect of Neuroscientific Evidence on Sentencing Depends on How One Conceives of Reasons for Incarceration' (2022) 17(11) *PLoS One* e0276237, 1–17.

Perry, D., 'Examining Child Maltreatment through a Neurodevelopmental Lens: Clinical Applications of the Neurosequential Model of Therapeutics' (2009) 14 *Journal of Loss and Trauma* 240–255.

Phelps, M. S., 'Rehabilitation in the Punitive Era: The Gap between Rhetoric and Reality in U.S. Prison Programs' (2011) 45 *Law & Society Review* 33–68.

Physicians for Human Rights, 'Emergency Medicine Association Finally Withdraws Its Approval of Policy Paper Endorsing "Excited Delirium" as Cause of Death' (*Physicians for Human Rights, Press Release*, 13 October 2023) <https://phr.org/news/emergency-medicine-association-finally-withdraws-its-approval-of-policy-paper-endorsing-excited-delirium-as-cause-of-death/>

Physicians for Human Rights, 'PHR Welcomes American College of Emergency Physicians (ACEP) Policy Reversal on "Excited Delirium", Calls for Further Actions' (*Press Release*, 9 May 2023) <https://phr.org/news/physicians-of-human-rights-welcomes-american-college-of-emergency-physicians-acep-policy-reversal-on-excited-delirium-calls-for-further-action/>

Physicians for Human Rights, 'PHR Welcomes National Association of Medical Examiners (NAME) Policy Reversal on "Excited Delirium" as a Cause of Death' (*Press Release*, 31 March 2023) <https://phr.org/news/phr-welcomes-national-association-of-medical-examiners-name-policy-reversal-on-excited-delirium-as-a-cause-of-death>

Pickar, D. B., 'Considerations Regarding Child and Parent Neurodiversity in Family Court' (2022) 60(3) *Family Court Review* 492–506.

Pinals, D. A., 'For Too Many with Mental Illness, Incarceration Is the Default' (*Trend Magazine*, 2023) <https://pew.org/49FnDpG> accessed 1 October 2024.

Pitman, S., 'Whangārei's New Court Tackles Unlicensed Driving among Young Adults' *New Zealand Herald* (Whangārei, 18 August 2024).

Pittsburgh Post-Gazette, 'Becoming Aware of Mental Illness: Pa. Law Requires Training for Police, Judges' (*Pittsburgh Post-Gazette*, 2015) <https://www.hmpgloballearningnetwork.com/site/emsworld/news/14043681/becoming-aware-of-mental-illness-pa-law-requires-training-for-police-judges>

Plomin, R., J. C. DeFries, V. S. Knopik, J. M. Neiderhiser, 'Top 10 Replicated Findings from Behavioral Genetics' (2016) 11 *Perspectives on Psychological Science* 3–23.

Policy Paper, *Government Response to the Law Commission Report on 'Unfitness to Plead'* (25 October 2023) <https://www.gov.uk/government/publications/government-response-to-the-law-commission-report-unfitness-to-plead>

Poythress, N. G. and others, 'Perceived Coercion and Procedural Justice in the Broward Mental Health Court' (2002) 25 *International Journal of Law and Psychiatry* 517–533.

Pullen-Blasnik, H. et al., 'The Population Prevalence of Solitary Confinement' (2021) 26 *Science Advances* eabj1928.

Queensland Government Statistician's Office, *The Overlap between Offending and Victimisation in Queensland: Crime Research Report* (Queensland Treasury, Brisbane, 2023).

Raine, A., *The Anatomy of Violence: The Biological Roots of Crime* (Vintage, New York, 2014).

Raine, A., L. Brodrick, 'Omega-3 Supplementation Reduces Aggressive Behavior: A Meta-Analytic Review of Randomized Controlled Trials' (2024) 78 *Aggression and Violent Behavior* 1–9.

Raine, A., A. Glenn, *Psychopathy: An Introduction to Biological Findings and Their Implications* (New York University Press, New York, 2014).

Ransom, J., A. J. Harris, 'How Rikers Island Became New York's Largest Mental Institution' (*The New York Times*, 29 December 2023) <https://www.nytimes.com/2023/12/29/nyregion/nyc-rikers-homeless-mental-illness.html> accessed 1 October 2024.

Ray, B., C. B. Dollar, 'Exploring Stigmatization and Stigma Management in Mental Health Court: Assessing Modified Labeling Theory in a New Context' (2014) 29 *Sociological Forum* 720–735.

Ray, L. A. and others, 'Combined Pharmacotherapy and Cognitive Behavioral Therapy for Adults with Alcohol or Substance Use Disorders' (2020) 3 *JAMA Network Open* e208279.

Rayasam, R., 'As More States Target Disavowed "Excited Delirium" Diagnosis, Police Groups Push Back' (*KFF Health News*, 18 March 2024) <https://kffhealthnews.org/news/article/excited-delirium-police-deaths-state-legislation-bans/> accessed 2 December 2024.

Redlich, A. D. and others, 'Enrollment in Mental Health Courts: Voluntariness, Knowingness, and Adjudicative Competence' (2010) 34 *Law and Human Behavior* 91–104.

Redlich, A. D. and others, 'Patterns of Practice in Mental Health Courts: A National Survey' (2006) 30 *Law and Human Behavior* 347–362.

Reed, C., 'Fighting the Demon: The Children of the Meth Epidemic' (*New Zealand Herald*, New Zealand, 10 May 2019).

Reeves, B., 'Census of State and Local Law Enforcement Agencies, 2008' (*Bureau of Justice Statistics*) <https://bjs.ojp.gov/library/publications/census-state-and-local-law-enforcement-agencies-2008> accessed 3 February 2025.

Regier, D. A., E. A. Kuhl, D. J. Kupfer, 'The DSM-5: Classification and Criteria Changes' (2013) 12 *World Psychiatry* 92–98.

Rêgo, X. and others, '20 Years of Portuguese Drug Policy—Developments, Challenges and the Quest for Human Rights' (2021) 16 *Substance Abuse Treatment, Prevention, and Policy* 1–11.

Reid, T. and others, 'Shock Tactics: As Taser Warns of Risks, Cities Bear a Burden in Court' (*Reuters*, 23 August 2017) <https://www.reuters.com/investigates/special-report/usa-taser-legal/> accessed 2 December 2024.

Reingle Gonzalez, J. M., N. M. Connell, 'Mental Health of Prisoners: Identifying Barriers to Mental Health Treatment and Medication Continuity' (2014) 104 *American Journal of Public Health* 2328–2333.

Reiss, F. and others, 'Socioeconomic Status, Stressful Life Situations and Mental Health Problems in Children and Adolescents: Results of the German BELLA Cohort-Study' (2019) 14 *PLoS One* 1–16.

Ricard, J. A. and others, 'Confronting Racially Exclusionary Practices in the Acquisition and Analyses of Neuroimaging Data' (2023) 26 *Nature Neuroscience* 4–11.

Rinne-Albers, M. A., J. N. Pannekoek, M. van Hoof, N. D. van Lang, F. Lamers-Winkelman, S. A. Rombouts, N. J. van der Wee, R. R. Vermeiren, 'Anterior Cingulate Cortex Grey Matter Volume Abnormalities in Adolescents with PTSD after Childhood Sexual Abuse' (2017) 27 *European Neuropsychopharmacology* 1163–1171.

Ritter, C., J. L. S. Teller, M. R. Munetz, N. Bonfine, 'Crisis Intervention Team (CIT) Training: Selection Effects and Long-Term Changes in Perceptions of Mental Illness and Community Preparedness' (2010) 10 *Journal of Police Crisis Negotiations* 133–152.

Ritzl, E. K., A. Saadi and others et al., 'AAN Position Statement on Excited Delirium' (*American Academy of Neuroscience*, 2024) <https://www.aan.com/advocacy/excited-delirium-position-statement> accessed 2 December 2024.

Roagna, I., *Protecting the Right to Respect for Private and Family Life under the European Convention on Human Rights* (Council of Europe, 2012).

Rohrer, B., T. P. Stratton, 'Continuum of Care for Inmates Taking Psychiatric Medications While Incarcerated in Minnesota County Jails' (2017) 23 *Journal of Correctional Health Care* 412–420.

Rosino, M. L., M. W. Hughey, 'The War on Drugs, Racial Meanings, and Structural Racism: A Holistic and Reproductive Approach' (2018) 77 *The American Journal of Economics and Sociology* 849–892.

The Royal College of Pathologists, *Forensic Science Regulator Guidance the Use of 'Excited Delirium' as a Cause of Death* (The Royal College of Pathologists, Birmingham, 31 October 2020).

Royal College of Psychiatrists, '"Acute Behavioural Disturbance" and "Excited Delirium"' (PS02/22, Royal College of Psychiatrists, Position Statement, September 2022).

Royal College of Psychiatrists, *Additional Submission to Justice Select Committee Inquiry into Children and Young People in Custody* (June 2020) <https://committees.parliament.uk/publications/2010/documents/19436/default/> accessed December 2024.

The Royal Society, *Brain Waves Module 4: Neuroscience & the Law* (Royal Society, 2011).

Russoniello, K., 'The Devil (and Drugs) in the Details: Portugal's Focus on Public Health as a Model for Decriminalization of Drugs in Mexico' (25 November 2021) *Yale Law School Legal Scholarship Repository* 371–431.

Rutherford, J., 'Juvenile Justice Caught between *The Exorcist* and *A Clockwork Orange*' (2002) 51 *De Paul Law Review* 715–742.

Ryberg, J., *Neurointerventions, Crime and Punishment* (Oxford University Press, New York, 2020).

Rymer, R., 'Murder without a Trace' (1990) *Health* 55–56.

Samuels Jr., C. E., 'Treatment and Care of Inmates with Mental Illness' (2014) *U.S. Department of Justice* 1–32.

San Francisco Service Guide, 'Resolve to Stop the Violence (Intervention Program)' (*San Francisco Service Guide*, 1997) <https://www.sfserviceguide.org/services/3234>

Sanders, L., 'New Electrodes Better Capture Brain Waves of People with Natural Hair | Science News' (*Science News*, 11 March 2020) <https://www.sciencenews.org/article/electrodes-brain-waves-eeg-black-african-american-natural-hair> accessed 6 August 2025.

Sapolsky, R. M., 'Neuroscience and the Law' (2021) 15 *University of St. Thomas Journal of Law and Policy* 138–161.

Sapolsky, R., *Determined: A Science of Life without Free Will* (Penguin Press, New York, 2023).

Saxena, K., A. Sahai, 'Understanding the Effectiveness of Cognitive Behavioural Therapy: A Study on Offenders' (2024) *Annals of Neurosciences* 1–6.

Schatz, E., K. Schiffer, J. P. Kools, 'The Dutch Treatment and Social Support System for Drug Users: Recent Developments and the Example of Amsterdam' (International Drug Policy Consortium, IDPC Briefing Paper, January 2011).

Schiavone, S. and others, 'Involvement of the NADPH Oxidase NOX2-Derived Brain Oxidative Stress in an Unusual Fatal Case of Cocaine-Related Neurotoxicity Associated with Excited Delirium Syndrome' (2016) 36 *Journal of Clinical Psychopharmacology* 513–517.

Schleim, S., 'Real Neurolaw in the Netherlands: the Role of the Developing Brain in the New Adolescent Criminal Law' (2020) 11 *Frontiers in Psychology* 1762, 1–5.

Schroeder, J. H. et al., 'The Neurobiology of Autism: Theoretical Applications' (2010) 4 *Research in Autism Spectrum Disorders* 555–564.

Schumann, M. et al., 'Amygdala Enlargement in Toddlers with Autism Related to Severity of Social and Communication Impairments' (2009) 66 *Biological Psychiatry* 942–949.

Schwarzer, W. W., 'Judicial Discretion in Sentencing' (1991) *Federal Sentencing Reporter* 339–341.

Scientific Working Group on Medicolegal Death Investigation, *Increasing the Supply of Forensic Pathologists in the United States* (Scientific Working Group on Medicolegal Death Investigation, 2012).

The Scottish Government, *International Approaches to Drug Law Reform: Research* (Justice Directorate, Scottish Government, 1 July 2021) <https://www.gov.scot/publications/international-approaches-drug-law-reform/> accessed 3 February 2025

Seltzer, T., 'Mental Health Courts: A Misguided Attempt to Address the Criminal Justice System's Unfair Treatment of People with Mental Illnesses' (2005) 11 *Psychology, Public Policy, and Law* 570–586.

Selvarajah, S. and others, 'Racism, Xenophobia, and Discrimination: Mapping Pathways to Health Outcomes' (2022) 400 *The Lancet* 2109–2124.

Sentencing Council, *Sentencing Children and Young People Definitive Guideline* (Sentencing Council, 1 June 2017).

Sentencing Council, 'Sentencing Council for England and Wales' <https://www.sentencingcouncil.org.uk/>

Sentencing Council, 'Sentencing Offenders with Mental Disorders, Developmental Disorders, or Neurological Impairments' <https://www.sentencingcouncil.org.uk/overarching-guides/magistrates-court/item/sentencing-offenders-with-mental-disorders-developmental-disorders-or-neurological-impairments/>

Sentencing Council (UK), *Imposition of Community and Custodial Sentences—Guideline Effective from: 01 April 2025* (SC, London, 2025)

Sententia, W., 'Neuroethical Considerations: Cognitive Liberty and Converging Technologies for Improving Human Cognition' (2004) 1013 *Annals of the New York Academy of Sciences* 221–228.

Sergiou, C. S. and others, 'Transcranial Direct Current Stimulation Targeting the Ventromedial Prefrontal Cortex Reduces Reactive Aggression and Modulates Electrophysiological Responses in a Forensic Population' (2022) 7 *Biological Psychiatry: Cognitive Neuroscience and Neuroimaging* 95–107.

Shapiro, D. L., L. Mixon, M. Jackson, J. Shook, 'Psychological Expert Witness Testimony and Judicial Decision Making Trends' (2015) 42–43 *International Journal of Law and Psychiatry* 149–153.

Shaw, E., 'Justice without Moral Responsibility?' (2019) 28(1) *Journal of Information Ethics* 95–114.

Shaw, E., 'Neuroscience, Criminal Sentencing, and Human Rights' (2022) 63(4) *William & Mary Law Review* 1409–1443.

Shaw, E., *Free Will, Punishment, and Criminal Responsibility*, PhD thesis (Edinburgh University, Edinburgh, 2014).

Shaw, E., *Punishment and Moral Uncertainty: Seeking Convergence on Criminal Justice* (Cambridge University Press, New York, forthcoming).

Shea, L. L. et al., 'Preventing and Improving Interactions between Autistic Individuals and the Criminal Justice System: A Roadmap for Research' (2021) 14(10) *Autism Research* 2053–2060.

Sherry, A., 'Colorado Strikes "Excited Delirium" from All Law Enforcement Diagnosis, Training Documents' (*Colorado Public Radio*, 1 December 2023) <https://www.cpr.org/2023/12/01/colorado-strikes-excited-delirium-as-law-enforcement-diagnosis/> accessed 2 December 2024.

Sherwin, J., *Initial List of Officers, Directors and Resident Agent* (Institute for the Prevention of In-Custody Death, Inc, 2005).

Shiroma, E. J., P. L. Ferguson, E. E. Pickelsimer, 'Prevalence of Traumatic Brain Injury in an Offender Population: A Meta-Analysis' (2010) 16(2) *Journal of Correctional Health Care* 147–159.

Shuman, D. W., 'Expertise in Law, Medicine, and Health Care' (2001) 26 *Journal of Health Politics.*

Shuman, D. W., 'Psychiatric and Psychological Evidence' (*Office of Justice Programs*, 1986) <https://www.ojp.gov/ncjrs/virtual-library/abstracts/psychiatric-and-psychological-evidence>

Sirotich, F., 'The Criminal Justice Outcomes of Jail Diversion Programs for Persons with Mental Illness: A Review of the Evidence' (2009) 37 *The Journal of the American Academy of Psychiatry and the Law* 461–472.

Skipworth, J., W. Brookbanks, 'New Justice System Responses to Mentally Impaired Defendants in New Zealand' (2022) 29(4) *Psychiatry, Psychology and Law* 549–562.

Slate, R. N., 'From the Jailhouse to Capitol Hill: Impacting Mental Health Court Legislation and Defining What Constitutes a Mental Health Court' (2003) 49 *Crime & Delinquency* 6–29.

Slavny-Cross, R. et al., 'Autism and the Criminal Justice System: An Analysis of 93 Cases' (2022) 15(5) *Autism Research* 904–914.

Smilansky, S., 'Determinism and Prepunishment: The Radical Nature of Compatibilism' (2007) 67(4) *Analysis* 347–349.

Smiley-McDonald, H. M. and others, '"All Carrots and No Stick": Perceived Impacts, Changes in Practices, and Attitudes among Law Enforcement Following Drug Decriminalization in Oregon State, USA' (2023) 118 *International Journal of Drug Policy* 104100.

Smith, L. and others, 'Developmental and Behavioural Consequences of Prenatal Methamphetamine Exposure: A Review of the Infant Development, Environment, and Lifestyle (IDEAL) Study' (2015) 51 *Neurotoxicology and Teratology* 35–44.

Smith, R. T., O. Whooley, 'Dropping the Disorder in PTSD' (2015) 14(4) *Contexts* 38–43.

Solitary Watch, 'Solitary Confinement in the United States: The Facts' <https://solitarywatch.org/facts/faq/>.

Sommaggio, P. and others, 'Cognitive Liberty: A First Step towards a Human Neuro-Rights Declaration' (2017) 3 *BioLaw Journal* 27–45.

Soto, D. et al., 'Neurorights vs Neuroprediction and Lie Detection: The Imperative Limits to Criminal Law' (2022) 13 *Frontiers in Psychology* 1030439.

Sparks, B. F. et al., 'Brain Structural Abnormalities in Young Children with Autism Spectrum Disorder' (2002) 59 *Neurology* 184–192.

Spranger, T., *Law and Neuroscience in the United States* (Springer-Verlag, 2012).
Spranger, T. (ed), *International Neurolaw: A Comparative Analysis* (Springer-Verlag, Berlin and Heidelberg, 2012).
Stare, B. G., D. M. Fernando, 'Black American Men's Treatment Experiences in Mental Health Court: A Phenomenological Analysis' (2019) 40 *Journal of Addictions & Offender Counseling* 17–35.
Start Taranaki, 'START Taranaki' <https://www.starttaranaki.co.nz> accessed 20 December 2024.
Stats NZ, 'Statistics New Zealand' <https://www.stats.govt.nz/topics/population> accessed 20 December 2024.
Stefan, S., B. J. Winnick, 'A Dialogue on Mental Health Courts' (2005) 11 *Psychology, Public Policy, and Law* 507–526.
Steinberg, L., 'The Influence of Neuroscience on US Supreme Court Decisions about Adolescents' Criminal Culpability' (2013) 14(7) *Nature Reviews Neuroscience* 513–518.
Steiner, A., 'Continuum-of-Care Programs Could Help Ex-Offenders Treat Their Mental Illness—and Stay Out of Jail' (*MinnPost*, Minnesota, USA, 13 November 2017) <http://www.minnpost.com/mental-health-addiction/2017/11/continuum-care-programs-could-help-ex-offenders-treat-their-mental-i/> accessed 14 February 2025.
Stevens, L. and others, 'EFA Supplementation in Children with Inattention, Hyperactivity, and Other Disruptive Behaviors' (2003) 38 *Lipids* 1007–1021.
Stiles, J., T. L. Jernigan, 'The Basics of Brain Development' (2010) 20 *Neuropsychology Review* 327–348.
Stone, N., 'Old Heads upon Young Shoulders: "Compassion to Human Infirmity" Following R v. JTB' (2010) 32(3) *Journal of Social Welfare & Family Law* 287–297.
Strömmer, E. M. F. and others et al., 'The Role of Restraint in Fatal Excited Delirium: A Research Synthesis and Pooled Analysis' (2020) 16 *Forensic Science, Medicine, and Pathology* 680–692.
Substance Abuse and Mental Health Services Administration, *SAMHSA's Concept of Trauma and Guidance for a Trauma-Informed Approach* (U.S. Department of Health and Human Services, Rockville, 2014)
Tadros, E. et al., 'Life in the Hole: The Impact of Solitary Confinement in the United States' (2023) *The Howard Journal of Crime and Justice* 374–390.
Taumaunu, H., 'Calls for Transformative Change and the District Court Response' (2021) 29 *Waikato Law Review* 115–140.
Taxman, F., 'The Partially Clothed Emperor: Evidence-Based Practices' (2018) 34(97) *Journal of Contemporary Criminal Justice* 97–114.
Teicher, M. H., S. L. Andersen, A. Polcari, C. M. Anderson, C. P. Navalta, D. M. Kim, 'The Neurobiological Consequences of Early Stress and Childhood Maltreatment' (2003) 27 *Neuroscience and Biobehavioral Reviews* 33–44.
Thekkumkara, S. N. and others, 'Psychosocial Interventions for Prisoners with Mental and Substance Use Disorders: A Systematic Review' (2022) 44 *Indian Journal of Psychological Medicine* 211–217.
Thomaidou, M. A., C. M. Berryessa, 'A Jury of Scientists: Formal Education in Biobehavioral Sciences Reduces the Odds of Punitive Criminal Sentencing' (2022) 40 *Behavioral Sciences & the Law* 787–817.
Thomaidou, M. A., C. M. Berryessa, 'A Mixed-Methods Analysis of the Influence of Bio-Behavioral Scientific Evidence on U.S. Judges' Reasoning and Sentencing Decision-Making' (2025) 102 *International Journal of Law and Psychiatry* [in press].
Thompson, M., F. Osher, D. Tomasini-Joshi, 'Improving Responses to People with Mental Illnesses: The Essential Elements of a Mental Health Court' (2007) *Bureau of Justice Assistance* 1–11.

Tonry, M., 'Community Punishments' in Erik Luna (ed), *Reforming Criminal Justice* (vol. 4, The Academy for Justice, 2017) <https://law.asu.edu/sites/default/files/pdf/academy_for_justice/10_Criminal_Justice_Reform_Vol_4_Community-Punishments.pdf>

Torrey, E. F., *Out of the Shadows: Confronting America's Mental Illness Crisis* (John Wiley & Sons, 1997) <https://www.pbs.org/wgbh/pages/frontline/shows/asylums/special/excerpt.html> accessed 1 November 2021.

Transform Drug Policy, *Drug Decriminalisation in Portugal: Setting the Record Straight* (Transform Drug Policy, 2016) <https://transformdrugs.org/blog/drug-decriminalisation-in-portugal-setting-the-record-straight> accessed 3 February 2025.

Trotter, S., 'Hope's Relations: A Theory of the "Right to Hope" in European Human Rights Law' (2009) 22(2) *Human Rights Law Review* 1–21.

Truscott, A., 'A Knee in the Neck of Excited Delirium' (2008) 178(6) *Canadian Medical Association Journal* 669–670.

Uhl, G. R., G. F. Koob, J. Cable, 'The Neurobiology of Addiction' (2019) 1451 *Annals of the New York Academy of Sciences* 5–28.

United Nations, 'Treatment of Drug Use Disorders for People with Drug Use Disorders in Contact with the Criminal Justice System' (Office on Drugs and Crime, United Nations) <https://www.unodc.org/unodc/en/treatment-and-care/webstories/2021/july/treatment-of-drug-use-disorders-for-people-with-drug-use-disorders-in-contact-with-the-criminal-justice-system.html> accessed 3 February 2025

United Nations Committee on the Rights of the Child, 'General Comment No 24' (CRC/C/GC/24, UN Committee, 2019).

United Nations General Assembly, 'United Nations Standard Minimum Rules for the Treatment of Prisoners' (Rule 44, A/C.3/70/L.3, 2015).

United States Courts, 'U.S. Probation & Pretrial Services Careers' (United States Courts, 2024) <https://www.uscourts.gov/careers/who-works-judiciary/us-probation-pretrial-services-careers>

United States Sentencing Commission, 'Chapter 5—Determining the Sentence' in *Federal Sentencing Guidelines 2018* <https://www.ussc.gov/guidelines/2018-guidelines-manual/2018-chapter-5>

U.S. Centers for Disease Control and Prevention, 'About Moderate and Severe TBI' (*Traumatic Brain Injury & Concussion*) <https://www.cdc.gov/traumatic-brain-injury/about/moderate-severe-tbi.html> accessed 22 November 2024.

U.S. Centers for Disease Control and Prevention, 'TBI and Correctional Facilities' (*Traumatic Brain Injury & Concussion*) <https://www.cdc.gov/traumatic-braininjury/healthequity/correctional-facilities.html> accessed 21 November 2024.

Valentiner, D., 'The Human Right to Sexual Autonomy' (2021) 22 *German Law Journal* 703–717.

Valentino-DeVries, J. and others, 'How Paid Experts Help Exonerate Police after Deaths in Custody—The New York Times' (*The New York Times*, 2021) <https://www.nytimes.com/2021/12/26/us/police-deaths-in-custody-blame.html> accessed 2 December 2024.

Van de Grift, C., 'Experts willen meer aandacht voor mogelijke hersenschade van verdachten' (*NOS*, 17 October 2022) <https://nos.nl/nieuwsuur/artikel/2448737-experts-willen-meer-aandacht-voor-mogelijke-hersenschade-van-verdachten> accessed 16 August 2024.

van den Berg, B., L. Klaming (eds), *Technologies on the Stand: Legal and Ethical Questions in Neuroscience and Robotics* (Wolf Legal Publishers, 2011).

van der Kolk, B. A. (ed), *Psychological Trauma* (American Psychiatric Press, 1987).

van der Kolk, B., L. M. Najavits, 'Interview: What Is PTSD Really? Surprises, Twists of History, and the Politics of Diagnosis and Treatment' (2013) 69(5) *Journal of Clinical Psychology: In Session* 516–522.

Van Ginneken, E., H. Palmen, A. Q. Bosma, P. Nieuwbeerta, M. L. Berghuis, 'The Life in Custody Study: The Quality of Prison Life in Dutch Prison Regimes' (2018) 4 *Journal of Criminological Research* 253–268.

van Laar, M. and others, *Report to the EMCDDA by the REITOX National Focal* (Netherlands Institute of Mental Health and Addiction, The Netherlands Drug Situation 2014, Ministry of Security and Justice, 2015) <https://www.trimbos.nl/wp-content/uploads/sites/31/2021/09/af1367-the-netherlands-drug-situation-2014.pdf> accessed 3 February 2025.

van Schalkwyk, G. I. and others, 'Antipsychotics for Aggression in Adults: A Meta-Analysis' (2018) 81 *Progress in Neuro-Psychopharmacology and Biological Psychiatry* 452–458.

Vardanyan, L., O. Hamuľák, H. Kocharyan, 'Personal Autonomy and Human Corporeality: What Protects the Right to Personal Integrity?' (2024) 27 *Internet of Things* 101279, 1–15.

Vidal, C. N. et al., 'Mapping Corpus Callosum Deficits in Autism: An Index of Aberrant Cortical Connectivity' (2006) 60 *Biological Psychiatry* 218–225.

Vilhauer, B., 'Free Will and Reasonable Doubt' (2009) 46(2) *American Philosophical Quarterly* 131–140.

Vilhauer, B., 'Taking Free Will Skepticism Seriously' (2012) 62(249) *The Philosophical Quarterly* 833–852.

Vilke, G. M., M. L. DeBard et al., 'Excited Delirium Syndrome (ExDS): Defining Based on a Review of the Literature' (2012) 43(5) *Journal of Emergency Medicine* 897–905.

Villiger, M. E., *Handbook on the European Convention on Human Rights* (Brill Nijhoff, 2022).

Volkmar, F. R. et al. (eds), *Handbook of Autism Spectrum Disorder and the Law* (Springer Nature, Switzerland, 2021).

Volkow, N. D., M. Boyle, 'Neuroscience of Addiction: Relevance to Prevention and Treatment' (2018) 175 *American Journal of Psychiatry* 729–740.

von Arnauld, A., K. von der Decken, M. Susi (eds), *Cambridge Handbook of New Human Rights: Recognition, Novelty, Rhetoric* (Cambridge University Press, Cambridge, 2020).

von Hirsch, A., A. Ashworth, J. Roberts (eds), *Principled Sentencing: Readings on Theory and Policy* (3rd ed., Hart Publishing, Oxford, 2009).

Voytko-Best, L., 'Daniel Prude's Autopsy Report Says "Excited Delirium," a Controversial Diagnosis, Contributed to His Death' (*Forbes*, 3 September 2020) <https://www.forbes.com/sites/lisettevoytko/2020/09/03/daniel-prudes-autopsy-report-says-excited-delirium-a-controversial-diagnosis-contributed-to-his-death/> accessed 29 November 2024.

Walker, A., H. Dewar, 'Cocaine-Sex Deaths in Dade Probed' (*Miami News*, 24 November 1988).

Walker, J. and others, 'Changes in Mental State Associated with Prison Environments: A Systematic Review' (2014) 129 *Acta Psychiatrica Scandinavica* 427–436.

Walsh, C., 'Youth Justice and Neuroscience a Dual-Use Dilemma' (2011) 51 *British Journal of Criminology* 21–39.

Walsh, T., H. Douglas, 'Sentencing Parents: The Consideration of Dependent Children' (2016) 37 *Adelaide Law Review* 135–161.

Wamsley, L., 'Taser Changes Its Name to Axon and Offers Free Body Cameras for Police' (*NPR*, 7 April 2017) <https://www.npr.org/sections/thetwo-way/2017/04/07/522878573/we-re-more-than-stun-guns-says-taser-as-it-changes-company-name> accessed 2 December 2024.

Wang, E. A. and others, 'Engaging Individuals Recently Released from Prison into Primary Care: A Randomized Trial' (2012) 102 *American Journal of Public Health* 22–29.

Wang, E. A. and others, 'Propensity-Matched Study of Enhanced Primary Care on Contact with the Criminal Justice System among Individuals Recently Released from Prison to New Haven' (2019) 9 *BMJ Open* 1–9.

Wang, E. A. and others, 'Transitions Clinic: Creating a Community-Based Model of Health Care for Recently Released California Prisoners' (2010) 125 *Public Health Reports* 171–177.

Ward, T., S. Maruna, *Rehabilitation: Beyond the Risk Paradigm* (Routledge, London, 2007).

Warth, P., 'Unjust Punishment: The Impact of Incarceration on Mental Health' (*New York State Bar Association*, 5 December 2022) <https://nysba.org/unjust-punishment-the-impact-of-incarceration-on-mental-health/> accessed 1 October 2024.

Wasserman, E. B., K. M. Guskiewicz, '§24C.02 TBI Defined' in *Forensic Sciences §24C.02* (vol. 1, Matthew Bender & Company, Inc., 2024).

Watson, A. and others, 'Mental Health Courts and the Complex Issue of Mentally Ill Offenders' (2001) 52 *Psychiatric Services* 477–481.

Wedell, K., C. Kelly, C. McManus, C. Fernando, 'George Floyd Is Not Alone. "I Can't Breathe" Uttered by Dozens in Fatal Police Holds across U.S.' (*USA Today*, 25 June 2020) <https://www.usatoday.com/in-depth/news/investigations/2020/06/13/george-floyd-not-alone-dozens-said-cant-breathe-police-holds/3137373001/> accessed 2 December 2024.

Wetli, C. V., D. A. Fishbain, 'Cocaine-Induced Psychosis and Sudden Death in Recreational Cocaine Users' (1985) 30 *Journal of Forensic Sciences* 873–880.

Wheable, V., J. Davies, C. Lewis, 'Investigating the Effectiveness of Forensic Case Formulation Recommendations' (2024) 30 *Psychology, Crime & Law* 823–841.

Wicks, E., 'The Right to Refuse Medical Treatment under the European Convention on Human Rights' (2001) 9 *Medical Law Review* 17–40.

Williams, D. R., S. A. Mohammed, 'Discrimination and Racial Disparities in Health: Evidence and Needed Research' (2009) 32 *Journal of Behavioral Medicine* 20–47.

Willmot, P., L. Jones (eds), *Trauma-Informed Forensic Practice* (1st ed., Routledge, Abingdon, 2022)

Wishart, H., R. Arthur, *International Perspectives of Neuroscience in the Youth Justice Courtroom* (Routledge, Oxon, 2025).

Wishart, H., C. M. Berryessa, *Neurolaw in the Courtroom: Comparative Perspectives on Vulnerable Defendants* (Routledge, Oxon, 2023).

Wishart, H., C. M. Berryessa, *Neuroscience in Criminal Justice: The Positive Impact of Neuroscience* (Routledge, Oxon, 2025).

Wolff, N., J. Shi, 'Childhood and Adult Trauma Experiences of Incarcerated Persons and Their Relationship to Adult Behavioral Health Problems and Treatment' (2012) 9 *International Journal of Environmental Research and Public Health* 1908–1926.

Woodhouse, E. et al., 'Identification and Support of Autistic Individuals within the UK Criminal Justice System: A Practical Approach Based upon Professional Consensus with Input from Lived Experience' (2024) 22 *BMC Medicine* Article 157.

Woodwark, S., N. Lynch, 'Decidedly But Differently Accountable? Young Adults in the Criminal Justice System' (2021) 1 *New Zealand Law Review* 109–140.

Woollard, F., 'The Doctrine of Doing and Allowing II: The Moral Relevance of the Doing/Allowing Distinction' (2012) 7(7) *Philosophy Compass* 459–469.

World Health Organization, *Clinical Descriptions and Diagnostic Requirements for ICD-11 Mental, Behavioural and Neurodevelopmental Disorders* (WHO, Geneva, 2024).

World Health Organization, *International Classification of Diseases, ICD-11* (WHO, Geneva, 2024).

World Health Organization, *International Statistical Classification of Diseases and Related Health Problems* (11th ed., WHO, Geneva, 2019).

World Population Review, 'Police Training Requirements by Country' (2024) *World Population Review* <https://worldpopulationreview.com/country-rankings/police-training-requirements-by-country>

Wren, G. L., 'Mental Health Courts: Serving Justice and Promoting Recovery' (2010) 19 *Annals of Health Law* 577–593.

Yang, S. and others, 'Doing Time: A Qualitative Study of Long-Term Incarceration and the Impact of Mental Illness' (2009) 32 *International Journal of Law and Psychiatry* 294–303.

Yehuda, S., S. Rabinovitz, D. I. Mostofsky, 'Essential Fatty Acids and the Brain: From Infancy to Aging' (2005) 26 *Neurobiology of Aging* 98–102.

Yen, C., C.-L. Lin, M.-C. Chiang, 'Exploring the Frontiers of Neuroimaging: A Review of Recent Advances in Understanding Brain Functioning and Disorders' (2023) 13 *Life* 1472–1485.

Yeung, B., 'Taser's Delirium Defense' (*Mother Jones*, March/April 2009) <https://www.motherjones.com/politics/2009/02/tasers-delirium-defense/> accessed 3 December 2024.

Yoon, I. A., K. Slade, S Fazel, 'Outcomes of Psychological Therapies for Prisoners with Mental Health Problems: A Systematic Review and Meta-Analysis' (2017) 85 *Journal of Consulting and Clinical Psychology* 783–802.

Young, G., C. Lareau, B. Pierre, 'One Quintillion Ways to Have PTSD Comorbidity: Recommendations for the Disordered DSM-5' (2014) 7(1) *Psychological Injury and Law* 61–74.

Young, S., B. Greer, R. Church, 'Juvenile Delinquency, Welfare, Justice and Therapeutic Interventions: A Global Perspective' (2017) 41 *BJPsych Bulletin* 21–29.

Youth Justice Board, *A Guide to Child First* (Youth Justice Board, 2022) <https://yjresourcehub.uk/wp-content/uploads/media/Child_First_Overview_and_Guide_April_2022_YJB.pdf>

Youth Justice Board, *Prevention and Diversion Scoping Survey* (Youth Justice Board, London, 2021).

'Youth Justice Statistics 2022–2023' (25 January 2024) <https://www.gov.uk/government/statistics/youth-justice-statistics-2022-to-2023/youth-justice-statistics-2022-to-2023-accessible-version#sentencing-of-children>

Yu, R. and others, 'Depression and Violence in Adolescence and Young Adults: Findings from Three Longitudinal Cohorts' (2017) 56 *Journal of the American Academy of Child & Adolescent Psychiatry* 652–658.

Yuan, J. and others, 'Machine Learning Applications on Neuroimaging for Diagnosis and Prognosis of Epilepsy: A Review' (2022) 368(4) *Journal of Neuroscience Methods* 109441, 1–14.

Yuste, R., J. Genser, S. Herrmann, 'It's Time for Neuro-Rights; New Human Rights for the Age of Neurotechnology' (2021) 18 *Horizons* 154–155.

Zalta, E. (ed), *The Stanford Encyclopedia of Philosophy* (Spring Edition, 2024). <https://plato.stanford.edu/archives/spr2024/entries/legal-punishment/>

Zielinski, M. J., M. K. Allison, L. Brinkley-Rubinstein, G. Curran, N. D. Zaller, J. A. E. Kirchner, 'Making Change Happen in Criminal Justice Settings: Leveraging Implementation Science to Improve Mental Health Care' (2020) 8(21) *Health & Justice* 1–10.

Zoorob, M. J. and others, 'Drug Decriminalization, Fentanyl, and Fatal Overdoses in Oregon' (2024) 7 *JAMA Network Open* e2431612.

Index

Note: page numbers in **bold** indicate a table on the corresponding page.